POWER AND POLITICS IN CALIFORNIA

POWER AND POLITICS IN CALIFORNIA

FOURTH EDITION

John C. Syer
*California State University
Sacramento*

John H. Culver
*California Polytechnic State
University, San Luis Obispo*

Macmillan Publishing Company
New York

Maxwell Macmillan Canada
Toronto

Editor: Bruce Nichols
Production Supervisor: George Carr
Production Manager: Valerie A. Sawyer
Cover Photographs: George Hall/Woodfin Camp & Associates;
Brian Barrette, California Department of Forestry and Fire Protection

This book was set in Century Schoolbook by V & M Graphics Inc.,
printed and bound by Quinn-Woodbine Inc. The cover was printed by
New England Book Components, Inc.

Macmillan Publishing Company
866 Third Avenue, New York, New York, 10022

Macmillan Publishing Company is part of
the Maxwell Communication Group of Companies.

Maxwell Macmillan Canada, Inc.
1200 Eglinton Avenue East
Suite 200
Don Mills, Ontario M3C 3N1

Library of Congress Cataloging-in-Publication Data
Syer, John C., 1940–
    Power and Politics in California / John C. Syer, John H. Culver.—
    4th ed.
        p.   cm.
    Includes bibliographical references and index.
    ISBN 0-02-326325-3 (paper)
    1. Political participation—California.   2. California—Politics
and goverment.   I. Culver, John H., 1945–   .   II. Title.
JK8795.S94   1992
320.9794—dc20
                                                                91-13670
                                                                CIP

Printing: 1 2 3 4 5 6 7   Year: 2 3 4 5 6 7 8

Preface

Since the third edition of this text, California has experienced significant changes in its politics. Failed efforts at campaign reform, difficult budget impasses, complex initiative battles, and corruption trials involving state officials marked the end of the 1980s and the beginning of the new decade. The 1990 statewide election produced a so-called "friendly" gubernatorial transition with Republican Pete Wilson replacing Republican George Deukmejian. This apparent continuity should not obscure the fact that California currently is undergoing a political transformation of serious proportions.

The present edition of *Power and Politics in California* has not been reorganized in terms of the sequence of chapters. However, this volume contains considerable updating in each chapter in order to keep pace with recent events. This edition asks whether the state's political institutions are capable of governing as large and as complicated a place as California.

To help explain the decline in public confidence in the institutions of state goverment, Chapter 1 now provides an account of political corruption in California. A constitutional amendment drafted in response to the corruption trials (SCA 32 later approved by the voters as Proposition 112) is discussed in detail in Chapter 3. As the proportion of ethnic minorities living in California continues to expand, it is increasingly important to assess the extent to which these populations are represented in state government. Chapter 4 examines the group life and the political agendas of California's minority communities. The impact of the 1987 court rulings on California's political parties is discussed in Chapter 5 together with an account of Governor Deukmejian's unusual battle with the *Los Angeles Times* in 1989.

The initiative wars of 1988 and 1990 receive extensive treatment in Chapter 6. The importance of absentee voting also is examined in this chapter along with an account of the collaspe of the campaign finance reforms contained in Propositions 68 and 73. Chapter 7 on the California Legislature now contains arguments for and against term limits as enacted in 1990 through Proposition 140. This chapter also includes an updated assessment of leadership in each chamber, including the upheaval caused by the Gang of Five in 1988. Besides introducing the Wilson administration, Chapter 8 now offers a comparison of the managerial styles of California's recent chief executives.

As California encounters ever more serious budgetary crises, citizens need to grasp the essentials of the state's finances. Resolution of the 1990 budget impasse is examined in detail to illustrate that high-level, private negotiations have replaced the traditional budgetary review of past years. The staggering workload of the California Supreme Court is described in Chapter 10 along with some methods for reducing this burden. The Lucas Court (a major legacy of George Deukmejian) is contrasted with the earlier Bird Court. The discussion in Chapter 11 highlights the fundamental differences between state government and the politics of its localities. At-large and districted elections are compared in this final chapter, and the prospects for regional government are assessed.

In the past, California was known for its ample natural resources and for its far-sighted political leadership. Neither of these items is assured any longer. Whether California's political institutions will be able to respond to the needs of a changing state is an open question. During a period of real testing for state government, it is important that Californians have a thorough understanding of the political changes now underway in the once Golden State.

J.C.S.   J.H.C.

Acknowledgments

Many generous individuals have contributed to the preparation of this edition. California is fortunate indeed to have political experts who are willing and able to share their knowledge of state government; they are public servants in the best sense of that phrase. We are indebted to Ann Bailey for her explanation of the ethics laws described in Chapter 3. Marilyn Miles, Bob Alvarez, Maeley Tom, Alice Huffman, and Kate Karpilow contributed a great deal to our discussion of ethnic and gender politics in Chapter 4. We are grateful to Rick Dunne, Tim Hodson, and Nettie Sabelhaus for furthering our understanding of legislative politics contained in Chapter 7. Peter Detwiler, Lorraine Okabe, and Mickey Richie provided valuable assistance to our treatment of local government in Chapter 11. We are most grateful to Adam Gottlieb, Jennifer Openshaw, and the late Otto Bos for their help in securing the photographs that appear in this edition.

We also acknowledge the stimulation and encouragement we have received from the members of the California Studies Association and from our colleagues at the Center for California Studies. The questions and comments of our students through the years have helped us to clarify our thinking about our subject. We appreciate the contributions of Lyndelle Fairlie, San Diego State University; Kenneth Kennedy, College of San Mateo; Duncan McGilvray, Palomar College; and Larry Wright, Sierra College, who reviewed the manuscript of this edition. Finally, we will never be able to thank the members of our families enough for their patience and their support throughout this undertaking.

Contents

CHAPTER 1

California: Institutions under Siege

It once was customary to sing the praises of government institutions in California. The legislature and the court system were considered among the finest in the nation. The civil service in California was highly regarded as well. The state was known for its leadership in areas such as environmental protection, higher education, coastal preservation, and freeway construction. Government worked.

In the late stages of the twentieth century, California has become the unquestioned national champion in the use of the ballot initiative—a process whereby voters, not public officials, make policy on a wide range of issues. At a time when more complicated and more costly problems are confronting the state, the effectiveness and performance of California's political institutions are being called into question. Here are words of alarm from some close observers of California politics:

> Anyone who isn't startled by the scandal of campaign financing, the distortion of the initiative process, the rapaciousness of reapportionment, the decline of the political parties, and the loss of citizen representatives simply isn't paying attention to what is happening.—We must start making some significant changes.
> Robert Monagan (1990)
> Former Speaker,
> California Assembly

> California's social and economic challenges cannot be met by a political system that is unproductive at best and at worst mired in systematic corruption.
> Dan Walters (1990)
> Columnist, *Sacramento Bee*

Such is the reality of California politics today. Whether we like it or not, more is being demanded of government. But government seems less able to respond.—Clearly, the policy analysis burden now being laid on the

1

average voter is far greater than even the most conscientious of us can shoulder.

> Walter Zelman (1990)
> Former Executive Director,
> California Common Cause

Plenty of problems cry out for answers in California, but even if the state regains the will to move on them, progress will be extremely difficult. Californians have put too many obstacles in their own paths. These obstacles can't be easily removed.

> Martin Smith (1990)
> Political Editor,
> *Sacramento Bee*

For a decade, the state has been marching at an increasing pace toward a political arrangement where everything of importance is put to a vote of the people and where every crucial post is independently elected. That can work in a New England town meeting or maybe in a Greek city-state. In a state of 30 million people, it's nuts.

> Peter Schrag (1990)
> Associate Editor,
> *Sacramento Bee*

As in 1911, it is time for Californians to save their representative government.

> Professor Eugene Lee (1990)
> University of California, Berkeley

This is a chorus of concern, not a single individual voicing gloom and doom. Although critics often have faulted one state policy or another in the past, it is unusual indeed to read such widespread agreement that California's entire political process is in need of change. The last major overhaul occurred 80 years ago when the Progressives instituted their comprehensive package of political reforms.

Paradise Lost

A review of public service levels and resource depletion rates suggests the gravity of the situation now facing California. Together with the State of Utah, California's K–12 classrooms are the most crowded in the country. Whereas classroom size in excess of 30 is common in California, some states have established maximums of 18 students per class. Some 37% of Californians entering high school drop out before receiving a diploma, whereas the national average for noncompletion of secondary education is 30%. (Drop-out rates of 50% are found in California's urban high schools where students are drawn largely from Latino and African-American populations.) Besides the questions of crowding and retention, schools are being asked to provide a broader array of services than was once the case. Since it is very difficult to teach a sick or hungry child, schools are now expected to provide nutritional and health services. With one of six children in California's K–12 schools born outside the United States, language difficulties are a major issue as well.

California is dead last among states in the Union for per capita expenditure on transportation. This is particularly troublesome given the tremendous escalation in the cost of building new roads and rail lines. Freeways could be built in the 1950s for about $1 million per mile; the Century Freeway was recently completed in Los Angeles at a cost of roughly $150 million per mile. The cost of building Bay Area Rapid Transit (BART) in the 1960s was about $21 million per mile, whereas the new Metro Line in Los Angeles cost some $625 million per mile to construct. Even though voters approved Proposition 111 in June of 1990 to generate some $18 billion in additional revenue to be spent on California's highway and rail systems, almost all of this money will be used to widen or to extend existing roads and lines. Little, if any, Proposition 111 money will be devoted to building new transportation facilities. Average speeds on California's freeways are expected to decline still further in the years to come. Partially as a result of traffic congestion, California has 8 of the 10 worst air pollution basins in the United States.

Although California's aqueducts and reservoirs are engineering marvels, serious problems are on the horizon for the state's water supply. Growers in the Central Valley have been pumping more water from underground aquifers than is naturally replenished each season. The long-term consequences of overdrafting may jeopardize the viability of one of the most, if not the most, productive agricultural regions in the world. Moreover, the chemicals used on cropland are moving through the soil and contaminating wells used for drinking water. Diversion of water onto fields, followed by chemical runoff entering streams and rivers, has cut the annual runs of bass and salmon to a fraction of what they once were. Despite being a major oil-producing state, California imports one-half of the petroleum it uses—primarily to operate thirsty automobiles. California is also a timber-growing state, yet the state must import 60% of the wood products it uses.

In addition to addressing low service levels and resource depletion, California must cope with rapid growth in population and with disasters (natural and otherwise). For a number of years in the 1980s, California had an annual population increase of nearly 700,000 people—that is tantamount to adding a city the size of San Francisco to the state each year. Drought, fires, and earthquakes all place heavy demands on the

Figure 1-1 The fight for the waterhole.
(Dennis Renault, *Sacramento Bee*)

state government. The Loma Prieta quake, which struck the Bay Area on October 17, 1989, killed 67 people and did an estimated $6 billion in damage. For a state already lacking in highway funds, the loss of the Cypress Freeway in Oakland and the Embarcadero Freeway in San Francisco, not to mention repairing the broken span of the Bay Bridge, was a costly blow. Apart from natural disasters, the state has to contend with cleaning up the results of human errors such as the 1990 oil spill at Huntington Beach. Over and above various physical catastrophes, there are political disasters as well.

Fall from Grace

Sometime after 10:00 P.M. on August 24, 1988, 30 agents and attorneys from the FBI and the U.S. Department of Justice commenced a search of offices in the State Capitol. They were looking for evidence that legislators were trading their votes in exchange for campaign donations and honoraria (speaking fees). When the investigators left the building near dawn, they took with them boxes full of memos, phone logs, campaign records, and desk calendars. This nighttime exercise, pursuant to bona fide search warrants, was the first public indication that a major investigation was underway. In fact, the FBI had been conducting an undercover investigation into political corruption in Sacramento for over $2\frac{1}{2}$ years prior to the so-called raid on the State Capitol. The patience and thoroughness exhibited by federal authorities throughout this episode no doubt contributed to the successful prosecution of public officials.

The U.S. Department of Justice in 1985 authorized an operation in Sacramento called "Brispec," which stood for bribery-special interest. In December of that year, the FBI formed the first of five bogus companies that were used in the investigation. Such sham firms as Gulf Shrimp

Figure 1-2 Collapsed roadway of Cypress Freeway near Oakland after the earthquake of October 17, 1989. (California Department of Transportation.)

Fisheries, Peachstate Capitol West, and Sunbelt Diversified were established in Georgia and Alabama. These businesses supposedly were interested in opening a shrimp processing plant in West Sacramento. First, however, they wanted the California Legislature to pass bills that would allow financial institutions to buy their corporate bonds and that would provide a state guarantee to investors in case the companies failed to repay their bonds. These measures were classic special interest bills in that they conferred benefits on a single proposed venture instead of throughout an industry as a whole. Phony tax returns and loan documents were prepared for the fictitious companies, and FBI agents with Southern accents came to the State Capitol masquerading as company officers and supporting the legislation. Due to the nature of the proposed business, the press and the public generally referred to this entire matter as "Shrimpscam."

To make contact with legislators, FBI agents began by developing relationships with legislative staffers who in turn could introduce the fake businesspersons around the State Capitol. After implicating himself in illegal activities, John Shahabian (an aide to then Senator Paul Carpenter) agreed to work with the FBI in exchange for immunity from prosecution. As they say in the movies, Shahabian consented to wear a wire and thereafter he taped a number of conversations with lawmakers. Representatives of the bogus companies also began dispensing campaign contributions and honoraria to various legislators.

Four legislators who were approached (i.e., Farr, Isenberg, Doolittle, and L. Greene) refused to author the legislation that the fake businesses wanted. Eventually, Assemblymember Gwen Moore (D, Los Angeles) agreed to introduce a measure for the companies. Moore's bill moved through the two houses of the California Legislature with practically no dissent. Tipped by the FBI that the bill was part of a sting operation, Governor George Deukmejian vetoed the bill. While the bill was still in the legislature, Senator Joseph Montoya (D, El Monte) agreed to support the legislation in exchange for a $3000 honorarium. At a breakfast meeting at Pennisi's Cafe not far from the State Capitol, the FBI videotaped Senator Montoya receiving a $3000 check while assuring a fake businessperson that he would promote the passage of Moore's bill. As it turned out, Senator Montoya had also asked for money to support bills in the areas of insurance, professional sports, and medical schools that were in no way related to the government's undercover operation.

On May 18, 1989, nine months after the search of the State Capitol, Senator Montoya (and his aide Amiel Jaramillo) were indicted on charges of extortion, money laundering, and racketeering. The government alleged that Montoya used his legislative office to conduct a criminal enterprise in violation of the Racketeer Influenced and Corrupt Organizations (RICO) Act. In addition to audio and video tapes, prosecutors obtained testimony from lobbyists that Senator Montoya had asked for money in exchange for his support of their bills. The legislator defended himself by arguing that he had simply accepted a perfectly legal honorarium for having breakfast with the representative of a business. On February 2, 1990, 17 months after the search of the State Capitol and some 5 years after the corruption probe began, Senator Montoya was convicted and sentenced to $6\frac{1}{2}$ years in prison. Thus ended a 17-year career in the California Legislature. At the sentencing hearing, Judge Milton Schwartz made the following comment about Montoya's conduct:

> The system can live with elected officials who are not very competent. It can live with waste and inefficiency. It can live with legislators who may be lazy. It can survive all these things. But it cannot survive legislators who say, "My vote is for sale. I'm here to vote the way I am paid and I will disregard the merits." (Bernstein, 1990a)

Former Senator Paul Carpenter (D, Norwalk) served in the legislature for a dozen years before winning election to the Board of Equalization in 1986 and 1990. On September 18, 1990, Carpenter was found

Figure 1-3   Nailed! (Dennis Renault, *Sacramento Bee*)

guilty of racketeering, extortion, and conspiracy for actions while he was a member of the California Senate. His defense was more elaborate than Montoya's. Carpenter's aide Shahabian had solicited $20,000 in campaign contributions from FBI agents posing as businesspersons, but the Senator maintained that his staffer was acting on his own. In addition, Carpenter claimed that he never promised any action in exchange for the donation. In fact, Carpenter did not even vote for the shrimp bill having abstained on the roll call on the Senate floor. He did acknowledge that he was more likely to meet with (or grant access to) lobbyists whose clients had contributed to his campaign fund. The government succeeded in proving that Carpenter went further than granting access to contributors; he actually solicited bribes from lobbyists by threatening *not* to meet with them unless they donated to his campaigns. Upon Carpenter's conviction, prosecutor David Levi stated the following in regard to extracting contributions.

> This case makes an important point that all citizens should enjoy equal access to the legislature. They shouldn't have to buy access. There should be no tollgate or teller's cage in front of a legislator's office. (Bernstein, 1990b)

As of now, the long-running investigation has not been completed. Additional elected officials may be brought to trial. Implicated staffers who cooperate with the prosecution are likely to receive immunity or reduced sentences; those who refuse to testify against their former bosses are likely to draw prison terms. The convictions of Montoya and Carpenter harmed the reputation of the California Legislature and contributed to the passage of a term limits initiative (Proposition 140) in November of 1990. However, these two cases are far from the entire picture of political corruption in California.

U.S. Senator Alan Cranston (D, California) was the subject of an extensive ethics investigation in 1990. Cranston intervened on behalf of Charles Keating (Lincoln Federal Savings and Loan) with federal regulators after receiving nearly $1 million from Keating in campaign donations and support for voter registration projects. Karl Samuelian, Governor Deukmejian's top fund raiser, influenced state regulators in the late 1980s to kill a new rule that limited risky investments by savings and loan institutions. Mayor Tom Bradley of Los Angeles, after accepting money as a paid consultant to the Far East National Bank, asked the city treasurer in 1989 to deposit $2 million in tax funds into the very same banking institution. A clumsy effort to cover up Bradley's involvement in the deposit decision was unsuccessful when investigators found his name had been whited out on key correspondence. Bradley quickly returned his salary to Far East National Bank, and he dropped off the Board of Directors of another savings and loan institution. Admitting that he had made an error in judgment, Bradley agreed to a civil (not criminal) settlement with the city attorney concerning his failure to properly disclose his financial situation. Though criminal penalties may never be handed down in these cases, many Californians view these actions as conflicts of interest and serious lapses of ethical behavior.

All of this is not to argue that honest people can no longer be found in state government. There are many dedicated and skillful public servants attempting to grapple with the mounting problems facing California. However, given the steady diet of news stories dealing with political corruption, it can come as no surprise that public enthusiasm for government as usual is lacking. Before discussing possible responses to the state's political predicament, let us turn to an examination of the demographic, economic, and cultural underpinnings of California.

Demographics

California's population growth in the 1980s was typical in some respects and atypical in others. Just as the number of residents boomed

Figure 1-4 "This is my friend, advisor and political fund raiser; I've never seen the other guy before!" (Dennis Renault, *Sacramento Bee*)

as a result of the Gold Rush and as a consequence of defense jobs during World War II, the 1980s marked a terrific surge in the state's population. Some 20 million people lived in California in 1970 and by 1979 the figure had reached 23.25 million. With California approaching 30 million people as of 1990, the rate of population growth in the 1980s doubles that of the 1970s. California has seen booms before, but this upsurge was not primarily from other states in the Union. Fully half of the population growth in California in the 1980s stemmed from immigration. (Forty percent of the new population came from the birthrate of existing residents and 10% came from elsewhere in the United States.) With over 3 million immigrants coming into California in the last decade, the state's Latino population grew by 55% and the Asian population by 75%. Political wits like to joke that it is California that inherits our nation's foreign policy mistakes. Whereas the nation as a whole grew by 10% in the 1980s, California grew by 25% in the past decade.

This population influx is not evenly distributed around the state. The lion's share of new residents appeared in the five megacounties of Southern California: Los Angeles (8.8 million overall population in 1990), San Diego (2.5 million), Orange (2.3 million), San Bernardino (1.4 million), and Riverside (1.1 million). The most populous counties in northern California—Santa Clara (1.5 million), Alameda (1.25 million), and Sacramento (1 million)—also grew steadily in the 1980s, but the great bulk of the population growth was in southern counties. Though small in terms of absolute numbers of new residents, some rural counties (e.g., Calaveras, Nevada, Amador, Lake, and El Dorado) had growth rates for the 1980s in the 40–50% range. This is possible because the base population for these counties at the beginning of the decade was small. What is most astounding is that the suburban counties of Riverside (47%) and San Bernardino (43%) had growth rates in the 1980s comparable to the rural counties despite having considerably more residents at the outset (Senate Office of Research, 1989:9).

As urban congestion worsens, some residents who can afford to relocate to rural California, or entirely out of the state, have begun to do so. This exodus from urban areas is mostly a white, middle-class phenomenon. Whereas long-time, white residents of California bemoan the longer commutes, the poor air quality, and the crowds at favorite attractions, recent immigrants find California to be cleaner and less populated than the conditions they left in Asia and Latin America. The president of the Portland Chamber of Commerce has said, "We're a trendy spot because we offer the lifestyle that California offered years ago" (McLeod, 1990). The favorite states for departing Californians are Oregon, Nevada, Arizona, Washington, and Florida.

Economics _____

As the state with by far the largest economy in the nation, California is frequently compared to national economies to give some sense of how immense the productive capacity of the state is. With a gross state product (GSP) of around $550 billion in the late 1980s, California was the eighth largest economy in the world. The gross national products (GNPs) of the United States, Soviet Union, Japan, Germany, France, Italy, and the United Kingdom exceeded the GSP of California as of 1987 (U.S. Bureau of the Census, 1990: 840). The British and Italian GNPs are within striking distance of California's economy, and it is interesting to note that their economic productivity is generated with roughly twice as many inhabitants as live in this state.

A brief account of economic life in California should touch on both the optimistic and pessimistic aspects of the situation. Because California does not have a single-industry economy, the state usually is spared regional economic downturns as sometimes seen in Michigan (automobile manufacturing) or West Virginia (coal mining). The wide variety of industries found in California includes defense production (weaponry), aerospace (civilian aircraft and space vehicles), electronics (computers and business machines), agriculture, tourism, entertainment, energy, construction (residential and commercial), chemicals and plastics, printing, furniture, and wearing apparel. Each major industrial sector is diverse within itself. The entertainment industry consists of movies, television, recording, videos, theme parks, and professional sports. In addition to oil and natural gas, the energy industry also is involved in geothermal, nuclear, solar, and wind generation of electrical power. Tourists flock to such diverse sights as Yosemite Valley, Disneyland, the wine country in Napa Valley, Universal Studios, Lake Tahoe, the San Diego Zoo, and the Big Sur coastline. Agriculture may well be the most varied industry in California, with important subsectors in citrus, livestock, cotton, timber, and specialty crops. California's climate and soils permit over 250 different commodities to be grown including rice, lettuce, tomatoes, grapes, nuts, apricots, peaches, olives, artichokes, avocadoes, and kiwi fruit. Agriculture also accounts for economic productivity in food processing, fertilizers and pesticides, and farm machinery.

In addition to the diversity of the state's economy, there is other good news. Until late 1990, California's unemployment rate ordinarily was below that of the nation as a whole. Hundreds of thousands of new jobs were created in California in the 1980s to provide employment for new residents. California provides a robust market for businesses wishing to sell their products. As a gateway to the Pacific trading area, California is the transshipment point for a growing volume of imports and exports.

Now let us turn to some of the less rosy aspects of California's economy. Diverse as this state's productivity is, California is not immune from national and global economic downturns. The national recession in the early 1990s curbed sales in California and reduced the revenues the state expected to collect. In addition, California has experienced an exodus of firms in certain sectors of business. Hughes Aircraft and Lockheed Corporation have opened plants in Georgia, Alabama, Mississippi, and South Carolina, and moved some California production to those areas. One aerospace executive said, "Every defense company worth its salt has looked at ways to move out, slip out, or slide out of the Los Angeles basin" (Vartabedian, 1990). Five major research and development projects that the state pursued in the 1980s were located elsewhere. The superconducting super collider project, a microelectronic consortium, a computer chip consortium, and an advanced computer research group all rejected bids by California. Even a national center to study earthquakes located in Buffalo, New York, of all places (Garcia, 1989).

California's major trading partners are Japan, Taiwan, South Korea, Singapore, Mexico, and Hong Kong. In the case of each of these countries, California exports less to them than these nations import into the state (*The State of California*, 1990: 24). The state's trade deficit has contributed to a hemorrhage of dollars abroad and the subsequent reinvestment of those funds in California. Japanese investors have purchased movie studios, the Pebble Beach resort, and the entertainment conglomerate Music Corporation of America (MCA). When Matsushita Electric (brand names Panasonic and Quasar) bought MCA in 1990, it purchased control of Universal Studios, recording artists, and television shows, among other properties. These acquisitions generated headlines, but no less significant is the fact that foreign investors own one-half the large downtown office buildings in Los Angeles and 25% of the state's total banking assets. Union Bank (owned by the Bank of Tokyo) and the Bank of California (owned by Mitsubishi Bank) are the fifth and sixth largest banks in California. Although it is true that foreign ownership is a vote of confidence in the state economy, profits from these businesses can now go abroad instead of staying in California.

The future of the defense sector and the quality of the state's labor supply are two other points of vulnerability for the California economy. Due to the massive deficit in the annual budget of the U.S. Government, closure of military bases and cancellation of the construction of weapons systems may produce major layoffs in the state. (Should defense industries be able to convert their technological know-how to producing renewable energy, sustainable agriculture, affordable housing, mass transit, clean air, and safe disposal of toxic wastes, the impact of Pentagon cutbacks will not be severe.) In the past, California has had a well-educated work force to offer to businesses. With the major population influx and the declining condition of the states's schools, quality labor in California is no longer assured. There will be sufficient labor for low-skill jobs, but will there be an adequate supply of highly skilled personnel for technical and managerial occupations? One economist has declared, "You cannot run an economy or a society successfully where 20–25 percent of the people are at risk of dropping out.—Ultimately California's prosperity depends most of all on the competitiveness of its labor force" (The Economist, 1990).

Political Cultures _____

California's political processes and outcomes are distinctive in several respects. After the Progressives weakened political parties and instituted ballot initiatives in 1911, California evolved into a media state. Professional campaign management originated in this state in 1934 to provide services to the backers of ballot propositions and to individual candidates. Lacking strong party organizations, office seekers ran personalized campaigns that featured image advertising. The vast size of the state discouraged face-to-face campaigns, and the mass media soon became indispensable in statewide races. As well-established media figures, Hollywood personalities have played a prominent role in California politics. Actors George Murphy (U.S. Senator, 1964–1970) and Ronald Reagan (Governor, 1966–1974; President, 1980–1988) won high office. Entertainers such as Charlton Heston, Clint Eastwood, and Steve Garvey are mentioned as potential candidates. Beyond running for office, Hollywood celebrities endorse ballot propositions and help raise the large sums that are needed to wage advertising campaigns. Media politics mean big-money politics. As we have seen, the preoccupation with raising money for reelection efforts can lead to illegal behavior and to neglect of the public interest.

Besides pioneering modern campaign management, California gave the nation the free-speech movement (Berkeley in 1964) and the tax-revolt movement (Proposition 13 in 1978). More recently, California has encouraged car insurance reform (Proposition 103 in 1988) and the term-limit movement (Proposition 140 in 1990)—matters that other states may take up as a result of the media attention lavished on developments in California. Will the California of the 1990s carry on the legacy of Ronald Reagan and Proposition 13? Political analyst and publisher Kevin Phillips does not think so.

The realignment in the Sun Belt isn't necessarily the conservative phenomenon so many expect.—State voters show signs of replacing tax-limitation populism with ballot-box harassment of the insurance, chemical, oil, and tobacco industries that's already spreading to other states. Overall, California may even emerge from the Goldwater–Nixon–Reagan era as more Democratic than the nation as a whole—and tilt U.S. politics accordingly. (Phillips, 1989).

Perhaps Phillips can foretell the future, but there is much history to overcome before the Democratic Party becomes dominant in California. There have been eleven presidential races since the end of World War II. Lyndon Johnson in 1964 was the only Democrat to carry California in his run for the White House. The Democratic Party has not nominated a Californian to either spot on the ticket in any of these 11 contests. Conversely, the Republican Party nominated Californians eight times during these same years (Earl Warren in 1948; Richard Nixon in 1952, 1956, 1960, 1968, and 1972; Ronald Reagan in 1980 and 1984). Phillips is correct that 1986 and 1988 witnessed losses for the chemical industry (Proposition 65), the tobacco industry (Proposition 99), and the insurance industry (Proposition 103). However, 1990 saw the agriculture and energy industries beat the environmental initiative Big Green (Proposition 128) and the liquor industry defeat the nickel-a-drink tax (Proposition 134).

Many Californians served in the administrations of President Richard Nixon (1968–1974) and President Ronald Reagan (1980–1988). Barring an unforeseen development, Californians will have to make their mark in Washington, D.C., in the early 1990s as members of the U.S. Congress. During the decade of the 1980s, California was entitled to 45 members in the U.S. House of Representatives. As a result of the 1990 census, California gained seven seats in the House for a total of 52 members of the House from this state. This is a most impressive figure as it represents as many House seats as are held by the 21 smallest states combined. Florida gained four house seats (total now 23) and Texas picked up three new districts (total now 30) to further demonstrate the shift of population to the Sun Belt. It came as no surprise that the states losing House seats were in the Rust Belt. New York had to give up three districts (total now 31). Pennsylvania, Ohio, Michigan, and Illinois each lost two seats in the U.S. House of Representatives as a result of the 1990 census. Whether a large congressional delegation will work to the advantage of California remains to be seen. An A.B.C. Syndrome—Anywhere But California—might emerge among representatives from other states. California may have lost research and development projects because of congestion and high-priced housing in this state, as well as because of the A.B.C. phenomenon.

California's role on the national stage would be heightened significantly if the state legislature were to move the state's presidential primary forward from June to March. By contesting its delegate selection for the national party conventions as late as June, California's voters have little, if any, part to play in the determination of presidential nominees. The standard bearers for each party ordinarily have been determined by the outcomes of primaries and caucuses in other states. Should the California Legislature change the date of the presidential primary, this state could become a key battleground in selecting national leadership. Since the GOP in California has retained the winner-take-all presidential primary in which all convention delegates would be awarded to one Republican candidate, the early primary would be especially pivotal for that party. (Democrats in California award their convention delegates on a proportional basis reflecting the strength of a candidate's popular vote in the primary.) With a House delegation of 52 plus the two U.S. Senate seats from the state, California now has 54 electoral votes—exactly one-fifth of the 270 votes needed to win the electoral college and the presidency. In the years to come, it will be increasingly difficult to enter the White House without carrying California.

From the standpoint of someone managing a statewide campaign, California can be viewed as a nation-state with a number of identifiable regions within it. The County of Los Angeles could very well be a state unto itself. With a population approaching 9 million, Los Angeles could be the ninth largest state in the Union—after California as a whole, New York, Texas, Florida, Pennsylvania, Illinois, Ohio, and Michigan. By the end of the 1990s, the Los Angeles metropolitan area is expected to exceed New York City in terms of population, employment, and total income. As financial and cultural centers, Los Angeles and Tokyo will be the anchors of the Pacific Rim in the future. Due to the immigration of the 1980s, Los Angeles is one of the most multicultural regions on earth.

In addition to Los Angeles, the Bay Area, the south coast counties of Orange and San Diego, the Central Valley, and the north coast are regarded as identifiable regions within the state. The distinctiveness of the Central Valley is clearly set forth by writer Gerald Haslam.

> Agriculture dominates and in this valley can hardly be referred to as "farming" in any traditional sense. Hereabouts it has developed its own terminology: farms are "ranches," farmers are "growers," and farming is "agribusiness."—This domain remains in many ways closer to Lubbock (Texas) and Stillwater (Oklahoma) than to Hollywood. (Haslam, 1990: 15 and 17)

The importance of environmentalism to residents of northern California is well known. Ernest Callenbach (1975) imagined the northern counties of California seceding from the Union and forming an environmentalist nation called Ecotopia with portions of what are now Washington and Oregon. Unlike parched areas elsewhere, this part of California has an abundant supply of water. Following Callenbach, Joel Garreau (1981) divided California into two so-called nations—the north being Ecotopia and the south being MexAmerica. Although it is possible to quibble over the precise boundaries of regions within a megastate such as California, it is clear that different appeals are needed to reach voters in various parts of the state. The entire matter of regional definition is complicated by the fact that Californians tolerate very lengthy commutes in search of affordable housing. Workers in Los Angeles commute from San Bernardino, Riverside, and Ventura. Some residents in the Central Valley communities of Stockton, Tracy, and Modesto drive to the Bay Area for their employment. Mayor Carol Whiteside of Modesto has said, "Whether we like it or not, our region is now far more closely linked to the Bay Area than it is to the rest of the Central Valley" (Haslam, 1990:26). Population shifts are changing the face of this state, but managers of statewide campaigns still are not likely to overlook the regional differences among California's voters.

Ongoing Challenges

The key to California's growth and agricultural productivity has been water. By means of a variety of dams, aqueducts, and canals, water has been brought from Northern California to Central and Southern California; from the Sierra to the Bay Area and Los Angeles; and from the Colorado River to the Imperial Valley, Los Angeles, and San Diego. Over the years, the political battles about moving water from one part of the state to another have pitted Northern Californians against Southern Californians; farmers against urban dwellers; California against Arizona, Nevada, and Colorado; and private power companies against the state and federal governments. The financial stakes have always been high and will continue to be so in the future given water's vital importance to land development.

The first canal was constructed at the turn of the century to divert Colorado River water into the Imperial Valley in the southeastern part of the state. A second canal was created in the same general area in 1905, but torrential rains washed away sections of it and the flood waters rushed into what is now known as the Salton Sea. Prior to the existence of the canals, the Imperial Valley was known as the Colorado Desert and the Salton Sea was the Salton Sink.

The most controversial and politically deceptive water diversion system came with the building of the Los Angeles Aqueduct. In 1904, plans were made between a member of the U.S. Bureau of Reclamation and Fred Eaton (the former mayor of Los Angeles) to channel water from the Owens Valley, on the eastern side of the Sierra, south to Los Angeles. Owens Valley residents thought the federal government was going to control drainage and establish irrigation facilities for farming in the valley, not that Los Angeles would be the recipient of the water. Prompted

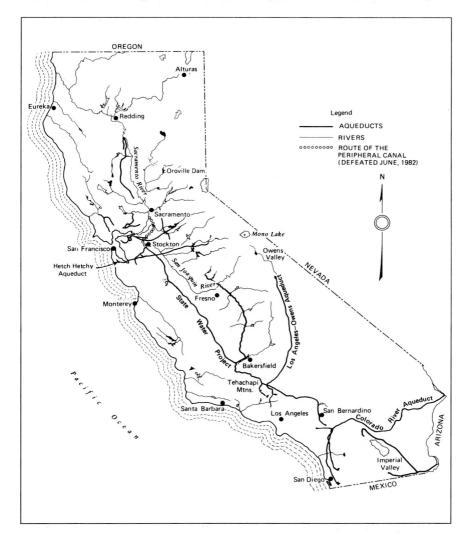

Figure 1-5 Major aqueducts in California.

by fears of a drought and encouraged by Harrison Gray Otis, the publisher of the *Los Angeles Times*, L.A. residents approved the issuance of municipal bonds to finance construction of the aqueduct. In the meantime, Otis and transportation baron Henry Huntington bought 16,000 acres of land in the San Fernando Valley for $35 an acre. With the opening of the aqueduct in 1913, water was now available to develop the San Fernando Valley, land that now had increased substantially in value with the arrival of the precious liquid. At its peak, the aqueduct provided Los Angeles with 80% of its water. Initially, the system only used the streams flowing into the Owens Valley. As Los Angeles grew, however, the streams flowing into Mono Lake were also diverted into the aqueduct along with underground water pumped from reservoirs below the Owens Valley. The level of Mono Lake dropped some 40 feet, and a lake shrimp (normally eaten by migrating birds) began to disappear. Plant life in the Owens Valley was adversely impacted when water was drawn below root level. With an ecosystem in jeopardy, the courts in the late 1980s ordered Los Angeles to allow four streams to empty into Mono Lake and to reduce the removal of underground water from Owens Valley.

Plans to irrigate the vast Central Valley were voiced as early as the 1870s. However, it was not until 1933, after a decade of false starts, that a proposal to construct the Central Valley Project was ratified by the state legislature as part of the State Water Plan (SWP). Because of the Depression, construction bonds could not be sold. The federal government assumed responsibility for the project, which, begun in 1937, involved the construction of three major dams, five canals, and two power transmission lines. Ninety-five percent of the water that flows through this massive system is used for agricultural purposes. In 1927, the legislature authorized the creation of the Metropolitan Water District of Southern California to bring Colorado River water to Southern California. By 1941, the 242-mile Colorado River Aqueduct was completed. As a result of a long-fought legal battle between Arizona and California, which was finally settled in the early 1980s, much of the Colorado River water that once quenched the thirst of Los Angeles must now be directed to meet the water needs of residents in Phoenix and Tucson.

Another addition to the State Water Plan (SWP) was initiated in 1960 when California voters narrowly approved Proposition 1 authorizing the sale of $1.75 billion in water resources bonds. One component of the SWP funded by Proposition 1 was the Oroville Dam on the Feather River in Butte County. It was intended to store spring runoff of melting snow for later release during the summer months. In addition to the major dam, SWP funds were used to build the California Aqueduct. This delivery system originates in the Delta (the confluence of the Sacramento and San Joaquin Rivers west of Stockton), travels south through the

Westlands (the arid side of the San Joaquin Valley opposite from the east side with its rivers flowing out of the Sierra Nevada), crosses the Tehachapi Mountains with the aid of giant pumping stations, passes through the Los Angeles metropolitan area, and terminates in San Diego County. Water agencies along the route of the California Aqueduct have contracts with the SWP for delivery of water.

In 1981, the legislature authorized construction of a peripheral canal as a part of the SWP. The 42-mile-long canal was to bring water from the Sacramento River to the California Aqueduct, which begins just south of Stockton. However, opponents of the controversial canal gathered enough signatures to force a referendum on the project. Critics charged that the canal would be too expensive (cost estimates ranged from $5 to $30 billion), environmentalists were concerned that the diversion of the fresh water into the aqueduct would increase the salinity of water in the Delta, and farmers were worried that the many water quality restrictions would render the water suitable only for urban residents. The peripheral canal was defeated by the voters in 1982.

Court decisions decreasing the flow in the Los Angeles Aqueduct from the Owens Valley and granting more of the Colorado River to Arizona have generated the need to reassess water delivery in California. Intense regional and economic rivalries occur whenever there is a fundamental review of water allocation in the state. Aside from developing

Figure 1-6 Before the rains in March of 1991, Folsom Lake near Sacramento stood at 16.5% of capacity. Several reservoirs in coastal areas were completely empty prior to the "March miracle." (California Department of Water Resources)

more supplies, great strides could be taken in agricultural conservation. A noted authority on water in California offers these basic facts.

> Eighty-five percent of the water goes to agriculture. According to state estimates, 40 percent of the remainder goes to industrial, commercial, and governmental uses. Roughly half of the 9 percent left over that goes to people's houses is used outdoors. That means that only about 4 percent of all the water that we have developed actually winds up being used in the home. (Kahrl, 1990)

Another challenge facing California is toxic contamination. Collectively, over 300 million pounds of pesticides are dumped on California soil each year. Although most farmers recognize the need to follow application guidelines closely, abuses are all too frequent and the number of field workers who become sick from pesticide exposure each year is increasing. The state also needs more locations to dispose of toxic materials. As of 1986, there were only six licensed toxic waste sites in the state and they were in violation of state and federal standards. Any toxic dump has to be located away from populated areas, away from any earthquake fault that could rupture the holding ponds, and on clay-like soil that prevents the toxic material from seeping into ground water. More sites are desperately needed. However, the further away such locations are from metropolitan areas, the greater the risk of accidents involving tankers carrying the wastes. The closest toxic dump to Los Angeles is in Casmalia, a small community of 200 residents located 10 miles west of Santa Maria in Santa Barbara County. The 225-acre dump opened in 1973, but by 1984 residents began complaining of headaches, nausea, and eye irritation. Health officials who monitored the residents found high levels of respiratory problems and neurological symptoms including loss of memory, depression, irritability, and abnormal fatigue.

With the generation of toxic materials at record levels and landfills available for disposal fast disappearing, the legislature and the governor crafted a compromise to deal with this problem. To clarify overlapping regulatory authority, the Integrated Waste Management Board was created in 1989. This board will establish policies to discourage excessive creation of toxic byproducts, and it will endeavor to break the logjam surrounding the licensing of new sites for the disposal of hazardous wastes. In an ever more populous state, questions of water supplies and toxic pollution are likely to be chronic issues facing the political system.

Institutional Change _____

The following chapters examine California's political institutions one by one. Sequential treatment could lead to the notion that institutional change in California might be dealt with on a piecemeal basis. The authorities cited at the beginning of this text suggest that a comprehensive, all-embracing package of reforms is worth undertaking given the dire condition in which California now finds itself. The extensive use of initiatives, the difficulty in passing state budgets, the loss of confidence in the state legislature, the strong disagreements among the independently elected executives, the overload facing the courts, and the crazy quilt of jurisdictions at the local level indicate that the institutional malaise is broad and deep.

To the contrary, some might argue that there is nothing inherently wrong with California's political institutions that the selection of a few capable leaders could not cure. Strong leaders have been known to succeed in deficient structures. Moreover, state government did respond to the Loma Prieta quake by establishing a relief fund (a $1/4$ cent increase in the state sales tax) and to the Huntington Beach oil spill by passing legislation setting up a clean-up fund and clarifying liability. It is true that state government acted in these instances, but it has been far less successful on matters such as car insurance, health insurance, water allocation, homelessness, and financial support for local government. No matter how capable a leader is today, there are difficult obstacles to surmount in attempting to govern California. Budgetary restrictions (detailed in Chapter 9) leave very little flexibility in allocating public funds. The two-thirds vote requirement to approve a state budget allows a minority in one house of the state legislature to stall the budgetary process. The governor is not responsible for administering upward of 40% of the state budget; the independently elected superintendent of public instruction is. Institutional strictures such as these place real limits on leaders, even if they are highly capable people.

This is not to argue that leadership is unimportant; it is to argue that it is not enough. California needs both excellent leaders and sound institutions—institutions that grant leaders the latitude and the power to solve public problems. Securing the services of effective leaders is itself an institutional matter as campaign finance laws, pensions and salary levels, and rules requiring politicians to disclose their personal assets all influence the quality of persons willing to enter public office. How might Californians respond to the need for institutional change?

A Constitutional Response

There are several ways in California to alter the basic law of the state. Depending on how sweeping the proposed changes are, one of the following forms of alteration may be undertaken.

1. **Legislative Constitutional Amendment.** After an assembly or senate constitutional amendment (ACA or SCA) has passed both houses of the legislature by a two-thirds vote, the proposed amendment is placed before the voters of the California electorate. A legislative constitutional amendment in California is adopted when a majority of those voting on that precise item approve it.

2. **Initiative Constitutional Amendment.** When signatures amounting to 8% of the total number of votes cast in the last gubernatorial contest are collected on petitions, an initiative constitutional amendment is placed before the popular voters at the next general election. An initiative constitutional amendment is adopted when a majority of those voting on that precise item approve it.

3. **Constitutional Revision Commission.** The state legislature may create a commission to review the basic law of California and to recommend changes to be made to the constitution. Changes proposed by the revision commission must be adopted by two-thirds votes of both houses of the legislature and by majority votes of those members of the electorate voting on the changes at statewide elections.

4. **Constitutional Convention.** The state legislature is empowered to call a constitutional convention on a two-thirds vote of both houses. A majority popular vote on the question of holding such a convention must be obtained from the electorate. After the convention drafts a new constitution, the proposed document must be approved by a majority of those voting on the issue. In other words, popular votes are required before and after a constitutional convention.

Legislative and initiative constitutional amendments tend to add length and complexity to the state constitution. Particular interests in California seek to place benefits for their group in the constitution because it is more difficult to change the basic law than it is to repeal an ordinary statute. Since California's present constitution was adopted in 1879, it has been amended 480 times as of 1990. About 100 of these constitutional amendments have been added since 1970. The more specificity incorporated into the document, the greater the need to adopt still more constitutional amendments to permit certain activities of government to take place.

Revision commissions and constitutional conventions usually are used to shorten the basic law and to modernize it. There are important differences between the two, however. Because revision commissions must send their recommended changes back through the legislature before they are set for popular approval, the California Legislature does not lose control of constitutional change if the revision process is used. In constitutional conventions, on the other hand, delegates especially chosen to attend the convention draft new language that then goes directly to the voters without passing through the legislature. A constitutional revision commission may be commenced simply by action of the legislature, but the voters must authorize the calling of a constitutional convention.

An interesting historical footnote in California pertains to the calling of constitutional conventions since 1879. During four elections (1898, 1914, 1920, and 1930) the voters of California refused to approve a legislative request to call a constitutional convention. In 1934, however, the voters narrowly approved a legislative request to hold a constitutional convention. This convention was never held because the legislature could not agree on the rules for selecting convention delegates. If the legislature were to agree on delegate selection methods today, a constitutional convention might be held without submitting the issue to the public again. In the opinion of some scholars, "The mandate of 1934 probably remains legally operative" (Jacobs and Sokolow, 1970:20).

In the 1960s, California did use the revision commission approach to alter the state constitution. Commission members appointed by the legislature included lawyers, academics, and members of the League of Women Voters, among others. Some three-fourths of the measures sent to the electorate were approved by the voters. As a result of the revision process, the length of the state constitution was cut in half. In the wake of the lengthy impasse regarding the state budget in 1990, the legislature instructed one of its committees to prepare a proposal for establishing a constitutional revision commission to modify language in the basic law dealing with fiscal affairs. Given the piecemeal additions to the state constitution through legislative and initiative amendments, is it unreasonable to engage in a full-scale review of the basic law about every quarter century?

California has amended its constitution more times than any other state with the exception of Alabama. Thought might be given to making it more difficult to amend California's basic law. Several alterations could be made. First, the percentage signature requirement to qualify an initiative constitutional amendment could be raised from 8 to 10 or 15% as is now the law in states such as Arizona, Arkansas, Michigan, Montana, Nebraska, Nevada, Ohio, Oklahoma, and South Dakota. Second, 12 states now require that legislative constitutional amendments be passed during two consecutive sessions of the legislature before the item is put out to ratification by the voters. Third, voter approval of constitutional amendments could be made more difficult by requiring a two-thirds popular vote for ratification as is now the law in New Hampshire. Alternatively, the voter requirement could be a majority of all those voting in the election as a whole as opposed to the majority of those voting on the amendment itself. If the vote is much heavier for president or governor at the top of the ballot than it is for a constitutional amendment at the bottom, this proviso would block amendments from slipping into the constitution with only a majority of a diminished electorate.

Depending on your view of the gravity of the present institutional crisis, and the amount of confidence you retain in the California Legislature, either a revision commission or a constitutional convention might attract your support. Should one of these constitutional responses be accepted, however, it is imperative that the politics surrounding such an undertaking not be neglected. The interests that benefit from the current constitutional arrangements will attempt to stop commissions and conventions from being convened; if these entities do come to life, entrenched interests will endeavor to control the selection of participants to these bodies. To pursue a constitutional response, it is advisable to have an agenda of institutional changes in mind and to have a base of support with sufficient power to see to it that suitable people are named to a revision commission or to a constitutional convention.

A Political Response

Perhaps the way to deal with the dilemmas facing California is not inside government. An institution already exists outside of government whose purpose is the selection of able leaders and the involvement of greater numbers of people in the political process. That institution, of course, is the political party. It is the job of political parties to register, to educate, and to turn out voters. Further, parties should nominate capable individuals for office and should provide their nominees with a clear platform of positions on the issues. If a party can speak directly to the needs of Californians, it should be able to win such a broad mandate at the polls that the executive and legislative branches would be controlled by the same party. A governing coalition of sufficient magnitude would not have to fear reprisals from narrow interests when the public good required taking action on such thorny issues as car insurance. A party with adequate campaign resources would alter the perception of some public officials that they need to engage in corruption to raise the money to win reelection.

Michael Woo, member of the City Council of Los Angeles, has called for "a collective application of courage" to deal with the problems facing California. That is precisely what parties could provide—a team of supporters to back up leaders when they tackle the tough issues. Woo has also lamented that, "We have a shortage of far-sighted shepherds at this time" (Woo, 1990). It is the work of parties to find effective leaders or shepherds. (Consistent with our earlier discussion, it is worth noting that even the best shepherds can have difficulty if too many streams and thickets are placed in the path of their flocks.)

Because California has been considered an antiparty state since 1911, there are long odds against party governance coming to pass. In addition to political parties, there are other forms of political activism that can have a profound impact. The environmental movement, the tax limitation movement, and the antinuclear movement have all jolted government institutions into action. After years of organizational effort, residents in the Sacramento Municipal Utility District voted in 1989 to close down the Rancho Seco Nuclear Power Plant despite heavy campaigning by district personnel to keep the facility open. Trying to imagine a homeless movement or a student movement suggests there are limits to this form of activism as well.

Summary

California is big and diverse. The state is huge in both population and economic terms. California is diverse ethnically, economically, and topographically. Unfortunately, the problems facing the state are also big and diverse. The once-vaunted political institutions of California may no longer be capable of resolving the issues confronting the state.

Having just begun your reading of this text, it is probably premature to expect you to decide which course of action will be most useful in the years ahead. Nevertheless, debating the merits and demerits of a constitutional convention, a constitutional revision commission, revitalization of California's political parties, and the efficacy of political movements is a worthwhile exercise. Creating the future politics of this state is not a spectator sport; it demands our active engagement.

References: Chapter 1

Bernstein, Dan. "Harsh Talk, Prison Term for Montoya." *Sacramento Bee* (April 27, 1990a).

Bernstein, Dan. "Carpenter Guilty on All Counts." *Sacramento Bee* (September 18, 1990b).

Callenbach, Ernest. *Ecotopia: The Notebooks and Reports of William Weston.* Berkeley: Banyan Tree Books, 1975.

The Economist. "How California Might Fare in an American Recession." *Sacramento Bee* (October 21, 1990).

Garcia, Phillip. "State Watches as Chips Fall Elsewhere." *Sacramento Bee* (October 25, 1989).

Garreau, Joel. *The Nine Nations of North America.* Boston: Houghton Mifflin, 1981.

Haslam, Gerald. *The Other California: The Great Central Valley in Life and Letters.* Santa Barbara: Capra Press, 1990.

Jacobs, Clyde and Alvin Sokolow. *California Government: One Among Fifty.* New York: Macmillan, 1970.

Kahrl, William. "Who's Conserving—And Who's Not—In the Drought." *Sacramento Bee* (April 29, 1990).

Lee, Eugene. "Hiram Johnson's Great Reform Is an Idea Whose Time Has Past." *Public Affairs Report.* Berkeley: Institute of Governmental Studies (July 1990).

McLeod, Roman. "Oregon Now a Trendy Destination." *San Francisco Chronicle* (December 18, 1990).

Monagan, Robert. *The Disappearance of Representative Government: A California Solution.* Grass Valley: Comstock Bonanza Press, 1990.

Phillips, Kevin. "A Growing Populism in California." *Sacramento Bee* (November 21, 1989).

Schrag, Peter. "The Plebiscitary Fun House." *Sacramento Bee* (May 14, 1990).

Senate Office of Research. *Does California Need a Policy to Manage Urban Growth?* Sacramento: State of California, 1989.

Smith, Martin. "The Triumph of the Status Quo." *Sacramento Bee* (September 2, 1990).

The State of California. *Economic Report of the Governor: 1990.* Sacramento, 1990.

U.S. Bureau of the Census. *Statistical Abstract of the United States: 1990.* Washington, D.C., 1990.

Vartabedian, Ralph. "Aerospace Industry Flees Southern California." *Sacramento Bee* (May 14, 1990).

Walters, Dan. "Political Reform Is First Order." *Sacramento Bee* (January 5, 1990).

Woo, Michael. "The New California: A Multicultural Society." Keynote address delivered at the California Studies Conference: Envisioning California II. Sacramento: February 8, 1990.

Zelman, Walter. "California's Stalemated Government." *Sacramento Bee* (August 5, 1990).

CHAPTER 2

California's History

The history of California is unique in several respects. Unlike Native Americans in some areas of the continent, the original tribes in California were peaceful. Although much settlement along the Atlantic seaboard stemmed from a desire for religious freedom, the impetus behind Spanish expansion into California was conversion of native tribes and military occupation of the region. Bypassing territorial status altogether, California experienced a staggering influx of people and rapidly became a state due to the discovery of gold. To make travel to the new state less arduous, and to better link areas within California, railroads rose to prominence. In response to the economic and political domination of the railroad, a period of major reforms took place. Even though these reforms are now eight decades old, they still form the basis of contemporary California politics.

Spanish and Mexican Rule

Although the Portuguese navigator Cabrillo explored the California coastline for Spain in 1542, permanent settlement by Europeans did not occur for another two centuries. At the time of Spanish exploration, some 300,000 Native Californians lived throughout California in numerous tribes. Indians had inhabited California for thousands of years, so the Spanish found anything but an empty landscape when they arrived. It was not until 1769 that Captain Portola and Father Serra led an expedition from the Spanish colony of Mexico to found a European settlement and Franciscan mission at San Diego. The chain of missions, which ultimately reached 21 in number, was confined to a narrow band of land bordering the Pacific shoreline. Native Californians in this area were either the object of missionary efforts by the Franciscan padres or displaced into the interior region of California.

Spanish rule, in its colony to the north of Mexico, was characterized by insufficient investment and uncertainty as to leadership and direction. Due to warfare on the European continent with France and England, as well as the remoteness of the colony itself, Spain was not able to provide ample support for the colonization effort. With the assistance of Native Californian labor, the missions grew economically powerful on the strength of cultivated crops and livestock herds. The military presidios and civilian pueblos did not thrive to such an extent, and discord between the military and religious authorities in California was common.

With Spain increasingly unable to administer its farflung colonial empire, Mexico successfully obtained its independence from Spain in 1821 and thereafter assumed control of California. Actually, Mexican control of its northern province was never complete. Years of inattentive administration by Spain had produced independent attitudes among the European residents of California. Governors sent from Mexico City found their authority was not accepted by local leaders. Although relatively bloodless in nature, military engagements between factions from northern and southern California did occur.

Two developments were of more long-term significance than the feuding among Mexican provincial officials. First, the Mexican government in 1834 decided to secularize the missions in California and to distribute the mission properties to those settlers desiring land grants. The Spaniards had dispensed a very limited number of land grants, but the pace of granting large parcels of land accelerated dramatically in the late 1830s and early 1840s. Grants of up to 48,000 acres were made to individuals; and, since the separate members of a family could each obtain a grant, vast ranchos—some reaching one quarter of a million acres in size—were accumulated by related persons. Second, citizens of the United States began to appear in California in greater numbers. Preceded by intrepid mountaineers and maritime traders, the first U.S. settlers to arrive over the Sierra Nevada in California were the members of the Bidwell party in 1841. Lieutenant John C. Fremont brought U.S. military expeditions into California in 1844 and 1846, thereby defying the authority and provincial rule of the Mexican government.

U.S. Military Occupation

As a result of a dispute concerning the location of the southern boundary of Texas, the United States declared war on Mexico in May of 1846. During this war, Commodore John D. Sloat occupied the Pacific port of Monterey for the United States, and General Stephen W. Kearny made his way across New Mexico and Arizona to take control of the southern portions of California. Los Angeles was initially entered without resistance because ranking Mexican officials had fled to Mexico. However,

Captain José Flores led those Mexicans who chose to stay and fight in a 5-month campaign against the U.S. forces. By January 1847, the United States was in full possession of California.

During the interim period in which U.S. military rule and the remnants of Mexican law prevailed, James Marshall discovered gold in January 1848 along the banks of the American River northeast of Sacramento. Later in 1848, the United States signed, and Congress ratified, the Treaty of Guadalupe Hidalgo. The treaty formally concluded the war with Mexico and ceded California to the United States. The treaty also provided that Mexican Californians wishing to become U.S. citizens could do so, and that titles to land established by earlier grants from Mexico and Spain would be honored. With legal responsibility for the area now transferred, and population rapidly mounting due to the frenzied search for gold, it became imperative for civilian government to be organized in California.

California's First Constitution

A constitutional convention was held in the fall of 1849 consisting of 48 male delegates representing various regions of California. It was a relatively youthful assemblage—the average age of the delegates being just under 38 years of age—with wide variation in length of residence in California. Seven delegates had spent all their lives in California, whereas 13 members of the convention had been in California for 1 year or less (Mason, 1973:87). From the standpoint of the document ultimately crafted, it was significant that the nonnative Californians at the convention had been born in 13 different states in the Union (as well as five foreign countries) and that they collectively had resided in 21 of the then 30 states. California borrowed heavily from other states in writing its first constitution. Largely due to the presence of a delegate who earlier had participated in Iowa's constitutional convention, the 137 sections of the California document contained 66 sections taken from basic Iowa law. Probably as a result of the fact that 12 former New Yorkers were convention delegates, 19 sections of the constitution of California originated in the Empire State.

The convention document, which was approved overwhelmingly by the voters in November 1849, established a government very much like today's. Unlike its national counterpart, where the provisions concerning a citizen's rights were attached at the end, the California constitution of 1849 began with a Bill of Rights. A plural executive branch of six separate officials chosen by statewide election was formed. A legislature with two houses—the senate and the assembly—was created. Unlike the other articles based on U.S. precedents, the section establishing the elected judicial branch with four levels of courts was borrowed largely from satisfactory experience with such an arrangement during the quarter century of Mexican rule. White males over 21 years of age were given the right to vote; Native Californians were denied this right pending a two-thirds vote of the legislature granting them the franchise. Official pronouncements and documents of state government were to be printed in English and Spanish. A provision of interest some 14 years later, when efforts were underway to build a rail line across the Sierra Nevada, was that the legislature could not incur a debt in excess of $300,000 without a vote of approval from the electorate. In the interest of solidifying its hold on the region, and perhaps dazzled by the mineral wealth being unearthed there, the U.S. Congress accepted the constitution of 1849 and on September 9, 1850, admitted California as the thirty-first state in the Union.

The Big Four

As the 1860s began, there was little indication that the chain of events about to be set in motion by four Sacramento merchants would have a profound and lasting impact on political life in California. The extraordinarily powerful transportation monopoly created at this time was to dominate state politics for over four decades. Its existence ultimately led to major modifications in California's political processes.

Leland Stanford, Collis Huntington, Charles Crocker, and Mark Hopkins formed the Central Pacific Railroad in 1861 for the purpose of building a rail line across the Sierra Nevada north of Lake Tahoe. Realizing the importance to the state and to the nation of a rail line between the east and west coasts, the group sought government support for its expensive undertaking. The U.S. Congress in 1862 (and later in 1864) made land grants and long-term loans available and named the Central Pacific as the corporation responsible for the western portion of the proposed line. Having run successfully for governor of California, Stanford used his office during 1862 and 1863 to secure outright monetary subsidies and additional loans from the state legislature for the railroad. Given the previously mentioned limitation on indebtedness in the state constitution, these financial arrangements were of questionable constitutionality. Fortified with public funds, together with private capital, construction commenced up the western slope of the Sierra in early 1863.

The leaders of the Central Pacific were a rare, complementary mixture of diverse abilities. Stanford enjoyed public office (he was later to be a U.S. senator) and served as corporate president of the Central Pacific. Huntington was the group's east coast representative and lobbyist in Washington, D.C. Tireless, yet shunning public attention, Huntington also planned the railroad's political operation throughout the length of California and held the position of corporate vice president. Although named only a director of the corporation, Crocker was the driving force behind the work crews laying track up and over very difficult mountain terrain. At first due to a labor shortage, but later due to their proficiency as workers and their lower wage demands, Crocker employed some 12,000 Chinese in the construction effort (Howard, 1962:235, 303). Less assertive than his three companions, Hopkins was treasurer of the Central Pacific and responsible for assembling the many supplies and materials needed to continue building the rail line to the east.

Given the size of California and the limited number of entry points to the state, transportation within and into the state was bound to be of crucial importance to the development of the region. Sensing this, the leaders of the Central Pacific—soon dubbed "the Big Four"—acquired railroad companies capable of linking regions within the state, as well as providing connections to Oregon and Arizona. One of these acquisitions, the Southern Pacific Railroad Company, later became the corporate identity by which the entire system was known.

Although people in California originally had supported the growth of rail transportation, the mood had changed by May 1869 when the Central Pacific linked with the Union Pacific at Promontory Point (north of the Great Salt Lake) to form the first rail line across the United States. By controlling 85% of the track in California, the Big Four possessed powerful economic leverage. Their principal economic tool was the ability to vary freight rates. If the railroad supported a particular business, it would provide secret discounts for shipments. Freight charges could also be raised to the point where a shipper would be unable to move goods by rail. Subsidies were expected from county and city governments for the privilege of rail service. Should such monies not be forthcoming, the local government in question would be bypassed entirely or a rival community would be established nearby to serve as a rail center. San Bernardino would not subsidize the Southern Pacific, so the company established the town of Colton for use as a depot (McAfee, 1973:123). Under these circumstances, localities wishing to prosper would generally subsidize the laying of track in their area. Note that the Southern Pacific received financial assistance from national, state, and, finally, local governments.

Efforts by disgruntled Californians to develop less expensive means of shipping were met head on by the Big Four. When shippers between San Francisco and Los Angeles shifted their freight to coastal steamships to avoid high rail rates, the Southern Pacific acquired the steamship line to eliminate the competition. Transportation companies traveling the inland waterways between San Francisco and Sacramento or Stockton met the same fate. If a rail line offering fair rates was established somewhere in the state, the railroad giant would temporarily cut its freight charges on that route to next to nothing. While the large corporation would recover its losses on that route by elevating its rates elsewhere, the upstart competitor would be forced out of business.

Apart from the above types of economic power, the Southern Pacific was by far the largest landholder in the state. Having received up to 12,800 acres from the public domain for every mile of track laid under provisions of federal laws passed in 1862 and 1864, the railroad came to control 11.5 million of California's 100 million acres (Robinson, 1948: 157). Although the railroad could not select acreage covered by a validated land grant made prior to statehood, the acquisition of so much land by the railroad was a genuine source of economic strength.

To forestall the implementation of governmental policies that might hamper their widespread interests, the Big Four and the Political Bureau of the Southern Pacific were thoroughly involved in politics at all levels of government. While Huntington sought favorable treatment for the corporation from the federal government, political agents of the railroad were active at the State Capitol in Sacramento and in country courthouses throughout the state. Since state party conventions were attended by delegates from localities, the railroad's operatives made every effort to see that representatives friendly to the Southern Pacific were selected. These meetings nominated candidates to run for state offices. By controlling nominating procedures, and by contributing heavily to pro-railroad candidates, many persons sympathetic to the Big Four took office.

Ample financial resources permitted the Southern Pacific to provide free train passes for officeholders and their families, to pay the expenses of the visits to San Francisco (the corporate headquarters) by political supporters, and to extend "legal fees" to lawyer–politicians. To obtain favorable press, the corporation subsidized those newspapers with the "correct" attitude about the railroad. Should a particular periodical be especially troublesome, not only would any subsidy then in effect be withdrawn, but efforts would also be made to have major shippers remove their advertising. In an unusually flagrant example of the use of money in politics, Leland Stanford's brother, Philip, openly paid voters on the streets of San Francisco to cast ballots in favor of a municipal stock subscription that would provide construction capital for the Central Pacific (Lewis, 1938:358). Finally, the political style of the Big Four is aptly illustrated by Governor Stanford's naming of Charles Crocker's brother, Edwin, to the state supreme court. Edwin Crocker was head of the railroad's legal department at the time of his appointment, and he did not relinquish this post when he joined the bench.

California's Second Constitution _____

During the mid-1870s, the state's economy weakened. Numerous businesses failed and the ranks of the unemployed grew. Resentment mounted against the Chinese as they returned from Utah and Nevada after helping to complete the transcontinental rail link in 1869. Corporations were criticized for controlling too much land, charging unfair rates, and encouraging the importation of Chinese laborers. The Workingmen's party was formed in San Francisco in September 1877 in response to these issues. Dennis Kearney, a 31-year old Irishman who supported himself by transporting goods around the city in a cart, became a vocal leader of this group. Kearney's statements included the following: "The rich have ruled us until they have ruined us. We will now take our affairs into our own hands," and "To an American, death is preferable to life on a par with the Chinese" (Swisher, 1969:11). Kearney served a brief jail term for threatening physical violence on a member of the Big Four, and for participating in a riot near the Nob Hill mansions of Stanford and Crocker in San Francisco.

Because of the lack of detail in the constitution of 1849 and the numerous changes in the state in the intervening decades, the state legislature called a constitutional convention in June 1878 to which delegates would be elected. Individuals with corporate interest turned their attention to the election of as many delegates opposed to Kearney's views as possible. Although the Workingmen's party (or Kearneyites) elected only one-third of the 152 delegates to the constitutional convention, their presence, and occasional alliance with small-farmer delegates, led to the adoption of a number of provisions dealing with corporations.

Some of the language approved for the new constitution dealt with corporations in general, and some with railroads in particular. Stockholders were made responsible for their share of the debts of a corporation; members of a corporation's board of directors were made liable for all monies embezzled or misappropriated by corporate officers; and no corporation could hold real estate unnecessary to its business for more than 5 years. The provisions regarding railroads forbade giving free passes to officeholders; prohibited raising rates that had been reduced to compete with a rival line; required that short haul fares be less than long haul fares traveling over the same track in the same direction; and, most importantly, established a railroad commission of three persons to be elected every 4 years to set transportation rates and to correct abuses by the carriers. The delegates wrote this regulatory commission into the constitution so that statutory action of the legislature could not disband it.

The delegates also approved an article prohibiting the employment of Chinese on public works projects, or by corporations chartered in California. This so-called Chinese exclusion provision remained in the state constitution until it was repealed in 1952. Although the all-male convention debated extending the right to vote to women, a motion to that effect was defeated. The California Constitution of 1879 remains in effect to this day, although it underwent major revision in the 1960s and 1970s. Through legislative constitutional amendment and initiative constitutional amendment, the 1879 constitution had been amended 480 times as of the November election of 1990.

The railroad had tried to block the constitutional convention of 1879, had argued against placing language on corporations and railroads in the constitution, and had urged voters to deny ratification of the finished document. Faced with the strong sentiment in favor of regulating the railroad, the Big Four instead "managed to 'influence' two of the three members of the state railroad commission (one by open bribery), and the entire machinery of regulation collapsed" (Lewis, 1938:404). Referring to the ultimate impact of the railroad commission, an authority on this era concluded: "Indeed, the railroads seemed to profit by the scheme, in that they appeared to submit to a political agency, which in fact they were themselves able to control" (Swisher, 1969:113). Celebrations over the supposed demise of the Southern Pacific were premature. Its period of dominance was only half completed. Although the antirailroad efforts of 1879 were not adequately implemented, they were the forerunners of major reforms three decades later.

Progressivism in California _____

By 1900 all the members of the Big Four had died, and the ownership of the Southern Pacific had passed to E.H. Harriman. However, with its control of the state legislature still intact, the transportation corporation saw to it that the state railroad commission was appropriated no funds to carry out regulatory activities. Determined to liberate their party and the legislature from the influence of the Southern Pacific, a group of reformers set about encouraging antirailroad delegates to attend the next Republican state convention. Partial success at this convention in 1908 led to the election of a significant number of state legislators who were not indebted to the rail company. During the legislative session of

1909, these progressive reformers enacted a direct primary law that removed from party conventions the responsibility of selecting nominees to run for public office. Whereas a small number of convention delegates, usually controlled by the railroad, had chosen candidates for various races prior to 1909, henceforth all registered voters in a particular party would participate in primary elections to determine the nominees of their party. Having instituted the primary system, the progressives moved quickly to take advantage of the opportunity it afforded.

Despite opposition from the Southern Pacific in both the Republican primary and the general election, progressive Republican Hiram Johnson swept to victory in 1910 to become governor of California. Declining to ride on trains and refusing to be identified in any manner with the railroad, Johnson traveled throughout the state in an automobile driven by his son. He campaigned on the theme that he would "kick the Southern Pacific out of politics." Since both houses of the state legislature had also become solidly progressive, the stage was set for the introduction of the most important political changes ever made in California.

Although a scholarly consensus is lacking concerning the meaning of the term progressivism, it is generally conceded the progressives believed in (1) taming unrestrained corporate influence in the political process, (2) regulating concentrated economic power, (3) expanding citizen participation in politics, (4) protecting the environment, and (5)

Figure 2-1 Governor Hiram Johnson. (State Library)

improving adverse working and living conditions stemming from industrialization and urbanization (Gould, 1974:2–5). Progressives hoped to rid government of corruption and to establish efficient, expert management in the public sector. The progressive point of view was not found exclusively among Republicans, nor were all Republicans necessarily progressive in their orientation. Democrat Theodore Bell, Johnson's opponent in the general election of 1910, was considered a progressive as well.

Under Hiram Johnson's administration, the following changes in political institutions were either placed in the state constitution, or enacted into statutory law, on the dates indicated:

1911— The Railroad Commission was expanded from three to five members; made appointive by the governor instead of elected; given jurisdiction over utilities (i.e., gas, electricity, and telephones) as well as railroads; and provided with the means to enforce its rate decisions.

1911— The direct democracy devices of initiative, referendum, and recall were made available to the people of California. (Please refer to Chapter 6 for extended discussion of these items.)

1911— Judicial and school board elections were to be nonpartisan, which meant that party labels could not appear next to candidates' names on the ballot.

1911— Women were extended the right to vote. (The U.S. Constitution was not amended to incorporate women's suffrage until 1920.)

1911— The party column ballot, which facilitated straight-ticket (i.e., selecting all the candidates of one party) voting, was eliminated in favor of the office bloc ballot.

1913— City, county, and special district elections were made nonpartisan.

1913— The leadership and operation of the official political parties in California were prescribed in detail thereby weakening these organizations. (Please refer to Chapter 5 for extended discussion of this point.)

1913— Candidates were permitted to "cross-file" into more than one primary election contest, which meant that a prospective officeholder might appear simultaneously on the ballot (and possibly win the nomination) of two or more parties (Olin, 1968; Mowry, 1951).

As is evident from this list, several reforms dealt with political parties. The progressives thought that parties were the vehicle by which the Southern Pacific exercised its domination over the state. Therefore, the reformers undertook to weaken them. Nonpartisan elections reduced the number of offices for which someone bearing a party label could run. Altering the ballot and introducing cross-filing made it more difficult for parties to be sure that their rank and file members were voting for party candidates. Governor Johnson and the legislature approved a bill in 1915 to do away with party labels for all state offices (legislative and executive), just as partisan elections had been eliminated at the local level. Essentially, this would have been a death blow to political parties in California, as only elections for national offices would have remained partisan. Ironically, the voters used a device made available by the progressives themselves—the referendum—to defeat this measure sponsored by the progressive leadership in the state.

Apart from changes in political institutions, the progressives attempted to curb industrial accidents, to improve conditions for immigrants and migrant agricultural workers, and to preserve the state's natural resources. Responding to an historic sentiment among some whites in California, the progressives put into effect an Alien Land Law in 1913, which prohibited Asians (but not Europeans) who were ineligible for citizenship from owning land. This law was declared unconstitutional in 1952. (Racial intolerance and insensitivity to the civil rights of nonwhites are the marked differences between progressives of the early twentieth century and liberals today.)

In 1914, Hiram Johnson became the first governor in the state's history to win a second election to office. However, he completed only 2 years of this term before moving to the U.S. Senate, where he served nearly 30 years until his death in 1945. The Republican lieutenant governor, William Stephens, finished Johnson's term and was elected to the chief executive post on his own in 1918. Although additional reforms were not instituted during his administration, Stephens did consolidate and preserve the progressive measures that had been introduced under Johnson. Attempts to reduce state regulatory power over corporations, and to alter the initiative and direct primary processes, were defeated in the last years of his governorship.

Antiprogressive sentiment had a resurgence in the 1920s, as progressives and their opponents battled on much more even terms than they had in the prior decade. Republican Friend Richardson, the state treasurer, was elected governor in 1922 and proceeded to cut funds supporting the work of the state regulatory commissions. His appointees to the regulatory bodies were sympathetic to corporate interests. After the legislative elections of 1924, the progressives rallied and kept Governor Richardson from further undermining their programs for the remainder of his term (Putnam, 1966:395–411). To thwart Richardson's bid for the second term, progressive Republicans backed the Republican lieutenant governor, Clement C. Young, in the gubernatorial primary of 1926. Young won the Republican primary and was elected governor. His administration had some progressive accomplishments in that he made the state bureaucracy more efficient and he had funds appropriated for the development of public hydroelectric power. Progressives were disappointed, however, with Governor Young's appointee as superintendent of banks. This superintendent approved the Bank of Italy's acquisition of numerous banks in the state, thereby leading to statewide branch banking and the eventual creation of the Bank of America. A. P. Giannini of the bank had endorsed Young's candidacy in 1926, but the governor maintained that this support was unrelated to the decision permitting the bank's aquisitions (James and James, 1954:180–184, 192–197). Given memories of the Southern Pacific, Young's allowing a large economic combination to come about did not sit well with progressives. With the victory of James Rolph over Young in the Republican gubernatorial primary of 1930, progressivism went into a period of eclipse. The repeal in 1930 of constitutional restrictions on corporations—that is, the 1879 provision limiting land ownership by corporations and the sections establishing liability of stockholders and directors—symbolized the basic shift toward less government regulation of business.

Politics during the Depression

As economic depression gripped the state, Governor James "Sunny Jim" Rolph—the nickname apparently a reference to his reputation as a jovial inebriate—opposed reform of corporate taxes and plans to develop public hydroelectric power in the state. He had especially close ties to the banking industry. After Rolph's death in 1934, conservative Lieutenant Governor Frank Merriam became the Republican candidate for governor by defeating several progressive challengers in the party primary. The ensuing gubernatorial contest offered Californians a genuine choice between candidates espousing highly contrasting policies. Upton Sinclair, the Democratic nominee and socialist author, advocated a program to End Poverty in California (EPIC) by putting the unemployed to work at state-operated farms and factories. Merriam countered by deriding the "empty promises in California" of his opponent. The gubernatorial race of 1934 was a prototype of the negative campaigns waged today. Because of his plan to tax their industry, owners of Hollywood studios unleashed distorted newsreels against Sinclair. (Newsreels were the television news of that day and age.) Sinclair backers were depicted as hobos and bums migrating to California, while Merriam's supporters were shown as responsible citizens. Though Merriam succeeded in defeating Sinclair in 1934, the continuing depression and the national tide against Republican officeholders led to the victory of Culbert Olson over Merriam in 1938. Olson was the first Democrat to be elected governor in California in the twentieth century. The year 1938 also provided a glimpse of the future as the district attorney from Alameda County, Earl Warren, became state attorney general by successfully using cross-filing to win the Republican and Democratic primary elections.

The Ascendancy of Nonpartisanship

Governor Olson intended to preside over a rebirth of progressive pro-grams—chief among them being public hydroelectric power, stronger government regulation of the oil industry, and compulsory health insur-ance—but conflict with the legislature precluded passage of his reforms. Olson lost the governorship to Republican Earl Warren in 1942. Through the appointment of Republicans and Democrats alike to state administrative positions, Warren typified the progressives' nonpartisan orientation to state government. His support of better pensions, unem-ployment insurance, and health insurance was also reminiscent of progressive policies. For the first and only time in the state's history, Warren carried the nonpartisan spirit to its zenith by winning the Republican and the Democratic nominations for governor in 1946 through a successful cross-filing effort. Warren became the only gover-nor of California ever elected to a third term in 1950, but he did not complete this term due to his appointment as chief justice of the U.S. Supreme Court in 1953. The major blemish on Warren's record was his support of the relocation of 110,000 Japanese-Americans during World War II. Of this he later wrote, "I have since deeply regretted the removal order and my own testimony advocating it, because it was not in keep-with our American concept of freedom and the rights of citizens" (War-ren, 1977:149).

Figure 2-2   Governor Earl Warren. (State Library)

Republican Goodwin Knight, the incumbent lieutenant governor, became governor on Warren's departure for Washington, D.C. Business interests thought Knight would be sympathetic to their point of view, but this proved to be only partially correct. Governor Knight did not support health insurance or create numerous new state programs, but he did permit increased appropriations for existing government activities (e.g., workmen's compensation and disability insurance) as well as embrace the aims of organized labor. The Democrats had climbed ahead of the Republicans in terms of registered voters in 1934. Migration of persons to California to work in military construction plants during World War II and the Korean Conflict further augmented the size of the state's Democratic party. Following Warren's example, Knight understood that to be retained as the state's chief executive he would need the votes of both Democrats and Republicans. Pursuing a relatively nonpartisan campaign, and with labor's backing, Knight was elected governor in his own right in 1954. The gubernatorial elections from 1942 to 1954 in California demonstrated that in terms of registration figures, the majority party could not always rely on its rank and file membership to vote for Democratic candidates. Voting for "the person, not the party" received impetus during this period. As we will see in Chapter 5, weak party loyalty in the voting booth during general elections is but one of the reasons for the lack of power on the part of California's political parties.

The Big Switch: 1958

The 1958 election was pivotal in California politics. Having just completed 8 years as state attorney general during the Republican administrations of Warren and Knight, Edmund G. (Pat) Brown was nominated as Democratic candidate for governor. Although Knight was planning to campaign for reelection, California's U.S. Senator William Knowland announced his intention to run in the Republican gubernatorial primary in his home state. To avoid a bitter split in the Republican party, and at the urging of then Vice President Richard Nixon and the *Los Angeles Times*, Knight decided to attempt an exchange of offices with Knowland by campaigning for the U.S. Senate instead of the governorship. The big switch failed as both Republican candidates lost. Unlike Warren and Knight before him, Knowland's reputation as a strongly partisan Republican hindered his appeal across party lines. In addition, an unofficial party organization called the California Democratic Council (CDC) was highly effective in urging Democratic voters to support their party's candidates in 1958.

Along with Pat Brown's victory in the gubernatorial race, the Democrats won control of both houses of the state legislature for the first time in this century. Once in power, the party that had fared poorly under cross-filing quickly eliminated this aspect of primary elections from future use in California. Saying that he hoped to lead California to accomplishments as significant as those made during the bipartisan administrations of Hiram Johnson and Earl Warren, Brown expanded aid to local educational districts, the highway system, and the state's university campuses. He inaugurated a consumer protection program to control unscrupulous business practices. Governor Brown also successfully advocated the State Water Project to build reservoirs on the Feather River north of Sacramento, and link them through an aqueduct with the central and southern portions of the state.

Following former Vice President Richard Nixon's unsuccessful attempt to unseat Governor Brown in the election of 1962, a number of problems plagued the incumbent's second term. Brown's conflict with the Democratic speaker of the state assembly, Jesse Unruh, hindered good relations with the legislature and weakened party cohesiveness in the state. The student protests surrounding the Free Speech Movement on the Berkeley campus of the University of California in 1964 and the African-American riots in the south Los Angeles ghetto of Watts in 1965 provided opponents with issues to use against Brown as he tried to duplicate Warren's feat of being elected to a third term. Campaigning on a platform to limit taxation and the growth of state government, as well as advocating firm measures to deal with student unrest, Republican Ronald Reagan defeated Pat Brown by one million votes in the gubernatorial election of 1966.

The Actor and the Seminarian

After decades of experienced leadership by the likes of Earl Warren and Pat Brown, 1966 marked the beginning of a 16-year period during which California's chief executives learned the job while occupying the governorship. Having never held public office, former actor Ronald Reagan endeavored to deliver on his campaign promises to cut government spending. He did reduce state appropriations for higher education and for mental health, but with inflation and population growth, Reagan was not able to stop the absolute growth of state expenditures. However, he claimed to have reduced the *rate* of increase in government spending. Having received strong campaign assistance from the business community, Reagan appointed numerous persons from industry to state posts formerly occupied by individuals supportive of labor, consumerism, or environmentalism.

The state legislature, which had been controlled by the Democrats since the realigning year of 1958, swung to a slight Republican majority in 1969. Governor Reagan hoped to use his reelection campaign in 1970 to help increase the Republican hold on the two legislative chambers. Reagan was elected to a second term as governor by defeating Democrat Jesse Unruh by one-half million votes. However, in a major disappointment to the Republican governor, both houses of the legislature returned to Democratic majorities by narrow margins. Reagan's party controlled the legislature for less than 2 of his 8 years as governor. This situation once again demonstrates the proclivity of California voters to forsake partisan loyalty by voting for a person, not a party. By splitting their tickets, voters returned a Republican to the governor's office while handing leadership of the state legislature to the Democrats.

The year 1970 also saw the election of the first African-American to statewide office as Wilson Riles became state superintendent of public instruction. Two individuals, who would later compete against one another for the governorship, won their first tries at statewide office as Republican Evelle Younger became attorney general and Democrat Edmund G. (Jerry) Brown was elected secretary of state. Two landmark measures protecting the environment became law early in the decade. The California Environmental Quality Act (CEQA), which required submission of environmental impact reports (EIRs) prior to government and corporate construction projects, passed the legislature and was signed into law in 1970. Two years later, California voters approved Proposition 20, thereby initiating what would eventually become the California Coastal Commission with powers to regulate access to, and development of, the state's shoreline.

Much of Governor Reagan's second term was spent in conflict with Bob Moretti, the Democratic speaker of the assembly. As Reagan did not intend to seek a third term, Lieutenant Governor Ed Reinecke and Controller Houston Flournoy announced their candidacies for the 1974 Republican nomination for governor. Rienecke virtually forfeited the primary to Flournoy when he was indicted for perjury in a U.S. government investigation of 1972 campaign finances, although he was subsequently acquitted on a technicality.

Sensing the public's support for political reform during the year of Richard Nixon's resignation from the presidency, Secretary of State Jerry Brown entered the Democratic gubernatorial primary against Mayor Joseph Alioto of San Francisco and Speaker Moretti, among others. Brown and his staff helped to draft the Political Reform Act, which appeared on the primary ballot in 1974 as Proposition 9. In brief, the ballot measure mandated public disclosure of campaign contributions and expenditures, amounts spent by lobbyists to influence government officials, and personal financial data pertaining to candidates and office-holders. During the campaign for the Democratic nomination for governor, Brown vigorously supported the reform initiative while his opponents were reluctant to do so. Both Brown and Proposition 9 swept to victory in June 1974. With a large early lead over Flournoy in the surveys of voter opinion, Brown ran a cautious campaign for the governorship. Given the handicap of being a Republican candidate when the Watergate scandal was forcing a Republican president out of office, Houston Flournoy lost the general election to Brown by a surprisingly narrow margin (i.e., 180,000 votes).

Governor Jerry Brown, whose father left the same public office 8 years earlier, announced at the outset of his administration that California faced an "era of limits" in which appropriate technologies would have to be employed to keep nonrenewable resources from being exhausted. In keeping with the notion of limits, Brown proposed few new government programs. He did play a major role in 1975 in the passage of an agricultural labor relations statute that established procedures for the conduct of union elections on California farms. Although Brown's legislative accomplishments were not numerous, his record in the area of appointments was indeed noteworthy. Jerry Brown appointed the first woman, the first and second African-Americans, and the first Latino to the California Supreme Court. His cabinet featured a number of female members. Brown named minorities and women to boards, commissions, and departments throughout state government. Environmentalists liked Brown's support of alternative energy programs (e.g., solar and wind) and his opposition to the licensing of PG&E's Diablo Canyon Nuclear Facility. His interest in energy conservation included discouraging the use of single-occupant motor vehicles and encouraging the use of mass transit and carpools. His spartan lifestyle (no limousine or mansion) and his penchant for asking tough questions of civil servants, each perhaps a reflection of his 3½ years in a Jesuit seminary as a young man, intrigued the public and contributed to his high standing in the polls during his first term.

The state's fiscal problems and his own ambition eventually eroded Jerry Brown's popularity. As inflation drove consumer prices and wage scales higher and higher, revenues generated from sales and income taxes correspondingly increased. Known for his tight budgets, Governor Brown did not permit state expenditures to keep pace with inflation. Because of the combination of increasing revenues and budget controls, the state accumulated a surplus in the range of $6 billion by 1978. This situation was perfectly tailored to the need of property tax reformers

Howard Jarvis and Paul Gann. Housing construction in California was not keeping pace with demand, so the assessed value of existing dwellings was skyrocketing. As county tax assessors placed higher values on real estate, property tax bills underwent precipitous increases. Although proposals to limit property taxes had been unsuccessful in the past, Jarvis and Gann in 1978 pointed out that property taxes could be slashed without serious consequences because of the existence of the large surplus at the state level. Proposition 13, authored and promoted by Jarvis and Gann, limited property taxes to 1% of a property's assessed value as of 1975. This limit reduced property taxes by 57% or roughly $6 billion per year. (The property tax is used primarily to fund local governments and school districts, whereas sales and income taxes predominantly support operations at the state level.)

Governor Brown publicly opposed Proposition 13 until its overwhelming passage (65 to 35%) in June 1978. In the same primary election, Attorney General Evelle Younger won the Republican gubernatorial nomination. Brown looked vulnerable in the general election because Younger had supported the passage of Proposition 13.

In one of the more adroit flip-flops in California history, Brown announced that he would implement Proposition 13 to the best of his ability. He imposed hiring and pay freezes throughout the state bureaucracy and supported the shift of the state's surplus to hard-pressed localities. Younger was unable to capitalize on his initial support of Proposition 13 and was soundly defeated by Brown (the margin was 1.3 million votes) in the 1978 general election. Though the legislature remained strongly Democratic, Republicans George Deukmejian and Mike Curb broke the Democrats' sweep by being elected attorney general and lieutenant governor, respectively.

Jerry Brown had waged a late, and ultimately unsuccessful, effort in 1976 to deny Jimmy Carter the Democratic presidential nomination. Having won reelection to the governorship in 1978, Brown devoted his energy to winning the presidential nomination of 1980. To attract the attention of the media in early 1979, he advocated calling a U.S. constitutional convention to write an amendment requiring a balanced federal budget. On top of his swift shift on Proposition 13, Jerry Brown's proposed constitutional amendment left other Democrats aghast. Assemblyman Willie Brown (D, San Francisco) said the Democratic governor sounded like Ronald Reagan. The state legislature, under Democratic leadership, refused to go along with the governor's request that the U.S. Congress be asked to convene a constitutional convention. Furthermore, the legislature overrode several of the governor's vetoes in the summer of 1979. The message to Jerry Brown was: Stay in California to help resolve the state's fiscal problems and drop your futile quest for the presidency. Instead, Brown pressed his campaign for national office in the Iowa and New Hampshire primaries, before finally dropping out after the Wisconsin primary.

Polls indicated that Brown's standing with the citizens of California began to decline dramatically during his second run for the White House. In spite of this, Brown thought he had a chance to move to the U.S. Senate into the seat vacated by S. I. Hayakawa (R). However, Jerry Brown was unable to recoup the support he had once had, and he lost to Mayor Pete Wilson of San Diego in the 1982 race for the U.S. Senate. Brown was fond of saying, "The first rule of politics is to be different." That he was.

A Squeaker

After 16 years (1966–1982) of governors possessing little governmental experience at the time they took office, 1982 featured a gubernatorial race between two veteran political leaders. With 9 years as Mayor of Los Angeles to his credit plus service on the City Council, Tom Bradley easily captured the Democratic gubernatorial primary against State Senator John Garamendi (D, Stockton) and former Health and Welfare Secretary Mario Obledo. In his come-from-behind win against Lieutenant Governor Mike Curb in the Republican gubernatorial primary, George Deukmejian highlighted his 20 years of experience in a variety of elective offices. Beginning in 1962, Deukmejian served 4 years in the Assembly, 12 years in the State Senate, and then 4 years in the statewide post of Attorney General. Once again overtaking an opponent in the closing days of a campaign, Deukmejian defeated Bradley by 93,345 votes out of some 7.8 million votes cast for governor. Despite losing the governorship and a U.S. Senate seat in 1982, Democrats retained control of both houses of the California Legislature and also captured all other statewide offices in the executive branch.

George Deukmejian faced a major crisis immediately on assuming the governorship in January 1983. As a result of lower than anticipated revenues caused by an economic downturn in 1982, the state lacked $1.5 billion to pay its bills for the fiscal year ending on June 30, 1983. Democratic legislators urged Governor Deukmejian to agree to a 1 cent increase in the state sales tax to obtain additional revenue. Having pledged not to raise taxes during his campaign, the governor refused to support an increase in general taxes (i.e., sales or income taxes). Instead, Deukmejian used a combination of techniques to weather the storm without a general tax hike. First, significant cuts were made in state spending for the remaining 6 months of the fiscal year. Second, new funds were obtained by accelerating the collection of certain taxes, by closing loopholes on heretofore untaxed (or undertaxed) sales and rentals, by delaying for 1 year the annual reduction in auto registration fees, and by raising fees for college students. Third, the remainder of the needed funding (about $750 million) was borrowed from banks with the stipulation that it would be paid back during the following fiscal year. Governor Deukmejian's solution to the 1983 fiscal crisis showed him to be a strong manager who could withstand pressure from the legislature.

Unlike his flashy predecessors, Governor Deukmejian ordinarily was characterized as unspectacular, bland, and predictable. His lack of charisma was so evident that Deukmejian himself joked about it. Despite his low-key style, Deukmejian used his budgetary and appointment powers to bring about new priorities in state government. Governor Deukmejian's budgets contained major increases for prisons and highways. Programs that suffered reductions included the state public defender, family planning, Medi-Cal, the Coastal Commission, the Agricultural Labor Relations Board, the Air Resources Board, and Cal-OSHA. By paying overtime to civil servants and by contracting out some tasks to the private sector, Deukmejian slightly decreased the number of employees working in state government during his first term. The governor especially appreciated the opportunity to appoint what he called "common sense" judges to the bench. He showed a preference for appointing former prosecutors and those with judicial experience to court vacancies.

Governor Deukmejian's record with the legislature during his first term was mixed. A compromise on workfare, a program to provide job training to welfare recipients, was reached in 1985. The governor's agreement in 1986 to curtail state investment in South Africa (due to that county's apartheid policies) won him favorable reviews in the legislature. However, no agreements were reached with the legislature during his first term on matters such as water delivery, reorganization of toxic enforcement agencies, or location of a state prison in Los Angeles County. Democrats in the California Senate refused to confirm Deukmejian's appointees to head the departments of Parks and Recreation, Industrial Relations, and Finance; and the names of directors for the Department of Fish and Game and Corrections were withdrawn when it became apparent that they would be rejected. Another reversal for Deukmejian in his first term came at the hands of the electorate. Hoping to create fairer district lines for GOP candidates than those drawn by the Democrat-controlled legislature, the governor's office proposed a new method of establishing legislative boundaries. During the 1984 general elections, California voters refused (45% yes, 55% no) to adopt Proposition 39, which would have created a redistricting commission staffed by retired appellate judges.

A Landslide

The 1986 general election saw three members of the California Supreme Court turned out of office. Although no appellate judges in California had ever lost a retention vote prior to this election, 1986 brought the defeat of Chief Justice Rose Bird (66% no) and losses by Associate Justices Cruz Reynoso (60% no) and Joseph Grodin (57% no). Bird had trailed in public opinion polls for a number of years, so her defeat was foreseen. However, Reynoso and Grodin did not show weaknesses in the polls until the late stages of the campaign. Although Bird's leadership abilities had been an issue since her appointment by Governor Jerry Brown in 1977, the defeat of Reynoso and Grodin as well suggested that the electorate viewed the retention vote as a referendum on the enforcement of the death penalty in California. All three justices had been criticized for failing to implement the state's capital punishment law. Republicans throughout the state supported the ouster of the Chief Justice, while Democrats split on her retention.

Prior to 1986, the major political parties in California had never nominated the same two candidates for governor in successive elections. As the incumbent with excellent job approval ratings according to Mervin Field's California Poll, George Deukmejian had no opposition in being renominated by the Republican Party. Surprisingly, Mayor Tom Bradley won the Democratic gubernatorial primary in June 1986 without serious opposition either. Democratic Senators Gary Hart (Santa Barbara) and John Garamendi (Stockton) gave consideration to contesting the primary with Bradley. However, Mervin Field's polling probably helped the senators decide against making the race. The California Poll released on August 16, 1985, showed Bradley six percentage points ahead of Deukmejian at that time, and the survey also indicated that the Republican governor was far ahead of any other potential opponent from the Democratic Party. In addition to discouraging challenges to Bradley in the Democratic primary, these poll results galvanized the governor's campaign into action. Since the party nominees were known over a year in advance of the November election, the 1986 gubernatorial campaign was one of the longest and most sustained in California history. Despite his momentary lead in the California Poll, Bradley waged an inept campaign in comparison with Deukmejian's well-organized and well-financed effort. The governor criticized Bradley for supporting Rose Bird during her narrow retention victory (51.7% yes) in 1978 and for taking no position on her reconfirmation in 1986. When Bradley portrayed Deukmejian as a friend of polluters, the governor struck back by pointing out that the mayor's own city had discharged waste into Santa

Monica Bay. In November 1986, Governor Deukmejian won reelection (61 to 38%) in a landslide of massive proportions. In winning by nearly 1.7 million votes, Deukmejian received over one-half million more votes than he collected in 1982. Mayor Bradley won one million fewer votes in 1986 than he did in 1982.

Governor Deukmejian's smashing triumph entitled him to appoint three new justices to the California Supreme Court. The governor first elevated Associate Justice Malcolm Lucas to Chief Justice, and he then named John Arguelles, David Eagleson, and Marcus Kaufman to the state's highest court. Even though Republicans had much to celebrate after the 1986 elections, Democrats won the offices of Lt. Governor (Leo McCarthy), Attorney General (John Van de Kamp), Treasurer (Jesse Unruh), Controller (Gray Davis), and Secretary of State (March Fong Eu). In a closely contested race, Democrat Alan Cranston retained his seat in the U.S. Senate over Republican Congressman Ed Zschau. Both the Assembly (44D, 36R) and the Senate (24D, 15R, 1I) stayed under Democratic control despite gains by Republicans of two or three seats in each house.

A struggle for the speakership of the Assembly, a significant ballot measure, and a key confirmation fight took center stage in 1988. With 44 members of the Democratic Party elected to the California Assembly, a dissident band of lower-house Democrats (known as the Gang of Five) withdrew their support from Speaker Willie Brown in 1988 thereby throwing the chamber into turmoil. Brown managed to survive the efforts to end his speakership, and attention shifted to some major proposition battles on the November ballot of 1988. With the active support of Bill Honig (Superintendent of Public Instruction) and the California Teachers Association, Proposition 98 narrowly won passage guaranteeing that some 40% of the state's general fund would henceforth be allocated to K–14 education. This measure was approved by the voters despite vocal opposition by Governor Deukmejian. Controversial car insurance reforms (Proposition 103) also won by a small margin in November 1988. Although convictions were not obtained until 1990, the FBI search of offices in the State Capitol to collect evidence of corruption took place on August 24, 1988.

Except for a relatively productive year in 1989, Governor Deukmejian's second term as chief executive featured intense conflict with the California Legislature. On the death of Democrat Jesse Unruh in August 1987, Governor Deukmejian appointed Representative Daniel Lungren (R, Long Beach) to the vacant post of state treasurer. Gubernatorial appointments generally require confirmation by the upper house of the state legislature. In the case of an appointment to a statewide elected post, however, both chambers of the legislature review the qualifications of an appointee. Although the California Assembly consented

Figure 2-3   (Dennis Renault, *Sacramento Bee*)

to Lungren's appointment, the California Senate rejected his name in February 1988. Deukmejian continued his struggle on behalf of Lungren by seeking a court ruling that confirmation by a single house was adequate for his appointee to take office. In June 1988, the California Supreme Court (including five justices appointed by Deukmejian) ruled that both legislative chambers need to approve gubernatorial appointments to statewide elective offices (i.e., that defeat in one chamber kills such an appointment).

The opposition to Representative Lungren stemmed from his record as a strongly partisan Republican. Ethnic groups, particularly Asian-Americans, fought his confirmation because he had voted in Congress against reparations (payments) for individuals who spent World War II inside internment camps. Viewed as a strong fund raiser and an energetic campaigner, Lungren was opposed by Democratic legislators who wanted to deny him a stepping stone to higher office. Some 16 months after Unruh's death, Thomas Hayes finally was confirmed as state treasurer in January 1989. Deukmejian's second appointee was a marked contrast to his first. As the former Auditor General of the California Legislature, Hayes was viewed as a nonpartisan technician who possessed great familiarity with California's finances.

Also in the first month of 1989, George Deukmejian announced that he would not seek a third term as governor in the elections of 1990. His decision to put an end to a career of 28 years in public service contributed to a more cooperative spirit with the legislative branch. During 1989, the governor and the legislature approved a ban on certain semiautomatic assault weapons, reforms in workers' compensation law, and a new regulatory commission for dealing with solid waste materials. The greatest achievement of 1989 was a grand compromise between Governor Deukmejian and legislative leaders to seek popular approval for gas tax increases and modifications in the state appropriations limit (the so-called Gann limit). This compromise was approved by the California electorate as Proposition 111 in June 1990.

Governor Deukmejian's final year as chief executive saw a return to bruising combat with the California Legislature. The state's economy entered recession in 1990 and actual revenues collected failed to meet projections. To cope with declining revenues, Governor Deukmejian proposed that the school funding guarantees contained in Proposition 98 be suspended. Legislators from both political parties refused to go along with the governor's request. Protracted negotiations finally produced a state budget 1 month into the new fiscal year. The revenue estimates contained in the budget agreement of August, however, failed to materialize in the state treasury as 1990 came to a close. Hoping to leave the state of California in better financial condition than he found it, Governor Deukmejian called the California Legislature into special session in December 1990 to address the revenue shortfall. Preferring to take their chances with a new governor, legislators refused one last opportunity to enact budgetary policies favored by George Deukmejian. An economic upturn allowed Deukmejian to weather the budget crisis in 1983, but the weak economy in 1990 saw him leave office with the state's books out of balance.

Toward Moderation _____

Aside from the obvious gender differences, the two major party nominees for governor in 1990 had much in common. Both Pete Wilson (R) and Dianne Feinstein (D) were centrists who shared the same positions on a number of issues. Both opposed offshore drilling, supported capital punishment, and claimed to be pro-choice on the matter of reproductive rights. Wilson had no major opposition in the Republican gubernatorial primary, whereas Feinstein needed to expend a great deal of money and effort in defeating Attorney General John Van de Kamp in the Democratic primary. Wilson ultimately prevailed in the general election by 49 to 46% on the strength of more seasoned campaign managers and superior funding. Feinstein's margin of defeat was less than pollsters had expected, and some columnists asserted that the international crisis in the Persian Gulf (which began in August) worked to her disadvantage.

In the closest race of the 1990 elections, Dan Lungren (R) edged Arlo Smith (D) for attorney general. Although Smith won some 29,000 more votes than his opponent on election-day balloting, Lungren eventually received 30,000 more votes than Smith after all absentee ballots were tabulated. Given his rejection for the office of treasurer in 1988, Lungren's victory must have been sweet indeed. Democrats won the other elective executive positions as Leo McCarthy (Lieutenant Governor), March Fong Eu (Secretary of State), Gray Davis (Controller), Kathleen Brown (Treasurer), and John Garamendi (Insurance Commissioner) were victorious.

Of the 28 propositions (constitutional amendments, initiatives, or bonds) that appeared on the 1990 general election ballot, only six passed. The highly publicized initiatives on the environment and the various propositions dealing with liquor taxes all lost. Voters essentially refused to act as legislators, and returned the problems to representative institutions. Of the six measures that did pass, the term-limit initiative (Proposition 140) was the most consequential. Ongoing headlines

Figure 2-4 Governor Pete Wilson. (Governor's Office)

about political corruption set the stage for voters to send a strong message of disapproval to Sacramento. Incumbent Senator Joe Montoya (D, El Monte) was convicted in February 1990, and former Senator Paul Carpenter (D, Norwalk) was found guilty in September 1990. Assorted other legislative staffers and lobbyists either engaged in plea bargaining or were awaiting trial. Given the heavy use of the initiative and the news of corruption, it is somewhat surprising that Proposition 140 did not pass by more than the 52% affirmative vote it achieved. The measure limited members of the California Assembly to 6 years in office, and members of the California Senate and the elected executives were limited to 8 years in their posts.

Although Attorney General Dan Lungren admittedly is not known for his centrist tendencies, Governor Pete Wilson's early actions may herald an era of moderation in state government. Unlike his predecessor, Wilson never made a pledge not to raise general taxes during the course of his campaign for the governorship. This allowed Governor Wilson flexibility in negotiating budgetary matters. In a move widely seen as an effort to restore harmonious relations with the educational establishment, Wilson selected Democrat Maureen DiMarco to serve as his secretary of education. Known as a technical expert, not as a strong partisan, Wilson's choice of former Treasurer Tom Hayes to head the Department of Finance was well received by the legislature. Appointments based more on merit than partisanship would have pleased Earl Warren.

Summary

With the prevalence of divided government (the legislature and the governorship under control of different parties), it is increasingly difficult to identify eras of party dominance in California politics. Except for 2 years in the late 1960s, the Democratic Party has controlled the the California Legislature continuously since 1958. Republicans Ronald Reagan, George Deukmejian, and Pete Wilson all served as the state's chief executive with the opposition party in control of the legislature. (During Reagan's tenure as governor, Republican Bob Monangan was Speaker of the Assembly from 1969 to 1970.) Although Governor Reagan had strong enough coattails to pull other Republican elected executives to victory in 1966 and 1970, neither Deukmejian or Wilson had Republican executive support—the exception being Attorney General Lungren in 1990. California voters obviously are comfortable with electing a chief executive of one party and a supporting cast of the opposition party. Split-ticket voting underscores how little value is placed on the party label in California campaigns.

References: Chapter 2 _____

Gould, Lewis L., editor. *The Progressive Era.* Syracuse: Syracuse University Press, 1974.

Howard, Robert W. *The Great Iron Trail: The Story of the Transcontinental Railroad.* New York: G.P. Putnam's Sons, 1962.

James, Marquis, and Bessie R. James. *Biography of a Bank: The Story of the Bank of America.* New York: Harper & Brothers, 1954.

Lewis, Oscar. *The Big Four.* New York: Alfred A. Knopf, 1938.

Mason, Paul. "Constitutional History of California." *Constitution of the State of California (1879) and Related Documents.* California State Senate, 1973: 75–105.

McAfee, Ward. *California's Railroad Era: 1850–1911.* San Marino, California: Golden West Books, 1973.

Mowry, George E. *The California Progressives.* Berkeley: University of California Press, 1951.

Olin, Spencer C. Jr. *California's Prodigal Sons: Hiram Johnson and the Progressives.* Berkeley: University of California Press, 1968.

Putnam, Jackson K. "The Persistence of Progressivism in the 1920s: The Case of California." *Pacific Historical Review* (November 1966): 395–411.

Robinson, William W. *Land in California.* Berkeley: University of California Press, 1948.

Swisher, Carl B. *Motivation and Political Technique in the California Constitutional Convention: 1878–79.* New York: Da Capo, 1969.

Warren, Earl E. *The Memoirs of Earl Warren.* Garden City, N.Y.: Doubleday, 1977.

CHAPTER 3

Group Power in California

There is such a profusion of groups represented in Sacramento that it almost defies description. Through the years, the State of California has come to regulate many areas of livelihood and recreational activity. All sorts of questions are brought to state government for resolution. What dates each year shall certain racetracks be open for running events and for betting? What specific chemicals shall be considered cancer-causing agents when they are released into supplies of public drinking water? Which precise parts of the human foot are properly treated by orthopedists and which parts by podiatrists? Shall the cleaning of dogs' teeth be carried out by pet groomers or by veterinarians?

Mainstream interests and professions such as the California Association of Realtors, the California Bankers Association, the California Bar Association, the California Cattlemen's Association, the California Dental Association, and the California District Attorneys Association are all represented in the State Capitol as you would expect. We also have three CMAs: California Manufacturers Association, California Medical Association, and California Mining Association. Likewise, there are three CTAs: California Taxpayers Association, California Teachers Association, and California Truckers Association. Unless you are very familiar with California politics, you may be surprised to learn that the Council of Acupuncture Organizations, the California Association of Midwives, the California Athletic Trainers' Association, the California Association of Photocopiers and Process Servers, and the California Association of 4-Wheel Drive Clubs also are represented in Sacramento.

The overwhelming bulk of groups at the State Capitol are considered to be selective-benefit organizations. Groups form around shared interests. Individuals join them in expectation of obtaining something in return that other Californians do not receive. (There are some collective-benefit organizations, but they are far less common. As examples, California Common Cause and the League of Women Voters are both interested in improving the political process and in educating voters. Members and nonmembers alike benefit from the work of these two groups.) In contrast to social groups, which have no involvement in the political process, interest groups or pressure groups are known for actively influencing government, public opinion, and other organizations. What determines the power of each pressure group?

Size of membership alone does not indicate the extent of a group's power. If the members of a group possess a monopoly on a crucial skill or hold special expertise, such as how to operate some complex machinery, they have more leverage economically and politically than laborers in low-skill occupations. Medical doctors, lawyers, and bankers usually have high credibility, which enables them to gain access to decision makers more easily than is the case for low-status workers and the unemployed. The presence or absence of strong opposition is also a significant aspect of a group's power. In addition to these determinants of group influence, two remaining factors stand out: organizational cohesiveness and financial resources. The more unified a group is, the more likely it is to act decisively in the political sphere. Individuals will not devote their time, talent, and monetary support to a group unless they are firmly committed to its goals. The development of consensus within a group underlies the donation of money and effort to the organization. With a strong financial base, groups are in a position to hire skillful leadership and to engage in all forms of political persuasion. After discussing the various techniques used by pressure groups in California, we will assess the power of major interests in the state.

Varieties of Influence

One of the more remarkable aspects of interest group politics in California is the utter flexibility and adaptability of these organizations in the face of changing political conditions. Political reforms come and go, but the power of interest groups in the state is not altered significantly. The blow suffered by political parties during the Progressive era enabled organized interests to fill a political void that they have not relinquished to this day. As we shall see in Chapter 5, some of the restrictions placed on political parties in 1911 were removed in the late 1980s. Nevertheless, the roots of group power today are too well entrenched in California to suffer diminution in influence. The key to the central role played by pressure groups in California is their varied and creative use of many forms of political action.

Election Support

In attempting to place friends in office, interest groups may donate money to election campaigns, offer the services of campaign volunteers, make endorsements of candidates and ballot measures, supply free publicity in group publications, and provide rent-free use of offices and telephones. In a hotly contested special election for a vacant seat in the California Senate (33rd District in 1987), organized labor made available hundreds of campaign workers to go door to door on behalf of candidate Cecil Green. The California Association of Highway Patrolmen donated $150,000 to Dianne Feinstein's campaign in 1990 after contribution limits were struck down by a federal judge. (Though ultimately unsuccessful, late contributions such as this did help Feinstein close the gap near the end of her race with Pete Wilson.) Some campaign money does come from individual donors and from candidates themselves or their spouses, but interest groups represented in Sacramento are the predominant source of election funds in California. Group leaders and their lobbyists decide each year how much their organization will contribute to various legislative and executive candidates. Law offices and real estate firms often donate their business telephone systems at night when they are not otherwise in use. Lest there be any doubt about the effectiveness of campaign support, consider the words of a longtime lobbyist in Sacramento.

> If everything else is equal and your opposition has a significant advantage in contributions, you are going to lose. It has to be equal on the merits, but I've seen votes change because of money. (Kushman, 1988a)

Appointment Politics

With so many areas of California life involving government regulation of one form or another, groups endeavor to win appointment for their friends to a wide variety of state boards, commissions, and agencies. California growers are particularly interested in who heads the California Department of Food and Agriculture. They were most pleased when Governor Pete Wilson named Henry Voss to direct the department. Voss was formerly the President of the California Farm Bureau Federation, the largest farm lobby in the state. Groups opposed to a particular gubernatorial appointee to such bodies as the Agricultural Labor Relations Board, the Air Resources Board, the Integrated Waste Management Board, or the Public Utilities Commission, ask the California Senate to deny confirmation of these individuals. Some of the most bruising battles in the State Capitol can be confirmation fights where major interests are arrayed on either side of the question.

Public Relations and Media Use

Apart from having friends in positions of power, it is advantageous to have popular opinion behind a group's goals. Public attitudes may be influenced by either paid or free means of communication. Besides promoting specific products, advertising is used to sell political ideas and to improve the image of a particular group. An ad showing a family with young children in front of a nuclear power plant is not intended to sell more of a product (i.e., electricity), but rather is designed to encourage attitudes that such plants are safe. Public relations firms also are hired to plan campaigns to reach the public through the so-called free media. Advocates for a group's viewpoint are scheduled to speak on radio and television talk shows, messages are prepared for dissemination during public service announcements over the electronic media, and packets containing information supporting a group's position are sent to newspapers with the aim of creating editorial support for the organization. Lacking the funds to use paid media, California Common Cause makes effective use of free media to disseminate information to the public and to put pressure on elected officials. This organization is known for publicizing the amounts of money donated to campaigns by affluent interests and for calling attention to any decision methods (i.e., agendas, hearings, and votes) that are not fair to all those involved in an issue—the so-called level playing field.

Lobbying

Since this topic will be examined in detail later in this chapter, suffice it to say at this point that attempting to influence decision makers, or applying pressure to them, is undertaken by many types of people in many sorts of ways. Some lobbying occurs in Sacramento and some at district or regional offices dispersed around the state. Some lobbyists are required by state law to register with the secretary of state and some are exempted from registration. Some lobbyists are considered to be professionals and some are not. In short, there is more to lobbying than that done by professional, registered lobbyists in Sacramento.

Initiative, Referendum, and Recall

Despite efforts to influence government officials and to place sympathetic persons in public positions, groups still may not obtain the policies they seek. When confronted with this predicament, an interest group may attempt to circumvent officeholders entirely, or to have them removed, by employing ballot propositions or recall procedures. Not all direct appeals to the electorate are successful by any means, but enough are to make the alternative of bypassing unresponsive elected officials a credible threat in an interest group's arsenal. This opportunity for political organizations is discussed at length in Chapter 6.

Legal Action

When a legislative enactment, an executive order, a ballot initiative, or a regulatory decision goes against a group's wishes despite the use of the foregoing methods of influence, an organization may file a law suit to impede implementation of the decision. When Proposition 103 (car insurance rate reduction) was passed by the voters in November 1988, insurance companies stymied its implementation by filing numerous legal actions. By spending well over $25 million in legal fees (Garcia, 1990), the industry won a court ruling that insurance companies are entitled to a "fair return" on their investment in California and that premium reductions cannot be applied to all carriers regardless of their financial condition. Insurance companies then submitted boxes of financial documents to the State of California to demonstrate that they could not make a fair return if they were compelled to give premium reductions to their policy holders. After frustrating the implementation of Proposition 103, one legislative staffer said the following regarding insurance businesses.

> They are an enormously powerful and wealthy industry. They never quit. You can drive a stake in their hearts and they never quit. (Kushman, 1990)

Protest

Hiring lawyers, lobbyists, and media consultants takes money. Some groups cannot afford to retain the services of such hired guns. For organizations lacking deep pockets, protest actions can be one of the few options available—in addition to donated or pro bono legal services. Environmentalists have draped huge banners from the roof of the State Capitol, and college students have marched on Sacramento to oppose fee hikes. During the budget impasse of 1990, disabled persons in wheelchairs blocked the entrance to the governor's office to protest proposed cutbacks in state services. Rallies outside the Capitol are commonplace and usually peaceful; disruptive protests inside the Capitol lead to arrest and to removal from the building.

Accurate assessments of group power must take into consideration the *cumulative* impact of the use, or threatened use, of all of the above types of behavior. Though the Political Reform Act of 1974 provides us with financial information on lobbying expenses and campaign contributions, there is little systematic information collected about the public relations and legal activities of interest groups. Affluent organizations are afforded many opportunities to expend their resources in the political arena.

Lobbying in California _____

According to the Political Reform Act of 1974, a lobbyist in California is anyone who is paid to communicate with state elective officials or their staffs, provided that a "substantial portion" of his or her activity is for the purpose of influencing legislative or administrative action. What is a substantial portion? The Fair Political Practices Commission, the body created to enforce the Act, has ruled that activity is substantial when either (1) a person earns $2,000 or more a month to influence officials; or (2) a person is paid less than $2,000 per month, but directly contacts state officials on at least 25 separate occasions in any two consecutive months. Persons meeting the above criteria must register as lobbyists with the secretary of state. Employees of the state executive branch, though they attempt to influence legislative action, are legally exempted from the requirement of registering as lobbyists (Government Code, Sec. 86300). The net effect of this legal definition of lobbying is that persons who are not paid to communicate are not lobbyists in the eyes of the law. Therefore, a corporate executive, a union leader, or a school principal who infrequently (less than 25 times in 2 months) communicates with legislative and executive officials need not register as a lobbyist. As we shall see, many people try to influence government action (i.e., lobby) who are not legally defined as lobbyists.

A negative stereotype persists about lobbyists. Registered lobbyists ordinarily do not use the word "lobbyist" on their business card. Instead we see businesses called California Advocates, Inc., Sacramento Advocates, Inc., Capitol Advocates, Inc., or Corporate Advocates, Inc., as well as firms with Governmental Relations and Public Relations in their business names. Despite the pejorative connotation some people place on their occupational label, lobbyists perform the necessary and constitutionally protected function of relating the views and the information of their group to decision makers in government. However, since registered lobbyists are compensated, not all groups can afford similar levels of advocacy in Sacramento.

There are no required degrees or credentials to become a lobbyist. Some would-be lobbyists mastered an issue area while working in an industry or profession and subsequently began representing their groups in the state capital. Other future lobbyists were formerly in elective or appointive positions in government. Some two dozen former legislators are now registered lobbyists in Sacramento. Robert Monagan was Speaker of the Assembly (1969–1970) before heading the lobbying operation for the California Manufacturers Association for many years. George Steffes was Governor Ronald Reagan's legislative aide before opening his own lobbying firm. Numerous legislative staffers have left government employment for the presumably greener pastures representing clients in the Capitol. Formerly a top staffer with the Assembly Agriculture Committee, George Soares now lobbies for 19 agribusiness clients.

Individuals and Firms

In years past, the conventional means of categorizing advocates consisted of determining whether an individual lobbyist represented one customer or several clients. Individuals representing one large business or one professional group usually were called either corporate lobbyists or association lobbyists. Advocates, on the other hand, who were retained by a multiplicity of diverse clients were referred to as contract lobbyists. An individual contract lobbyist might have worked for anywhere from 5 to 10 clients.

The past 20 years have witnessed the rise of the lobbying firm, although there are still plenty of individual practitioners in Sacramento. These firms may consist of approximately three to six registered lobbyists who represent from 25 to 40 clients. Individual lobbyists (with fewer clients) believe that they are able to provide more personal attention to the needs of their clients and decision makers than is the case with lobbying firms, where a junior partner might be assigned to handle a particular issue. Firms obviously can devote more lobbyists to a crucial vote should the need arise.

Aside from the above differences between firms and individual practitioners, there are two matters worth noting. First, the greater the number of clients represented by a firm, the greater the likelihood that some of the clients might be on opposite sides of the same issue. (Such conflicts can happen to individual practitioners, but are more likely to occur when a firm represents dozens of clients.) Firms attempt to avoid such client conflicts by exercising care when accepting new customers. If this is not sufficient to avoid problems, lobbying firms attempt to reconcile the differences among their clients or advise certain customers to retain other representation. Second, the more numerous the clients, the larger the role of the lobbying firm in guiding campaign contributions to public officials. A Common Cause official noted the following:

> When Clay Jackson (25 clients) lobbies you on something that is important to him, you are not simply talking to one of his employers. You are relating to Clay Jackson, who has the campaign financing resources of ten or twenty significant players (Kushman, 1988a).

Mr. Jackson of Jackson/Barish and Associates represents Anheuser-Busch, California Hotel and Motel Association, NCR Corporation, and the American Insurance Association, among other clients. The combined total of campaign contributions given by all of the clients of Jackson/Barish in 1987 was $2.5 million. Will public officials act against Jackson's wishes on a given issue and risk losing campaign support from his lengthy list of clients?

Inside Lobbying

Inside lobbying is partly communicating information and partly cultivating friendships. Drafts of bills, amendments, speeches, and regulations are given to decision makers by lobbyists. In addition, cost estimates, economic ramifications, and social and environmental impacts are transmitted to public officials. Besides materials bearing on the substance or merits of the issue at hand, lobbyists provide procedural and political information as well. They advise lawmakers concerning the appropriate vehicle (a bill, a resolution, or control language in the state budget) for a specific matter, and they may be of assistance on parliamentary rules. Lobbyists provide political intelligence that is extremely useful to decision makers concerning who opposes and who supports a measure both inside and outside of government. Lobbying organizations prepare precise headcounts of votes at various points along the legislative process to be of service to authors carrying their bills and to find out where more work needs to be done.

Even seemingly minor bits of information ultimately may have political uses, so sophisticated lobbying operations have files of several types. *District characteristic files* can be maintained to assist lobbyists in determining how a given legislator's constituents will react to a bill. *Personal data files* can be kept on public officials. Is the decision maker a pilot or a hunter, is the public servant the parent of a handicapped child, does someone in the family have a drug problem, or is a family member a school teacher or other type of public employee? Such background material may aid a lobbyist in finding a sympathetic ear in government. *Topic or issue files* contain information on specific areas that is used to show decision makers that there is ample justification to support a measure on its merits alone. It may be necessary for lobbyists to stress different points with different officials. Lastly, though it may or may not be placed in a file, competent lobbyists make mental notes about the most effective way to gain access to particular officials. It may be that approaching a decision maker through his or her staff, through a particular legislator, through the director of an executive department, or through a respected person in an interest group or political party is preferable to having the lobbyist contact the official personally.

Based on thorough understanding of the issues and in-depth knowledge of the personalities of the key decision makers, lobbyists serve as guides through the complicated labyrinth of the governmental process. The unwritten code of lobbyists is well known to registered advocates in Sacramento. Trying to undo a decision that has been taken is most difficult, so lobbyists endeavor to be as timely as possible in their communication. The accuracy of presentations is crucial because political allies should never be embarrassed by repeating incorrect information. As the saying goes in the Capitol, "Credibility is like virginity—once you lose it, it's tough to get it back" (Kushman, 1988b). Sacramento lobbyists also adhere to the notions that advocates should never speak ill of each other and never engage in trying to steal clients from one another.

The term "lobbyist" misleadingly suggests that advocates communicate with public officials in hallways and corridors. A bit of last-minute input is conveyed in the halls outside meeting rooms, but far more information is delivered outside public view. Lobbyists make sure that officials receive written communication concerning their clients' positions on issues pending decision. Telephone conversations and private visits are used to follow up position letters. Lobbyists are free to testify at committee hearings held by the California Legislature, but many advocates decline this opportunity because they are confident that the votes are already in place for their clients' positions. The importance of early, private communication is reflected in these comments by a former legislative staffer.

> My college textbooks had emphasized that a legislature's real work is not accomplished on the floor, but in committee. But I observed very few instances where thoughtful substantive change occurred either on the floor or in committee. Rather the formal hearings merely reflected the gritty negotiations that actually took place beforehand. . . . One of the most striking aspects of legislative decision-making is that the basic, formative decisions which shape a major program are made before the formal legislative process ever begins (BeVier, 1979:102–103, 218).

Besides providing information to decision makers, the other main aspect of inside lobbying is the cultivation of friendships. Despite the limitations on lobbyists' spending that are discussed at the conclusion of this chapter, it is still possible for lobbyists to meet with public officials on golf courses, on tennis courts, or in exercise clubs. Provided that proper disclosure takes place and that appropriate persons pay the bills, representatives of interest groups may engage in socializing with public officials. Pressure groups continue to provide the bulk of campaign funds used by candidates in California. Developing friendships with decision makers increases the likelihood that lobbyists will be able to speak with officials on short notice.

Though known primarily as communicators, some registered lobbyists really are closer to coordinators. By managing an association or coalition, by finding appropriate witnesses to testify at hearings, and by organizing grassroots input to decision makers, much of the lobbyists' time today is spent coordinating the activities of others rather than communicating face to face with government leaders.

Outside Lobbying

Whereas inside lobbying is largely performed by registered lobbyists, outside lobbying is usually accomplished by persons who volunteer their time. Registration with the secretary of state as a lobbyist is not required if (1) the advocate is unpaid, or (2) the advocate makes fewer than 25 contacts with public officials in a 2-month span and is paid less than $2,000 per month. Bankers, teachers, farmers, and realtors, among others, lobby in Sacramento periodically. Outside lobbying has two basic forms: letter-writing campaigns and personal visits. Each form has several variations.

When organizing letter writing to a government official, it is best if letters are individually written instead of appearing to be form letters. Specificity is crucial. The recipients of letters should be asked precisely what they like and dislike about given bills or regulations. Officials should be asked pointedly what their positions are on particular items, so that there is less chance that they will respond in a vague manner. Letters from a legislator's home district are thought to have more impact than those from other constituencies. Letter writing can be undertaken by a small number of influentials (the rifle approach), by the general membership of an interest group (the shotgun approach), or by soliciting participation from the public at large through the use of newspaper ads (the grapeshot approach). However broad or narrow the source of letters is, it is important to maintain control over the content of the correspondence. An amendment to a measure might necessitate the reversal of a group's position on the issue.

Personal contacting likewise may be undertaken by the few or the many. Interest groups have established *key contact* systems in which carefully selected members of organizations are assigned the responsibility of cultivating, and later communicating with, particular officials. The California Association of Realtors has a "Legislative Tree" program that identifies realtors who have personal, professional, fraternal, or other ties with officials so that these contacts may be exploited (Lofland, 1982:33–34). Individuals belonging to the same social and religious organizations as a given lawmaker are used as key contact persons. The California Medical Association (CMA) designates from 8 to 12 physicians in each legislative district to personally contact local representatives. The linkage between the CMA operation in Sacramento and the key contacts around the state is tight. Position papers on issues affecting the medical profession are sent to the selected physicians, contacts with legislators are made, and the CMA in Sacramento is informed of the outcome of these conversations. After votes on medical legislation, a legislator's support or opposition is made known to key contacts so that campaign contributions can be provided or withheld as the case warrants. Skillful use of the key contact system has enabled the CMA to thwart the efforts of the California Podiatry Association and the California Chiropractic Association to expand the areas of their service into procedures legally confined to CMA members. The California Bankers Association also operates a statewide lobbying system in every legislative district. The association has a key contact training program to prepare two bankers in each district for interaction with legislators.

If inside lobbying and key contacts are insufficient, an interest group may engage in *crowd lobbying*. Mobilization of a group's members to appear in Sacramento may be done on an emergency basis timed to influence a specific decision or conducted on an annual basis to remind government officials of the group's presence. Swarms of people in the Capitol for a one-time event may or may not be effective depending on the level of preparation and coordination they display. The California Association of Realtors (CAR) had its members come to Sacramento to help defeat a tax bill that they thought would depress housing sales, and the United Professors of California (UPC) mobilized its members to lobby for collective bargaining bills (Lofland, 1982:24 and 27). The CAR and UPC efforts were successful because participants were carefully briefed and given fact packets by their group's lobbyists, appointments were arranged with legislators, and several attempts were made to contact lawmakers if the initial appointment was missed. The California Teachers Association (CTA) has mobilized educators to visit Sacramento, but CTA crowd lobbying has come away with poor marks. Instead of arranging appointments in advance, many CTA members called legislators out of meetings and engaged in sometimes heated conversations standing in hallways. A close student of crowd lobbying concluded that, "the larger the swarm, the less the likelihood there was of prearrangement and the greater the degree of confusion, milling, abrasive contact with officials, and the likelihood of people wandering off and sightseeing in and around the Capitol" (Lofland, 1982:26).

Because political meetings are often postponed and rescheduled, it can be very difficult to effectively time an emergency mobilization. Alternatively, groups may decide to hold the annual meeting of their association in Sacramento. One aspect of an annual gathering might be a Legislative Day. At such an event, group members are briefed by their lobbyists concerning pending issues and then meet with public officials at prearranged appointments. Groups also may hold receptions or dinners honoring legislators at which officeholders sit with group members

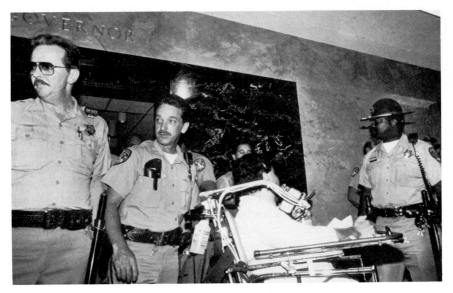

Figure 3-1 Crowd lobbying: Proposed budget cuts in rehabilitation services triggered this protest outside the governor's office in 1990. (Photograph by Michael Williamson).

from their districts. Finally, more in the vein of a working session than a social function, the California Manufacturers Association has conducted Legislative Conferences involving elected officials and top corporate executives. Such meetings are held in rented space, like the Sacramento Convention Center, to draw officeholders away from their Capitol turf and its interruptions.

Size is not everything in crowd lobbying; style of operation is just as important as sheer numbers, if not more so. Groups lacking competent inside lobbyists cannot count on legions of outside lobbyists to rescue their case in Sacramento. Given the careful planning that is needed to make crowd lobbying work, groups that have hired capable registered advocates are the very ones that are most likely to organize effective outside pressure as well. Grassroots lobbying complements inside lobbying; it does not replace it.

The Major Interests

Business interests possess distinct advantages in California politics. Considering the status, wealth, and organization of corporations, as well as the weakness of their opposition, business manifests considerable power in this state. A former head of California Common Cause stated, "Business is always mobilized and the general public is not" (Kushman, 1988a). Economic incentives provide strong motivation for political involvement by business. A relatively small investment in politics can yield substantial economic rewards. For instance, an aircraft company avoided a $1 million increase in taxes due to the skillful work of their lobbyist. The oil industry contributes hundreds of thousands of dollars a year to state legislative races. To the extent that this spending discourages the imposition of a $300–500 million per year oil severance tax, these campaign donations are an excellent investment. Scientific Games provided major financial backing for the successful lottery initiative in 1984 in the anticipation of winning lucrative contracts with the state for years to come. Infant industries in California, such as computer and solar energy firms at one time, have won preferential treatment in the state tax code. All individuals and groups need clear reasons to become involved in state politics; the clearer an economic benefit is, the stronger the likelihood of full commitment to political action. The financial health of real estate businesses throughout California is impacted directly by state laws concerning lending rates, land use, and rent control. Because of this, the California Association of Realtors (CAR) has this credo: "We have to be active in politics, or we will be out of business." During our survey of the organizational and financial strength of various groups in California, we should bear in mind the pronounced motivational edge that inclines businesses to exercise power.

General Business Organizations _____

Although there is considerable economic diversity in California, the different sectors of the state's economy typically are not political competitors. The agriculture, energy, defense, computer, entertainment, and tourism industries seldom conflict in Sacramento. Rather than going their separate ways politically, however, there is significant organizational interlocking among California's businesses. Several multiindustry linkages exist that suggest that the overall business community is better described in terms of collaboration and cooperation than in terms of competition and disagreement.

Some business groups are concerned with long-term policy planning or agenda setting, and some focus on day-to-day lobbying in Sacramento. In what is regarded as one of the most prestigious events anywhere, some 2,000 prominent businessmen (women are excluded) meet for 2 weeks each summer at the Bohemian Grove encampment near Monte

Rio north of San Francisco. Along with major industrial and financial leaders in California, these gatherings have included presidents, governors, and cabinet members. Camp rules supposedly forbid discussing business at the encampment, but "political appointments are made and corporate directors are chosen from among the men who gather around Grove campfires" (Van der Zee, 1974:130). The Bohemian Grove affords business leaders an excellent opportunity to discuss the future course of national and state politics.

Another pinnacle group is the California Roundtable. This organization consists of less than 100 chief executive officers from the state's major corporations. The leaders of business giants such as Hewlett-Packard (largest electronics firm in the world), the Bechtel Corporation (largest construction company in the world), and the Bank of America (formerly the largest bank in the world) discuss ways to enhance the business climate in California. A noteworthy fact about the California Roundtable is that the chief executives themselves occasionally lobby decision makers in Sacramento, rather than relying solely on their corporations' registered lobbyists. The status and knowledgeability of these corporate executives make them outside lobbyists of unequaled influence.

The two most visible general business organizations in Sacramento are the California Manufacturers Association (7 lobbyists in 1989) and the California Chamber of Commerce (11 lobbyists). The two bodies differ in membership and organizational structure. The California Chamber has approximately 600 chapters at the county, city, and neighborhood levels, including 120 chapters in the Los Angeles area alone. Membership in these chapters includes local industries, retail and service businesses, motels and restaurants, and even individual attorneys and accountants. The state chamber conducts lobbying operations in Sacramento and disseminates information to local units. If several localities are seeking highway project funding or construction of a state facility in their area, it is difficult for the state chamber to take a position. Since its broad membership sometimes limits activity, the California Chamber of Commerce is viewed as a lowest-common-denominator organization.

Unlike the Chamber of Commerce, which is built on local chapters, the California Manufacturers Association (CMA) consists of some 800 major corporations operating in the state. Companies such as U.S. Steel, IBM, Xerox, General Motors, Lockheed, Douglas Aircraft, Hunt-Wesson, Continental Can, Kaiser Industries, R.J. Reynolds, Hewlett-Packard, Mobil, Arco, Shell, Exxon, and Standard Oil of California form the membership of CMA. Even foreign companies, such as Sony and Toyota, are members of this association. Roughly two-thirds of the industrial work force in California is employed by member companies. Both the California Chamber and the CMA divide their lobbying corps into specialized areas, such as energy, transportation, taxation, environment, employee relations, workers' compensation, and unemployment insurance. Both groups include agriculture, but exclude banking.

The CMA is active on matters that are overwhelmingly supported or opposed by its member companies. When corporations are divided on given issues, they turn to their individual advocates or lobbying firms to represent their interests in Sacramento. At first glance, the increased use of lobbying firms by individual companies could be construed as a loss of power for CMA. However, the sheer presence of more business lobbyists in Sacramento is useful to CMA when it is time to form broad coalitions in support of, or in opposition to, certain policies. In a clear example of coordinated activity, the CMA conference room each Monday morning is the setting for a meeting involving CMA's lobbyists together with those employed by member firms and other business organizations represented in Sacramento.

The CMA engages in outside lobbying by hosting events in Sacramento to allow executives from member firms to meet politicians. The annual CMA conference is usually addressed by the governor. Monthly CMA forums permit corporate executives to meet with officials such as the attorney general, the superintendent of public instruction, the governor's chief of staff, and legislative leaders. CMA has a political action committee that raises money and dispenses it to candidates. The association also advises member companies concerning their political contributions.

Agricultural Organizations _____

The productivity of this state's farms is well known. California is the national leader in 48 crops (e.g., lettuce, tomatoes, almonds, walnuts, lemons, peaches, sugar beets, strawberries, figs, and olives). The state's production of oranges is second only to that of Florida, and the production of cotton is second only to that of Texas. This incredible agricultural output is not produced on small, family farms. Ever since the days of Spanish and Mexican land grants, California has been noted for large landholdings. As agriculture has become increasingly mechanized, it has been the large farming enterprises that have been able to purchase expensive harvesting equipment. Corporate farming is commonplace in California.

California agriculture is represented in Sacramento in three ways: by individual agribusiness firms, by associations reflecting the interest of one commodity or service, and by general farm organizations. The California Farm Bureau Federation (9 lobbyists in 1989), the Agricultural Council of California (3 lobbyists), and the Western Growers Association (2 lobbyists) are the most active general farm organizations. By including livestock ranchers, crop farmers, and suppliers of related services, the California Farm Bureau Federation (CFBF) has the widest scope of membership, although it is not involved in food-processing issues. The Agricultural Council of California represents the grower-owned cooperatives that process and market fruits and vegetables. The Western Growers Association (WGA) consists of landowners directly involved in growing fruits and vegetables, and its special area of interest is agricultural labor law. These three organizations are not mutually exclusive as citrus growers, for instance, belong to all three groups and have their own commodity organization as well.

CFBF has an active lobby in the state capitol. The 52 farm bureaus at the county level send recommendations on political issues to the state farm bureau in Sacramento. Each of CFBF's nine lobbyists specializes in a policy area, such as water, land use, farm labor, commodities, pesticides, natural resources, and taxes. The organization's political action committee, which makes contributions to candidate and ballot measure races, is called FARM-PAC. Like the California Chamber of Commerce, CFBF is a lowest-common-denominator organization. When agriculture as a whole is affected, CFBF is in a position to represent the entire industry. If, on the other hand, grain farmers want high prices for their products and livestock owners prefer low feed costs for their animals, it is difficult for CFBF to take a clear position for agriculture.

When narrow agricultural constituencies find that general farm organizations are unable to advocate their interests effectively, they turn to commodity associations for representation. Some of the most expert advocacy in Sacramento emanates from commodity organizations. Besides being highly knowledgeable about their crops, commodity lobbyists are noted for patiently cultivating long-term relationships with decision makers. The California Association of Winegrape Growers (vineyardists) and the Wine Institute (bottlers) use tours of their facilities to educate legislators to the needs of modern agriculture. This approach is not designed to influence a particular vote, but rather is intended to develop in decision makers an underlying sensitivity to the problems facing growers and processors. Knowing the importance that legislators place on communication from home, the inside lobbyist for the Wine Institute frequently uses vintners from members' districts as outside tools of persuasion. The Gallo brothers winery in Modesto is the world's largest, and it was the first to introduce computerized production processes and stainless steel storage containers. California is the source of 90% of our national production of wine.

Besides general farm organizations and commodity associations, the agricultural sector consists of many businesses that supply services to farmers. Advocates are in Sacramento representing seed and fertilizer companies, pesticide and herbicide manufacturers, tractor and irrigation-equipment firms, marketing corporations, container businesses, and grocery chains. Chemical companies play an especially active role on decisions concerning pesticides. Despite the wide variety of groups in California agriculture, coordinated activity is encouraged. One morning each week, lobbyists from the various agricultural organizations gather for breakfast in Sacramento. The proliferation of commodity associations might suggest splintering within the ranks of agriculture, but many of these narrow groups employ the same lobbyists to represent them. The client list of George Soares includes commodities such as avocados, citrus, cotton, eggs, lettuce, kiwifruit, pistachio nuts, and rice. More remarkable, Soares also represents the Western Agricultural Chemicals Association and the Pest Control Operators of California. Soares is in an excellent position to coordinate the activity of the various interests he represents.

Two groups that oppose corporate agriculture in Sacramento are California Rural Legal Assistance (4 lobbyists in 1989) and the United Farm Workers (no registered lobbyist). The former is known more for its judicial and regulatory strategies than for its legislative advocacy. In 1975, CRLA won court-ordered revision of occupational safety regulations to prohibit the use of the short-handled hoe in California fields. Use of the tool had caused ligament, disc, and vertebrae damage to the backs of laborers. When it was suggested in 1985 that field hands be allowed to use the tool for 5 minutes each hour, the proposal was rejected. Cesar Chavez organized the UFW in 1966 to improve the low wages and unsafe working conditions of farm workers. When growers refused to bargain with the union, the UFW declared nationwide boycotts of table grapes and other California produce. By the time Governor Jerry Brown (D) assumed office in 1975, grocery chains had prevailed on growers to support the creation of an Agricultural Labor Relations Board (ALRB) to reduce labor turmoil. The ALRB's role is to supervise the election of bargaining agents for the farm workers. After Governor George Deukmejian (R) took office in 1983, the ALRB budget was cut by 27%, thereby reducing its ability to investigate allegations of unfair labor practices.

While agribusiness must now contend with CRLA and UFW, a review of subsidies, taxes, and regulatory policies should dispel the notion that the power of corporate agriculture in California is waning. Government-supported research has aided agribusiness immeasurably. The University of California has provided the industry with improved harvesting machines, fertilizers, pesticides, and plant seeds. New strains of fruits and vegetables, most particularly the tomato, have been developed by university scientists to withstand mechanical harvesting. The value of this subsidized research pales alongside the water and electricity provided to farmers by the state and federal governments at well below market rates. Growers are charged about one-seventh the amount that

Figure 3-2 "Here comes Santa Claus, here comes Santa Claus, right down Santa Claus Lane—" (*Dennis Renault, Sacramento Bee*)

residential and industrial users pay for water. When California's watermelon growers were forced to take all their 1985 production off the market due to unsafe levels of the chemical aldicarb found in some of the crop, the state government compensated these farmers to the tune of $6.2 million for their losses.

One of the more favorable policies toward agriculture in California is the low tax on wine. Since 1937, California taxed wine containing 14% or less alcohol at the rate of 1 cent per gallon. Wine with more than 14% alcohol was taxed at 2 cents per gallon. For purposes of comparison, Arizona's wine tax is 42 cents per gallon and Oregon's is 65 cents per gallon. Efforts in 1983 and 1990 to raise taxes on wine met with failure, but the wine tax was raised to 20 cents per gallon in 1991.

In addition to subsidies and tax policy, the regulatory activity of state government has been congenial to agriculture. Under state law, the California Department of Food and Agriculture (CDFA) is supposed to maintain files on the toxicity of pesticides and on the amounts of chemicals applied to agricultural land in California. CDFA has been criticized for not having the toxicity studies on file and for incorrectly tabulating the levels of pesticides being used. Even though these lapses imperil consumers and farm workers, efforts to shift responsibility for enforcement of pesticide regulations to the Department of Health Services (an agency without close ties to growers) have not been successful. When Governor Wilson established a California EPA in 1991, pesticide regulation finally was shifted out of CDFA and assigned to the new agency.

The Energy Industry

Several different components of the energy industry are in evidence in Sacramento. The majors (i.e., Arco, British Petroleum, Standard Oil of California, Exxon, Mobil, Shell, and Texaco) are well represented in the State Capitol. Midsized companies (e.g., Beacon Oil, Phillips Petroleum, Santa Fe Energy, Unocal Corporation, and Wickland Oil) also retain lobbyists in Sacramento. The smaller independents that specialize in drilling operations and in the construction of pipelines and offshore platforms have advocates working state government as well. Energy companies are unified on some issues, but there are instances when particular firms feel the need to break ranks.

By way of background, it is interesting to note the variety to be found within the industry. Largely as a result of agreements negotiated with Saudi Arabia in 1932 by Standard Oil of California, the majors import a great deal of petroleum. They also have broadened their energy interests into uranium, coal, and solar generation, as well as investing in chemicals, agriculture, department stores, and container fabrication. In short, the majors are diversified conglomerates with global operations. The independents, on the other hand, are still mainly petroleum businesses that do most of their drilling within the United States. The different segments of the industry stand together on issues such as taxation and air-quality standards adjacent to industry facilities. However, the majors resent the independents' efforts to undersell them, so there is friction concerning bidding procedures and marketing policies.

For many years, the major energy companies retained a single lobbyist to represent their interests in the State Capitol. In the late 1980s, however, the use of a single spokesperson for big oil faded into history. The majors have chosen to be represented by several individual practitioners and lobbying firms. Some of the most prestigious lobbying firms in Sacramento now list major energy concerns as their clients. Exxon is represented by George Steffes, Inc.; Standard Oil of California (Chevron) retains the services of the noted law firm of Pillsbury, Madison, and Sutro; and Mobil uses the well-connected lobbying firm of Franchetti and Swoap. Although there is no longer one industry lobbyist as such, the combined efforts of the various firms representing the energy industry remain impressive.

The energy industry is in the enviable position of having favorable government policies already in place. Rather than needing to build political support to alter unsatisfactory policies, the energy lobby has the simpler task of killing hostile measures. A good example of an obliging policy is the lack of a mineral extraction tax. Even though all other petroleum-producing states have an oil severance tax, California has defeated all attempts to enact one. A study of campaign contributions indicated that legislators who voted against the oil severance tax received four times as much in industry donations as those voting to initiate the new revenue device. The former chairperson of California Common Cause commented, "If $2.5 million in contributions can stave off a $500 million severance tax, the money will be very well spent. The amounts are trivial for the industries involved" (Asimov, 1983).

Other Interests

Commercial banks in the state are represented by the California Bankers Association (3 lobbyists in 1989). The major in-state banks, such as Bank of America, Security Pacific, and Wells Fargo, also retain company lobbyists in Sacramento. Out-of-state banking institutions (i.e., Chase Manhattan Bank and Citicorp) have retained contract lobbyists to argue their case for access to the California market. The state's savings and loan institutions belong to either the California Federal Savings and Loan Association (2 lobbyists), the California League of Savings Institutions (3 lobbyists), or the California Association of Thrift and Loan Companies (4 lobbyists). One dozen insurance firms are registered to lobby in Sacramento, and an additional 12 political associations hire lobbyists to represent the varied interests of insurance agents, brokers, and companies.

The major public utilities in the state each employs five to six lobbyists apiece to represent their views in Sacramento. Pacific Gas & Electric, Southern California Edison, Southern California Gas, and San Diego Gas & Electric lobbyists direct much of their attention to the Public Utilities Commission where rate increases are decided. Pacific Telesis (three lobbyists), GTE (two lobbyists), AT&T (two lobbyists), and MCI Telecommunications (one lobbyist), make up the telephone lobby in Sacramento.

Health-related organizations are worthy of a chapter by themselves. Advocates are retained for basic interests such as hospitals, insurance carriers, laboratories, pharmaceutical firms, and practitioners. Looking just at the last category, there are lobbyists in Sacramento representing doctors, chiropractors, podiatrists, dentists, opticians, nurses, and veterinarians. Focusing on doctors alone, there are separate lobbies for specialists such as obstetricians, orthopedists, anesthesiologists, pathologists, and radiologists. Some of the traditional associations in the health area are the California Medical Association (7 lobbyists), the California Dental Association (2 lobbyists), the California Nurses Association (3 lobbyists), and the California Pharmacists Association (10 lobbyists). However, the foregoing associations are being challenged by a host of other groups eager to increase their earnings in the lucrative health industry. The California Medical Association, which represents physicians in the state, is a lowest-common-denominator organization in cases in which its members split on political issues. That is, this association functions best when there is consensus among medical doctors.

The legal profession has fewer groups in Sacramento than are in evidence for the health field. In the criminal law area, the California District Attorneys Association squares off against the California Public Defenders Association, with American Civil Liberties Union lobbyists likely to side with the public defenders. The California Trial Lawyers Association is the largest law-related lobby, and it is one of the heaviest contributors to campaigns in the state. CTLA opposes the insurance industry's efforts to limit the size of damages awarded in personal injury and medical malpractice cases. The State Bar of California protects the profession from interlopers who try to provide legal advice without a license. The State Bar is active on measures dealing with disciplinary procedures for lawyers, and a committee of this organization evaluates the qualifications of gubernatorial nominees to the appellate bench.

The Sierra Club (3 lobbyists) is the largest and most powerful environmental group working in the state; half the club's membership resides in California. Together with advocates for the Planning and Conservation League, the Environmental Defense Fund, and the Defenders of Wildlife, the entire environmental lobby consists of around a dozen registered representatives in Sacramento. A favorite tactic of environmentalists is to publicize the voting records of friends and foes of the environment. These positive and negative endorsements are a far cry from the campaign contributions that businesses are able to lavish on candidates. John Zierold, the first registered lobbyist ever to represent the Sierra Club in Sacramento in 1964, said the following on his retirement twenty years later: "There are certain roads in politics that are followed only by paying a toll; the business interests are paying that toll, and we can't" (Jones, 1984).

Lastly, mention should be made of government entities lobbying each other. Although the advocates for executive departments at the state level direct a tremendous volume of communication to the legislature, these individuals are exempted from registering as lobbyists. Every department in state government has somewhere between 1 and 6 lobbyists working on legislative relations. Unlike lobbyists for departments of state government, lobbyists for local governments must register. Although some localities have used professional advocates in Sacramento for many years, the decline of property tax revenues due to the passage of Proposition 13 in 1978 has caused greater numbers of local governments to retain lobbyists at the State Capitol. Some 50 cities and 26 counties now employ registered advocates in Sacramento to add to the services they receive from the League of California Cities (7 lobbyists) and the County Supervisors Association of California (7 lobbyists).

Regulation of Lobbyists

Rules governing the activity of lobbyists in Sacramento were written in the wake of two scandals. First, California voters approved the Political Reform Act (PRA) in June 1974 at the height of the Watergate episode in Washington, D.C. Second, the electorate passed Proposition 112 (ethics) in June 1990 some 6 weeks after the sentencing of former Senator Joseph Montoya (D, El Monte) following his conviction for extorting money in exchange for his legislative votes. Technically, Proposition 112 dealt more with restrictions on legislators and legislative staff than with lobbyists; but the provisions of this legislative constitutional amendment altered the working conditions under which lobbyists operate.

The PRA requires lobbyists to register with the secretary of state every 2 years at the beginning of each new legislative session. Registration includes providing a list of all a lobbyist's clients, from which a directory is prepared. In addition to registration, lobbyists must file quarterly reports disclosing how much they have personally received in salary and expenses, as well as how much they have spent on particular government officials. The PRA also prohibits *registered lobbyists* from giving gifts (including food and beverages, travel expenses, or anything else of value) in excess of $10 per month to any legislative or administrative official. Note that the $10 limit applies only to registered lobbyists—that is, about 800 people in the entire state. Members of pressure groups (other than officially registered lobbyists) do not have to abide by this $10 limitation. The PRA does limit nonlobbyists to giving no more than $250 in gifts per calendar year to each decision maker. Campaign donations are not considered to be gifts under the law.

While the PRA was causing a great amount of information to be collected on the cost of lobbying and campaigning, several types of salaries were being used from 1975 through 1990 to convey money to decision makers. Beyond campaign donations, interest groups—not their lobbyists—were allowed to pay honoraria (speaking fees) to officeholders, to retain lawyer legislators as legal counsel, to put elected officials on salary as political consultants, to provide lavish travel arrangements for state officials, and to employ public decision makers the day after they left state service. Making an explicit exchange of a vote for money is an illegal bribe. Through 1990, however, it was perfectly legal to accept a high-paying job from a grateful group immediately on retiring from state government—in effect, a deferred bribe. Financial ties such as these gave the appearance of impropriety, even if actual illegality could not be proven.

Figure 3-3 "Got seventy-five cents for a cup of cofee, Senator? Or, for a three thousand dollar honorarium, I'll have breakfast with you." (Dennis Renault, *Sacramento Bee*)

When the U.S. Attorney and the FBI began what were to be success-ful cases against public officials, the leadership of the California Legis-lature realized the need to stop the erosion of public confidence in state government. Legislators drafted and passed a constitutional amend-ment that altered many of the financial practices that had existed for decades. This measure was placed on the ballot in June 1990 for voter ratification. Proposition 112 wrote the following provisions into law.

1. No elected state official (legislative or executive) may accept an honorarium. Professional employees of the Legislature are also prohibited from receiving honoraria.
2. State officials may be reimbursed for transportation expenses in connection with travel for a legislative or governmental purpose. Either one of the following conditions must apply for travel reimbursement to be legal.
   a. Travel payments are for the day before, the day of, or the day after a speech delivered by an official.
   OR
   b. Travel payments are provided by a domestic or foreign government, an educational institution, or a charitable organization.
3. No elected state official (legislative or executive) may accept compensation for appearing before a *state* board or agency, although officials may continue to represent clients before courts and *local* boards and agencies.
4. Legislative and executive officials may not accept compensation from any individual or group that has been under contract within the past year with their respective branch of government.
5. Former legislators are prohibited from lobbying in the California Legislature for a period of one year after leaving office. (This prohibition does not apply to former legislative employees.) Former elected executives and department directors are prohibited from lobbying in the executive branch for one year after leaving office (California Legislature, 1991).

It is the intent of Proposition 112 to remove some of the financial temptation surrounding decision making in the State Capitol. No longer should it be possible for a state official to make brief remarks before a group and then receive a $10,000 honorarium. The 1-year cooling off period after government service should slow down the so-called revolving door where officials are making law one day and lobbying it the next. The new travel rules should reduce the outright recreational trips that had little, if any, government purpose. The restrictions contained in Proposition 112 should curtail the use of financial blandishments that had been in the arsenal of group tactics for many decades.

Summary _____

Interest groups wield considerable power in California for several reasons. Even though groups no longer are allowed to dangle honoraria, consulting fees, and immediate future employment in front of state officials, many other bases of group power remain in effect. Groups are still free to spend as much as they like on inside and outside lobbying, on public relations campaigns, on court cases, on ballot measures, and on candidate races. Business groups are at a great advantage in California not only because their money allows them to use all of the above methods, but also because corporations have superior access to officials and are better organized than other groups in the state.

References: Chapter 3 _____

Asimov, Michael. "Tax the Oil and Beverage Industries." *Sacramento Bee* (May 19, 1983).

BeVier, Michael. *Politics Backstage: Inside the California Legislature.* Philadelphia: Temple University Press, 1979.

California Legislature. *A Guide To Laws on Official Conduct for Legislator's and Legislative Staff.* Sacramento: State of California, 1991.

Garcia, Philip. "In Proposition 103 Fight, Lawyers Win." *Sacramento Bee* (June 3, 1990).

Jones, Robert. "Sierra Club's Man in Sacramento." *Los Angeles Times* (November 6, 1984).

Kushman, Rick. "The Business of Lobbying: Part I." *Sacramento Bee* (February 14, 1988b).

Kushman, Rick. "The Business of Lobbying: Part II." *Sacramento Bee* (February 15, 1988a).

Kushman, Rick. "Why Proposition 103 Fell Short." *Sacramento Bee* (July 1, 1990).

Lofland, John. *Crowd Lobbying: An Emerging Tactic of Interest Group Influence in California.* Davis: Institute of Governmental Affairs, 1982.

Van der Zee, John. *The Greatest Men's Party on Earth: Inside the Bohemian Grove.* New York: Harcourt Brace Jovanovich, 1974.

CHAPTER 4

Ethnic and Gender Politics

It is difficult in the space of one chapter to do justice to the many ethnic and gender groups that make up California, but even an introduction to the profound variations in this state's population should be useful. California is the destination of 46% of all the refugees who enter the United States. For every nationality, except for Poles and Cubans, California is the favorite state in which to settle. Nonwhite students began to outnumber white students in California's K–12 schools beginning in 1988. If overall population tends continue as presently projected, nonwhites will exceed whites in California by the year 2003.

As we examine the various ethnic and gender groups in California, it is worth considering the political resources and the unity that each of these groups brings to the political process. The control of information and finances that typifies corporate California is difficult to match. Moreover, the political objectives of business are more easily attained than those of the populations discussed in this chapter. Corporations (or associations of similar firms) often seek a small change in the state revenue code that saves an industry millions of dollars in taxes. If lobbied skillfully, such a revenue code revision may attract little adverse attention and be dealt with by decision makers as a noncontroversial, technical item. In contrast, many of the requests put forth by ethnic and gender populations in California require the creation or expansion of state bureaucracy. Such proposals as these, even if lobbied with care, are quite controversial and susceptible to concerted opposition. Given the difficulties they face, ethnic and gender groups need considerable resources to be successful.

TABLE 4.1   California Population by Race/Ethnic Group (in percent)

	1990	2003	2020
White	58	50	41
Latino/Hispanic	25	31	38
Asian/Pacific	10	12	14
African American	7	7	7

Source: Department of Finance Report 88 P–4.

Native Americans _____

There were Native Americans living in California for at least 13,000 years prior to the beginning of European settlement in San Diego in 1769 (Chartkoff and Chartkoff, 1984:36). When the Spaniards arrived to start the first of the 21 missions along the coast, the California Indian population is estimated to have been 310,000 persons (Cook, 1976: 42–44). In slightly more than 80 years (1769 to the mid-1850s), the population of Native Californians dropped sharply to 30,000 individuals and their ways of life were threatened with extinction. According to the U.S. Census of 1980, the number of Native Americans in California has rebounded to some 200,000; but only 12% (or 24,000) of this census figure are California Indians (Moisa, 1988:8). The great majority (88%) of Native Americans in California today relocated here from tribal areas outside of this state.

Although romanticized in some quarters, the mission period had a devastating impact on Native Californians. The California Indians that the Spaniards encountered in the late 1700s were extraordinarily diverse peoples (some 104 native languages were spoken) who lived in very small communities. Through specialization and coordination of labor (primarily hunting, gathering, and processing of foods), Native Californians were able to accumulate surpluses of provisions for use in trade or during seasonal shortages. In ceremonies and dances distinct to each native community, California Indians expressed their reverence for the earth and the creatures on it. Into these native settings of harmony and balance came Franciscan missionaries who were either oblivious to the cultures they were meeting or calculatedly destructive of them.

The Spaniards badly needed California Indians to build their missions and to tend their crops and livestock, not to mention needing converts to Catholicism to justify the entire missionary effort along the Pacific Coast. Once baptized, it was expected that natives would continue to labor at the missions. Indians who ran away were tracked down, returned to the missions, flogged, and placed in chains. The European diseases of measles, diphtheria, small pox, and syphilis decimated Native Californians. Even if the Indians had been allowed to leave the missions and to try to recreate their native villages, soon too few natives were available to operate the cooperative economic relationships that had existed for centuries among these Native Americans. For the indigenous peoples who had inhabited the region for thousands of years, "The missions of California were places of defeat and death—not only physical death, but cultural and spiritual death as well" (Margolin, 1989:33).

Unlike tribes in the Great Plains and in New England, California Indians did not have warrior chiefs who organized grand alliances to fight the

Europeans. Despite lacking traditions of warfare, California Indians did rebel in 1824 at Mission Santa Ynez, Mission La Purisima (near Lompoc), and Mission Santa Barbara. Troops were brought in from Monterey to quell the revolt, but many Indians left these missions to live in the San Joaquin Valley. Two years later, an Indian named Estanislao encouraged natives to leave Mission San Jose and join him in the interior. This group raided Mexican livestock herds for 3 years before Mariano Vallejo led an expedition that finally overwhelmed their stronghold (Hurtado, 1988:37, 43). Sanctuary for Native Californians in the Sacramento and San Joaquin Valleys was temporary at best as the Indians increasingly encountered American trappers in the region during the late 1820s. These Americans are thought to have been the source of the terrible small pox epidemic of 1830 that took the lives of 60,000 Native Californians. Pressured from both the West Coast and from the settlers and trappers entering California from the east, Native Californians suffered immensely as a result of the Gold Rush.

> Before the gold discovery, Indians had outnumbered whites by nearly ten to one.—The gold rush changed this picture dramatically. By the early 1850s whites outnumbered Indians by perhaps two to one.—In 1848 the richest gold-bearing regions in the state contained the most native people. Gold hunters consequently ventured directly into the territory of Indians who had previously been independent of white control. The United States Army, supposed to protect both white and Indian people, was severely weakened by desertion because the soldiers proved no more immune to "gold fever" than their civilian counterparts. Therefore, the mining districts became the scenes of boisterous disorder without sufficient police power to control Indian or white communities (Hurtado, 1988:100–101).

Well-armed civilians in search of gold had scant respect for the territorial rights of Native Californians. Denied land bases they needed to hunt and to gather, Indians sometimes avoided starvation by stealing the livestock of white settlers. With or without provocation, hundreds of Native Californians were massacred by the U.S. Army or by armed civilians at Clear Lake (1850), at the Russian River (1850), at Hayfork on the Trinity River (1852), and at Humbolt Bay (1860). Peter Burnett, California's first governor after statehood, stated in 1851 that, "A war of extermination will continue to be waged between the two races until the Indian race becomes extinct" (Heizer and Almquist, 1977:26).

Despite acts of brutality and violence, the remaining Native Californians survived by hiding in the mountains or working in agriculture. Even though the California Constitution of 1849 explicitly prohibited slavery or involuntary servitude, the California Legislature in 1850 passed a law that allowed whites to hold Indians as indentured servants. This act permitted natives to be worked against their will by the same employer for periods of 10 to 15 years. Native American children were kidnapped and sold to whites with no specified termination date for their work obligation. The constitutional protection against involuntary servitude simply was not enforced. It was not until halfway through the Civil War and 4 months after President Lincoln issued the Emancipation Proclamation that California repealed this indentured servant law in 1863. Two authorities on this period conclude, "This was a legalized form of slavery in California Indians. No other possible construction can be made of the facts" (Heizer and Almquist, 1977:57). In addition to the possibility of involuntary servitude until 1863, California Indians were not allowed to testify against whites at trials until 1872 and not allowed to vote until 1879.

Native Californians had a glimmer of hope of obtaining officially recognized homelands in 1851. Three U.S. Government commissioners negotiated treaties in which California Indians relinquished all claims to land in California and in which they placed themselves under the protection of the federal government in exchange for 8.5 million acres of reservation land in the state. The California Legislature communicated to the U.S. Congress that the proposed reservation lands were too valuable to grant to the native population. The U.S. Senate secretly refused to ratify these treaties in 1852—a fact that did not become publicly known until 1905. It took just 83 years (1769–1852) for Native Californians to be entirely dispossessed of their ancestral lands. Many years later in 1944 and 1968, the U.S. Government paid Native Californians a total of $34 million "as compensation for the taking of the lands properly belonging to the California Indians" (Heizer and Almquist, 1977:136).

A primary goal of Native Californians today is to secure and to retain tribal *acknowledgment* or *recognition* from the U.S. Government. With such acknowledgment, a particular California Indian community is entitled to the services, programs, and benefits that are made available by the U.S. Congress to all officially recognized tribes in the United States. Some 94 California tribes had recognition as of 1990; another 36 tribes in California were attempting to secure acknowledgment. An unrecognized tribe may continue to function as a unit, but it will not receive government assistance. Acknowledgment is worth having because recognized tribes have an advantage in securing lands and their rights as Indians are protected under guardianship of the U.S. Government. To obtain acknowledgment, a tribe must prepare a fully documented application that lists their members, describes their tribal government, and demonstrates their continuous and historic tribal identity from early times. If there has been a lapse of time during which a tribe no longer functioned as such, federal recognition may be withdrawn. In the late

1950s, the U.S. Congress terminated the acknowledgment of 60 tribes in California. Seventeen of these tribes had their recognition reinstated by winning a law suit in 1984 (Slagle, 1987:21).

Due to ongoing disagreements with the U.S. Bureau of Indian Affairs concerning its failure to acknowledge many California tribes, Native Californians are requesting that the U.S. Congress pass statutes to settle the long-standing recognition disputes. Given that recognition questions are now being fought in all three branches of the Federal government, it is safe to say that acknowledgment has become a legal morass. To apply for acknowledgment, or to fight termination of recognition, is such a detailed and expensive process that a special field of law has developed on the issue. California Indian Legal Services (CILS) was established in 1967 to help Native Californians with acknowledgment applications and with other legal matters.

Beyond the legal question of acknowledgment, Native Californians are active in several issue areas to preserve their culture and heritage. Tribal representatives are requesting that universities and museums return the remains of California Indians and their artifacts for reburial and respectful preservation. The Native American Heritage Commission, a state panel that advises the governor's office, has prepared guidelines for the protection of California Indian remains that are found at construction sites. Due to the forced labor and punishment practices at California missions, some Native Californians are opposing the canonization of Father Junipero Serra.

CILS obtained an injunction to stop the U.S. Forest Service from building a road from Gasquet to Orleans in the Siskiyou Mountains. The so-called G–O Road was to pass through an area that Native Californians held sacred. Many generations of California Indians had come to this high country to perform religious rituals and to communicate with their Creator. Although lower courts ruled that building the G–O Road would infringe on the religious rights of Native Californians, the U.S. Supreme Court in April 1988 disagreed and held that First Amendment protections did not preclude building the road. As of 1990, the injunction blocking construction of the road was still in effect because the U.S. Forest Service had not yet shown that the planned route met environmental and water quality standards.

Native Californians lack elected representation in California, and they do not have well-funded lobbyists advocating their interests. As a small minority, California Indians face a difficult task in achieving electoral and legislative majorities. Given these realities, the judicial strategy followed by CILS makes sense. By helping Native Californians to win and to keep federal recognition, CILS postpones assimilation of California Indians into the general population and encourages preservation of indigenous cultures.

Latino/Hispanic Americans _____

Are the Latinos of California the once and future rulers of this region? Once rulers—yes. Mexico ruled California for a quarter of a century (1821–1846) following over 50 years (1769–1821) of Spanish control. Future rulers—that remains to be seen. Projections suggest that Latinos will exceed the Anglo population in California not long after the year 2020 (refer to Table 4–1). Whether sheer numbers will translate into political power for the Latino population must await historical developments. There may never again be a transition in power as rapid and as fundamental as that set in motion by the gold rush.

The Treaty of Guadalupe Hidalgo in 1848 made California part of the United States and entitled Mexicans then living in the area to become American citizens. These Spanish-speaking residents of this new American possession became known as Californios. For a brief period, Californios and Anglos worked together cooperatively. Eight of the 48 delegates to California's constitutional convention of 1849 were Californians of Mexican descent. A section of the California Constitution of 1849 required that all legislative enactments be printed in Spanish as well as English. This experiment in bilingualism and biculturalism did not last long, however. The size of the Yankee immigration brought to California by gold fever soon had a devastating effect on Californios living in the northern (i.e., mining) portion of the state; the way of life of Californios in southern areas of the state was not nearly as disrupted by the frantic search for gold.

The Spanish-speaking miners who journeyed to the gold fields from Chile, Peru, and Mexico, as well as local Californios, soon encountered discrimination from Yankee miners. "The Spanish-speaking miners knew how to mine gold, worked hard, lived frugally, were often successful, and in this way acquired the resentment of the Yankees, who were inexperienced, required more amenities, and had poorer returns as a group since there were more of them" (Heizer and Almquist, 1977:144). English-speaking Americans thought that the gold belonged to white settlers, not to foreigners. Californios were lumped together with immigrants from South and Central America for purposes of determining who was entitled to mine gold and who was not. Mining claims filed by Spanish-speaking prospectors were not honored, and the California Legislature passed a Foreign Miners Tax in 1850 to discourage non-white miners. This tax was repealed after just 1 year when it turned out that California merchants were hurt by it. Rather than leaving the state with their gold, most foreigners spent their new wealth or provisions and entertainment inside the state. The commitment to bilingualism faded rapidly in the mining region and the California

Legislature in 1855 failed to appropriate money for the translation of its statutes into Spanish. When California's second constitution was drafted in 1879, there was no section in it requiring Spanish versions of official documents.

Spanish-speaking Californios retained their way of life for three decades longer in southern California than had been the case in the north. The ranchos south of the mining regions continued to operate as in earlier times. Whereas Anglo immigrants were the overwhelming population majority in the north, Californians of Mexican ancestry were the largest population group in the south. As a minority in southern California, Anglos adopted the majority culture there. "These Yankees (in southern California) became Mexicanized—spoke Spanish, at times married Mexican wives, and in general adopted the social customs of the majority group, which remained a majority until the 1870s" (Heizer and Almquist, 1977:150). Californios from the south were elected to the state legislature, and they served as alcaldes (mayors) and as other local officials in southern California. With the construction of railroads into southern California, particularly the Santa Fe line in 1887, a flood of white immigrants began to buy up the ranchos and the rule of the Californios came to an end. As southern California becomes increasingly Latino today, it is worth remembering that this area was governed by Spanish-speaking people for over three decades after California's admission to the Union in 1850.

With Anglos now dominant throughout California, Mexican Americans in the state assumed the role of manual laborers. To secure better working conditions in the fields, some 40 agricultural unions were created in the 1930s. These unions were the forerunners of the United Farm Workers of today. There was considerable labor-management strife in California agriculture during the Great Depression. During the war years, a serious outbreak of anti-Mexican violence occurred in 1944. Despite the fact that Latinos in the military were fighting and dying for the United States in World War II, Anglo sailors and soldiers attacked Mexican Americans wearing pegged (narrowed) pants and lengthy sport coats during the so-called zoot suit riots. Latino males were dragged out of movie theaters and pulled off of public transportation before being beaten. The theatrical production of *Zoot Suit* by Luis Valdez is based on these events.

After training as a community organizer in urban areas, Cesar Chavez launched the United Farm Workers (UFW) union in 1962 in Delano in the southern San Joaquin Valley. Migrant farm workers suffered from low wages and deplorable living conditions. Unlike industrial workplaces, employers in California agriculture had not recognized unions to bargain on behalf of field hands or workers in packing sheds. As growers resisted recognizing a union for farmworkers, Chavez organized nationwide boycotts against the purchase of California table grapes and lettuce. The UFW further asked shoppers not to patronize any chain of markets that carried boycotted produce—in effect, a secondary boycott. Chavez received support from major Anglo politicians, such as U.S. Senator Robert F. Kennedy (D, New York) who was campaigning in California's presidential primary in 1968. Many leaders in the Catholic Church lent their assistance to the cause of union recognition. Supermarket chains eventually prevailed on California's growers to sit down and bargain with the UFW, though there would be several years of contested elections over which union would serve as bargaining agent. (Secondary boycotts against markets-as-whole are no longer legal; boycotts of specific products within markets are still lawful.)

At the point that the UFW was achieving its first solid contracts with the growers of table grapes in 1970, long-festering problems in the urban barrios (neighborhoods) ignited. Latino high school students in East Los Angeles had been protesting inadequate educational programs during the late 1960s. The fact that a disproportionate share of Latino men were being drafted and later killed in Vietnam was well known in the barrios. On August 29, 1970, the National Chicano Moratorium organized a large rally (an estimated 20,000 persons attended) at Laguna Park in East Los Angeles at which speakers were planning to urge resistance to the draft and renewed commitment to achieving social justice. Before speeches could be delivered, an altercation broke out when police attempted to arrest someone at the edge of the crowd. Rocks and bottles were thrown at law enforcement officers, and protesters dispersed in several directions smashing shop windows and setting fires as they went. Believing that someone with a gun was in the Silver Dollar Cafe, police fired tear gas projectiles into the establishment. One such shell hit Ruben Salazar in the head and killed him. An award-winning reporter for the *Los Angeles Times* with experience in both the Saigon and Mexico City bureaus, Salazar's last assignment was to report on the Mexican-American community in Los Angeles. He was also news director for a Spanish-language television station. With a high-profile victim such as Salazar as an example, the focus of demonstrations changed from draft resistance to police brutality. In January 1971, a peaceful rally outside of Parker Center (headquarters of the Los Angeles Police Department) to protest police conduct also turned into a riot.

Throughout the 1970s and 1980s, there have been around half a dozen Latino/Hispanic members of the California Legislature. Since the overall size of the state legislature is 120 members, the Latino contingent has been roughly 5% of the whole body. With the Latino/Hispanic portion of the state population in 1990 at 25% and climbing, this ethnic group is underrepresented in the California Legislature. Although Mexican-American legislators have chaired some important committees, they have yet to serve as a major legislative leader in the manner of

Speaker Willie Brown—an African American. Richard Alatorre and Gloria Molina both won election to the Los Angeles City Council after serving in the California Assembly; Molina was the first Latina ever elected to the state legislature in 1982. In an effort to make the most of their small members, an Hispanic Legislative Network has been established. Organized by the Latino/Hispanic legislators in the State Capitol, the network consists of Hispanic activists in cities around the state. These individuals provide policy ideas to Latino members of the state legislature, and they may generate support for legislation once it has been introduced. This network is expanding the number of Latinos who are familiar with the intricacies of the legislative process.

The situation in the executive branch is bleak. Asian-American and African-American candidates have won statewide executive posts in California in the last two decades, but no Latino/Hispanic office seeker has been elected to state executive office in the twentieth century. (Romualdo Pacheco did serve as Treasurer, Lieutenant Governor, and Governor during the 1860s and 1870s.) Turning to the composition of the state civil service, again Hispanics are underrepresented. Whereas other minority populations have achieved parity in the civil service with their numbers in the overall work force in California, Latino employment in the bureaucracy is below the share of Hispanic workers in the statewide labor pool (Green, 1989).

Certain issues are of interest to most ethnic groups. For instance, education and employment are central concerns of most minority citizens. Some 45% of Latino students entering high school do not graduate, and Hispanic workers earn considerably less in wages than others in the labor force. There are other issues, however, that are of much more interest to Latinos than to others. Latino/Hispanic Californians recently have been focusing on election rules, language issues, and immigration law. Depending on laws in effect in each locality, candidates for local offices may run throughout a municipality to garner votes (the at-large method) or just campaign in a delimited portion of the city (the distinct method). Some 95% of all city council and school board elections in California are contested under at-large rules (Johnson, 1989:28). Latino candidates for local office have not done well under the at-large system. For example, the locality of Watsonville near Monterey Bay had not elected a Latino candidate to its city council before 1985 despite the fact that the population of the town was half Hispanic. A law suit was filed in 1985 challenging the at-large method of election. While the case was working its way through the federal courts, Tony Campos won election to the Watsonville City Council in 1987 under the at-large system. Despite this victory by Campos, the 9th U.S. Circuit Court of Appeals in 1989 ruled that Watsonville's at-large elections violated the U.S. Voting Rights Act because racially polarized voting by Anglos denied representation to Latinos. Somewhat surprisingly, the first election using districts in Watsonville did not produce change in the ethnic composition of the city council; but the turnout of Latino/Hispanic voters increased dramatically, nearly tripling in one Latino district. The City of Salinas voluntarily switched to the district system and elected the first Latino ever to its city council in 1989. Interestingly, the turnout in Hispanic districts in Salinas was slightly higher than that in Anglo districts. When the chances of success are greater, it appears that Latino voters participate at a higher rate. Latino lawmakers in the State Capitol won passage of bills in 1989 to require district elections for large school districts and for community college districts, but Governor Deukmejian vetoed these enactments.

District elections by themselves do not guarantee that minority candidates will enter office. There is the secondary question of how the district lines are drawn. Even though the population of Los Angeles County is one-third Hispanic, no Latino before 1990 had ever occupied one of the five district seats on the board of supervisors. A lawsuit was filed claiming that the board intentionally dispersed Latino voters into several districts to dilute their strength. In August 1990, a federal district judge ordered the five supervisional districts of Los Angeles County to be redrawn thus establishing a district with 72% Hispanic population. Leaving her seat on the city council, Gloria Molina was elected to this newly drawn district on the Board of Supervisors of Los Angeles County in early 1991. The state legislature is elected on a district basis, but Latino representation in the State Capitol is far from the Hispanic share of California's population. For this reason, Latino/ Hispanic politicians and activists are focusing intently on legislative redistricting as the 1990s begin in hopes of securing district lines that are more favorable to Latino candidates.

In 1986, the voters of California adopted Proposition 63 by a whopping margin of 75 to 25%. This initiative made English the official language of California. The ballot measure is a statement of general sentiment, but it has the potential to be implemented through legislation (if introduced and passed) in areas such as education, elections, and employee compensation. From 1972 to 1987, California had state-supported bilingual education programs for limited English proficiency (LEP) students. Efforts to continue the state bilingual education programs after 1987 were passed by the legislature, but were vetoed by Governor Deukmejian. In the absence of a state law mandating that bilingual programs be provided to LEP students, most local school districts have maintained bilingual programs on their own. Controversy has surrounded bilingual education since its inception. Critics contended that there were not enough competent teachers to conduct bilingual instruction. Moreover, there was disagreement concerning the ultimate objective of bilingual education. Was it only to hasten the acquisition of fluency in English or was it to maintain proficiency in the native language as well? The supporters of bilingual education strongly favor cultural pluralism.

Latino activists recounted numerous instances in which primary school teachers had "anglicized" their names or in which they had been punished by school authorities for speaking Spanish to their playmates on the school grounds.—Proponents of bilingualism pointed out that the United States had never been a monolingual, monocultural nation and they argued that efforts by state agencies (such as public schools) to make it such through "forced" assimilation into the dominant culture amounted to nothing less than "cultural genocide." Many Latinos and other minority group activists wanted to be treated as full and equal members of American society without having to give up their linguistic and cultural identities (Schmidt, 1989:11–12).

Proposition 63 (English as official language) might pose a threat to the provision of ballots and voter pamphlets describing initiatives in languages other than English. Although the U.S. Voting Rights Act of 1975 requires that bilingual voting materials be made available, California voters in 1984 requested that the national government drop this requirement. (As of 1990, ballots and pamphlets in languages other than English were still being prepared at state expense in California.) Another issue involving language is whether bilingual public employees should receive extra compensation for their linguistic skills. Opponents argue that bilingualism is an accident of birth and should not be regarded as a special skill. Supporters of salary differentials for speaking a second language contend that the additional work demands placed on bilingual employees merit financial reward.

Immigration law is a federal question, but the impacts of this law are felt at the state and local levels. The influx of non-English-speaking peoples to California places demands on the state's schools and electoral processes as just discussed. Health and welfare agencies provide services until immigrants become self-sufficient. With national budget deficits a continuing problem, federal reimbursement to California for refugee expenses is shrinking every year. Major revisions in immigration law were adopted at the national level in 1986. Employers were no longer allowed to hire alien workers, and individuals illegally in the country since 1982 had the opportunity until 1990 to apply for citizenship through an amnesty program. Despite the passage of the immigration reform package in 1986, more immigration bills were being considered by the U.S. Congress as the 1990s began.

Several organizations reflect Latino/Hispanic viewpoints in California. The Mexican American Legal Defense and Educational Fund (MALDEF) has an effective lobbying operation at the State Capitol, but the organization is best known for initiating the successful districting cases in Watsonville and in Los Angeles County. Besides its legal arm, MALDEF conducts research on opportunities for Latino students and is involved in raising scholarship assistance. The Southwest Voter Registration Education Project (SVREP) trains organizers to conduct voter registration drives and get-out-the-vote campaigns. This group also promotes changes in election and redistricting law to increase Latino/Hispanic participation in the electoral process. Both MALDEF and SVREP were first established in San Antonio, Texas, but each has opened a number of offices in California. The Mexican American Political Association (MAPA) has local chapters organized around the state. MAPA is not well known for lobbying in the State Capitol, but the organization actively endorses candidates for offices at all levels of government. The League of United Latin American Citizens (LULAC), like MAPA lacking a paid lobbyist in Sacramento, is active in efforts to increase the numbers of Latino/Hispanic citizens on the voter rolls. California Rural Legal Assistance (CRLA) is known for its litigation on behalf of farmworkers. There are several other organizations that represent the special interests of Latino teachers and lawyers. Increasing the extent of Latino/Hispanic participation on decision-making bodies in California will require persistent legal advocacy and skillful political organizing.

Asian/Pacific Americans

Immigration from Asia to California occurred in several distinct eras. Each period involved peoples from different parts of Asia, and each stage featured discrimination toward populations of Asian origin. The first Asians to arrive in California were the Chinese in 1848. They were met by white miners who passed resolutions that limited the mining of gold to persons of European descent. As a result, many Chinese entered service occupations where they served as cooks and laundry workers. A few Chinese mined for gold in areas that white miners were not interested in prospecting (Heizer and Almquist, 1977:154–155).

Chinese labor was crucial to the completion of the transcontinental railroad in 1869, but white workers sought and obtained restrictions on Asian laborers thereafter. The California Constitution of 1879 prohibited employment of Chinese by any government entity or corporation in California. (This provision remained in the state constitution until 1952.) The U.S. Congress suspended Chinese immigration for a period of 10 years in the Chinese Exclusion Act of 1882. Many Chinese homes and businesses were burned to the ground as some Californians took the passage of the Exclusion Act as a license to engage in hostile acts against the Asian population. The prohibition against Chinese immigration was extended for 10 more years in 1892 and then made indefinite in 1902. When the United States and China were allied against Japan in World War II, the U.S. Congress finally repealed the Chinese Exclusion Acts in 1943.

These state and national laws induced some Chinese to return to their homeland. The Chinese population in California reached 75,000 persons in 1880, and then began to decline. Incredible as it may seem, there were fewer than 100 Japanese in the entire state during this same year. With the Chinese population decreasing and with demand for low-wage labor still present, the stage was set for a strong surge of Japanese immigration. By 1920, Japanese population figures almost equalled those of the Chinese 40 years earlier. During this period, Japanese males in California contemplated going to Japan to find spouses to bring back to the United States. However, these men would not be readmitted to California after going to Japan. This prohibition against reentry led to the custom of picture brides in which marriages were arranged without loss of residency in California (Jensen and Lothrop, 1987:70).

At the turn of the century, the Asiatic Exclusion League urged limitations on Japanese immigration. The San Francisco School Board precipitated an international incident in 1905 by planning to put Japanese students in separate schools from other students. Japan protested this segregation plan as a violation of treaty commitments made by the United States. Ultimately, the school board rescinded its segregation plan in exchange for President Theodore Roosevelt issuing an executive order prohibiting new arrivals from Japan. Anti-Japanese sentiment also was reflected in the passage of the Alien Land Law of 1913 by the California Legislature. This statute prohibited Asians (but not European nationals) from owning land in California. (This state law remained on the books until 1952.) The U.S. Congress enacted the Immigration Act of 1924 that barred persons of Japanese descent from settling in the United States; henceforth, only short-term visas to study and to travel in the United States would be issued to people from Japan.

The crowning blow to persons of Japanese ancestry in California was the signing of Executive Order 9066 by President Franklin Roosevelt 2½ months after Japan's attack on Pearl Harbor on December 7, 1941. The order required all individuals of Japanese descent (whether U.S. citizens or not) to relocate away from coastal areas to internment camps either in eastern California or in other states of the Union. Since an internee could take to camp only what he or she could carry, Japanese Americans lost many possessions as well as their homes and businesses.

Fred Korematsu, whose family lost its nursery business in Oakland, defied the evacuation order and continued working at his welding job in a shipyard. As a U.S. citizen, Korematsu considered relocation to be illegal because it was not based on proof of any wrongdoing by the 110,000 persons touched by the order. After his arrest, Korematsu was found guilty of residing in an out-of-bounds area and sent to the Topaz internment camp in Utah. On appeal at the U.S. Supreme Court in 1946, the justices decided the case on the technical basis of whether or not Korematsu was in an off-bounds area; the high court did not consider whether the executive order itself was too sweeping or was unwarranted under the circumstances (Korematsu, 1990). A respected account of internment commented as follows:

> The recommendation (to relocate) was made despite advice from Army and Navy authorities that a sustained Japanese attack on the coast was "impossible" and that even enemy raids, although possible, "would be sporadic and would have little, if any, bearing on the course of the war."—The total inability of the FBI to uncover saboteurs among the Japanese population was frankly admitted by (U.S.) Attorney General Biddle in a memorandum to President Roosevelt (tenBroek et. al., 1968:86, 92).

Japanese-American men fighting in the U.S. Army's 442nd Regimental Combat Team were the most decorated soldiers of World War II, yet the records of the American judicial system long after the war was over continued to reflect that people of Japanese descent were disloyal and needed to be relocated for military necessity. To reclaim his own good name and that of his people, Korematsu returned to court in 1983. His lawyers, the Bay Area Attorneys for Redress, demonstrated that the government purposely suppressed evidence showing that Japanese Americans were not a security risk at the time of Korematsu's wartime trial. In late 1983, the 9th U.S. Circuit Court of Appeals overturned Korematsu's original conviction and found that the government had deliberately attempted to tarnish all Japanese Americans as disloyal in 1942. Former internees held reunions at Korematsu's legal proceedings in the 1980s and Japanese Americans felt vindicated by the outcome. Having been wronged, what redress should Japanese Americans receive?

Governor Jerry Brown signed a bill in 1982 authorizing payment of $6000 each to some 80 Japanese-American state workers who were fired from their jobs in 1942 because of their ancestry. In August 1988, President Ronald Reagan signed federal legislation that formally apologized for internment and also authorized payment of reparations in the amount of $20,000 to each of the 60,000 internees still thought to be alive. California curriculum guidelines now require discussion of internment in high school, and some schools recognize February 19th as a Day of Remembrance when Executive Order 9066 was signed in 1942. Are apologies and reparations sufficient response for the injustices done? More than an attack on legal and property rights, internment was also an attack on a culture. "Attorney General Warren (of California) sweepingly condemned as anti-American the language schools, religious organizations, and vernacular press of the resident Japanese, and considered the Japanese tongue itself a suspicious bond with the old country" (tenBroek et al., 1968:94). As the following excerpts indicate, Japanese Americans seek respect for their way of life.

> The fact of the matter is that assimilation for us has meant giving up our Japanese heritage, without being accepted into the spiritual and emotional life of this country in return.—Being Japanese is a matter of mind, spirit and style. And the essence of this style is manners and consideration for others.—What we want is not fame and glory, not money and official apologies. We don't want to take. We want to give. And what we want to give is more than our loyalty, more than the fruits of our many professional talents and skills. We want to be able to give those special gifts of the heart, those emotional gifts of love and affection that we ourselves value above all. But these are gifts that can only be given between equals (Tanaka, 1990).

The aftermath of internment consists of more than legal vindication and financial reparations. Though half a century has passed, political repercussions are still being felt. Political figures who do not favor reparations can expect strong opposition from Japanese Americans. Governor Deukmejian's first appointee to the vacant office of state treasurer, U.S. Representative Dan Lungren, failed to win confirmation in the California Senate in 1988 after being roundly criticized for his failure to support reparations. Japanese Americans formed a coalition with other Asian/Pacific peoples, as well as with other minority populations, to spearhead the battle against Lungren's confirmation. Lungren subsequently went on to win his bid for the office of attorney general in 1990.

The federal government relaxed restrictions on Asian/Pacific immigration in the mid-1960s. Stimulated by the U.S. withdrawal from Vietnam in 1975, the extraordinary diversity of the Asian/Pacific peoples coming to California in the last two decades sets the present period apart from past eras of immigration. Some 70% of the Asian/Pacific persons now living in California were born outside of the United States in countries such as Cambodia, Laos, Vietnam, Singapore, Hong Kong, the Philippines, Taiwan, Korea, and many Pacific island nations. In the same vein as Chinatown, Koreatown, and Little Tokyo, the Southeast Asian immigrants settling near Garden Grove in Orange County have built Little Saigon—a mall of restaurants and shops featuring items of

Vietnamese culture. As California's schools strain to educate children speaking over a hundred different native languages, younger immigrants in particular are torn between two cultures. Although urged to be successful in their new country, immigrant youths are also expected not to lose their original cultural roots. For older immigrants, the politics of their homelands may well be more prominent in their minds than concern for political developments in their adopted country. For instance, immigrants who lived through the lengthy conflict in Vietnam vehemently disagree with each other concerning whether or not to send aid to friends and families still inside Vietnam (Hecht, 1990). Does such aid prop up a despised regime they left behind?

The most recent wave of Asian/Pacific immigration to California has not faced the sort of legal harassment suffered by the Chinese and the Japanese. Despite not being inflicted with exclusionary laws, Asian/Pacific peoples in California have been the target of discriminatory practices and hate crimes. In the late 1980s, Chancellor Michael Heyman of U.C. Berkeley formally apologized for allowing admissions policies to exist that caused a decline in Asian enrollment; steps have been taken to modify admissions policies. In January 1989, Patrick Purdy opened fire with an AK-47 assault rifle at the Cleveland Elementary School in Stockton, killing five Cambodian children and wounding 30 other people before taking his own life. Legislators and the governor used these deaths as a catalyst to adopt legislation banning assault weapons, and the racial aspect of the murders was downplayed. In February 1991, a member of the Compton Police Department responding to a report of a domestic disturbance fired 20 shots into the bodies of two unarmed Samoan brothers as they were in the process of kneeling in front of the officer as ordered. The police officer claimed that the brothers tried to seize his weapon, but the Samoan-American population characterized the deaths as unwarranted executions. After such episodes as these, Asian/Pacific peoples cannot be blamed for thinking that some Californians bear them malice.

Immigrants from countries such as Vietnam, Laos, Cambodia, and Thailand also have been subjected to violence and robbery at the hands of Asian gangs. A gang called the Oriental Boys is known to take valuables from the homes of Asians living in California. In a break with precedent, four members of the Oriental Boys in Sacramento seized 41 hostages at The Good Guys stereo store in April 1991. Frustrated by their inability to find steady employment in California, these Asian teenagers demanded millions of dollars and a plane to take them out of the country in exchange for releasing their captives. Before losing their own lives when sheriff's deputies retook the store, gang members killed three hostages and wounded eleven others. The dead perpetrators were all born in Vietnam and arrived in California as youngsters in 1980. In this case, the dream of golden opportunities in California certainly did not materialize.

Californians of Asian descent have had mixed success in winning elective office. The long-standing populations (Chinese and Japanese) have won offices at all levels of government, but Southeast Asian peoples have yet to win public office. When economic security and fluency in English are assured, perhaps the younger generation of Southeast Asians will produce some candidates for office. After the mid-1960s and throughout the 1970s, there were always two or three Asians seated in the California Legislature. Al Song, a Korean American, was elected to the California Assembly in 1962 and moved up to the California Senate in 1966. (Senator Song failed to win reelection in 1978.) March Fong Eu, a Chinese American, was the first woman of Asian ancestry ever elected to the California Assembly in 1966. She left the Assembly in 1974 on her election as Secretary of State, an office to which she was reelected in 1978, 1982, 1986, and 1990. Tom Hom, a Chinese American Republican, served briefly in the California Assembly from 1969 to 1970. Hom is noteworthy because he did not share the Democratic Party registration of other Asian American state legislators. Paul Bannai and Floyd Mori, both Japanese Americans, served in the California Assembly in the latter half of the 1970s. With Senator Song defeated in 1978 and with Assembly members Bannai and Mori leaving the legislature in 1980, not a single state legislator was Asian American during the decade of the 1980s. Democrats Norman Mineta and Robert Matsui, both Japanese Americans, repeatedly won reelection to the U.S. House of Representatives in the 1980s; and Republican S. I. Hayakawa, also Japanese American, represented California in the U.S. Senate from 1976 to 1982. Michael Woo, a Chinese American, became the first Asian American at the Los Angeles City Council in 1985. The 1990s began with the important appointment of Chang-Lin Tien, a naturalized U.S. citizen who was born in China, to serve as Chancellor of U.C. Berkeley on Michael Heyman's retirement.

In recognition of the lack of Asian-American representatives in the state legislature during the 1980s, President pro Tem David Roberti (D, Hollywood) created the Office of Asian/Pacific Affairs in the California Senate in 1987. While African-American and Latin-American legislators naturally receive inquiries and requests from Californians of their ethnic background, this office serves the same function for the growing numbers of Asian/Pacific peoples in California. A wide assortment of Asian/Pacific organizations exists outside the state legislature, such as the Asian Law Caucus, the Chinese American Citizen Alliance, the Chinese Chamber of Commerce, the Japanese American Citizens League, the Nisei Farmers League, the Korean American Political Association, and the California Lao Association. The Office of Asian/Pacific Affairs actively reaches out to these groups instead of passively waiting to be contacted by them. With the multiplicity of languages spoken in the nine major subethnic groups within the Asian/Pacific population, each linguistic or subethnic group is too small to be heard in statewide politics. By coalescing the many Asian/Pacific peoples together, the resulting 10% of the state's population (as of 1990) is much more likely to be politically effective. Some issues obviously are unique to peoples such as Filipinos, Samoans, or Laotians, but there are other issues on which Asian/Pacific Americans can agree. Access to quality education and multilingual instructors, immigration laws that do not discriminate against Asians, and strong law enforcement to deter hate crimes are all issues that draw Asian/Pacific peoples together.

African Americans

People of African ancestry began arriving in California during the mission period (1769–1834). Africans were brought to Mexico as slaves by the Spaniards, and the descendants of these Africans were among the founders of the pueblo at Los Angeles in 1781. Other blacks entered California as paid servants or as slaves of white settlers from the United States and by jumping ship when their vessels put into Pacific coast ports. Miners of African descent, who struck it rich in the gold fields, purchased their freedom from slave owners rather than return to the South. The black population of California during the 1800s was very small—some 1% of the state's population (Lapp, 1987:27). This proportion was considerably smaller than the numbers of Native Californians and Chinese then in the state.

The California Constitution of 1849 outlawed slavery in California, but it did not allow people of African descent to vote or to testify against whites in court. The early organizing among black residents in California occurred in churches and in groups advocating the right of black people to testify at trials. The law forbidding African Americans to testify was repealed by the state in 1863, but the California Legislature continued to deny black citizens the franchise. Finally, the 15th Amendment to the U.S. Constitution extended the right to vote to African Americans in 1870. Securing the right to vote did little to improve conditions for black Californians in the short run, as is evident from the following description of the early 1900s.

> While blacks continued to migrate to California, once arrived they found the state something less than an interracial paradise. In the large cities

there were hotels that would not receive them, restaurants that would not serve them, and innumerable public places, such as swimming pools and parks, that would not admit them.—In the rural areas of the state the segregation of blacks was even more intense. The degree of racial prejudice among rural Californians, many of them originally from the South and poorly educated, was more pronounced than in the urban areas (Lapp, 1987:45).

The California chapter of the National Association for the Advancement of Colored People (NAACP) was established in 1913 to work for civil rights. The NAACP assumed a high profile quickly by attacking the negative characterization of African Americans in motion pictures. A California affiliate of the Urban League was soon formed to improve social services and employment opportunities. Newspaper publisher Frederick Roberts became the first person of African descent to be seated in the state legislature when he was elected to the California Assembly in 1919. He was known for his efforts to remove racist materials from textbooks used in California's schools. Probably in recognition of the Republican party's role in ending slavery, Roberts ran successfully as a GOP candidate until 1934. The severe unemployment during the depression years caused black voters to switch party allegiance, and Democrat Augustus Hawkins (also of African descent) ousted Roberts from the California Assembly. The black Californians who have been elected to the legislative and executive branches since Roberts have all been Democrats.

African-American migration to California rose dramatically during World War II as black laborers found employment in defense industries. The NAACP won battles to guarantee equal rights for black workers in labor unions and to prohibit de jure (in law) restrictive covenants that kept black home buyers out of white neighborhoods. Housing and employment discrimination continued on a de facto (in fact) basis nonetheless. Black Assemblymember Byron Rumford (D, Oakland) successfully carried a Fair Housing Act in 1963, but the California electorate overturned the legislation in 1964. The California Supreme Court and the U.S. Supreme Court invalidated this election result, and reinstated the statute, to uphold the equal protection clauses in the state and federal constitutions.

Any illusion of racial harmony in California was abruptly shattered in the Watts riot in 1965. Six days of violence that August resulted in 34 deaths, over 1,000 injured, and property damage amounting to more than $40 million. Located in south-central Los Angeles, Watts seemed an unlikely area for a riot on the surface, especially when the single-family bungalows were contrasted with the crowded tenements of ghettos in eastern cities. The riot, which began over a routine drunk-driving arrest involving a white law enforcement officer and a black driver, symbolized the crumbling relations between black citizens and the police and public officials in Los Angeles. From 1965 to 1968, other cities in the state, including San Bernardino, Bakersfield, Riverside, San Francisco, Oakland, and San Diego, also experienced sporadic violent outbursts from the black community.

Despite some improvements (e.g., the building of the Martin Luther King Hospital), Watts continues to be plagued by chronic unemployment, low literacy levels, heavy gang activity, high drug use, and strained police–community relations. In the wake of the above urban upheavals, the Black Panther party was formed around the ideas of protecting African Americans from police brutality and of providing food and black pride to community members. Some black activists favored a confrontational approach with white-dominated institutions, whereas other Californians of African descent chose to compete in the electoral arena. The early 1970s were a time of considerable success for African-American candidates.

Wilson Riles became the first black Californian elected to statewide executive office when he won the race for Superintendent of Public Instruction in 1970. (Riles won reelection as school's chief in 1974 and 1978 to serve three terms in statewide office.) The next major breakthrough was the election of Tom Bradley as mayor of Los Angeles in 1973. Bradley's victory received national attention as it was the first for a black candidate in a predominantly white city. A former police officer and member of the city council, he was defeated initially in the 1969 mayoral race by incumbent Sam Yorty who characterized Bradley as a militant black activist. In fact, Mayor Bradley became known for his conciliatory style and his ability to work with people of all types. He is credited with securing major private investment in downtown Los Angeles and with tirelessly seeking federal funds for the city. (Bradley won reelection as mayor in 1977, 1981, 1985, and 1989.) In 1974, black legislator Mervyn Dymally won election to the post of Lieutenant Governor to join Riles in statewide office. Lionel Wilson, a black superior court judge, was elected mayor of Oakland in 1977. (Wilson won reelection in 1981 and 1985.) Wiley Manual became the first black member of the California Supreme Court in 1977 on appointment by Governor Jerry Brown.

The success of Americans of African descent in statewide executive races dramatically declined in the late 1970s and throughout the 1980s. Lieutenant Governor Mervyn Dymally lost to Republican Mike Curb in 1978. In the same year, Yvonne Brathwaite Burke, a black woman who served in the California Legislature and later the U.S. Congress, lost her bid to become the state Attorney General to Republican George Deukmejian. In the state elections in 1982, Bill Honig ousted Wilson Riles as Superintendent of Public Instruction, and Attorney General

George Deukmejian narrowly defeated Mayor Tom Bradley for the governorship. In a rematch for the governor's office in 1986, Deukmejian won overwhelmingly. In 1990, not a single African-American candidate was nominated by either major party for any of the eight elected positions in the executive branch.

Despite setbacks in statewide races, African Americans were successful in other areas. After serving in the lower house since 1964, Willie L. Brown, Jr. (D, San Francisco) was selected Speaker of the Assembly in December 1980. With every day he continues in this powerful position, Brown establishes a record as the person to serve the longest as Assembly Speaker. After the elections of 1990, Brown was joined by six other African Americans in the California Assembly and by two in the California Senate. At the local level, Alameda County Supervisor John George became the first black person to lead a county board of supervisors in the state in 1982. Charles Byrd was elected the state's first black sheriff in 1986 in sparsely populated Siskiyou County.

Tom Bradley's loss to George Deukmejian in the 1982 race for governor still generates debate concerning the role of racial campaigning. Deukmejian stated several times that he had no intention of raising race in the campaign, and Bradley expressed satisfaction in having received some 3.7 million votes for governor—the majority from white voters. However, all other Democrats running for statewide offices in the executive branch in 1982 were victorious. Two writers who examined the 1982 election closely comment as follows:

> Subtle, racially charged code words and slogans slipped into the 1982 campaign. Deukmejian used a slogan that frequently appears in various forms in campaigns against black candidates: "He can represent all Californians." Such a slogan implies that a black person cannot represent the state's white citizens.—Less subtle were radio ads for Deukmejian aimed at older white voters in California, many of whom have southern roots. In a radio spot aired repeatedly in southern California, Slim Pickens, an actor with a "country" accent, declared "Daddy told me never to trust a skunk or a politician." "Skunk" was a derogatory term for blacks commonly used in the South before World War II.—When Deukmejian took pains in the final debate to link Tom Bradley and Willie Brown, he was intentionally evoking race on the eve of the election (Pettigrew and Alston, 1988:33, 35).

As the 1990s begin, Speaker Brown and Mayor Bradley are the major African-American political figures in California. Both are veteran politicians with full careers behind them. Whatever the impact of code words and slogans may be in future campaigns, it is going to be a real challenge to elect successors to Brown and Bradley into high-profile leadership positions in the years to come.

Black officeholders, even in alliance with white politicians, have not been able to make a great deal of headway on problems facing African Americans in California. Unemployment among black Californians continues to be high, and the competition for jobs is intense as newly arrived immigrants add to the labor supply. The president of the Los Angeles chapter of the Urban League is quoted as saying, "At times it appears that our government leaders give a higher priority to welcoming new immigrants than to helping those folks who are already here" (Lapp, 1987:97). In the early 1980s, a Japanese-owned electronics firm in Compton had to be ordered by the state to stop giving preference to Asian job applicants and to begin hiring African Americans.

Americans of African descent encounter California's criminal justice system far more frequently than whites do. Though hardly confined to one ethnic population, the toll of drive-by shootings, the drug industry, and gang activity on black Californians has been heavy.

> If you are a black Californian, your chances of being arrested are seven times as great as a white person's. Your chances of being sent to prison are nine times as great, and your chances of getting a death sentence are twelve times as great (Cooper, 1988).

The case of Don Jackson, a black police officer from Hawthorne, reinforced the fears of African Americans and received national publicity as well. While on leave from his police job and dressed in civilian attire, Jackson and a black correctional officer drove into Long Beach one night in January 1989 to test that city's reputation for police brutality. Jackson's car was pulled over by two white officers of the Long Beach Police Department. Though he complied with the instructions of the Long Beach police, Jackson was assaulted and his head was pushed through a window pane. Unbeknownst to the arresting officers, Jackson had arranged to have NBC news follow him that night. The entire incident was placed on videotape. As a result of the outpouring of criticism of the Long Beach Police Department when the tape was shown, charges against Jackson of resisting arrest were quickly dropped and the two white officers were charged with assaulting Jackson and filing false reports of the event. The assault charges against the two police officers were dismissed in May 1991 due to a hung jury. There are no plans to conduct another trial in this case.

Rodney King, a 25-year-old black motorist, received a severe beating by four officers of the Los Angeles Police Department in the early morning hours of March 3, 1991. After being pulled over for speeding and for running red lights, King was ordered out of his car. Though it is unclear whether King made threatening moves toward police officers, there is less doubt about the behavior of the members of the LAPD because their actions were recorded on videotape by a local resident. King was struck

Figure 4-1 (Dennis Renault, *Sacramento Bee*)

by two electric-shock darts, hit 56 times with police batons, and kicked 7 times. He suffered a broken right cheekbone, a shattered right eye socket, fractured right sinus bones, additional skull fractures, and a broken ankle. There was worldwide revulsion in response to the airing of the videotape. As of June, 1991, the four officers who inflicted these injuries on King were awaiting trial on charges of assault with a deadly weapon and unnecessarily beating a suspect (i.e., excessive force).

To address issues such as police misconduct, unemployment, school completion rates for black youth, affordable housing, and adequacy of health care, a number of groups have been founded to represent the different segments of the African-American population in California. The long-standing organization in the judicial arena is the NAACP, and the Urban League is noted for its work in developing job opportunities. Black civil servants have their own group, and there is a California Black Chamber of Commerce for individuals in business. There are groups for black Californians who are elected officials of cities, counties, and school boards. To foster coordinated action among all these groups, the Black Americans Political Association of California (BAPAC) was formed in 1978. BAPAC is a nonpartisan, umbrella organization that embraces black Californians from the most humble grassroots level to the highest public officials. African Americans in the Republican Party are welcome in BAPAC, although it must be said that Democrats heavily outweigh the GOP in the black constituency. A real strength of the organization is its 32 local chapters throughout the state. BAPAC holds an annual meeting in Sacramento at which a legislative agenda is drafted. Although BAPAC's tax status as a nonprofit entity will not allow it to employ a lobbyist, members of the local chapters do write and phone state leaders when the interests of black Californians are threatened. The various chapters of the organization are active in local politics as well. BAPAC also conducts voter education and registration activities, and it regularly prepares information pamphlets on upcoming ballot measures. Effective African-American organizations will be of considerable importance should black Californians encounter continuing difficulty with local police departments.

Women and Politics

For nearly half of the 140 years of statehood in California, no women were chosen to hold state offices. It was 68 years after admission to the Union before the first women won seats in the California Legislature in 1918. Well over a century of statehood passed before Ivy Baker Priest became the first female elected to a statewide executive position as treasurer in 1966. Pollster Mervin Field has heralded the 1990s as "The Decade of the Women." After the 1990 general elections, the number of women elected to statewide executive posts (two) and to the California Legislature (21) were at all-time highs. These successes, however, should not obscure the decades of political toil that preceded them.

Although Native California women assumed leadership of some Indian communities, the role of European women in California at the time of statehood was distinctly subordinate. Only 2% of the early immigration of whites into California was female. With this tremendous imbalance of white males to white females, many miners and ranchers fathered children with Native California women. If forced to mate with white males, some Indian mothers killed their mixed-blood offspring out of resentment. It was not until 1910 that white women reached population parity with white males (Jensen and Lothrop, 1987:9, 17, 37).

The economic and legal status of California women continued to be subordinate to that of men throughout the remainder of the nineteenth century. Refusing to accept jobs as earlier women had in saloons and brothels, some females began careers in teaching, nursing, and textile fabrication. Men in these fields assumed the higher paying positions of school principal, medical doctor, and factory manager. Girls of 11 to 14 years of age in California worked on textiles in poorly lighted and inadequately ventilated sweat shops for 11 hours per day. Older women were locked inside cannery sheds for 50 to 70 hours per week to make sure crops were processed before they spoiled (Davis, 1967:31, 124). In addition to the economic situation of women, state law made fathers the guardians of children and also did not permit wives to draw up wills—under the law, all the property of a wife went to her husband on her death. Until 1878, it was against California law for women to become lawyers. A male attorney for Hastings Law School in 1879 argued that Clara Shortridge Foltz should be denied admission because "lady lawyers were dangerous to justice inasmuch as an impartial jury would be impossible when a lovely lady pleaded the case" (Jensen and Lothrop, 1987:44). Gender bias exists in the California judiciary to this day as we shall see, but Foltz did win admission to Hastings by arguing that women should not be barred from public institutions.

By 1870, the economic and legal deprivations experienced by women in California spawned the suffrage movement. The most effective way to change state laws was by power at the ballot box. Women were unable to secure the right to vote in the California Constitution of 1879, but a state constitutional amendment extending the franchise to women was placed on the ballot in 1896. This amendment passed in all counties of California except San Francisco, where it lost so heavily that the amendment was defeated statewide by 13,000 votes. Since many suffragists were also members of the Women's Christian Temperance Union (WCTU), opponents of female suffrage argued that women wanted the right to vote in order to take alcoholic beverages away from men. In response to this criticism, women eventually formed equal suffrage clubs (purposely separate from the WCTU) in localities all over California. Suffragists organized at conventions every year from 1870 to 1910, brought in well-known speakers such as Susan B. Anthony to give addresses in California, and mailed prosuffrage literature to newspapers throughout the state. When another state constitutional amendment to enfranchise women was placed on the ballot in 1911, the amendment passed by a slender 3,587 votes. The strong margins in Southern California were enough to offset the continued opposition of San Francisco. Despite its reputation today, San Francisco was not a pacesetter regarding women's suffrage. By approving this constitutional amendment in 1911, California became the sixth state in the Union to grant women the right to vote—following Wyoming, Colorado, Utah, Idaho, and Washington.

Four women were elected to the California Assembly in 1918. Through efforts they began, California law was eventually changed to give females the right to make wills and to give women equal rights in guardianship of children. After this first cohort of women legislators retired in 1926, decades passed when as few as one or two women were elected to the Assembly. It was not until 1976 that five women at the same time would be elected to the lower house. In the same year, Rose Ann Vuich became the first woman ever elected to the California Senate. Since the rebirth of women's representation in 1976, the number of females in the Assembly has grown to 16 and in the Senate to five at the conclusion of the 1990 general elections.

Numbers do not tell the whole story, however. It is one thing to be elected; it is another thing to be a power player. Women have not yet headed a powerful fiscal or judiciary committee. (Female legislators have chaired a variety of the committees including local government, environmental safety, banking, education, and consumer protection.) Women legislators were not key players in the great budget impasse of the summer of 1990. Female members have been subjected to insulting introductions made by their male colleagues (i.e., references to the sex lives and marital status of women legislators). On one occasion, a male committee chairperson told a woman Senator that he resented her "mindless blather" (Buck, 1986:47). This incident precipitated the formation of the Women Legislators' Caucus in 1985 to provide unity in the face of disrespectful and demeaning behavior by male legislators. All women elected to the Assembly and the Senate are welcome at caucus meetings. As a bipartisan gathering (there are nearly equal numbers of

Figure 4-2   First Five: Together with the year of their election to the upper house, the above are the first women to serve in the California Senate. From left, Senators Diane Watson (1978), Rose Ann Vuich (1976), Lucy Killea (1989), Rebecca Morgan (1984), and Marian Bergeson (1984). (Photo by Adam Gottlieb.)

Democratic and Republican women in the legislature), there are many issues on which the women do not share common positions. However, there is considerable agreement among the women legislators on matters such as child care, crimes against women, child abuse, failure to pay child support, and family law. The caucus members agree that sexist remarks and behavior are unacceptable.

Although females constitute 51% of the employees in the state executive branch as a whole, it has been calculated that women held just 25 or 26% of the top-level, administrative positions in the state bureaucracy in 1988. "This means that women are concentrated in the lower levels of the bureaucracy in the clerical, subprofessional, and technical categories" (Bayes, 1989:106). The number of women in high management positions in state government increased dramatically during Jerry Brown's two terms as governor (1974–1982). To recommend potential appointees to him, Brown named Carlotta Mellon to be his appointments secretary—a position of considerable influence over the ultimate composition of the higher levels of the executive branch. Governor Brown also named Mary Ann Graves as director of the Department of Finance, the powerful agency responsible for preparing the governor's budget proposal. In a move that was nearly as controversial as his appointment of Rose Bird as Chief Justice of the California Supreme Court, Brown appointed Adriana Gianturco to direct the Department of Transportation. George Deukmejian did not appoint women at as high a rate as Jerry Brown, but Jan Sharpless (environmental affairs) and Shirley Chilton (state and consumer services) did serve in the Republican governor's cabinet.

As women assume greater leadership in the state bureaucracy, they encounter problems related to their gender. "Having a family is clearly a barrier to advancement for many administrative women in California.— Another attitude that the successful women in the California (interview) sample projected was one of down-playing their identity as women" (Bayes, 1989:140). There is an ongoing debate concerning whether or not women can have both successful careers and fulfilling personal lives. This is known as the "having it all" question. There is evidence that high-ranking women in state service have to work harder at their jobs than men and that women executives forego families and children more often than their male counterparts (Bayes, 1989:133, 136). Women have not been equally successful in gaining leadership roles in all departments of state government. The traditional female areas of health and welfare reflect a much higher incidence of women in top positions than is the case for male-dominated departments such as forestry, fish and game, and water resources. Surprisingly, given the abundance of male engineers in the organization, over half of the senior positions at the Department of Transportation in 1988 were held by women. This is probably attributable to Gianturco's influence as director and to the fact that many retirements in the department produced more hiring opportunities.

In addition to posts in executive departments of state government, there are some 3,000 appointments available on advisory panels and regulatory bodies known collectively as boards and commissions. In 1988, women held 27% of the appointments to boards and commissions in California (Karpilow, 1989). Again, women were more likely to be appointed to health, welfare, and education boards than to commissions dealing with public safety and construction projects. Because women with extensive service in appointive positions make stronger candidates in elections, pushing for greater numbers of females on boards and commissions ultimately is likely to produce electoral gains for women. Female legislators have introduced bills to require that appointments to boards and commissions reflect gender parity. Dianne Feinstein and Pete Wilson debated the issue of gender and ethnic appointments during the 1990 gubernatorial campaign.

Even though the role of the judiciary is crucial in attaining equal justice, gender bias is evident in California's courts. As of 1990, women held 13% of the judgeships in California. The behavior of males serving as judges, attorneys, and clerks has interfered with women using the judicial process. For example, when male judges repeatedly refer to female attorneys as "sweetie, sweetheart, honey, dear, and baby," they undermine the professional credibility of women lawyers in front of their clients and members of juries (Judicial Council, 1990:Sec. 4:15). Some males on the bench have little patience with matters of importance to females such as protection from domestic violence and provision of child and spousal support. "Too few judges are assigned and too few courtrooms are available to resolve family law matters in California.—A judge remarked that he would not take family law assignments until the court got rid of women lawyers" (Judicial Council, 1990:Sec. 1:18; Sec. 2:3). A move toward gender parity in judicial appointments would provide a larger pool of women judges willing to hear family law cases.

Outside of government itself, most of the portrayal of women in California politics is created by male reporters. Female membership in the press corps at the State Capitol is practically nonexistent. While elderly males in the legislature are never described in such terms, older women legislators resent being characterized in print as "grandmotherly." The female role in political parties and campaigns has not received attention commensurate with the substantial contributions made by California women. For example, Clara Shirpser organized Democratic Party clubs up and down California to spearhead the revival of that party in 1953–1954. Her grassroots work is largely overlooked as Alan Cranston is credited with having brought the club movement to life in the form of the California Democratic Council (Shirpser, 1981:59–63). The 1990s may see increasing numbers of women in California step in front of microphones instead of laboring in obscurity on political mailings and telephone banks.

The interest group arena has seen a flowering of women's participation in the last two decades. First, females as of 1989 comprised over one-fourth (206 of 785) of the registered lobbyists in the State Capitol. Women lobbyists once emphasized the education and health fields, but female advocates today handle corporate clients as well. The most lucrative lobbying firms are still in male hands; however, lobbying is no longer the male preserve it once was. Second, women have formed their own pressure groups to interact with state government.

After the equal suffrage clubs accomplished their mission in 1911, the next major group development was the establishment of the League of Women Voters (LWV) in California in 1921. In its early years, the League supported safety measures for female and child laborers and the legal equality of men and women in the writing of wills. When many soldiers were out of California during World War II, the LWV prepared an information sheet to help absentee voters in the military services. From the preparation of these wartime materials, the League has become a major player in matters of voter education. Besides the useful pro and con summaries of ballot initiatives prepared by the group, the LWV arranges debates and forums pertaining to crucial campaigns and issues of the day. Multilingual election materials prepared by the League will become more and more necessary as an increasingly diverse population attempts to educate itself about the highly complex matters appearing on California ballots. Nonpartisanship always has been an important tenet of the LWV. When the League endorsed Proposition 119 (a proposed commission to conduct redistricting instead of the legislature drawing district lines), the LWV's reputation for nonpartisanship was called into question. Since the Republican Party backed this initiative in June 1990 to remove redistricting from the Democratic-controlled legislature, Speaker Willie Brown (D, San Francisco) chastised the League for supporting a GOP measure. Whether or not the LWV will be able to retain a nonpartisan image, there is no denying that many women candidates for local and state offices began their political careers as members of the California League of Women Voters.

In terms of both issue positions and operating tactics, there is considerable variety in women's organizations. California Elected Women's Association for Education and Research (CEWAER) is made up of female officeholders at the state and local levels. This association holds retreats and conferences for women officials, as well as compiling data on the extent to which women occupy public office in California. Although the group actively encourages women to run for (or to seek appointment to) public office, CEWAER's nonprofit tax status precludes it from lobbying measures in the State Capitol or from donating money to candidates. On the other hand, California National Organization for Women (NOW) endorses candidates for election, contributes funds to campaigns, lobbies decision makers throughout state government, and issues report cards on the voting records of lawmakers. Whereas CEWAER must take into account the divergent opinions of a wide array of women in office, NOW puts forth solid feminist positions supporting the need for an Equal Rights Amendment (ERA) and the right of women to choose whether or not to have an abortion. (Abortion was a felony in California from 1850 to 1967, when Governor Ronald Reagan signed therapeutic abortion legislation allowing termination of pregnancies when a mother's mental health is endangered.) The antifeminist Women's Lobby supports the pro-life position in the State Capitol. There are also state chapters of the American Association of University Women (AAUW) and Business and Professional Women (BPW) in California.

The degree of unity among California women has been adversely impacted by the fact that the organizations discussed above have not been broadly inclusive of females from all races and economic levels (Jensen and Lothrop, 1987:68, 80). Besides differences in background, women have been divided on important issues. Some women refused to support the ERA because it would have removed protective statutes that safeguarded female and child workers. (These statutes were invalidated by the courts in 1972.) Women continue to disagree on the issue of the sanctity of life versus reproductive rights. Also, there is no consensus among women concerning whether or not to limit pornography. Those wishing to restrict the distribution of obscene materials contend that pornography is degrading and potentially dangerous to women. On the other hand, female defenders of the First Amendment do not want the government involved in censoring expression—no matter how repugnant it might be. There is one matter on which most women's groups agree: More women need to be elected to, or appointed to, public offices in California.

Women achieved electoral success at the local level earlier than at the state and national levels. Major cities such as San Diego, San Jose, San Francisco, Sacramento, and Fresno all had women mayors in the 1970s and 1980s. Female majorities existed for a time on the city councils of both San Jose and Sacramento. As of August 1990, women comprised 27% of all those elected to county supervisional seats and 26% of all persons elected to city councils throughout California (Karpilow, 1990). In comparison, women were 17.5% of the California Legislature after the general elections of 1990. The victories of Treasurer Kathleen Brown and Secretary of State March Fong Eu in November 1990 are noteworthy, but whether or not the 1990s merit the title "Decade of the Women" depends on further inclusion of females throughout all branches and levels of government. California women solidified bases in local government and the state bureaucracy during the 1980s. Will the 1990s bring substantial improvements in the role of women in the California Legislature, the state judiciary, and elective executive posts?

Lesbian and Gay Politics

In the first half of this century, gay and lesbian people were not highly visible in politics. It was not uncommon for police to harass patrons of gay bars in the 1960s. When gays fought back against police at the Stonewall Inn in New York City in 1969, the modern gay liberation movement was born. No longer content with personal acceptance of their sexual orientation, lesbians and gays henceforth sought acceptance by society as a whole.

A substantial migration of young, white males from throughout the United States to San Francisco occurred in the 1970s. (Gays lived in other California cities as well, but their political significance was not as great as it was in San Francisco.) Many of these immigrants to San Francisco settled in an old Irish neighborhood known as the Castro. A gay economy soon developed featuring bankers and insurance agents, legal and medical professionals, and merchants and restaurateurs. One arrival to the Castro in the early 1970s was Harvey Milk, a Navy veteran and former investment analyst from Long Island. Milk opened a camera store, but his great interest was politics. Running as an openly gay candidate, Milk twice ran for the San Francisco Board of Supervisors (1973 and 1975) and once ran for the California Assembly (1976)—losing all three contests. Milk's energy and speaking ability made him a strong campaigner, and he eventually won election to the San Francisco Board of Supervisors in 1977.

In November of 1978, Milk was instrumental in defeating Proposition 6, an initiative to prohibit gays and lesbians from teaching in California's schools. He toured the state debating the initiative's sponsor (then State Senator John Briggs). It was generally agreed that Milk's oratorical skills allowed him to win these exchanges. Three weeks after this triumph on Proposition 6, Milk was dead. Dan White, a supervisor who regularly opposed Milk's gay rights proposals, had resigned from the board of supervisors and then changed his mind. White asked Mayor George Moscone to reappoint him to the board. Milk urged Moscone to appoint someone other than White who would be a friendlier vote to their agendas. On learning that he would not be reappointed, White entered City Hall through a basement window in order to evade metal detectors at the main entrance. White killed Mayor Moscone with four shots. After reloading, he shot Supervisor Milk five times. Supervisor Dianne Feinstein was the first person to find Milk's body; she announced the deaths of Moscone and Milk to the City Hall press corps.

To the outrage of the gay community, Dan White was convicted of voluntary manslaughter (not first-degree murder) in 1979; he received the maximum sentence under the law of 7 years and 8 months in prison. Milk's friends gathered at City Hall in protest against what they considered to be a lenient outcome for White. After breaking windows at City Hall and setting police cars on fire, the protesters returned to the Castro. Police raided gay bars that evening and administered beatings to many patrons.

Dianne Feinstein, elevated to mayor on Moscone's death, appointed Harry Britt to Milk's seat on the Board of Supervisors. Britt had left a marriage and the ministry in Texas to settle in the Castro in 1971. Although Feinstein received gay support during her mayoral campaign in 1979, she incurred the wrath of lesbians and gays by vetoing Britt's domestic partners legislation in 1982. This ordinance would have granted gay partners rights similar to those of spouses in straight marriages. After several successful reelection campaigns, Britt was president of the San Francisco Board of Supervisors as of 1990. After the November elections of 1990, Carole Midgen and Roberta Achtenberg joined Britt as openly gay/lesbian members of the Board of Supervisors in San Francisco. A ballot measure also passed allowing gays and lesbians to register their domestic partnerships at City Hall.

Three openly lesbian/gay candidates won election to the five-member City Council of West Hollywood in 1984. Valerie Terrigno, a lesbian social service worker, became the mayor of West Hollywood; but she was forced from office after being convicted in 1986 of embezzling federal funds from a counseling project she managed. Through the 1990 state elections, there were no openly gay members of the California Legislature. There is a gay and lesbian staff caucus that is open to employees of the state legislature. Gays have been appointed to judgeships and to the Board of Regents of the University of California.

During his life, Milk endeavored not only to unite lesbians and gays, but also to build coalitions among gays, ethnic groups, and low-income people. The rapid influx of well-educated, white-collar professionals into San Francisco in the 1970s drove up housing prices and a number of minorities were no longer able to afford to live in the city. Not only did a cross-cultural coalition fail to materialize, unity among lesbians and gays weakened during the 1980s. Acquired Immune Deficiency Syndrome (AIDS) was first identified by the U.S. Center for Disease Control in 1981. The disease is not transmitted by casual contact or through the air; there must be an exchange of bodily fluids (i.e., blood, semen, or vaginal secretion) for the virus to spread. There is agreement among lesbians and gays that more money must be spent on AIDS research and patient care. However, the consensus does not extend to which methods to use to gain more funding or to the issue of whether to close public bath houses patronized by gay customers. Gay residents of San Francisco were badly divided over the bath house question; some argued these establishments were a health risk due to unsafe sex practiced therein and others claimed that closing the baths was an unwarranted interference with gay life-styles. The baths in San Francisco were closed in 1984, but not before gay unity was shattered.

As the 1990s begin, there are other sources of stress in lesbian and gay politics. Some gay activists condone the practice of "outing" and others do not. Outing is the public disclosure (against his or her will) of an important person's sexual orientation. Gains for the movement are won at the expense of the privacy of individuals. There is also much disagreement concerning the confrontational tactics employed by AIDS Coalition to Unleash Power (ACT UP)—a group founded in 1987 to encourage faster public and private action against the disease. This organization blocked traffic on the Golden Gate Bridge and disrupted the opening night of the San Francisco Opera in 1989. ACT UP members contend that shocking and offending people is justified to improve the chances of AIDS patients. Critics of these militant tactics claim they are counterproductive. The Lobby for Individual Freedom and Equality (LIFE) is an organization for lesbians and gays in the State Capitol that carefully follows friendly and hostile legislation. In the area of campaign donations, Bay Area Municipal Elections Committee (BAYMEC) and Metropolitan Elections Committee of Los Angeles (MECLA) are two influential groups that funnel gay and lesbian contributions into the political process. There are also ethnic-specific organizations, such as the Gay Latino Alliance (GALA), and numerous lesbian and gay clubs within the political parties.

The gay and lesbian agenda consists of more than addressing the AIDS epidemic. Unlike 24 states that still prohibit sodomy, California does not restrict the kinds of sex practiced by consenting adults in private. The California Legislature passed a measure in 1984 prohibiting discrimination against lesbians and gays in the workplace, but Governor Deukmejian vetoed this bill. Some California cities have laws against job bias based on sexual orientation. Lesbians and gays favor a state law barring discrimination because such a statute would remove the need to work for ordinances in hundreds of localities. In addition to fair employment, gays and lesbians want to secure couples' rights similar to those that now exist in straight marriages. Gays and lesbians want the law to recognize their entitlement to inheritances, medical benefits, and child custody. Some churches now perform weddings for gays and for lesbians;

they would like these marriages to be honored and accepted under state law. With much time, effort, and money being devoted to combating AIDS, it may be several years before there is success regarding the other items on the lesbian and gay agenda.

Summary

What is the likelihood of the creation of a multicultural, gender-equal polity in California? Professor Steven Erie (UC San Diego) has said, "Demography is destiny—at some point, twenty or thirty years from now, the day of ethnic political reckoning is coming" (Clifford, 1990). Other observers, such as Arnoldo Torres of LULAC, contend that California's power structure is not changing with its demographics (Rodriguez, 1989). There are both hopeful and discouraging signs. Resistance to multiculturalism should not be underestimated.

> Old prejudices die out slowly, and they can be transmitted through the generations for a very long time.—The tenacity with which people hold convictions about superiority and inferiority permits one to say today that such ideas have not been replaced by alternative and more rational beliefs in equality. The old biases and intolerances still exist in latent form, and they can be aroused when a cause appears (Heizer and Almquist, 1977: 200–201).

A legislative committee examining ethnic tensions on UC campuses found evidence of racist graffiti, "slave auctions" held by social groups, fights caused by racial epithets, and posters ridiculing gays and lesbians (California Legislature, 1988). It is discouraging that some college-educated citizens exhibit intolerance, but at least the state legislature is publicizing a problem that needs to be addressed. Curriculum changes to provide a multicultural perspective for students are being made, but the task of diversifying faculties is proceeding very slowly. It is encouraging to read Chancellor Tien's remarks on his appointment in 1990 to lead UC Berkeley.

> Excellence and diversity are not in conflict—they are complementary. I don't think we can achieve and maintain greatness without the widest possible ethnic and cultural diversity (Walker, 1990).

Sometimes advances in diversity are rolled back by the tide of events. Chief Justice Rose Bird (1977–1986) and CSU Chancellor W. Ann Reynolds (1982–1990) held very important appointments, but both were removed from office amid much antagonism. Their appointments were controversial from the outset. However, not long after these two women left state government, women were nominated to run for the offices of governor, lieutenant governor, treasurer, and secretary of state.

Unless there are fundamental changes in voting turnout by ethnic groups, white voters will continue to control statewide elections in California. Even when the white population ceases to be a majority in California sometime around the year 2003, white voters still are expected to be casting over 70% of the votes in statewide elections. Educational attainment on the part of ethnic students, among others, is crucial if California is to have informed voters and a skilled workforce. "No one group (can) fully and justly represent and make laws for another group no matter how good their intention" (Jensen and Lothrop, 1987:61). Increasing the ethnic and gender diversity of officeholders in California is proceeding much more slowly than the diversification of the population as a whole.

Inadequate financial resources mean that most ethnic organizations cannot afford to rent office space and hire lobbyists in Sacramento. These same organizations also cannot compete in the area of campaign donations. For the foreseeable future, court challenges and registering voters are viable strategies. As to the matter of group unity, there are signs that Pan-Indian and Pan-Asian cohesion may take hold; but multiracial coalitions are another matter. The competition for college admissions and for employment, not to mention for political office, is likely to produce tensions that will make cross-cultural coalitions difficult to build. If and when multiracial coalitions are formed, who will benefit from them? Although it is true that Mayor Tom Bradley was helped by a biracial coalition during his elections, it is by no means clear that African Americans in Los Angeles have benefitted from this coalition in terms of improved municipal services. The creation and maintenance of multiethnic coalitions will require the highest levels of skill, commitment, and goodwill.

References: Chapter 4 _____

Bayes, Jane. "Women in the California Executive Branch of Government." In Mary Hale and Rity Mae Kelly (editors), *Gender, Bureaucracy, and Democracy*. New York: Greenwood Press, 1989:103–142.

Buck, Shelley. "Beyond Blathergate." *Sacramento Magazine* (March, 1986).

California Legislature. "Hearing on Racial/Ethnic Tensions and Hate Violence on UC Campuses." Senate Special Committee on UC Admissions (October 4, 1988).

Chartkoff, Joseph L., and Kerry Kona Chartkoff. *The Archaedogy of California*. Stanford: Stanford University Press, 1984.

Clifford, Frank. "Barriers to Power for Minorities." *Los Angeles Times* (May 7, 1990).

Cook, Sherburue F. *The Population of the California Indians: 1769–1970*. Berkeley: University of California Press, 1976.

Cooper, Claire. "Justice's Scales Way out of Balance for Blacks." *Sacramento Bee* (March 6, 1988).

Davis, Reda. *California Women: A Guide to their Politics 1885–1911*. San Francisco: California Scene, 1967.

Green, Stephen. "State Offices Lag in Hispanic Hires." *Sacramento Bee* (June 29, 1989).

Hecht, Peter. "Refugees Build New Lives in Teeming Little Saigon." *Sacramento Bee* (April 29, 1990).

Heizer, Robert F., and Allan F. Almquist. *The Other Californians: Prejudice and Discrimination under Spain, Mexico, and the United States to 1920*. Berkeley: University of California Press, 1977 (paper).

Hurtado, Albert L. *Indian Survival on the California Frontier*. New Haven: Yale University Press, 1988.

Jensen, Joan M., and Gloria Ricci Lothrop. *California Women: A History*. San Francisco: Boyd and Fraser, 1987.

Johnson, Bob. "Watsonville's New Crop." *Golden State Report* (September, 1989).

Judicial Council. *Achieving Equal Justice for Women and Men in the Courts: Advisory Committee on Gender Bias in the Courts*. Sacramento: California Judicial Council, 1990.

Karpilow, Kate. *California Women, Get on Board!: A Report from the California Board and Commission Project*. Sacramento: Joint Publications, 1989.

Karpilow, Kate. "Stats from CEWAER." Sacramento: California Elected Women's Association for Education and Research (October, 1990).

Korematsu, Fred. "The Legacy of Internment." Remarks delivered at the California Studies Conference: Envisioning California II. Sacramento: February 9, 1990.

Lapp, Rudolph M. *Afro-Americans in California*. San Francisco: Boyd and Fraser, 1987.

Margolin, Malcolm. "Introduction." *Monterey in 1786: The Journals of Jean Francois de La Pérouse*. Berkeley: Heyday Books, 1989.

Moisa, Ray. "The BIA Relocation Program." *News from Native California* (May–June, 1988):8.

Pettigrew, Thomas F., and Denise A. Alston. *Tom Bradley's Campaigns for Governor: The Dilemma of Race and Political Strategies*. Washington, D.C.: Joint Center for Political Studies, 1988.

Rodriguez, Rick. "Minorities Feel Left Out in Cold." *Sacramento Bee* (December 12, 1989).

Schmidt, Ronald. "Language Policy in California: What's Really at Stake?" Paper prepared for the California Studies Conference: Envisioning California I. Sacramento: February, 1989.

Shirpser, Clara. *Behind the Scenes in Politics*. Portola Valley: American Lives Endowment, 1981.

Slagle, Allogan. "A Byline of Political and Legal Concerns." *News from Native California* (November–December, 1987):20.

Tanaka, Ronald Phillip. "The Invisible Minority—A Japanese-American's Angst." *Sacramento Bee* (May 6, 1990).

tenBroek, Jacobus, Edward Barnhart, and Floyd Matson. *Prejudice, War and the Constitution.* Berkeley: University of California Press, 1968.

Walker, Bill. "Chinese-born Scholar Will Lead UC Berkeley." *Sacramento Bee* (February 16, 1990).

CHAPTER 5

Political Parties and the Press

Interest groups, political parties, and news organizations all serve to link Californians to their government. Each is distinctive. Interest groups attain benefits for their members. As discussed earlier, groups need not encompass large numbers to be effective; they tend to be homogeneous or exclusive in character. Cohesive and well-organized groups are highly capable of winning favorable policies for the numerous minorities they represent. Political parties and news organizations, on the other hand, serve a much wider and more heterogeneous audience. Because their paramount goal is electing their candidates to office, political parties are open and inclusive by nature as they continually try to amass a majority of voters. Akin to parties, news organizations endeavor to maximize their circulation and their educational objectives, so their appeal is to the broad public as well. Aside from the breadth of people served, these linking mechanisms differ as to the extent of public accountability they afford. By shifting one's vote to candidates of another party or by utilizing another source for the news, it is possible to hold political parties and press organizations accountable for their actions. In contrast, it is very difficult to compel accountability on the part of an interest group unless one is a member—and a leader at that.

California's political parties perform governmental and electoral functions both inside and outside of state government. Democrat and Republican officeholders organize (i.e., pick floor and committee leadership) the California Legislature, name appointees to vacancies in the executive and judicial branches, enact public policies, and serve as the loyal opposition to the party in power. In the area of policy making, party legislators play a major role in the design of California's campaign laws. For instance, redrawing the boundaries of legislative districts each decade, determining the ballot access of minor parties, and establishing the date and type of primary elections to be used in California are all matters decided by party legislators in Sacramento. In the electoral realm outside of government, party activists recruit candidates to run for office, coach office seekers and provide them with background information on the issues, register voters, raise money, adopt resolutions and platforms, distribute election materials, and get out the vote. Whereas party officeholders inside government are powerful in California, party activists involved in electoral work outside government are weak.

Causes of Weak Parties

What is meant by saying California's political parties in the electoral sense are weak? If a political party is able to control the name of persons appearing on the ballot and if a party can strongly influence the selection of persons entering public office, such a political party is strong. When a political party cannot affect elections in this manner, it is weak. Some of the reasons for party weakness in California can be traced to constitutional and statutory law in this state; other reasons have more to do with a general decline in party influence nationwide.

1. A key reason for weak parties in California is the nonpartisan nature of local elections (California Constitution, Art. II, Sec. 6). Consider the number of offices filled by partisan election as opposed to those filled by nonpartisan election. Partisan races for seats in the U.S. Senate (2), U.S. House of Representatives (52), the state legislature (120), state executive (11), and the U.S. President (1) total a mere 186 contests where the party label is attached to candidates. Nonpartisan races for city council, county board of supervisors, special districts (including school districts), and judicial elections total well into the thousands. With party labels not legally allowed in thousands of local contests, a firm foundation for political parties at the grassroots level is missing. With parties on the sidelines in local politics, interest groups (e.g., merchant organizations and service clubs) recruit and support candidates for city, county, and special district offices. In the absence of parties at the local level, press endorsements take on more importance.

2. From 1913 to 1987, the state elections code (Sec. 11702) forbid official party organizations at the state and local levels to "endorse, support, or oppose, any candidate for nomination by that party for partisan office in the direct primary election." For 74 years following the progressive era, official party bodies were silenced in primary campaigns. Even though this prohibition on preprimary endorsements was lifted on constitutional grounds in 1987, the advantage that interest groups in California have developed in terms of endorsing and bankrolling candidates is likely to persist. It will take many years before party organizations can begin to rival interest groups as a source of campaign contributions.

3. Language in the elections code formerly required that state party chairpersons serve only a 2-year term and that they not be allowed to succeed themselves. The party chairperson once was required by state law to alternate every 2 years between northern and southern California. These legal provisions inhibited the development of effective party leadership in California. The elections code also instructed the state party when to meet, where to meet, and what its composition would be. Although these restrictions on party organization were lifted by the 9th U.S. Circuit Court of Appeals in 1987 (and affirmed by the U.S. Supreme Court in 1989), California's backwardness in matters of party development may take decades to overcome. After an exhaustive study of all 50 states, one authority concluded that, "California is about the last place anybody would look to find traditional party organizations, and in fact none turns up in records of the last half century" (Mayhew, 1986: 185).

4. California is one of 23 states to possess the direct democracy devices of initiative, referendum, and recall. Direct democracy runs counter to strong parties. Should persons elected to state and local offices not be responsive, interest groups may bypass public officials by using initiatives to make public policy or by using referenda to undo laws with which they disagree. Interest groups may also attempt to remove officeholders through the use of recall. Having invested considerable effort in electing their nominees to office, political parties are understandably depressed by the prospect of their officeholders either being circumvented by the initiative process or removed from office by recall. Direct democracy provides interest groups with a useful means by which to threaten party officials in government.

5. California's political parties are fragmented into three components. First, the officeholder segment is comprised of party members elected to partisan posts in government. Second, electoral activists (in both official and unofficial organizations) help party candidates win elections. Third, the party rank and file is made up of all registered voters affiliated with a given party. These three wings within a party often disagree. Party officeholders in California are not particularly interested in enhancing the power of electoral activists with whom they disagree. California's rank and file party voters have notoriously low levels of loyalty as indicated by their propensity to vote for candidates from other parties. Split-ticket voting is a clear manifestation of the weakness of California's political parties.

6. Beyond California's own antiparty environment, political parties nationwide are experiencing increasingly difficult times. Changes in campaign technology have made it easier for candidates to run personalized campaigns instead of running as one member of a

slate of party nominees. Computerized direct mail and television permit candidates (provided they have the money) to reach voters without benefit of a party apparatus. As more and more government positions come under civil service procedures for hiring and promotion, political parties have far fewer patronage appointments to dispense to party campaign workers.

Party Rank and File

Of 19 million Californians over the age of 18 who are eligible to vote, some 13 million of the state's residents have registered as voters. As of mid-1990, the great bulk of these voters affiliated with the Democrat (49.7%) and Republican (39.1%) parties. Registrants with all the minor parties and persons declining to list a party preference made up the remaining 11.2% of the electorate. The registration percentages for the major parties are misleading, however, because some people who have ceased to vote are still registered and because some registered Democrats vote Republican without bothering to change their registration. Perhaps a more meaningful gauge of party strength in California comes from public opinion surveys. In August 1990, pollster Mervin Field found nearly identical proportions of voters identifying themselves with each of the major parties: 43% identify with the GOP and 45% with the Democrats. Secretary of State March Fong Eu (D), in February 1987, went so far as to say that "California has become a Republican state" (Raimundo, 1987). Others disagree with Eu, pointing out that Democrats won all the statewide offices in 1986 except the governorship. The Democrats' large registration advantage of 22.6% in 1976 after Watergate had dropped to 10.6% by 1990.

From 1909 to the present, California has employed a closed primary ballot that restricts participation in party nominating elections to rank and file voters registered in the respective parties. (As we shall discuss, the closed primary law may be revised in the future.) The cost of printing ballots and tabulating primary election results is borne by the state and its counties. To avoid the expense of conducting primary elections for parties with very few members, one of three criteria must be met to qualify a party for the holding of a primary election at public expense.

1. One statewide candidate of a party must receive at least 2% of the total vote in the last gubernatorial election, or
2. A party must have registered within its ranks at least 1% of the number of persons voting in the last gubernatorial election, or

3. A petition requesting a primary election must be signed by voters equal in number to 10% of the total vote in the preceding gubernatorial election.

Under these criteria, two major parties and three minor parties now qualify to have their primaries conducted at taxpayers' expense. In terms of registered members and offices held, the Democrat and Republican parties are the major ones in the state. During the past two decades, three minor parties also have managed to qualify for primaries. The American Independent and the Peace and Freedom parties qualified for state-supported primaries in 1968 and are considered to have roots in the civil rights and Vietnam issues of the 1960s. The Peace and Freedom Party was opposed to U.S. involvement in Vietnam and strongly supportive of equal rights for ethnic minorities; the American Independent Party reflected the opposite position on these issues. More recently, the Peace and Freedom Party has advocated greater public services for the disadvantaged, heavier taxes on corporations, and gay and lesbian rights. The American Independent Party is tempering its issue stances on race and aid to the truly needy to appeal to a broader segment of voters. The Libertarian Party became the third minor party to qualify for state-run primaries in 1979. Libertarians espouse minimal government intervention in the economy and minimal government regulation of the lives of private citizens. Their critics jokingly allude to Libertarians as "anarchists in three-piece suits." Beyond these three minor parties that qualify for primaries operated at state expense, there are several other minor parties that do not qualify: Citizens Party, Equalitarian Party, La Raza Unida, Prohibition Party, Socialist Labor Party, and Socialist Workers Party. These tiny parties nominate their candidates by means of caucuses and conventions, not primary elections.

Even though the minor parties taken together register only 2.15% of all voters in California, votes going to their candidates can be determinative in close races between candidates of the major parties. In the general elections of 1990, a member of Congress (Doug Bosco) lost his seat when 15% of the vote went to a Peace and Freedom candidate. Likewise, Assemblymember Sunny Mojonnier (R, San Diego) lost her seat when a Libertarian candidate won 11% of the district vote. With a combined 5% of the gubernatorial vote going to three minor party candidates, Governor Pete Wilson won only 49% of the overall vote in 1990. Though it has not passed as yet, legislation has been introduced to raise the number of registrants required in a party in order to preserve that party's status as one qualified to hold state-supported primaries. Newspaper editorials have denounced such legislation as a blatant attempt to stifle electoral competition from the minor parties.

Electoral Activists: Official _____

The party activists who prompt the party rank and file to vote are of two types: official and unofficial. Official party organizations were highly regulated by state law from 1913 to 1987, whereas unofficial party bodies were regulated to a far lesser extent. The titles of the organizations, the membership, the selection of officers, and the time and place of meetings of official party units were all provided for in the state elections code. The names, composition, leadership, and meeting arrangement of unofficial party bodies were not determined by state law. Official party units were not allowed to "endorse, support, or oppose" candidates in party primaries, but unofficial party organizations engaged in precisely such activities. With the restrictions on official parties having been lifted in 1987, the distinctions between official and unofficial party organizations will no longer be significant.

The main elements of the official parties are the state central committees and the county central committees. The state central committees for the two major parties carry out quite similar responsibilities, but they differ somewhat in composition. The official state committees may undertake the following activities:

- Conduct campaigns for party nominees.
- Raise funds for party nominees.
- Consent to the use of the party's name by organizations using such labels to solicit campaign donations.
- Register new rank-and-file party members.
- Monitor pending legislation in Sacramento.
- Research the records of opposition party candidates.
- Pass resolutions on behalf of the state party.
- Draft and approve a state party platform.
- Elect the officers of the state party.

In addition, following federal court rulings in 1987 and 1990, the state central committees may

- Endorse candidates in partisan primary election.
- Endorse candidates in nonpartisan local and judicial elections.

In *Eu* v. *San Francisco County Democratic Central Committee*, the 9th U.S. Circuit Court of Appeals (1987) and the U.S. Supreme Court (1989) ruled that the preprimary endorsement prohibition and the other organizational restrictions placed on California's official political parties were unconstitutional. Not only do parties have the right to free political expression, they also are entitled to organize themselves as they see fit. The courts held that a state must be able to assure fair and orderly elections, but that this does not include regulating the internal operations of political parties. As private associations (not government agencies), political parties are allowed to select their leaders by rules established in party bylaws—not imposed by state law. The courts reasoned that allowing state legislators from Party X to enact state laws governing the internal operations of Party Y gives Party X the opportunity to cripple the effectiveness of a rival party through the drafting of state statutes.

How have the major parties responded to being deregulated? They have reacted differently, which is precisely what the courts wanted parties to have the freedom to do. If a party establishes internal rules for itself that hamper its success, so be it—at least state laws have not brought about the demise of the party. The California Democratic Party chose to make endorsements before party primaries, whereas the California Republican Party decided not to follow this path. Republican leaders believed that granting an endorsement to one GOP candidate in a primary (and denying it to others) would be divisive and make it more difficult to pull the party together for the general election campaign. Recollecting the nomination of a Ku Klux Klan member in a Democratic congressional primary in 1980, Democrats saw the endorsement as a means to alert rank-and-file party voters to the presence of an unacceptable candidate in their midst.

Early experience with preprimary endorsement by official Democratic Party bodies suggests that party voters may not be especially swayed by the endorsement. To make an endorsement in a statewide primary race, rules of the California Democratic Party require that a candidate receive 60% of the delegate votes at the annual convention of the Democratic State Central Committee. Attorney General John Van de Kamp narrowly won endorsement by party delegates (60.3% after a recount) during the Democratic gubernatorial contest in 1990, but he was convincingly defeated by Dianne Feinstein (52 to 41%) when rank-and-file Democrats voted the day of the primary election. Similarly, the Contra Costa County Democratic Central Committee endorsed challenger Sunne McPeak over incumbent State Senator Dan Boatwright in a legislative primary in 1988, but Boatwright won the nomination with Democratic voters nonetheless. Clearly, voters in primary elections are willing to ignore the endorsements of party central committees.

At the local level, the major parties both have county central committees that register voters, raise money, conduct campaigns, and make preprimary endorsements. The bylaws of the California Republican Party do not allow the state or county central committees in the GOP to endorse; however, this no-endorsement rule could be difficult for the party to enforce on all of its county central committees. The Santa Clara County Republican Central Committee made an endorsement in a congressional primary in 1988 without receiving severe repercussions from the state party. Besides the county central committees of both major parties, Democrats also convene caucus gatherings in each of the 80 Assembly districts in California. These meetings are open to any registered Democrat who wishes to attend. Party caucuses such as these select rank-and-file Democrats to be delegates at the annual convention of the state party as well as mobilizing support for party nominees. Republicans have yet to make use of the Assembly district caucus idea.

When the courts voided state laws limiting the length of service of state party chairpersons to 2 years, the Democrats promptly revised their bylaws to extend the term of their party chair to 4 years. Though now free to set whatever term length they wish for their party leadership, California Republicans have decided for the time being to stay with a 2-year term for their party chair. With a longer term of office and a greater party role in primaries, former Governor Jerry Brown actively sought, and won, the position of chair of the California Democratic Party in 1989. He entered this party leadership post proclaiming the need to enlist a large number of nonvoters into the ranks of the Democratic Party. Brown said, "It is a high priority of mine to expand the base of (party) registration" (Richardson, 1989). However, a year and a half after assuming leadership of the California Democratic Party, Brown

Figure 5-1 "What are you shaking for?" (Dennis Renault, *Sacramento Bee*)

could not point to gains in Democratic registration. In fact, the Democratic share of overall registration dropped to its lowest point since 1934. As is evident from the following quote, registration and get-out-the-vote (GOTV) expert Marshall Gans was highly critical of Brown's stewardship of the party.

> There was just no effort to reach minorities among Democrats in California. What brings people to the polls, especially people without past political experience, is personal contact: someone at the door talking to them, someone they may meet two or three times. It has to be done with people, not TV ads or mail cards. (Leary, 1990)

Brown defended his leadership by pointing out that Democrats won five of seven statewide executive races in 1990, as well as gaining seats in the state legislature. In addition, legislative leaders prevailed on Brown to divert registration and GOTV funds in an attempt to defeat two redistricting initiatives in June and two term-limit propositions in November. After serving two years of his four-year term as party chair, Brown resigned this post to seek election to the U.S. Senate in 1992.

Electoral Activists: Unofficial

Unofficial or volunteer party organizations developed in California to circumvent the legal prohibition against preprimary activity (1913–1987) by units of the official party. The first such organization to be founded was the California Republican Assembly (CRA) in 1934. Cross-filing (a candidate running in the primaries of both major parties) was in use at the time, and the Republicans wanted to reduce the likelihood of a Democrat winning the GOP primary. By having the CRA endorse one Republican in their primary, the chances of a vote split among GOP candidates (thereby allowing a Democratic cross-filer to win) was lessened. Although Democrats were largely frustrated in their cross-filing efforts due to the CRA endorsement, Republicans cross-filed into Democratic primaries with considerable success because there was no Democratic counterpart to the CRA in the 1940s and early 1950s. It was 1953 before Democratic volunteers finally organized the California Democratic Council (CDC) to make endorsements in their primaries. CDC endorsement made successful GOP cross-filing into Democratic primaries more difficult. After the Democrats swept to power in Sacramento in 1958, they abolished the practice of printing the names of nonparty candidates on primary ballots. Cross-filing is not entirely dead, however, as it is still possible for a candidate to run in an opposition party primary by means of a write-in campaign. In June 1982, one member of the state Senate and two incumbent members of the Assembly won the nominations of their own party plus the nominations of the opposition party by waging successful write-in efforts.

Two other unofficial GOP organizations also are active in California. The United Republicans of California (UROC) and the California Republican League (CRL) were created in 1963 and 1964, respectively. UROC members regarded the CRA as not conservative enough, while the CRL preferred to take more liberal positions than the CRA. All three unofficial Republican organizations are more conservative today than at the time of their founding, but the differences among them persist with UROC being the most conservative, the CRL the most moderate, and the CRA somewhere in between. As an example of its conservative stances, the UROC has urged the United States to withdraw from the United Nations and has advocated the discontinuation of the federal income tax. In 1990, CRL endorsed Pete Wilson for governor in the GOP primary. CRA refused to endorse Wilson in this primary because he was not conservative enough for the organization's taste.

From 1976 to 1986, the Campaign for Economic Democracy (CED) may have been an unofficial Democratic Party organization along with CDC. An outgrowth of Tom Hayden's unsuccessful primary race for the U.S. Senate in 1976, CED devoted much of its attention to local politics in places such as Santa Monica, Chico, and Santa Cruz. The organization supported renters' rights, solar energy, environmental protection, and corporate democracy. After initial successes at the city level, most CED loyalists were swept out of office by the mid-1980s. Despite Hayden's election to the California Assembly in 1982, CED was formally disestablished in 1986. In its place, an entity known as Campaign California was established to work on ballot issues and candidate races. How active Campaign California will be in Democratic Party politics remains to be seen.

Despite the elimination of printed cross-filing in 1959 and the removal of restrictions on political parties in 1987, much remains of the original Progressive package that weakens parties in California. Popular primaries, nonpartisan local government, office block ballots, strong civil service, the initiative process, and private campaign businesses all continue to reduce the influence of parties in California. Depending on one's idea of the proper role to be played by political parties, a number of options exist for increasing or decreasing the power of parties in California.

Weakening Parties

Closed primaries limit voting rights in nominating elections to rank and file members of a particular political party. Persons registered with outside political parties or as independents (i.e., decline to state) are excluded from closed primaries. A *fully* open primary system could be established to allow independents and registrants from opposite parties to vote in the party primary of their choice. Less sweepingly, independents alone could be allowed to vote in whatever party primary they wished, while party registrants would be required to vote in the primary corresponding to their party affiliation. This arrangement would be an open primary for independents, and a closed one for party registrants—essentially a *partially* open primary. The role of the party rank and file would be lessened in selecting nominees because voters from outside the party could tip the balance in close primary contests. (The most drastic means of weakening parties would be to institute nonpartisan offices and nonpartisan primaries at the state level similar to the situation now used at the local level.)

One of the strongest incentives to register with a party is to gain a role in selection of party nominees during primary elections. If primaries are partially opened and independents are allowed to vote in any party primary they like, there will be much less reason to affiliate with a political party. As pollster Mervin Field sees it, "There would still be considerable incentive for many California voters to change their registration from one of the major parties to 'decline to state' because the latter designation would still allow them to vote in either party's primary election" (Field, 1987:103). The larger the ranks of independent voters become, the greater the chance that the will of the party rank and file will be overridden. Opening party primaries, either fully or partially, weakens the role that party members have in naming their nominees and in holding them accountable.

Strengthening Parties _____

A number of steps may be taken to increase the power of political parties in California. The party column ballot might be reinstituted to encourage straight-party (not split-ticket) voting. Selected portions of local government, perhaps county supervisors as an example, might revert from nonpartisan to partisan offices. The number of executive positions covered by civil service might be reduced by a small percentage to give party officeholders more appointments to dispense to party activists. Given the antiparty mentality that prevails in much of California, the likelihood of these ideas being adopted is remote.

Another approach to increasing the clout of political parties in California is to build on the recently bestowed right of the parties to endorse candidates before primary elections take place. Having agreed to recommend one office seeker in a given primary race, parties might also coordinate volunteer workers and fundraising on behalf of the selected individual. To make the endorsement more meaningful, endorsed persons might be listed first on the ballot or carry an asterisk next to their name to highlight the party's support. Parties in California might endeavor to upgrade the role of the endorsing convention and downplay the importance of the primary election. Models in other states suggest how to do this. The system used in Utah allows only one person to be listed on a party's primary ballot if that individual succeeded in obtaining the support of 70% of the delegates at the endorsing convention. If no candidate wins 70% of the delegate votes, then the top two vote winners at the party convention move on to the primary (Hrebenar and Thomas, 1988:4). Utah's nomination rules assure that an individual with the strong support of party workers will be nominated. A so-called media candidate, perhaps a wealthy and charismatic person, would not be able to deny the nomination to the consensus pick of party activists.

Instead of establishing a high threshold for avoiding a contested primary, it is possible to set a minimum level of convention support needed to enter a party's primary. Connecticut employs this approach. The winner at the party convention in Connecticut is listed first on the ballot with an asterisk beside his or her name. No other name besides the convention winner's will appear on the primary ballot in Connecticut unless another candidate is able to win the support of at least 20% of the delegates at the party endorsing meeting. Establishing a 20% floor, or a 70% upper threshold of convention support, would not have changed Democratic Party outcomes in California in 1990 because Van de Kamp and Feinstein split the convention delegates 60–40%. The party rules in Connecticut discourage primaries crowded with numerous candidates out of which voters might elect a plurality (not a majority) winner. Like Utah, a candidate in Connecticut with a well-funded personal campaign (but lacking even 20% convention support) would not be able to prevail. If there is a strong frontrunner (70% threshold), or if there is not a viable competitor (20% floor), then the party convention is determinative and the nominee is allowed to save his or her money for the general election. On the other hand, should there be fairly evenly matched candidates at a party convention, then the Utah and Connecticut methods allow more than one person to advance to the primary election.

If their long-run objective was to weaken political parties in California, the Progressives did their work well. California is known as a media state and as a state with interest groups that are highly professional and influential. Candidates who enter office using personalized media campaigns can easily become beholden to these powerful forces. Such officeholders need ample amounts of groups' money to wage expensive media campaigns. Conversely, a person elected as a member of a party team is better able to resist the blandishments of organized interests. Instead of being picked off one at a time as individual officeholders, vital parties permit elected officials to collectively withstand group power that is bent on attaining selfish ends. Unlike groups, political parties encourage broad coalitions to be forged across economic, regional, and racial lines. With the legislative and executive branches of California government frequently under the control of different partisan labels, parties are the most likely political institution to mobilize voters into a sweeping mandate that would allow paralysis to be overcome and chronic policy problems to be addressed.

The Power of the Press

The feeble condition of California's political parties stems largely from the efforts of journalists during the first decade of this century. After witnessing the railroad's domination of the 1907 legislative session, Edward Dickson of the *Los Angeles Express* and Chester H. Rowell of the *Fresno Republican* formed the Lincoln–Roosevelt League. This reform group succeeded in electing roughly half the membership to the 1909 legislative session. When this legislature abolished nominating conventions and instituted the direct primary, Rowell was instrumental in encouraging a reluctant Hiram Johnson to run for governor in 1910. During the subsequent period of party-weakening enactments, Rowell was a close confident of Governor Johnson's as well as a key theoretician and activist in the progressive movement.

Although it has long been thought that then Vice President Richard Nixon engineered the attempted switch in offices between U.S. Senator William Knowland and Governor Goodwin Knight in 1958, the *Los Angeles Times* also placed great pressure on Knight to have him vacate the GOP gubernatorial primary in favor of Knowland. Kyle Palmer, the powerful political editor of the *Times* for 40 years, phoned Knight daily urging him to withdraw from the governor's race and even threatened to publish reports of scandal in the Knight administration if he did not comply (Halberstam, 1979:265–266). Incumbents and challengers routinely schedule appointments with editorial boards in pursuit of newspapers' endorsements. What is noteworthy about the Rowell and Palmer examples is that they went beyond simple endorsement to actively encourage and discourage candidates for the highest office in California.

In addition to campaign involvement, news organizations shape public decisions both by actual reporting and editorializing and by the mere threat to publicize events. When major party legislators introduced bills in 1979 and 1981 to make it more difficult for the Peace and Freedom

Party to conduct its primary election at state expense, critical editorials from around the state culminated in the measures being dropped. A rash of unfavorable stories regarding the amount of campaign money received by legislators who approved the so-called New Cities bill in 1981 led to its veto by Governor Jerry Brown. Sometimes the press exercises power without lifting a pen or tapping a keyboard; the presence of reporters at an event can be enough to forestall action. When hasty approval was sought in 1986 for the removal of a parcel of state land from the Coastal Zone, a hurriedly convened committee declined to act due to the attendance of reporters at the meeting. Given the importance of favorable coverage to officeholders and aspirants, the press can be watchdogs with a powerful bite. Assembly Speaker Willie Brown has gone so far as to say that "The press has as much influence on public policy as I have" (*California Journal*, January, 1986:13).

Capitol Correspondents Association _____

Journalists covering the U.S. Congress must view proceedings from press galleries one story above the floors of the two legislative chambers. Contrastingly, political reporters in Sacramento are allowed on the floors of the Senate and the Assembly provided they remain in designated areas. To gain this access to the floor of each house, it is necessary for correspondents to be accredited members of the Capitol Correspondents Association. Employees of the national wire services, of metropolitan daily newspapers throughout California, of radio and television stations, and of a specialized news service pertaining to state government are members of the Association.

The types of news organizations making up the Association have not changed a great deal over the years. However, there have been marked shifts in the number of personnel assigned to each outlet's Capitol bureau. Whereas the *Los Angeles Times* had a single accredited reporter in the State Capitol in 1957, the number had risen to 11 by 1985. Backed by vast advertising revenues and a weekday circulation in excess of one million copies, the *Times* has endeavored to become the best paper in the state—if not the nation. The *Times* provides an extensive historical record of state political events as well as in-depth, interpretive pieces and reports on the members of the Los Angeles delegation in Sacramento. The only other daily to attempt to be as comprehensive in its coverage of state government as the giant from Los Angeles is the *Sacramento Bee*.

With the exception of the *San Francisco Chronicle* and its five accredited reporters, most other metropolitan dailies have either one or two reporters in their Sacramento bureaus. These smaller operations tend to focus their coverage on legislators representing their region and on stories not disseminated by the wire services. Rural and suburban newspapers without an accredited reporter in the State Capitol may supplement wire service reports by reprinting state news stories obtained from the Capitol News Service. Interestingly, given the growth of the state and its government, both the AP and UPI wire services have operated with between 8 and 10 employees for the past 30 years.

Despite its size, there is no lack of competition for the *Los Angeles Times*. By featuring human interest stories and hometown angles as opposed to comprehensive, global perspectives, some pesky rivals are contesting circulation turf with the *Times* in specific regions. The *Orange County Register* outsells the *Times* nearly 2-to-1 in its county, the *Long Beach Press-Telegram* is much stronger than the *Times* in the harbor area, and the *Daily News* is a vital competitor for the *Times* in the San Fernando Valley (Reinhardt, 1986).

Unlike the print media, the participation of the electronic media in the Capitol Correspondents Association has undergone dramatic ups and downs. With the arrival of Ronald Reagan as governor in 1967, television coverage of state politics entered its glory days. The three major television stations in Los Angeles each staffed bureaus in Sacramento

Figure 5-2 Impromptu Press Conference: Speaker Willie Brown surrounded by television cameras. (Photograph by Adam Gottlieb.)

at that time. Each bureau consisted of a minimum of three people including a camera operator, a sound person, and a correspondent. During the 1970s, so-called news doctors (i.e., market researchers who suggest ways for stations to improve their ratings) recommended that television covererage of hard news from the State Capitol be reduced. Thereafter, the Los Angeles channels closed their bureaus in Sacramento. Television coverage of the State Capitol today is left to Sacramento stations, with occasional visits by Los Angeles, San Francisco, and San Diego channels on temporary assignment.

Although both print and electronic reporters are accredited with the same organization, newspaper and television correspondents have significantly different working conditions. Television news thrives on good visuals, its equipment is much more intrusive than pencil and notepad, and it has the potential to do live coverage. However, news reports read on television are a great deal shorter than newspaper accounts, and the sheer number of print reporters in the State Capitol overwhelms the representatives from the electronic media. Californians with the highest levels of interest in politics rely far more on the print media for their news than they do on television. Just the reverse is true of individuals with low levels of interest in state government.

Journalistic Access _____

The members of the Capitol Correspondents Association have very different levels of access to the various parts of state government. Much legislative activity is open to reporters, but there are also important meetings that correspondents cannot cover. Floor sessions, committee hearings, fiscal subcommittees, and conference committees are open to the press. On the other hand, meetings of the legislative party caucuses, party leadership gatherings, and meetings of top legislators with the governor are closed to the press corps. The executive branch is much less accessible than the legislature. The correspondents attend the State of the State speech delivered by the governor each January, as well as periodic press conferences and bill signings held by the state's chief executive. However, the press does not have access to the governor's cabinet meetings, the daily gatherings of the governor's senior staff, any of the meetings at which the governor's budget is prepared, any of the deliberations concerning major gubernatorial appointments, or any of the discussions in the governor's office regarding the use of general or item vetoes. With respect to the judiciary, reporters may listen to the submission of evidence at trial court proceedings and to the oral arguments made before appellate courts. Journalists may not listen to jury deliberations or to the conferences held by appellate jurists where they discuss cases and make their decisions on them. Even though they are both considered private associations under the law, political parties are more open to press coverage than interest groups. Annual party conventions and party primary elections receive a good deal of attention from journalists, though it is true that legislative party caucuses are off-limits to the press. Conversely, meetings of lobbyists and their interest group clients are not open to reporters.

Complete access would bring state government to a standstill. Confidential meetings are necessary if detailed information about the strengths and weaknesses of a potential high-level appointee is to be communicated to the governor. When the governor and legislative leaders meet privately to negotiate the annual budget or a major policy bill, they are able to be more flexible in search of consensus if correspondents are not likely to reveal the contents of their discussions to the public. Care must be exercised with the privacy-produces-results argument; excessive use of it may deny specific interests and the general public their right to know.

Beyond attendance at meetings, there is a vast quantity of information that correspondents have access to under open records and public disclosure statutes. The sources and amounts of campaign donations, the type and value of gifts given to politicians, and the sorts of assets possessed by state and local officials are all public information. Reporters from the *Sacramento Bee* produced some eye-popping articles concerning the salaries of legislative staffers and university administrators—all from readily available documents filed with public agencies. It would be beneficial to the public if more journalists acted on the phrase, "All good stories begin in the library."

What Is Newsworthy?

What ultimately constitutes the news from the State Capitol is not solely determined by the press corps, but also is influenced by public information officers (PIOs) working for state government. Legislators and executive departments all have someone designated to handle relations with the news media. Individuals occupying these positions frequently carry the title of press secretary, but they are commonly referred to as "flaks" around the Capitol. The job of PIOs is to project favorable messages through the media to the public. Some flaks, perhaps those who were once journalists themselves, understand press deadlines and know how to alert reporters to fresh stories. Other PIOs are criticized for disseminating too much information of marginal interest and for protecting their bosses from press inquiries. The extent to which reporters utilize PIOs varies. Correspondents who have developed their own sources within offices need not work through flaks, whereas reporters who are new to a beat may have to rely more on PIOs. How much information from official sources (i.e., from officeholders and their flaks) eventually finds its way into finished stories is up to members of the press. Journalists who rely too much on PIOs soon become lapdogs, not watchdogs.

One of the primary functions of PIOs is the preparation of press releases. These bulletins contain the five Ws (who, what, when, where, and why) in the first paragraph because it is most likely that news organizations will cut material from the bottom of the submission. It is a good idea to incorporate a snappy quote from an important person if possible. Press releases are of three types. *Advisory* releases alert the press corps to an upcoming event, such as a press conference. So that reporters are able to plan for the following day, these advisories should be released at least 24 hours in advance of the event. *Perfunctory* releases note that certain stages in a sequence of events have taken place. For instance, bill introductions and amendments to pending legislation are routinely the subject of press releases. Many perfunctory releases are thrown away by reporters, but it is important to send out such releases nonetheless to avoid the appearance of trying to keep information from the public. Furthermore, research has shown that decisions of the California Supreme Court were much more likely to be reported in the press if they had been the subject of a press release (Hale, 1978). *Reaction* releases are issued when a PIO's boss wishes to make a statement about a recent development. The press is attentive to these releases because they contain strong rhetoric and because they frequently generate controversy, which is to say they make news.

Besides issuing press releases, PIOs undertake several other responsibilities. Press conferences and other media events (e.g., elected officials visiting grammar schools or riding in helicopters on raids of areas suspected of marijuana cultivation) are carefully arranged by the flaks. Contingency plans are prepared for handling hecklers and for dealing with hostile questions from the press. Whereas all members of the Capitol Correspondents Association are invited to press conferences, PIOs also put together background briefings and interviews with top officials for selected members of the press corps. Journalism is a competitive business where breaking stories is infinitely better than chasing your rivals. Being in position to grant exclusive access to handpicked reporters, therefore, gives PIOs a powerful card to play in cultivating key correspondents.

The three largest flak operations in the State Capitol belong to the Office of the Governor, the Speaker of the Assembly, and the President pro Tem of the Senate. They compete with each other to obtain the greatest media exposure for their leader. In addition to these three, PIOs working for other legislators and managers in state government are attempting to gain attention for their superiors. Throw in the media specialists employed by corporations, associations, and unions, and what we have is a blizzard of advisory releases announcing events. A central decision for reporters each day is selecting which events to cover. Journalists consult a log of the day's events prepared by the Associated Press (AP) as well as the Daily Files announcing legislative committee meetings and floor sessions. News organizations with large bureaus in Sacramento, such as AP itself or the *Los Angeles Times*, hold staff meetings to assign reporters to specific events. In the case of single-person bureaus, the correspondent chooses which items to cover with varying degrees of input from an editor or a producer.

What guidelines do reporters use in selecting among events? Since most members of the press see themselves as serving the public, incidents with a wide impact on the population are considered newsworthy. Professional pride, if not concern for the financial health of their news organization, leads journalists to try to beat the competition to what is new, unique, unusual, and sometimes sensational. Correspondents focus on what is controversial, especially when the public may need to participate in the resolution of the issue. The public and private lives of celebrities are considered news by most members of the press.

Figure 5-3   Press Briefing: Formal meeting with Capital Correspondents Associaton. Note the lack of ethnic and gender diversity in the press corps. (Photograph by Adam Gottlieb.)

When the general guidelines above are insufficient to determine what is news, additional criteria are employed. As an example, a great many candidates run for office in primary and general elections. Instead of expending time and space on aspirants who have no chance of election, reporters cover the "serious" candidates. These newsworthy politicians are selected by the amount of money they have raised and by their standing in public opinion polls. Furthermore, both convenience (i.e., the time and place an event is scheduled) and the habit of using established sources help determine what news is. In the interest of maintaining access inside government, reporters may decide that news is what their sources say it is. Television correspondents' judgments about newsworthiness of course are influenced by the quality of visuals related to events. Selecting what to run as "news" is a judgment, so it is understandable that news decisions may generate disagreements.

During the 1985–1986 legislative session, reporter Dave Willman of the *San Jose Mercury News* found out what can happen when journalists and politicians disagree over what matters deserve coverage. As a prelude, Willman had written an article about Speaker Willie Brown (D, San Francisco) serving as legal counsel to Southern Pacific at the same time he was supporting their legislative measures, thereby giving the appearance of a conflict of interest. When Speaker Brown later announced his intent to give a major address the day before Governor Deukmejian's constitutionally mandated state of the state speech, Willman quoted Senate President pro Tem David Roberti (D, Hollywood) as opposing Brown's plans. Willman customarily checked with television channels around the state to see how many planned to air the governor's address, and he proceeded to do the same survey regarding the speaker's speech. Willman found that only three small stations intended to carry Brown's speech live, and he publicized this information, which was then picked up by other newspapers. Speaker Brown believed that Willman was encouraging stations not to broadcast his speech. Thereafter, Brown refused to answer Willman's inquiries at gatherings with the press. Brown also asked other members of his party to deny interviews to Willman, and Assemblyman John Vasconcellos (D, San Jose), Chairman of the Ways and Means Committee, did in fact cancel an appointment with the reporter. The rest of the press corps rallied to Willman's defense, but he soon left the Sacramento bureau of the *Mercury News* and dropped the state government beat. When relations between legislators and journalists become especially frayed, rumors circulate in the Capitol that the press may lose their privilege to gather news directly on the floors of each legislative chamber. Although reporters today may be somewhat more inclined to write hard-hitting pieces than during past decades, they know that it may cost them access to particular politicians.

Journalistic Ethics

Heaven from the point of view of PIOs is the printing or broadcasting of their press releases without any changes. However, reporters ultimately tire of dealing with spokespersons; correspondents want interviews with high-level officials themselves. Reporter Robert Scheer, whose work has appeared in the *Los Angeles Times*, gives the following advice to frustrated journalists:

> Politicians try to prevent you from knowing what's going on because that's how they survive. And they have lots of people employed to help them. The journalist's job is to get the story by breaking into their offices, by bribing, by seducing people, by lying, by anything else to break through that palace guard (Goldstein, 1985:114).

Although most reporters do not endorse the methods recommended by Scheer, there is broad agreement that stonewalling the press is a serious problem in covering both the business sector and political institutions. Many employees of state leaders have been told simply, "Do not talk to the press."

Journalists' efforts to inform the public and to serve as watchdogs have aroused the ire of both the speaker and the governor's press office. Whereas Speaker Brown has lashed out at the press in public statements, Governor Deukemjian's press secretary took complaints about press coverage directly to the editors and publishers of offending newspapers (Salzman, 1984). The speaker believes that reporters lack an accountability mechanism such as legislators face with periodic elections. Willie Brown probably would agree with media writer David Shaw's comment that "The press is still a powerful institution dedicated to the critical examination of every powerful institution but itself" (Goldstein, 1985:185).

The press does exercise restraint or self-censorship in some areas. For years reporters have voluntarily withheld from the public information about alcoholism, other drug abuse, and adultery involving high-ranking officials. Many journalists regard these subjects as smut, and they do not believe that these matters deserve coverage unless it can be shown conclusively that such behavior adversely impacts job performance. It is difficult to know whether reporters avoid these stories because of a sense of ethics or a fear of libel suits and a loss of access at the State Capitol.

Rather than regarding the friction between the press and politicians as dysfunctional, it may well be that the public is best served by one powerful institution challenging another. Columnist Dan Walters of the *Sacramento Bee*, who has been in his share of confrontations with powerful leaders, thinks that criticism of the news media should be worn as a badge of honor. According to Walters, "If Willie Brown is upset by the way the Capitol press corps is performing of late, it means that the political press is having some impact" (Walters, 1985).

Setting Agendas

News organizations play a significant role in setting public agendas by assigning investigative teams to explore certain topics and by editorializing about problems that need attention. During the spring of 1985, the *San Francisco Examiner* published a series of articles concerning the backlog of disciplinary cases involving attorneys that were not being heard in a timely manner by the State Bar Association. Over 5,000 incomplete cases were on file and some complaints were over a decade old. As a result largely of the impetus provided by the *Examiner*, reforms were enacted in 1986 to improve the processing of complaints against lawyers. Another example pertains to the *Los Angeles Times*, which published news stories and editorials throughout 1983 detailing the failure of social service departments to protect youngsters from child abuse. Investigations were launched and an Assembly Select Committee on Child Abuse was formed in Sacramento. By the time several employees and the owner of the McMartin Pre-School in Manhattan Beach were charged with sexual molestation of children in March 1984, the *Times* had been giving prominent coverage to the issue for a year. In a chilling example of the power of the press, the district attorney hurriedly prosecuted seven defendants without adequate preliminary investigation. When initial stories could not be corroborated with other testimony, charges against five of the defendants had to be dropped. The trials of the remaining defendants did not result in convictions, and it cost taxpayers over $15 million to conduct these prosecutions. It must be acknowledged that the press itself eventually became skeptical of the allegations against the defendants, but by that time it was too late to stop the whole chain of events from happening.

Research findings on public reaction to investigative reporting strongly indicate that exposés change citizens' views (Cook, 1983). Where victims are graphically depicted and villains are identified as clearly as possible, readers and viewers become convinced that action is necessary. For example, an investigative team from television station KRON in San Francisco dug into a proposed housing development in 1984. They found that the planned community was located on a flood plain and downwind from a chemical plant. The resulting uproar caused the financial backing for the project to be withdrawn. The corruption trials of state legislators in 1989 and 1990 are the fallout of the many newspaper reports and columnist articles calling attention to the questionable practices that were going on in the State Capitol throughout the 1980s.

People inside government frequently assist reporters in setting agendas. Providing tips or leaks to the press is a common practice at all levels of government. For example, someone with access to Governor Ronald Reagan's state tax forms let it be known around the Capitol that he had paid no California income tax for 1970. At a press conference held on May 4, 1971, reporters asked the governor about both his state and federal tax payments and urged him to make his tax returns public. Reagan's reply that business losses had offset any state tax liability for 1970 did not stop several days of embarrassing stories carried in newspapers around the country. He chastised the press for invading his privacy by using information they knew was confidential. Legislators often suggest that journalists investigate a certain matter, such as who will profit from the purchase of land by the state, in order to hurt the opposition. Campaign managers always are eager to have reporters examine an alleged weakness in an opponent's record or background. By bringing particular issues to center stage, reporters are much more than mere observers. They are important participants in state politics as well.

Editorial Influence

In addition to assigning investigative teams, editors also exercise influence by the timing and emphasis given stories and the contents of the editorial page. As to the timing of a major story, consider the case of former Chief Justice Rose Bird's first retention election in November 1978. On election day, the *Los Angeles Times* published allegations that the California Supreme Court had delayed the release of the controversial Tanner ruling. Bird had no opportunity to respond to the article. Critics contend that the *Times* "nearly blew her out of office in 1978" (Taylor and Richardson, 1986:452). Despite the release of the Tanner story, Bird was narrowly retained that year.

The *Times* has also been criticized for emphasizing Mayor Tom Bradley's racial background in its coverage of the 1982 gubernatorial campaign. Besides noting his ethnic group in numerous headlines, the *Times* gave extensive attention to a remark made by George Deukmejian's campaign manager. Bill Roberts stated, "If we are down only five points or less in the polls by election time, we're going to win (because of) the hidden anti-black vote" (Payne and Ratzan, 1986:302). Having pledged not to inject race into the campaign, Deukmejian promptly fired Roberts. Bradley downplayed the remark and its aftermath, but the *Times* highlighted the incident by running related articles for five straight days. Bradley's backers were probably reminded of the old saying in journalism that editors can create a crime wave any day of the week by simply instructing their reporters to write stories about every felony arrest.

Apart from the play given the statement by Roberts, Bradley may have been hurt as much, or even more, by the editorial decision of the *Times* not to endorse any candidate for governor in 1982. Since Bradley had spent his entire political career in Los Angeles, the failure of the leading newspaper in the state to endorse him was a blow to his campaign. Though editorial endorsements are especially influential in local races where information about candidates is scarce (St. Dizier, 1985), politicians at all levels eagerly seek the blessing of editors. A newspaper's summary of candidate endorsements, and approved positions on ballot measures, usually appears on the editorial page a few days before the election. A study of the *Santa Barbara News Press* found that 39% of its readership generally carried the newspaper's summary of endorsements directly into the polling booth on election day (Gregg, 1965: 536–537).

Aside from candidate endorsements or the lack thereof, editorial boards are free to criticize whatever they wish at any time. An editorial in the *Los Angeles Times* on February 17, 1989, initiated an unusual exchange between the state's chief executive and the major newspaper in California. In response to the editorial, which faulted his fiscal policies, then-Governor George Deukmejian wrote a letter to the editor of the *Times* (published on March 15, 1989) explaining why turning California into a high-tax state would be detrimental to the economic growth. Deukmejian concluded his letter by suggesting that the *Times* voluntarily contribute some of its $332 million in after-tax profits for 1988 to the state's general fund. The newspaper answered with printer's ink, not its checkbook. After publishing the governor's letter, the *Times* ran three lengthy editorials (March 15–17) setting forth methods by which essential programs could be funded. Deukmejian wrote the *Times* again (March 30, 1989) to observe that his original letter was only 10 column inches in length whereas the newspaper's three editorials in response totaled some 87 column inches. He also noted that the newspaper had yet to send in its voluntary donation to the state's coffers. The *Times* did not run an editorial opposite the governor's second letter. However, not to be left out of the fray, the editorial board of the *Sacramento Bee* (March 31) castigated Deukmejian for spending too much time corresponding with the *Times* and not enough time securing funds for the state's programs. George Deukmejian clearly ignored the old injunction not to fight with people who buy ink by the barrel.

Other than editorials, the op-ed pages also contain the work of cartoonists and syndicated columnists. Unlike reporters, these individuals are not required to be objective or balanced in their approach; having strong opinions on the editorial page is fine. Editorial slant is created by the kinds of writers and cartoonists that a paper carries, such as pro-growth versus environmentalist or Democrat versus Republican. The damage done to former Governor Jerry Brown's image on editorial pages is worthy of note. One cartoonist consistently drew Brown with Mickey Mouse ears and columnist Mike Royko of the *Chicago Tribune* dubbed him "Governor Moonbeam." Such characterizations contributed to Brown's eventual reputation as a flaky politician.

Summary

California's weak political parties provide an excellent opportunity for news organizations to exercise power. With the absence of party labels in local races, on ballot propositions, and in party primaries, many voters rely heavily on editorial recommendations. Because of a chronic lack of time on television news as well as a lack of space in the print media, news coverage of state politics is a very compressed version of actual events. Through selecting and emphasizing certain stories, news organizations determine what the vast majority of Californians know about political developments. Officeholders always are mindful of journalists' power. Politicians frequently weigh the advantages of complying with party leaders and campaign contributors as opposed to the disadvantages of attracting negative press coverage.

While the members of the Capitol Correspondents Association are covering events in Sacramento, Californians must not lose sight of the major role in politics being played by news organizations throughout the state. Just as the press watches the government, the public should watch the press. If reporters make excessive use of material from PIOs in service of the powerful, letters to the editor should demand coverage of views held by the less influential. If news organizations filter events too heavily, greater efforts must be made to schedule debates and to arrange free media time for direct communication between public figures and the electorate.

References: Chapter 5

Cook, Fay Lomax. "Media and Agenda Setting." *Public Opinion Quarterly* Spring, 1983.

Field, Mervin. "Will Independents Vote in Partisan Primaries?" *California Journal* (February 1987).

Goldstein, Tom. *The News at Any Cost*. New York: Simon and Schuster, 1965.

Gregg, James E. "Newspaper Editorial Endorsements and California Elections: 1948–62." *Journalism Quarterly*, Autumn, 1965.

Halberstam, David. *The Powers That Be*. New York: Alfred A. Knopf, 1979.

Hale, F. Dennis. "Press Releases vs. Newspaper Coverage of California Supreme Court Decisions." *Journalism Quarterly*, Winter, 1978.

Hrebenar, Ronald, and Clive Thomas. "Political Parties in the West: Competition, Organization and Change." A paper delivered at the annual meeting of the Western Political Science Association. San Francisco: March 9–12, 1988.

Leary, Mary Ellen. "California's Non-Voters: Hispanics, Blacks, Asians." *Sacramento Bee* (November 19, 1990).

Mayhew, David. *Placing Parties in America Politics: Organization, Electoral Setting, and Government Activity in the Twentieth Century*. Princeton, N.J.: Princeton University Press, 1986.

(No Author). "Mr. Speaker: A California Journal Interview." *California Journal*, January 1986.

Payne, J. Gregory, and Scott C. Ratzan. "Did the *Times*' Coverage Cost Bradley the 1982 Election?" *California Journal*, June 1986.

Raimundo, Jeff. "Eu Warns Democrats on Future." *Sacramento Bee* (February 2, 1987).

Reinhardt, Richard. "Not the *Los Angeles Times*: Who Dares to Challenge the Giant?" *Columbia Journalism Review*, May/June 1986.

Richardson, James. "Party Chairman Now Has Some Real Muscle." *Sacramento Bee* (February 12, 1989).

Salzman, Ed. "Press Corps Battles with Duke's Aide." *Sacramento Bee* (April 15, 1984).

St. Dizier, Byron. "The Effect of Newspaper Endorsements and Party Identification on Voting Choice." *Journalism Quarterly*, Autumn 1985.

Taylor, Rivian, and James Richardson. "Stalking the Wily Chief Justice." *California Journal*, September 1986.

Walters, Dan. "Press Drawing Criticism?" *Sacramento Bee* (November 17, 1985).

Weinstein, Henry. "Parties Can Endorse in Nonpartisan Races." *Sacramento Bee* (August 15, 1990).

CHAPTER 6

Elections in California

Elections are the hallmark of democracies. Voting allows Californians to select the men and women who will occupy public office (representative democracy), and it permits the electorate to govern itself through initiatives and referenda (direct democracy). Each qualified voter has an equal say in the polling booth, but the lengthy campaigns preceding elections provide ample opportunity for the powerful to exercise influence in the electoral process. Whether it be giving a fee to workers for each new voter they register, paying signature gatherers to qualify ballot measures, commissioning voter surveys to be conducted by pollsters, purchasing mailers to be sent to voters, or buying television time, the role of money is pervasive in California elections. Political parties, which make use of activist volunteers, are more and more being replaced by candidate-centered campaigns featuring professional managers and media consultants. Businesses profit handsomely from waging campaigns; companies offering election assistance are a growth industry in California. This chapter begins with a description of the nature of the voter in this state and continues with an examination of the various campaign techniques used to persuade voters.

The California Voter

Any 18-year-old citizen of the United States who has resided in the state for at least 29 days may vote in California elections. (Persons with fewer than 29 days residency in California may vote for president and vice president of the United States, but not for other offices.) In addition to these general qualifications, neither felons in prison or on probation nor persons institutionalized as mental incompetents may vote.

During the first 70 years of this century, a person had to be literate in the English language to be eligible to vote in California. In 1970, the state supreme court struck down this limitation on voting rights in *Castro v. the State of California*. In conformity with the U. S. Voting Rights Act, state law now stipulates that non-English-speaking citizens shall be encouraged to vote. To implement this provision of the law, ballots and other election materials are available on request in Spanish and Chinese as well as English. In Inyo County, oral translations of voting documents are provided for Native Americans who do not possess a written language.

Beyond meeting the qualifications as to age, citizenship, and residency, it is necessary to register to vote to be eligible to receive and mark a ballot on election days. A registration form must be filled out and received by the county clerk before the close of registration, 30 days prior to elections. The completed forms may be returned by mail or left with a deputy registrar of voters—any registered voter may serve as a deputy registrar—for delivery to the county clerk. Getting on the voter rolls is one thing; getting off is another.

Prior to 1974, an automatic purge deleted voters from the rolls for chronically failing to vote. This purging process made the voter lists relatively accurate reflections of the active electorate. Since 1974, however, voters have been stricken from the rolls only when notice is received that a registrant has died, left the county, or has asked to be removed from the voter lists. Merely failing to vote on election day no longer leads to a purge of the voter rolls. With so-called "deadwood" now remaining on the rolls, it is possible that 1 to 2 million of the 13 million Californians officially registered really are nonvoters. This no-show factor can contribute to errors by pollsters and lead to misuse of precious resources by campaign managers.

Political parties periodically conduct voter registration drives, often paying workers one dollar or more for each new registrant. However, registering individuals is no guarantee that they will vote, let alone vote for the party that registered them. Despite registration drives, only about 68% of Californians over the age of 18 are registered to vote. As of 1990, 11 million of the 30 million overall residents in California were ineligible to register due to age (under 18) or lack of citizenship. Of the 19 million Californians old enough to register to vote, only 13 million (68%) have done so. Only a portion of these registrants bothers to vote. In the primary elections in June of 1990, the turnout was roughly 40% of registrants or 5.7 million voters. During the general election in November 1990, the turnout was around 56% or 7.26 million voters statewide. The electorate in California is substantially smaller than the overall population of the state. The preeminent pollster in California has made the following observation.

> Today, "taxpayers" and "voters" are frequently distinctly different groups. —Taxpayers represent everybody, almost 100 percent of the adult population. Any person, citizen or not, voter or not, pays taxes. But only a small proportion of all taxpayers—a proportion declining each year—decides what the tax level should be (Field, 1990:9).

The social composition of California's electorate deviates considerably from the nature of the state's population. The electorate consists of more white voters, more older voters, and more better educated voters than their proportions in the overall state population would suggest. Conversely, nonvoters are likely to be young, poorly educated, and nonwhite. As indicated in Table 6.1, African-American voters participate in California elections in the same proportion as their presence in the overall state population. However, white voters are overrepresented, and Latino and Asian voters underrepresented in the California electorate. Language barriers may impair progress in school and thereafter contribute to low voter registration rates among some nonwhites. New citizens may place greater effort in attaining economic security than in gaining political representation. Although the reasons for refusing to vote are not well understood, there is speculation that the length of ballots, especially the number and complexity of ballot measures, together with negative campaigning contribute to the incidence of nonvoting.

Exit polls of voters leaving polling places in November 1990 found distinct voting patterns among the different ethnic populations in California. African-American voters exhibited strong loyalty to the Democratic Party by casting well over four-of-five of their votes (some 86%) for Dianne Feinstein. Latino voters also favored Feinstein, but by a slender margin of 53 to 47%. White voters went for Republican Pete Wilson— also by 53 to 47%. Asian-American voters gave Wilson his greatest margin by supporting him 58 to 42% (*S.F. Chronicle*, November 8, 1990). Given the many subethnic populations within the Asian-Pacific Islander peoples, it is hazardous to generalize about this portion of the electorate. Columnist Martin Smith has written that Korean-American and Vietnamese-American voters identify with the Republican Party because of the GOP's strong anticommunist record, whereas Filipino-American and Japanese-American voters are inclined to support candidates of the Democratic Party (Smith, 1989).

In addition to ethnic trends, there are regional voting patterns in California. Looking at the county-by-county returns for the presidential race

TABLE 6.1   California Population and Voting Participation by Race/Ethnicity: June 1990 Primary

Race/Ethnicity	Percent of State Population	Percent of Voters in June 1990 Primary
White	58	83
Latino	25	7
African American	7	7
Asian American	10	3

Source: Field and DiCamillo (1990:5).

in 1988 and the gubernatorial contest in 1990, there is remarkable consistency in the areas of strength and weakness for the two major parties in California. Both Dianne Feinstein (1990) and Michael Dukakis (1988) carried the Bay Area counties and Los Angeles County for the Democratic Party. On the other hand, the remaining counties in southern California (San Diego, Orange, San Bernardino, Riverside, Imperial, and Ventura) were bastions of Republican strength. The counties in the Central Valley, generally considered to be pivotal to statewide victories because they hold the balance of power between Republicans in the suburbs and Democrats in the cities, were solidly in the Republican column in 1988 and 1990. The mountain counties of the Sierra Nevada also gave strong majorities to President George Bush (1988) and to Governor Pete Wilson (1990)—both Republicans. Coastal counties were split in 1988 and 1990 with Mendocino and Sonoma voting Democratic, but Del Norte, Santa Barbara, and San Luis Obispo voting Republican.

So as not to waste scarce campaign resources, considerable effort is expended to determine which Californians are likely to vote and which are not. Further, it is important to gauge which voters are susceptible to switching their normal party allegiance. It makes sense to spend money trying to win so-called "swing voters" that gravitate between the two major parties. Likewise, there are "swing districts" in legislative contests that may be won by either political party. (In contrast, "safe seats" are so strongly Republican or Democratic that they seldom, if ever, change party control.) The number of swing districts is not large. Looking at the 80 Assembly races contested in November 1990, only 10% (eight) of the districts were highly competitive—that is, where the winner had under 55% of the votes cast. Interestingly, there were also eight Assembly districts in 1990 that were uncontested—the safest of seats. In California elections, most money and attention are directed at swing voters and swing districts.

The Absentee Voter

Prior to 1978, voting by mail was limited to housebound persons and to individuals physically absent from the precinct on election day (e.g., soldiers and travelers). However, these rules were relaxed in 1978 to allow any registered voter who so desired to vote by mail. This change in the Elections Code has produced a tremendous upsurge on absentee voting. Whereas only 4% of the statewide vote was absentee in 1976, some 14% of the vote in 1988 and 20% in 1990 was not cast at polling places on election day (DiCamillo, 1989). The absentee vote has been decisive in several major elections. George Deukmejian lost the precinct voting on election day to Tom Bradley in the governor's race in 1982, but ultimately prevailed due to his large margin in absentee ballots. Likewise,

Dan Lungren (R) lost the election-day vote to Arlo Smith (D) in the race for attorney general in 1990, but Lungren's edge in absentee votes secured him the overall victory. Republicans are not alone in successfully employing the absentee strategy. Lucy Killea (D) of San Diego won a special election to the California Senate in 1989 on the strength of her absentee vote, after narrowly losing the election-day vote to Carol Bentley (R). In January 1990, a special election to fill a vacant Assembly seat from Modesto featured more votes cast by the absentee method than by walk-in voters on election day—Sal Cannella (D) was the victor. California elections today now consist of two campaigns: one an outreach to in-home voters and the other to turn out voters on election day.

Supporters of absentee voting point out that it allows citizens to take as much time as they like to work through the complicated ballot. Some voters prefer not to venture into unfamiliar neighborhoods to vote or are too weary from a long commute to bother voting at a polling place. Campaign managers like absentee voting because once a ballot is mailed that voter can no longer be swung to the opposition on the basis of last-minute appeals. Critics of absentee voting dislike the slow and costly tabulation of such votes. Also, absentee voters may miss some late-breaking developments in campaigns by voting several days before election day. The most serious allegation, however, is that campaign workers or party activists may mark absentee ballots or heavily coach the in-home electorate. As 1990 drew to a close, election officials were investigating ways to limit fraud in the absentee voting process.

Recall: Removal from Office

In the vast majority of cases, a person's name appears on the ballot as a result of his or her own actions. Would-be officeholders get on the ballot by taking out nomination papers, having them signed by 20 to 100 registered voters (the number varies with the office being sought), and filing them with a county clerk or the secretary of state. There are some instances, however, when an individual faces the voters without having personally filed papers of candidacy. For example, state law requires that the secretary of state place the names of all persons generally recognized to be candidates for the U. S. presidency on the presidential primary ballots of the major parties. Should a person not wish to remain on the ballot in a certain presidential primary, that individual may withdraw his or her name by notifying the secretary of state at least 64 days prior to the election. In this situation, persons are not kept on the ballot against their will—they have the opportunity to avoid the voters if they so wish. By using a device instituted in California in 1911 by the Progressives, registered voters are able to put officeholders' names on the ballot whether they like it or not and there is no way such officials can avoid a day of reckoning with the electorate.

Elective officials, including judges, at all levels of government in California are subject to being recalled (removed) by popular vote during their term of office. Recall has two major phases, with several steps in each. The *qualifying phase* entails notifying a county clerk or the secretary of state that an effort will be made to unseat an official. The proponents of a recall must submit a brief statement of reasons for the removal attempt, although any reason is legally acceptable. Petitions are then circulated to obtain a legally specified number of signatures within a legally fixed time period. The larger the size of the district in which a recall is attempted, as may be seen in Table 6.2, the lower the percentage of signatures required and the longer the period to obtain them.

Should sufficient signatures be collected within the prescribed number of days, the *election phase* of recall then commences. Voters are asked: "Shall (name of official) be removed from the office of (title)?" If the affirmative votes are in the majority, the individual is removed from office. When a recall is successful, which is about half the time, the vacancy is filled by appointment on the part of other officeholders or by election. To avoid the expense of holding two elections in the event removal is successful, it is common to hold the election to fill the possible

TABLE 6.2 Recall Requirements in California

Type of Office	State Officeholders	
	Percentage of Last Vote for the Office Required to Sign Petitions	Number of Days Allowed to Obtain Signatures
Executive	12	160
Legislative	20	160
Judicial	20	160

Number of Registered Voters in Local Unit	Local Officeholders	
	Percentage of Registered Voters in Local Unit Required to Sign Petitions	Number of Days Allowed to Obtain Signatures
Fewer than 1,000	30	40
1,000 to 10,000	25	60–90
10,000 to 50,000	20	120
50,000 and above	10–15	160

Sources: California Constitution, Art. II, Sec. 14; Elections Code, Sec. 27210 and 27211.

vacancy at the same time the recall vote is being conducted. If the public official in question survives the recall effort, the outcome of the race to fill his or her post is immaterial. A recalled official may not run to replace himself or herself. This fact leads to a somewhat awkward possibility. The yes–no vote on recall is a *majority* decision, whereas the contest to replace a recalled official may have a *plurality* winner if more than two candidates file for the race. A recalled person may have received the support of 49% of the electorate and still have to surrender office to someone who received only 30% of the vote in a crowded field.

Local officials in California have good reason to fear recall. Three or four members of the same local government body occasionally have been swept out of office, so the recall threat is very real for officeholders on schoolboards and city councils. Mayor Frank L. Shaw of Los Angeles was recalled in 1938, but Mayor Dianne Feinstein of San Francisco easily turned back a recall effort (the vote was 4-to-1 in her favor) in 1983. In rare instances, recall petitions are circulated against officials at the state level; seldom do they acquire enough signatures to call for a popular vote. Former Chief Justice Rose Bird was the subject of several unsuccessful recall petition drives, but she was removed from the California Supreme Court at a regularly scheduled general election.

Several alterations to California's recall procedures have been discussed. First, to curb petitioning on petty grounds, would it be advisable to require that petitions contain specific allegations of misconduct by an official? Second, should a recalled officeholder be able to run against his or her challengers in the replacement election? Third, given the function of the judiciary to defend minority rights, should judges be subject to recall by the majority? Fourth, given the importance of decisions made by various boards and commissions (e.g., the Public Utilities Commission), should some high-level appointive posts be subject to recall?

Initiative and Referendum

In addition to electing candidates, Californians have the opportunity to vote on several types of propositions. Ballot measures at the state level are identified by number (i.e., Proposition 13), whereas issues on local ballots are referred to by letter (i.e., Measure A). Issues are placed on the ballot either due to legislative action or to successful signature-gathering drives. Whereas some 23 states possess the initiative process, California is considered the prime user of ballot measures originating from the circulation of petitions. Propositions bypass the legislative and executive branches of state government, but the judiciary may review the legality of ballot measures.

Legislative in Origin

There are three types of legislative action that must be presented to the electorate. First, any legislative enactment that places the state or its localities in debt is automatically put on the ballot to be sure residents wish to assume the burden of repayment. In the 1980s, California voters agreed to the sale of state bonds (long-term indebtedness) for the purpose of raising funds to construct new prison facilities, to build new schools, and to acquire land in the Lake Tahoe vicinity. A bond proposal to finance improvements in state highways failed, but voters did approve an increase in the gasoline tax for the same purpose. Earlier in California's history, voters approved the sale of water bonds for the construction of such facilities as the Los Angeles Aqueduct and the State Water Project. Second, whenever amendments to the state constitution or to local charters are proposed by legislators, such items go directly on the ballot without any need to collect a specified number of signatures. Third, legislative amendments to laws initially passed as ballot measures also go on the ballot automatically. This is intended to guard against legislative tinkering with statutes created by the voters. Since it is mandatory that the public be given the opportunity to review legislative action in these three instances, ballot measures stemming from these legislative actions are called *compulsory referenda*. If a local jurisdiction wishes to gauge public sentiment (i.e., conduct a straw poll) on a controversial issue, an *advisory referendum* may be placed on the ballot. Advisory referenda are just that—they are not legally binding.

It is far more common for ballot measures to originate in the legislature than it is for them to begin through petition drives. Over 70% of the propositions appearing on the state ballot have resulted from legislative action. Numbers are not everything, however. Though less numerous, initiatives stemming from the gathering of signatures on petitions receive more attention than compulsory referenda. Propositions originating through petition are more controversial (e.g., Big Green and term limits), involve heavier campaign spending (e.g., car insurance reform and liquor tax increases), and have more far-reaching consequences (e.g., coastal zone management and property tax limitation) than ballot measures prompted by legislative action. In short, hot issues avoided by the California Legislature become initiatives.

Petition in Origin

There are three devices by which registered voters may place issues on the ballot. These methods of enacting or nullifying laws are known as *direct democracy* because legislators and executives are bypassed. With the exception of possible review by the judiciary, laws adopted directly by the electorate do not require approval by elected representatives. If a change is desired in the state constitution, proponents of the alteration may sponsor an *initiative constitutional amendment*. Advocates of an addition to the state's statutory code may author and attempt to pass an *initiative statute*. If any state or local legislative body has enacted a statute with which there is strong disagreement, opponents of the legislation may carry out a *protest referendum* to give voters the opportunity to nullify the legislative enactment. A statewide protest referendum had not been held in California for 35 years until four referenda qualified for the ballot in June 1982. The legislation authorizing the Peripheral Canal (SB 200) and three enactments that redrew the boundaries of Congressional districts, State Senate districts, and State Assembly districts were placed on the ballot due to strong reservations concerning the legislature's action. The electorate nullified the work of the legislature in all four instances. Despite speculation about its vitality, the protest referendum device obviously has a potent kick when it is put to use. The state constitution (Art. II, Sec. 9) does not allow the protest referendum to be used on urgency statutes or on revenue or appropriations bills. An urgency statute takes effect immediately (instead of January 1 of the year following passage) and requires a two-thirds vote in the legislature. Having been rejected by the electorate in June 1982, legislators passed another set of redistricting laws for the Senate and Assembly (not Congress) in December 1982 as urgency statutes to forestall the possibility of more protest referenda.

All three of the direct democracy devices originate with proponents drafting a ballot measure and giving notice of intent to gather signatures. At the state level, the attorney general gives a title to the measure and prepares a brief summary of it for use at the top of each signature petition. Each of the three devices has slightly different requirements regarding the number of signatures to be gathered and the time allowed to circulate the petition.The total gubernatorial vote in the most recent general election is the basis for calculating the required number of signatures. After the gubernatorial election of 1990, the 5% signature requirement needed to qualify a statewide initiative *statute* for the ballot amounted to 384,971 persons. The 8% qualifying figure for initiative *constitutional amendments* called for 615,953 valid signatures on petitions. Both forms of initiative (statutory and constitutional) are allowed 150 days to obtain signatures. Under the direction of the secretary of state, who is the chief elections official in California, city and county clerks verify that persons who have signed petitions are indeed registered voters. (Clever people circulate petitions outside polling places on election days to be sure they are gathering valid signatures.) When sufficient valid signatures have been collected within the proper time frame, the measure is placed on the ballot. Protest referenda have a 5% signature requirement, but are allowed only 90 days for circulation of the petition. If people opposed to a legislative enactment do not mind its going into effect briefly, they can sponsor an initiative statute to repeal a law (instead of employing the protest referendum) to gain 60 more days to circulate petitions. When the Rumford Fair Housing Act was nullified by the California electorate in 1964, the ballot measure was an initiative statute to repeal the law—not a protest referendum.

Initiative Wars

The primary and general elections in California in 1988 and 1990 witnessed a pronounced proliferation in the number of initiatives qualifying for the statewide ballot. Combining the June and November ballots, 18 initiatives that were qualified by petition faced the voters in *each* of these years. (Voters decided on bond acts and legislative constitutional amendments as well.) Before 1988 and 1990, the greatest number of initiatives in a single year was in 1914 when 17 qualified. To place 18 initiatives in a single year in an historical context, note how many initiatives qualified for the ballot during entire decades prior to the 1980s. As is evident from the figures in Table 6.3, the initial fascination with the statewide initiative faded in the 1950s and 1960s. More initiatives (18) were presented to California voters in 1988 and 1990 than qualified for the ballot in each of those two decades (12 and 9). If initiative use remains at the 1988 and 1990 levels, the present decade could see 80 or 90 initiatives qualified for the ballot in California. The steep increase in initiative use of late has generated critical comment from both academic

Table 6.3 Initiatives Qualified via Petition in California by Decade

Years	Initiatives Qualified for Ballot
1912–1919	30
1920–1929	35
1930–1939	37
1940–1949	20
1950–1959	12
1960–1969	9
1970–1979	21
1980–1989	48

Source: California Secretary of State (1988:9, 10).

and political quarters. Professor David Magleby of Brigham Young University, an authority on ballot measures, has said, "I think the initiative process is out of control. The numbers exceed the ability of all but a few voters to gather the necessary information to make informed choices" (Matthews, 1990). Senator Barry Keene (D, Benicia), majority leader of the California Senate, has commented as follows.

> We are faced with a constitutional crisis in California.—The initiative process is making more policy than we (legislators) are (*Sacramento Bee*, July 15, 1990). The large and poorly written body of law created by initiatives over the past several elections is characterized by anger, simplicity, extremism, hidden agendas, unintended consequences, and polarization (Matthews, 1990).

What has contributed to the increased use of the initiative in California? The inability of the California Legislature to fashion policies in areas such as car insurance reform and tax reform prompted some people to turn to the initiative process. However, much more than legislative inactivity has fueled the initiative binge. The initiative has become an attractive option, and it is difficult for interest groups and politicians to resist. An initiative may contain precisely the content its sponsors

Figure 6-1 "Get an initiative; we're only the government!"
(Dennis Renault, *Sacramento Bee*)

desire with no concessions and no compromises that might have been extracted by lobbyists and public officials during legislative review. Sophisticated technology now enables initiative users to identify their financial supporters, likely petition signers, and potential voters during elections. Many profitable businesses (e.g., signature gathering, media buying, and direct mail) exist to supply services to those advancing initiatives. Although the Progressives who gave California the initiative in 1911 probably intended it for the use of ordinary citizens, the results of a blockbuster proposition can be so stunning (e.g., Proposition 13 in 1978) that candidates and officeholders have sponsored quite a few initiatives as well. Legislators have qualified initiatives in areas such as campaign regulation and tax increases on cigarettes and liquor. John Van de Kamp, unsuccessful candidate for the Democratic Party nomination for governor in 1990, caused three initiatives (i.e., Big Green, criminal justice reform, and term limits and legislative ethics) to be qualified that he thought would help him win the governorship. Politicians use initiatives for two purposes: to make policy and to win votes.

Instead of viewing the initiative as a safety valve to be used only in emergencies when representative institutions fail, it is now common practice in California to use the initiative as the major approach to making law. In short, the initiative became a first resort, not a last resort. When this reality could no longer be denied, the era of the counterinitiative descended on California. Concerned that voters might adopt a particular initiative, opponents of that idea qualify rival measures for the ballot as the best way to stop the original proposition from passing. In essence, initiatives beget still more initiatives. Examples of counterinitiatives abound. In June 1988, Proposition 68 authorizing public financing of campaigns in California was countered by Proposition 73, which explicitly forbid the practice of public financing in candidate races. In November 1988, five separate initiatives dealing with car insurance reform (Propositions 100, 101, 103, 104, and 106) all qualified for the ballot. Some of these measures were pro-consumer, whereas the remainder were viewed as measures advanced by the insurance industry. In November 1990, the nickel-a-drink tax increase initiative (Proposition 134) was countered by two measures supported by the liquor industry (Proposition 126 and 136). Also in November 1990, the so-called Big Green environmental initiative (Proposition 128) restricting the logging of old-growth redwoods and the use of cancer-causing pesticides was countered by two industry-backed measures (Proposition 135 and 138). Although not strictly speaking counterinitiatives, the two redistricting reform initiatives in June 1990 (Propositions 118 and 119) and the two term-limit measures in November 1990 (Propositions 131 and 140) certainly attest to the proliferation of initiatives. Every aspect of the initiative process has drawn the attention of critics.

Drafting Stage

Despite the use of the term "direct democracy" to refer to the initiative process, there is little involvement of the people in drafting ballot measures. Small, self-appointed committees gather to decide on the wording of measures. Initiative writers are not required to consider objections that may be raised by persons who are not involved in the drafting process. Although the attorney general must prepare an abbreviated summary of each initiative and give each proposal a title, drafters are not required to negotiate the content of their measures with this official. Once the signature-gathering process begins, no changes whatsoever may be made in the proposal. Under these rules, it is not surprising that drafting errors are found in initiatives. Proposition 140, for example, which limited the number of terms state legislative and executive officials are allowed to serve, left out one statewide executive post (insurance commissioner) under the provisions of the act. One lawyer has had this to say about the drafting of the landmark initiative lowering property taxes in 1978.

> I like to call Proposition 13 "The Lawyers' Relief Act of 1978." Never in the history of California electoral politics has an initiative been so sloppily drafted. And that is saying a mouthful, given how many ballot measures appear to have been written by one person over the course of a weekend he or she spent in a closet. Proposition 103—the insurance initiative that passed—is the latest example of the phenomenon (Ulrich, 1990).

In addition to the inclusion of errors in ballot measures, initiative drafting has been faulted for its length and complexity. Big Green (Proposition 128 in 1990) ran to 20,000 words, or roughly three times the length of the *U. S. Constitution*. This measure dealt with redwoods, pesticides, offshore drilling, recycling of paper, reduction of the greenhouse effect, and the creation of the post of environmental advocate. The *California Constitution* states: "An initiative measure embracing more than one subject may not be submitted to the electors (voters) or have any effect" (Art. II, Sec. 8d). Despite this constitutional language, Big Green did indeed occupy a place on the ballot. Multisubject initiatives put voters in a real dilemma when they agree with part of the proposal, but disagree with the remainder.

Qualifying Stage

Petition circulators must be registered voters in the State of California. Of the three methods now in use to obtain signatures on petitions, one would please Progressives and the other two would not. Having citizens volunteer their time to circulate petitions is what Progressives would endorse. Beyond this method, groups with ample financial resources may hire signature-gathering firms or employ direct-mail houses to solicit signatures. Hired crews, usually paid at least 75 cents a signature, circulate petitions at malls, sporting events, unemployment lines, or outside polling places. (The more difficult a signature is to obtain on a petition, the higher the price charged by firms.) The direct-mail approach consists of sending minipetitions to selected addresses with a request that signatures and a campaign donation be returned in the envelope provided. The organizations engaging in these activities are businesses, so they are interested in making a profit. It is hardly likely that such firms will discourage clients from attempting to qualify measures for the ballot. An editorial in the *Sacramento Bee* condemned the so-called initiative industry in the following terms.

> Never before has money played so large a part in determining what gets on the ballot; never before has that money distorted the issues so greatly. . . . As the initiative was originally conceived, signatures were to be gathered by volunteers going door-to-door persuading equally concerned friends and neighbors . . . It has become an industry dominated by professional political technicians, big money interests, and flimflam men (November 7, 1984).

Campaigning Stage

Two aspects of initiative campaigns have drawn critical attention: deceptive campaign advertisements and wide disparities in the amounts of money spent on the pro and con sides of these races. Given the complexity of the issues facing the voters, there is an incentive to simplify choices with catchy slogans. These memorable phrases frequently distort the proposition in question. For instance, the opponents of Big Green referred to it as "The Hayden Initiative" in an attempt to associate the measure with Assemblymember Tom Hayden's (D, Santa Monica) controversial past as an antiwar activist. John Van de Kamp, then attorney general, was a prime sponsor of Big Green, but his name lacked the negative campaign value attached to Hayden's. Earlier in 1990, the battle over two redistricting reform initiatives (Propositions 118 and 119) was twisted from what entity ought to draw legislative district lines (either the legislature or a commission) to a question of protecting the environment. Since the two proposals might have reduced the number of coastal districts in California, the Sierra Club voiced its opposition to the two propositions. This led to advertisements saying, "Stop the big corporations from despoiling the environment." Neither initiative dealt with the environment. The state lottery (Proposition 37 in 1984) was sold to the electorate as "a vote for children" in that a portion of the proceeds was earmarked for education, and the issue of legalized gambling was avoided. Two initiatives in 1978 and 1980 designed to limit indoor smoking were defeated by using the antigovernment theme: "They are at it again." The tobacco industry skillfully shifted the issue from the danger of secondhand smoke to the question of state regulation.

Initiative races in California feature heavy, yet disparate, spending. For the general election in November of 1988, some $129 million was spent on ballot measure contests. To put this initiative spending in some context, it is three times as much as the $43.5 million combined spending of Pete Wilson and Dianne Feinstein in the 1990 gubernatorial race. Spending on propositions is anything but equal on either side of the issues. The insurance industry spent $55 million to enact no-fault insurance (Proposition 104) in November 1988 against virtually no opposition spending, yet still lost the measure. After the final tallies were recorded, the insurance industry had spent $23.36 per vote in losing Proposition 104 (California FPPC, 1989). In 1990, the liquor industry was unable to pass its Propositions 126 and 136 despite heavy spending on their behalf. Outcomes such as these confirm the conventional wisdom that large campaign expenditures cannot guarantee passage of propositions.

Until 1986 and 1988, it was thought that heavy negative spending could defeat initiatives. Strong spending against indoor smoking restrictions (1978 and 1980) and against gun control (1982) had prevailed. However, heavy negative spending was not enough to defeat three key initiatives in the late 1980s. Proposition 65, requiring identification of cancer-causing chemicals, won in 1986 despite disproportionate negative spending by the chemical industry. Proposition 99, the quarter-a-pack cigarette tax in 1988, also won even though backers were outspent by tobacco companies $1.8 million (for) to $21.2 million (against). Proposition 103, allegedly a pro-consumer car insurance proposal creating an elected commissioner, won as well in 1988 regardless of heavy opposition spending by the insurance industry. These three may prove to be exceptions to the general rule that heavy negative spending is effective. In 1990, Big Green (Proposition 128) was defeated after major opposition spending by the timber and agriculture industries, and the nickel-a-drink alcohol tax fell to strong negative spending by the liquor industry. Whether or not heavy spending against propositions is decisive, there is no doubt that massive amounts of money are raised and spent in the initiative wars.

Voting Stage

The California electorate is faced with an overwhelmingly difficult task in attempting to cast informed votes on initiatives. More than having to decipher individual multisubject propositions, voters also must grasp the interconnections among several initiatives on the same ballot. For instance, voters might have favored one of the two initiatives to raise taxes on liquor in 1990 (Proposition 126 and 134), but unwittingly nullified their preference by voting for a so-called "poison pill" measure (Proposition 136) further down the ballot. Had the poison pill passed, which it did not, a two-thirds popular vote would have been required to enact either of the foregoing tax increase propositions.

While conscientious citizens grapple with the interrelated intricacies of the ballot measures, they also must be on guard concerning deceptive campaign advertisements. The poison pill measure in 1990 (Proposition 136) was officially titled "State and Local Taxation." Proponents of this item labeled it the "Taxpayer's Right to Vote Initiative" in all the publicity they generated on its behalf. Remember Proposition 136 would have eliminated a simple majority's right to raise taxes and allowed a minority of voters (one-third plus one) the power to block tax hikes. Regarding the interwoven complexity of the 1990 general election ballot, Professor Larry Berg of the University of Southern California stated "A few years ago I was a strong proponent of the initiative—not anymore. This has got to stop or it will destroy the whole state" (Kushman, 1990b).

Registered voters in the state are provided with a lengthy voter's pamphlet assembled by the secretary of state. In addition to the language of each ballot measure, the pamphlet includes statements submitted by proponents and opponents of each proposition. The voter's pamphlet normally is from 50 to 80 pages in length, but so many detailed initiatives were on the 1990 general election ballot that this pamphlet had to be issued in two separate sections totaling over 200 pages.

> Confronting 28 propositions, let alone the 222 pages analyzing them that voters are sent by the state, is like that persistent nightmare people have for years after college—of facing an exam without having taken the course. In this case the nightmare is finding you've been *transformed into a legislator* who must do a whole term's worth of voting in one nauseating sprint.—Small wonder people don't vote. I have always been pious about voting,—but I no longer feel the same anger toward people who don't vote. I can understand how turned off they feel, because I now feel it too. (Kaplan, 1990, italics added.)

Adding all the candidate races and local initiatives together with the statewide initiatives we have been discussing, it is probable that voters will be asked to make over 60 decisions on their ballots. When highly educated members of the electorate experience ballot fatigue, low turnout among the broad spectrum of voters cannot be considered surprising.

Judicial Review

Although initiatives bypass the legislative and executive branches, the judiciary reviews propositions when cases are filed. For the most part, courts do not intervene in the initiative process prior to the popular vote. However, on rare occasions, judges have revised propositions and ballot pamphlet arguments where their language was found to be blatantly misleading. Most judicial review occurs after the popular vote has been tallied. For groups that just lost at the ballot box, the battle may be continued in the courts. When Proposition 103 passed in 1988 requiring rate reductions in car insurance, the insurance industry spent an estimated $25 million in legal fees in the next year and a half endeavoring to block implementation of the initiative (Garcia, 1990). The proliferation of initiatives ultimately leads to more work for the courts.

The courts have two traditional tools for reviewing initiatives, and additional legal concepts are evolving at the present time to assist the courts in these matters. First, if an initiative violates provisions of the federal or state constitutions, it may be struck down. The California Supreme Court overturned a popular vote by reinstating the Rumford Fair Housing Act in 1964 after it had been nullified by the electorate. (It is possible that the U. S. Supreme Court might overturn tax-cutting Proposition 13 in the future on the grounds that it denies equal protection of the law by allowing unequal tax assessments on properties of similar value.) Second, the courts may invoke the single-subject rule to invalidate an initiative. Historically, judges have been reluctant to enforce the single-subject rule. The so-called Victim's Bill of Rights (Proposition 8 in 1982) contained sections on school safety, restitution (payment) to victims, bail reform, and plea bargaining, among other matters. Asked to review this measure, the state's highest court ruled that Proposition 8 contained only one subject. The single-subject rule in practice has meant one *broad* subject (e.g., crime or the environment). In a decision that could have major consequences, the 1st District Court of Appeal in February of 1991 struck down Proposition 105 (truth in advertising) on the grounds that it contained unrelated topics. The measure dealt with warning labels identifying toxics in household products, protection of senior citizens against fraud in insurance policies, and disclosure by companies doing business in South Africa. If upheld by the California Supreme Court, this ruling may begin to curb the use of multi-subject initiatives.

Given the disinclination to strictly apply the single-subject rule, the courts may dust off an old concept and use it in the contemporary period. Proposition 115, a criminal reform measure passed in 1990, contained dozens of amendments to the state constitution. It also stipulated that criminal defendants in California shall have only those rights provided by the *U. S. Constitution*, not rights independently derived from the *California Constitution*. Initiatives may amend the state constitution, but they may not *revise* it. Should the courts find wholesale changes in the state constitution to be revisions instead of amendments, the unruly beast of multisubject initiatives may be curtailed to an extent.

When conflicting initiatives both pass, as happened with Proposition 68 and 73 on campaign reform in 1988, the courts historically have attempted to blend portions from each measure into the law. (Where provisions on the same subject directly conflicted, the courts accepted the language that received the most votes. However, if the proposition receiving fewer votes had provisions that were not contained in the other measure, that language too would be enacted into law.) Evidencing some frustration in its efforts to reconcile the two successful propositions of 1988, the California Supreme Court ruled in 1990 that only the top vote-getting initiative is operative because it is a "comprehensive regulatory scheme" that cannot be merged with another full-blown plan to regulate campaign financing. Therefore, Proposition 73 prevails and Proposition 68 is not in force. (While this case was being resolved by the state's highest court, a federal district court judge was hearing a separate challenge to Proposition 73 and finding aspects of it invalid.)

With Proposition 13 (property tax decrease), Propositions 68 and 73 (campaign finance reform), Proposition 103 (car insurance reform), and Proposition 140 (term limits), among others, all brought before the courts, it is clear that victory at the polls is no longer conclusive. Does the saying "pay me now or pay me later" come to mind? Avoiding legal counsel early on may produce faulty drafting and subsequently lead to the need to retain attorneys when an initiative is taken to court. On the other hand, perhaps initiative warfare today is really a "pay me now *and* pay me later" situation wherein even the most carefully drafted measures are taken to court.

Reforms

On concluding that direct democracy in California is no longer democratic, Professor Eugene Lee of the University of California (Berkeley) proposed a package of changes to the state's initiative process. To permit alterations to be made to initiative proposals, Lee recommends that much more extensive review of measures occur *prior* to the commencement of the circulation of petitions. (The legislative hearings that are currently held on propositions occur *after* the initiatives have qualified for the ballot—meaning that the hearings cannot lead to changes in the wording of ballot measures.) Besides moving legislative review forward in the process, the attorney general could be empowered to refuse to title and summarize any measure containing more than one subject. Any such ruling could be appealed in the courts.

After the drafting stage, Lee advocates that the sources of donations favoring initiatives be reflected on the qualifying petitions and in the ballot pamphlets. Lee also suggests that the percentage of signatures required to qualify constitutional amendments be raised, that initiatives appear only on the general election (November) ballot where the turnout is higher, that it be made easier for the legislature to amend initiatives after their passage, and that the courts more strictly apply the single-subject rule (Lee, 1990:2).

The role of paid signature gathers has drawn the attention of other reformers. The State of Colorado completely forbid the use of paid signature gatherers for over 30 years, but the U. S. Supreme Court in *Meyer v. Grant* overturned Colorado's prohibition in 1988. If paid gatherers can no longer be outlawed, possibly there are other ways to reduce the role of money in buying ballot access. Assemblymember Jackie Speier (D, South San Francisco) has carried legislation—it has not yet passed—that would require compensated workers to wear badges saying "Paid Petition Circulator." Professor Dan Lowenstein of UCLA Law School has promoted the idea that higher percentages should be required to qualify through paid circulators than through volunteer workers. Alternatively, volunteer petition circulators could be given a longer time frame in which to qualify their proposals.

Such reforms would be rendered unnecessary in some respects if California's courts and electorate acted decisively. Judicial enforcement of the single-subject rule would clarify choices for voters, although it might increase the number of initiatives in circulation. Voters approved only 3 of 13 initiatives on the November 1990 ballot, and only 1 of 5 insurance propositions passed in November of 1988. A hefty number of "No" votes could do more than anything else to discourage the proliferation of initiatives.

Campaign Professionals _____

When the firm of Whitaker and Baxter handled a ballot measure in 1933, California introduced to American politics the concept of professional campaign management. Whitaker and Baxter did not confine themselves to proposition campaigns on behalf of corporate clients; they also worked for gubernatorial candidates. The growth of campaign management businesses in California was hardly surprising. Given the legal restrictions on political parties during partisan primaries and the nonpartisan nature of local elections, there was much need in such contests for organizations possessing electioneering skills. Proponents and opponents of ballot measures also required professional campaign assistance.

As the campaign industry has grown in size and complexity, more and more job titles have come into use. We now have media buyers, media producers, media coaches, pollsters, direct-mail houses, and focus groups, not to mention the traditional speech writers, schedulers, and advance teams that handle preparations for candidate appearances. Let us first endeavor to clarify such commonly used terms as campaign manager, campaign director, campaign chairperson, and campaign consultant. The first three of these titles usually refer to an individual who actually runs the day-to-day operations of *one* campaign. This person ordinarily is responsible for the detailed implementation of campaign tactics, and he or she generally hires and supervises the campaign staff. On the other hand, campaign consultants usually work with *several* candidates and ballot measures at the same time. Consultants provide advice on major themes to be followed, but generally try not to become bogged down in the particularities of campaign administration. Confusion occurs, however, because some consultants occasionally consent to take on the direct management of campaigns. The career of consultant Richie Ross demonstrates what an up-and-down business campaign consulting is. Ross was most successful in the early 1980s giving advice to Democratic candidates in Assembly races. However, a good number of his legislative clients were defeated in 1986. Ross got back on the winning track in 1987 by managing the successful campaign to elect Art Agnos as Mayor of San Francisco. In his biggest campaign to date, Ross was unable to pull John Van de Kamp to victory in the 1990 gubernatorial primary of the Democratic Party. The firm of Woodward and McDowell prefers to specialize in initiative races because, as they say, ballot measures do not have drinking problems and they do not make ill-advised remarks to the press. Woodward and McDowell have had good years and bad years, similar to Ross with his candidate campaigns.

The rise of consultants has added an important set of players to the electoral process. In the precampaign period before massive efforts are undertaken to reach voters, a candidate's ability (or inability) to place a well-known consultant under contract for an upcoming campaign confers instant credibility (or the lack thereof) on a candidacy. Campaign donors and journalists take a candidate much more seriously if he or she has signed with a well-known consultant. In a most unusual move in the fall of 1989, consultant Clint Reilly publicly dissolved his contract with gubernatorial candidate Dianne Feinstein, saying she lacked the commitment to wage a victorious campaign. Reilly's conduct was faulted by others in the consulting field, and some Democrats have since refused to use his firm because of his slight to Feinstein. Consultants Michael Berman and Carl D'Agostino (BAD Campaigns) were in the spotlight in 1988 for writing indiscreet memos to a client that insulted Mayor Tom Bradley's intelligence. When consultants do their jobs properly, they are not the story—their clients are.

Campaign consultants prepare a strategy (or plan) to be used by a candidate or by one side of a ballot measure contest. At the outset, consultants provide recommendations on ways to discourage the entry of other viable candidates into a race in the first place. Later, ideas are developed on the overall theme or message of the campaign and the timing of media saturation. Should a candidate commit a blunder during a campaign, consultants provide advice on methods of damage control. If a consulting firm offers a broad range of services, it may manage almost all areas of a campaign. More commonly, specialized firms are retained to handle specific parts of a campaign. For instance, Dick Wirthin's DMI (Decision Making Information) may be used to conduct surveys of voter opinion; Computer Caging Corporation or Below, Tobe & Associates may be signed to carry out direct mail operations; and Focus Media or Western International Media may be asked to purchase television time. With the growing expense of campaigns, it is important that consultants and managers not waste money on fruitless endeavors. Many people will not vote on election day and others are unlikely to change strongly held views. In short, targets must be selected. Skillful campaigns identify persuadable voters as well as the issue that will help secure their support. Survey research is instrumental in establishing the target groups and the target issues.

Polling

Most political polls today are conducted over the telephone by part-time interviewers under the direction of professional supervisors. Firms maintain lists of competent interviewers to assist in the collection of unbiased information from the public. Initial polls are used to determine the strengths and weaknesses of a candidate's image and to learn the voters' views on various issues. This information will help consultants tentatively settle on a campaign theme. Well-funded campaigns for major offices never stop polling throughout the course of a race, so that immediate adjustments may be made should slippage be detected. Pollsters gauge public reaction to televised commercials and to mass mailings—all the while hoping to find the key idea that can be used to harvest a particular cluster of votes. Although Berman and D'Agostino are known for not using or trusting polls, most contemporary practitioners would agree with consultant David Townsend that "You would not run for dogcatcher without a poll" (Kushman, 1990a).

The results of some polls are disseminated in the mass media, whereas other surveys are kept private and used strictly within a campaign.

The California Poll, founded by Mervin Field in 1947, is syndicated to newspapers throughout the state. Several metropolitan dailies, including the *Los Angeles Times* and the *Sacramento Bee*, also conduct voter studies and publish the outcomes. The release of polling data presumably fascinates viewers and readers. The public, similar to spectators at a horse race, likes to see who is gaining and who is dropping back. Upward momentum in the polls produces an influx of campaign donations, whereas stable or declining ratings tend to reduce contributions. Because candidates and consultants realize how crucial poll results are, they attempt to manipulate survey outcomes by unleashing flurries of advertising just before pollsters sample public opinion. For this reason, Mervin Field and other survey researchers have become very secretive about the precise dates they intend to conduct interviews.

Endorsements

Given a long ballot containing federal, state, and local races plus ballot measures and judicial elections, voters are faced with the task of informing themselves on many questions before election day. To ease the search for election information, voters are receptive to cues or shorthand signals that will expedite their decision making. In nonpartisan races and initiative contests in which no party label appears on the ballot as a quick and easy guide for voters, a newspaper endorsement can be an important stimulus to vote a certain way. The *Sacramento Bee* ran a summary of its candidate and proposition endorsements for three straight days in November 1990. Also, interest groups and influential people are only too happy to offer guidance. Groups as divergent as the California Farm Bureau and the Sierra Club endorse candidates for public office. Celebrities from the entertainment industry lend their seal of approval as well. James Garner and Jack Lemmon helped defeat Propositions 118 and 119 (redistricting reforms) in 1990, but Angela Lansbury was unable to stop the passage of Proposition 140 (term limits). Michael Landon, Ted Danson, and Ed Begley, Jr., were unsuccessful in attempting to pass Big Green. Jane Fonda secured the support of Melissa Gilbert, Ally Sheedy, Judd Nelson, Tom Cruise, Kelly McGillis, Demi Moore, and Emilio Estevez in helping to pass Proposition 65 (clean water) in 1986. The endorsement of Proposition 103 (car insurance) by Ralph Nader was crucial to its passage. Remember that Propositions 65 and 103 both overcame heavy industry spending against them. In all likelihood, these two measures would have failed without celebrity endorsements. In the defeat of Big Green in 1990, however, the former Surgeon General of the United States was skillfully used to counter the impact of Hollywood celebrities.

Campaign Media _____

Although the cost of polls, travel, and telephones is not to be dismissed lightly, the great bulk of campaign money is expended on media. Most statewide campaigns allocated 60 to 80% of available funds to the purchase of media of all kinds. The production and airing of television advertisements used to receive the lion's share of this allocation, but increasingly money is being directed to printing and mailing campaign materials directly to voters.

Direct Mail

Computers have many applications in campaigning. Aside from tabulating voter survey results with dispatch, computers enable campaign professionals to segment the electorate and then direct highly refined messages to each component of the voting public. With the large memory capacity that is now available, computers can store information on voters' age, gender, income level, occupation, party affiliation, race, magazine subscriptions, and sexual preference. Much of this information is readily available through published sources such as the census, voter rolls, and employee listings. The more difficult task of building ethnic and gay data bases (known as dictionaries) is painstakingly derived from phonebooks, precinct visits, and expert judgment. As firms such as Below, Tobe & Associates acquire more and more knowledge of the electorate over the years, their ability to help candidates increases. When recent polling data and election results are analyzed together with the socioeconomic information already on file, campaign consultants are able to say with some assurance what attitudes are held by certain categories of voters. To put it succinctly, targeting has improved immensely in recent years.

Direct mail is particularly cost-effective in legislative district races. First, direct mail does not waste money outside the legislative district as television advertising frequently does. Second, mail targets persuadable voters (not others) very precisely inside the district. In the past, it was common to send out the same campaign brochure to a district-wide audience. This practice may have done more harm than good if broadly worded mailers contained language that offended almost every recipient. The direct mail of today targets narrow groups and highlights carefully selected issues. Mailers are designed to work on voters' partisan, religious, ethnic, and occupational predispositions. In addition, the letterhead printed at the top of a campaign letter can be adjusted to appeal to the targeted audience. For instance, influential Latinos are shown as campaign committee members on letters going to Spanish-speaking neighborhoods, whereas prominent persons in business are shown as sponsors of mailings into affluent communities. Great effort is expended on the design of envelopes to keep recipients from throwing mailers into the wastebasket unopened.

There is considerable conjecture that targeted mail facilitates the use of highly negative brochures called "hit pieces." By carefully planning when a piece is to be mailed, it is possible to blast an opponent in the last days of a campaign and to deny that person sufficient time to design, print, and mail a response. Knowing that a piece is being sent primarily to a sympathetic audience (i.e., is not for mass consumption) may incline direct mail operatives to use stronger language and graphics. To reiterate, one of the reasons so much effort is being put into encouraging absentee voting is to minimize the damage from hit pieces late in the campaign.

The precise targeting now possible with computers may be connected to other delivery methods besides mail. Some campaigns have experimented with sending video cassette recordings to selected voters. With detailed knowledge of particular residents, personal contact can be made through phone banks and precinct walkers. It is best to use local callers and canvassers if possible, since there can be resistance to outside mercenaries. Well-coordinated ground operations that promote the use of absentee ballots can blunt the effectiveness of late hits delivered by direct mail and television advertising.

Television Commercials

One 30-second political advertisement in a metropolitan area will reach more Californians than a candidate could meet by walking precincts for a year. We should hasten to add that such a commercial would also cost $30,000 or more if aired on the popular "Cosby Show" in Los Angeles. The price of air time is related to the number and type of viewers tuning in a given channel. The time of day or night, the size of the media market, and the popularity of the program during which an ad is run all influence cost. Though more difficult to target than direct mail, it is possible to some degree to focus televised commercials. Specialists in buying media like to obtain slots near news broadcasts and public affairs programs because people watching these shows are more likely to vote. Further, conservative voters are thought to be viewers of police dramas, whereas young and liberal members of the electorate presumably are the audience of "Saturday Night Live." (In the radio market, various types of listeners can be reached by placing ads on Spanish-language broadcasts, all-news shows, and sports coverage—not to mention the different audiences available on rock, country, and classical stations.) It is not uncommon for statewide candidates to spend half of their media budgets at television stations in Los Angeles. The signals from these channels carry to San Diego, San Bernardino, Riverside, Orange, Ventura, Santa Barbara, and Kern Counties. Media buyers have begun to place ads on cable channels because the cost is low and the ability to target is superior to that available over the major networks.

The typical campaign advertisement on television is a 30-second spot. After careful review of polling data, a concept for the piece and a closing tag line are developed. Tag lines are what consultants hope the voters will remember. Some examples include: "Vote NO on the Hayden initiative." "Great governor, great state." "They're at it again." Unless faced with catastrophe, the fundamental theme is not altered in mid-campaign. Next, an eye-catching video is shot, sound is recorded, and charts or other graphics are prepared. When all the ingredients have been mixed and edited, the results are shown to focus groups to determine their reaction. Test audiences made up of a cross section of the electorate view a number of commercials and comment on what they like and dislike about each. Actors, dialogue, and tag lines are all evaluated for their ability to put across the desired message. Given the brevity of spots, it is common for these ads to oversimplify complex propositions and to focus more on candidates' images than their issue positions. Whereas television adver-

Figure 6-2 Garbage in—garbage out. (Dennis Renault, *Sacramento Bee*)

tisements usually present a grand theme for a campaign, many sub-themes tailored to fit specific segments of the electorate are typical of direct mail.

Rather than positive and accurate, some television spots are negative and deceptive. Of many examples that might be cited here, one will have to suffice. The redistricting commission proposed by Proposition 39 in 1984 was to be composed of retired appellate justices. The television ads used to defeat this initiative showed judges (with party bosses peering over their shoulders) taking their oath of office saying "I swear to uphold my-my-my political party." These commercials conjured up judicial corruption and entirely avoided the issue of unfair lines for legislative districts. Speaker Willie Brown (D, San Francisco), an opponent of Proposition 39, later admitted that the negative commercials, "had absolutely nothing to do with Proposition 39; they were the most extensive collection of con jobs I've ever seen" (*Sacramento Bee*, November 22, 1984). In the primary and general elections of 1990, several major newspapers in California pointedly analyzed television commercials as to their accuracy and truthfulness. This innovation is thought to have made the producers of television spots somewhat more careful in making charges about opponents. Negative campaigning is by no means at an end, however, because far more voters watch television than read newspapers.

Free Media

Not all media exposure is by means of paid advertisements. Campaign managers endeavor to have their candidates appear as often as possible on news broadcasts, on talk shows, and in newspapers. In addition to press conferences to attract media coverage, staged or pseudo-events are carefully organized for the same purpose. Candidates visit elementary schools, watch space shuttle landings in person, engage in long hikes along the state's highways, and take rafting trips to provide interesting visual situations that news editors would be likely to use. Though considerably less expensive than paid media, expenditures for advance work by staff, telephoning, and travel can make media events anything but free.

So-called free media have their drawbacks, however. Candidates and ballot measure advocates need the cooperation of news organizations. An international crisis, a strike, or a sensational crime may push a staged event off the news. Publishers and editors who are opposed to the point of view of those seeking free exposure can deny coverage of particular media events. Candidates with money to buy media improve their standing in voter surveys and thereafter receive more coverage by the news media. In essence, paid media produces free media. Since newsworthiness is related to standings in voter surveys, it is difficult for someone trailing badly in the polls to use free media to improve his or her position. Lately, candidates are holding press conferences to screen their television spots for reporters. This is a clear example of paid media begetting free media.

Ordinarily, the message projected at a media event cannot be as easily controlled by a candidate as the language in a paid commercial. Lately, however, candidates have achieved a measure of control of their free media by tightly scripting the event and refusing to take questions from the press. When news organizations become frustrated with such canned performances, they can force spontaneity out of candidates by refusing to air their highly planned events.

Candidate debates are a variation of free media. These events are staged for media coverage, but the power of news organizations to edit is lessened provided debates are shown in their entirety. (Later newscasts, of course, show selected excerpts from debates.) There were debates between the major gubernatorial candidates in 1974, 1978, and 1982. George Deukmejian refused to debate Tom Bradley in 1986, but Pete Wilson and Dianne Feinstein had one televised debate in 1990. It is never easy to secure a wide audience for debates because commercial channels dislike losing the advertising revenue they normally would make during prime viewing hours. (Refer to pages 224–226 for discussion of the 1990 gubernatorial contest.)

Campaign Money

The cost of campaigns in California has skyrocketed. Jerry Brown was reelected to the governor's office, both primary and general elections, in 1978 on a budget of $4.6 million. When Governor Deukmejian was reelected in 1986, he spent $13.4 million to retain his office. Pete Wilson spent some $24 million in winning the governor's office in 1990—more than five times what Brown spent 12 years earlier. While winners and losers for 100 legislative seats spent slightly over $20 million in 1978, combined spending for legislative races in 1988 reached $68 million. In November 1984, $32.4 million was spent on ballot propositions—then a record. With the initiative wars hitting their stride, $129 million was spent on propositions in November 1988 followed by over $91 million on ballot measures in November 1990. Campaigns are a multimillion-dollar business in California. When the insurance industry spent $74 million or more on five car insurance initiatives in 1988, consultant Clint Reilly collected over $9 million in commissions on these races. Perhaps his peers resent this payday more than his unceremonious dumping of Dianne Feinstein as a client.

Several techniques are used to raise money. First, direct solicitation of major donors is carried out in a variety of ways. When someone such as David Packard of electronics giant Hewlett-Packard allows his name to be used on a candidate's letterhead, or makes phone calls for an office seeker, substantial contributions are forthcoming. Being endorsed by a well-known industrialist can be as important as signing with a top campaign consultant. Under campaign disclosure laws now in effect, it is now possible to obtain printouts of major contributors. With a U. S. President or other national party leader headlining an event, tickets to fundraising dinners are sold for $1,000 or more per person. A single well-organized dinner can raise over $1 million in contributions. Second, small donations today are solicited through direct mail. Using lists of people who are interested in a specific issue (e.g., Gun Owners of California), mail pieces are carefully crafted to bring in donations in the $10–$25 range. Third, candidates in California are beginning to raise money nationwide. Jerry Brown raised money from the oil industry in Texas when he was governor, and both Tom Bradley and Dianne Feinstein obtained donations in major cities on the East Coast.

Figure 6-3 Friendlier Circumstances: Mayor Dianne Feinstein presented U.S. Senator Pete Wilson an award in 1985 for his endeavoring to locate the *USS Missouri* in the Port of San Francisco. Five years later they opposed each other in the race for the governorship. (Governor's Office)

Campaign Regulation _____

The status of campaign law in California is most uncertain as Pete Wilson assumes the governorship. Provisions of the Political Reform Act of 1974 are in force, but the legality of two campaign finance propositions that were passed by the voters in June 1988 is in tatters. The general election of 1990 was contested under campaign finance rules that changed almost weekly as various legal challenges progressed through the state and federal courts. Having undergone judicial review in the late 1970s, we can be more confident in describing the 1974 law than the 1988 measures.

The Political Reform Act (approved by the voters in 1974 as Proposition 9) addressed the role of money in California politics in three ways. First, the statute required that lobbyists register with the secretary of state and file quarterly reports concerning their salaries and expenses. Second, the Political Reform Act established requirements that campaign contributions and expenditures be disclosed to the public. Third, the law obliged candidates and officeholders to disclose their investments and income so that it may be determined if they ever illegally participate in government decisions leading to their own enrichment. The Fair Political Practices Commission (FPPC) was established to carry out the intent of the Act.

Campaign Disclosure

All campaigns at the state and local levels in California—whether they be candidate or proposition contests—must file detailed reports on campaign contributions and expenditures. So that opponents and the public may know the source of a campaign's funding, two reports must be submitted before election day—one report 2 weeks prior to balloting and the other 6 to 8 weeks before that. A final, postelection report is also required. The reports contain totals regarding all monetary and nonmonetary contributions as well as particulars concerning any loans extended to the campaign. The *actual* source of donations must be reported. (W. Patrick Moriarty of Red Devil Fireworks was convicted in 1986 of channeling campaign contributions to candidates through his friends and relatives—a process called "laundering"—to conceal his own involvement.) Anyone contributing $100 or more to a campaign in a calendar year must be listed, and all expenditures of $100 or more must be itemized. To facilitate possible audits, all contributions and disbursements of $100 or more must be in check form—cash transactions being difficult to trace. Small, anonymous donations may be accepted by a campaign, but any anonymous contribution of $100 or more in a calendar year must be handed over to the secretary of state.

Conflict of Interest

During campaigns, candidates are required to disclose information about their personal assets. Once elected, officeholders are obliged to file periodic reports of a similar nature. The conflict-of-interest requirement applies not only to elective officials, but also to high-level appointees whose decisions could lead to their own financial gain. Senior university officials and city managers are obliged to file conflict-of-interest statements. By having information on officials' real estate holdings, investments, and income available to the press and the public, it is more likely that public servants will abstain from participation in decisions in which they have an economic interest.

Contribution Limits

When voters approved Proposition 68 and 73 in June 1988, it appeared that California had ended an era in which campaign donations of an unlimited size were lawful. Both measures limited individual donors to state legislative races to giving $1,000 per election (primary and general campaigns considered as two separate elections). Under each proposition, large-donor political action committees (PACs) could give only $2,500 per election, and small-donor PACs were allowed $5,000 per election. Both initiatives also forbid the transfer of campaign funds from one legislator (or candidate) to another. This prohibition was designed to stop legislative leaders from transferring large sums from their campaign accounts to candidates in difficult races. Neither proposition placed contribution limits on ballot measure races, which fed speculation that big money henceforth would be donated to the initiative wars.

Apart from their similarities, Proposition 68 and 73 differed in significant respects. Proposition 68's contribution limits applied only to legislative races, whereas Proposition 73's limits pertained to both legislative and executive contests. Because incumbents established an unfair advantage by accumulating 99% of all contributions raised in nonelection years, Proposition 68 banned nonelection-year fundraising altogether. In an effort to reduce the sense of obligation that officials felt toward their contributors, Proposition 68 instituted a public financing program for legislative races with funds generated by a check-off system administered on the personal income tax form. In the presence of publicly subsidized campaigns, the U. S. Supreme Court (*Buckley* v. *Valeo*) allows expenditure limits to be imposed and Proposition 68 contained these limits as well. In contrast, Proposition 73 was silent on nonelection-year contributions and explicitly prohibited public financing (and by extension expenditure limits).

As previously discussed, the California Supreme Court endeavored to sort out the various provisions of these two successful propositions. Since Proposition 73 passed by a larger margin, its prohibition of public financing clearly negated the language on that topic in Proposition 68. Since Proposition 73 failed to mention fundraising in nonelection years, it was initially thought that Proposition 68's prohibition of such activity would hold. However, the state's highest court in November 1990 struck down Proposition 68 in its entirety saying that two comprehensive regulatory schemes regarding campaign financing could not be grafted together. At about the same time, a federal district court judge ruled that the contribution limits set forth in Proposition 73 were illegal because they gave an advantage to incumbents. Proposition 73's limits were applied on a fiscal year basis (July 1– June 30); the primary election fell in one fiscal year and the general election in the next. Most incumbents raise campaign funds throughout their term of office — potentially in four different fiscal years. Challengers ordinarily commit to making a race about a year prior to the general election. Given these realities, challengers miss some fiscal years in which to raise the allowable maximums. (If contribution limits were applied to the entire preelection period, presumably challengers would be less disadvantaged.) To cut a complicated story short, and pending further legal developments, it appears that neither Proposition 68 nor parts of 73 will apply in the 1990s. How about that for writing law through the initiative process?

Reforms

At the end of 1990, California had little more campaign regulation on the books than the public disclosure of donations and expenditures mandated in the Political Reform Act of 1974. There is a very weak public financing provision—hardly worthy of the name really—dating from 1982, which allows taxpayers to add contributions to their political party at the time they file their state income tax return. Since practically no money is raised in this manner, this cannot be considered a meaningful public financing program.

In the wake of the wreckage of Propositions 68 and 73, it is worthwhile to consider the suggestions of Robert Monagan in the area of campaign reform. Having been in the California Assembly for 12 years and having served as its Speaker (1969–1970), Monagan understands the practicalities of running for office every 2 years. Although he is not a supporter of contribution limits or public financing, his ideas would help lessen the advantage that incumbents possess through building massive warchests during their years in office. First, no fundraising whatsoever would be allowed until after an individual has filed papers of candidacy. This would eliminate nonelection-year fundraising. Second, contributions could not be transferred to any other candidate. This would reduce the role of legislative leaders in making huge transfusions of money into closely contested races. Third, funds raised for a given election would be spent on that election—any surplus in a campaign account 30 days after an election would be sent to the general fund of the State of California. Fourth, violation of the above rules would lead to forfeiture of office (Monagan, 1990:144). Although it might be argued that these suggestions do not go far enough, they are direct and workable ideas that would not be costly or difficult to implement.

Summary

There are 13 million registered voters in California, yet it is the actions of a handful of individuals that are crucial to electoral outcomes. Professional petition circulators frequently determine which propositions qualify for the ballot. Pollsters and key business leaders are instrumental to a candidate's ability to raise the vast sums of money that are now spent on campaigns. Wielding the technology of targeted persuasion and mass communications, consultants have centralized the direction of campaigns as never before. Failing the enactment of reforms, incumbents will continue to amass large warchests to discourage challengers in upcoming elections.

References: Chapter 6

California Fair Political Practices Commission. "Campaign Spending Records Set." Sacramento: State of California (March 30, 1989). Release 89-07.

California Secretary of State. *A History of the California Initiative Process.* Sacramento: State of California (December 1988).

DiCamillo, Mark. "The Rise of Absentee Voting in California." San Francisco: The Field Institute (September 29, 1989).

Field, Mervin. "Falling Turnout—A Nonvoting Majority." *Public Affairs Report.* Berkeley: Institute of Governmental Studies (March 1990).

Field, Mervin and Mark DiCamillo. "A Digest on California's Political Demography." San Francisco: California Opinion Index of the Field Institute (August 1990).

Garcia, Philip. "In Proposition 103 Fight, Lawyers Win." *Sacramento Bee* (June 3, 1990).

Kaplan, Marty. "28 Propositions and $57 Million." *Sacramento Bee* (November 14, 1990).

Kushman, Rick. "Candidates Today Trust Polls." *Sacramento Bee* (April 1, 1990a).

Kushman, Rick. "Dueling Initiatives Spell Big Headache for Voters." *Sacramento Bee* (September 24, 1990b).

Lee, Eugene. "Hiram Johnson's Great Reform Is an Idea Whose Time Has Passed." *Public Affairs Report*. Berkeley: Institute of Governmental Studies (July 1990).

Matthews, Jon. "Experts Fear Complex Ballot May Discourage State's Voters." *Sacramento Bee* (September 9, 1990).

Monagan, Robert. *The Disappearance of Representative Government: A California Solution*. Grass Valley: Comstock Bonanza Press, 1990.

Smith, Martin. "GOP Gains Asian Support." *Sacramento Bee* (October 31, 1989).

Ulrich, Roy. "Proposition 13: Taxing Courts, Rolling Back Logic." *Sacramento Bee* (March 30, 1990).

CHAPTER 7

The California Legislature

The California Legislature is an institution in transition, if not decline. The 1980s opened with a major leadership battle in the California Assembly and a protracted fight over redistricting. The decade closed with another leadership donnybrook in the Assembly, budgets passed long after the constitutional deadline, and the commencement of corruption prosecutions. The legislature was criticized for being more concerned with raising campaign funds than with making public policy. In the past 10 years, seven separate initiatives qualified for the ballot that dealt with changes in legislative operations. Four of these measures (Propositions 14, 39, 118, and 119) concerned removing the redistricting process from the legislature; all of these proposals were defeated at the polls. Another measure (Proposition 24) changed the powers of leadership in the legislature. This proposal was accepted by the voters, but was invalidated by the courts on the grounds that the state constitution entitles the legislature to adopt its own rules of internal operation. Finally, two term-limit measures (Propositions 131 and 140) were placed on the ballot in November 1990. Of these two items, Proposition 140 was approved (52% yes) by the voters in California.

As the majority party in both houses of the California Legislature throughout this period, the legislative leadership of the Democratic Party endeavored to defeat the above seven initiatives. Having succeeded in blocking the first six of these measures, it is ironic that the one item now in effect (Proposition 140) is the most damaging of the entire set of initiatives. Unless Proposition 140 is successfully challenged in court, the term limits and staff reductions mandated by this measure will lead to significant changes in the California Legislature.

Legislative Districts

California has had a bicameral or two-chamber legislature throughout its statehood. The 80 members of the state assembly (lower house) are elected to 2-year terms. A ballot measure to extend terms in the assembly to 4 years was defeated by the voters in 1960. The 40 members of the state senate (upper house) serve a 4-year term with half of the senate districts conducting elections every 2 years. Besides the 120 legislative districts represented in Sacramento, California will have 52 congressional districts (2-year terms) in the U.S. House of Representatives in Washington, D.C., during the 1990s. (California's two U.S. Senators run statewide, not from smaller districts within the state.) After the U.S. Census Bureau completes its work each decade, the California Legislature redraws the lines of the state assembly, state senate, and congressional districts. To comply with the U.S. Supreme Court's *Reynolds* v. *Sims* (1964) ruling that legislative districts must approximate each other in size (i.e., one person, one vote) and to take into consideration population shifts during the past 10 years, the state legislature must enact redistricting maps every 10 years for all three types of districts. The California Legislature must draw four seats for the Board of Equalization as well.

By a process known as *gerrymandering*, the majority party in a state legislature sometimes draws district lines to maximize its own strength and to minimize that of the minority party. This entails placing high numbers of minority party registrants in the same district in order that the majority party will have a better chance to win the surrounding districts. In the wake of the 1970 census, the Democratic majority in the legislature drew new districts that Governor Ronald Reagan viewed as unfair to his fellow Republicans. Reagan vetoed the maps. Due to the deadlock between the legislature and the governor, then under the control of different parties, the judicial branch had to accomplish redistricting.

The Democratic majority in the state legislature after the 1980 census pushed through new districts in 1981 without benefit of adequate public hearings and, in some cases, without presenting maps of the new districts until after votes had been taken. With Democrat Jerry Brown in the governorship instead of a Republican, the redistricting bills of 1981 were signed into law. The Republicans fought back by qualifying all three sets of district lines for referenda votes (Propositions 10 –12) on the June ballot in 1982. The electorate rejected the 1981 maps enacted by the legislature in all three instances, thereby necessitating the drawing of new lines. Hoping to avoid further flagrant gerrymandering, the Republicans and California Common Cause qualified Proposition 14 for the November ballot in 1982 to create a redistricting commission to assume the legislature's power to redraw district lines. When Proposition 14 unexpectedly lost (45% in favor; 55% against), the Democrats hurriedly passed new districts lines in December 1982 so that Democrat Jerry Brown could sign them into law before Republican George Deukmejian was sworn into office.

Why not put the 1982 district lines before the voters as referenda as well? With the help of some Republican legislators who were given safe seats, the maps of late 1982 for the two houses of the state legislature were passed as urgency measures (two-thirds vote required) to block another referenda effort. (The California Constitution does not permit popular votes on urgency measures.) With referenda no longer possible, Assemblymember Don Sebastiani (R, Sonoma) qualified an initiative containing new legislative boundary lines that were more favorable to the GOP. The Sebastiani lines could not be used in the legislative elections of 1984, however, unless they could be approved by the voters sometime in 1983 at a specially called election. Democrats in the legislature tried everything (including delaying the state budget for over 1 month) to discourage Governor Deukmejian from calling a special election. In July 1983, the Republican chief executive scheduled a popular vote on the Sebastiani initiative.

In a last-ditch attempt to save their preferential lines, the Democrats turned to the California Supreme Court, which ruled in September 1983 that the Sebastiani initiative could not be presented to the electorate. The state's highest court reasoned that redistricting is supposed to take place only once each decade, and that frequent changing of legislative district lines causes electoral chaos. Hoping to reverse the outcome of Proposition 14 in 1982, Governor Deukmejian helped qualify Proposition 39 in 1984. This measure would have created a redistricting commission of retired appellate judges, but it too was rejected by the voters.

Fearful that unfair district lines would again be enacted after the 1990 census, Republicans supported two initiatives on the primary ballot in June of that year. Proposition 118 would have required a two-thirds legislative vote (not a simple majority) to enact redistricting maps. Proposition 119 would have established a 12-member redistricting commission. Neither initiative passed. The Republican Party then obtained the best possible insurance against a Democratic Party gerrymander by winning the governorship with Pete Wilson in November 1990. Governor Wilson, like Governor Reagan before, has the power to veto redistricting maps prepared by Democrats in the Legislature. Acknowledging that the redistricting process in 1981 and 1982 was flawed, particularly as to the maps for the districts in the U.S. House from California, Democrats promised that the 1991 map making would involve public hearings held throughout the state.

Two sorts of decisions determine how redistricting will be conducted. First, what body will be responsible for drawing lines? Should it be the legislature, a commission, the courts, or the electorate through the initiative process? Second, what types of guidelines or criteria will govern the work of the decision-making body? There are some guidelines currently required by law. For instance, districts must be contiguous and numbered from north to south, districts must contain equal population, and districts must meet the requirements of the U.S. Voting Rights Act

Figure 7-1 Political Poker. (Dennis Renault, *Sacramento Bee*)

of 1965. This federal enactment (as amended in 1982) prohibits the drawing of district lines in such a manner as to diminish minority voting rights. Though not yet required by law, map makers also could be asked to respect terrain features and communities of interest, instructed to draw compact districts, and required to place two state assembly seats perfectly inside one state senate district—a process known as *nesting* (see Cain, 1984:32–77). Adding criteria such as these reduces the artistic freedom of map makers to gerrymander for partisan advantage.

Legislative Functions

Legislators have several responsibilities besides their function of enacting laws. Deliberating on the nearly 7,000 bills introduced in each 2-year session is work enough, but assembly and senate members must attend to other business as well. These additional duties are not altogether separate from making laws because ideas obtained in the course of nonlegislative work can easily be incorporated into legislation. Describing the various responsibilities of legislators is intended to provide a well-rounded picture of their activities, and it is also meant to show why they are not able to devote more time to considering legislative proposals.

Lawmaking

Each member of the assembly and of the senate may introduce bills, resolutions, and constitutional amendments. By introducing a measure, a legislator becomes known as its "author." Unfortunately, this terminology gives quite a misleading impression of the actual work done by elected members. Legislators themselves seldom undertake serious writing. What they do, in fact, is discuss with their staffs the desirability of introducing legislation on certain topics. After consultation with legislators' offices, the detailed drafting of legislative measures is accomplished by the Office of Legislative Counsel—literally the legislature's own law firm. Legislators themselves are far from the only source of ideas for new legislation. With only 120 individuals in California possessing the power to introduce legislative measures, numerous lobbyists, state executives, private citizens, and legislative staffers contact legislators with ideas for new laws. While putting a legislator's name on a bill allows it to be introduced as a piece of legislative business, a member's signature does not indicate how much (if at all) an officeholder will actually work for a measure's passage. Legislators sometimes introduce a measure as a courtesy, and they have no intention of expending effort on its behalf. In short, "authoring" really means "introducing."

Some legislators agree to introduce nearly 100 bills during a 2-year session, whereas other members may "author" only 10 or so. The volume of measures introduced by a member is not a valid indicator of legislative competence for several reasons. First, bills differ greatly in terms of the degree of difficulty associated with their passage. A comprehensive, pathbreaking piece of legislation entails far more work than several technical bills to correct minor flaws in existing statutes. Second, if the objective is to record a high number of introductions, it is a simple matter for a legislator's office to levy numerous bill requests on the Office of Legislative Counsel. This office dutifully will draft whatever members have requested, so high introduction levels do not necessarily reflect a great deal of effort on the part of a member. Third, the real test of an effective lawmaker is whether a legislator is capable of "working" or "carrying" a measure through *all* phases of the legislative process, not whether he or she authored a large number of bills. Some legislators inflate their bill introduction totals to appear competent to casual observers of state politics. However, serious students of the California Legislature, such as lobbyists and members of the press corps, know which officeholders are capable of pushing major legislation through and which are not.

Once the decision to introduce a proposal has been made by a legislator, the proper vehicle must be selected. If changes in the state's body of statutory law (known as the California Code) are desired, assembly bills

(ABs) or senate bills (SBs) may be introduced. Constitutional amendments originating in the legislature, not to be confused with initiative constitutional amendments, may be introduced in the assembly (ACAs) or in the senate (SCAs). Resolutions may be introduced in either chamber to make the views of the California Legislature known to the U.S. Government, to establish rules and committees within the state legislature, and to express the sentiments of legislators (as in condolences and congratulations).

Appropriations

Since the annual budget is taken up as a bill, it could have been discussed in the foregoing section on lawmaking. However, passage of the budget is such an important and distinctive legislative responsibility that it deserves separate treatment. The budget is a massive document that is written in the executive branch. The governor transmits a revenue and spending plan to the legislature each year on or before January 10th. The state constitution (Article IV, Section 12) instructs the governor to suggest new taxes whenever a proposed budget has higher expenditures than revenues. The legislature must pass a balanced or surplus budget; it may not approve a deficit budget. Like the extraordinary majorities needed for constitutional amendments, for urgency measures, and for overrides of gubernatorial vetoes, passage of the state budget and other appropriations bills requires a two-thirds vote in both chambers of the state legislature. The budget must be sent back to the governor by June 15th, so the legislature has slightly more than 5 months to review billions of dollars of state expenditures. The June 15th deadline frequently has been missed by the legislature in recent years. (For an expanded discussion of budgetary politics, see Chapter 9.)

Confirmations

Members of the California Senate have the responsibility of approving or rejecting, by simple majority vote, hundreds of gubernatorial appointments. Persons named to head the cabinet agencies, as well as the department directors beneath them, must be confirmed by the senate. In addition, gubernatorial appointments to such bodies as the Public Utilities Commission, the Water Resources Control Board, the Air Resources Board, and the Agricultural Labor Relations Board are subject to senatorial confirmation. First, the five-member Senate Rules Committee studies appointees' backgrounds, hears testimony on the fitness of nominees, and recommends approval or disapproval of job candidates to the full membership of the upper house. Second, at least 21 votes on the senate floor are needed to confirm an appointment. Governor George Deukmejian was unable to win confirmation for his original appointees to direct the Departments of Finance, Industrial Relations, and Parks and Recreation. After hard-fought battles, he did secure confirmation for controversial appointees to direct the Department of Motor Vehicles and to serve as special counsel to the Agricultural Labor Relations Board. (As discussed in Chapter 2, the assembly joins the senate in evaluating nominees to vacant statewide, elected posts.)

There are important exceptions that do not require senate confirmation. For instance, the governor's personal staff (i.e., chief-of-staff, press secretary, legislative liaison, appointments secretary, scheduling personnel, and legal affairs secretary) need not be confirmed by the senate. Likewise, the California Senate does not approve or block judicial appointments by the governor. Appellate court appointments are confirmed by the Commission on Judicial Appointments, and trial court nominations are reviewed only by the electorate.

Constituent Relations

Legislators and their staffers allot a substantial portion of their time to cultivating positive impressions among voters. When a district resident notifies his or her legislator of a problem with the state bureaucracy, the member's office endeavors to resolve the dilemma by contacting the relevant executive agency and then communicating with the citizen. This process is known as *constituent casework*. Beyond providing this service, legislators go to great lengths to project a competent image in their districts. They conduct polls of their constituents' attitudes, respond to letters requesting their positions on pending legislation, and write congratulatory notes to district residents who have recently won awards or celebrated anniversaries—all at taxpayers' expense. They prepare press releases (perhaps on bills they have introduced) and write letters to editors of local newspapers in hopes of obtaining free media. Legislators frequently spend Fridays and weekends in their districts meeting with specific groups, holding townhall meetings open to the public, and receiving constituents in their district offices. These image-building activities improve legislators' reelection chances, and they also compensate for any unpopular votes members may have cast in Sacramento.

Oversight

Members of the legislature oversee or monitor the manner in which the executive branch carries out statutes passed during earlier sessions. If the legislative intent behind a certain program is not being met due to faulty implementation, lawmakers can investigate the situation and urge corrective action. If simple publicity is insufficient to bring about the desired change in the executive branch, more drastic steps may be taken. The legislature may delete from the budget the salaries of recalcitrant directors of departments. Budget control language requiring that specified actions be taken may be attached to an agency's appropriation. The state constitution grants the assembly the power to vote articles of impeachment on statewide executives, as well as on members of the state judiciary. Impeached officials are tried in the state senate where a two-thirds vote is needed for conviction and removal. Careful monitoring of executive agencies consumes a great deal of member and staff time, and it is not clear from the outset that such effort will yield a legislator publicity that is commensurate with the work involved. In short, it is easier to appear competent by introducing bills and handling constituent problems than it is by engaging in oversight of the bureaucracy.

The Legislative Process

After a measure has been introduced by its author in either the assembly or the senate, it is numbered and referred to a committee. To allow members of the public and the press to become informed about a specific proposal, no committee action may take place until a bill has been in print for 30 days. Committee hearings permit interested individuals, lobbyists for organizations in the private sector, and legislative liaison from state executive departments and local governments to give their views concerning a particular bill. The members of the committee may recommend approval of a bill and send it to the chamber floor without alteration, may recommend modifications to a bill and recommend that it be passed on the floor as amended, or allow a bill to die in committee. The great majority of items that fail to be enacted into law are killed in committee.

After having been sent to the floor, a measure is debated by the membership of the chamber. Amendments to a bill may be made by the legislators prior to the vote on the issue. Approval of legislative business ordinarily requires a simple majority of the full membership of each chamber (41 in the assembly and 21 in the senate). There are, however, several instances in which an extraordinary majority is needed for passage. To repeat, legislative amendments to the state constitution, appropriations bills and the annual budget, urgency measures to take effect immediately on passage, votes to override a gubernatorial veto, and—in the case of the senate—votes to convict an impeached official, all require a two-thirds vote (54 in the assembly and 27 in the senate). The most significant area needing two-thirds approval is monetary bills. Since one party seldom controls 67% of the legislative seats in a chamber, the effect of the two-thirds requirement on budgetary matters is to necessitate bipartisan support for financial outlays.

Given the bicameral structure of the legislature, bills must pass both chambers in identical form before being sent to the governor for acceptance or veto. As soon as a bill has passed one chamber, it is immediately sent to the other house for its committee review and floor action. Because bills may be amended both in committee and on the floor, it is likely that a bill passing the second-to-act chamber will contain different language than the bill that passed the chamber of origin. To resolve differences in wording, the first-to-act chamber may simply concur in the changes made by the other house, in which case both chambers will have passed identical bills. Failing concurrence, a conference committee consisting of three senators and three members of the assembly is established to recommend common wording for the bill. The report of the conference committee is sent to the floor of each chamber where it must be accepted in its entirety to be adopted. If either chamber refuses to accept the conference committee report, a new conference committee is selected and another report with compromise language is prepared. Three conference committees—meeting one at a time, not simultaneously—may be attempted on a single bill. If the report of the third conference committee is not accepted by both chambers, the bill dies.

The above account of the legislative process suggests an orderliness that often is not evident in actuality. Political compromises may not have been achieved at the point when a measure is introduced. To reserve a number and to have a bill begin meeting the deadlines contained in the legislative calendar, members sometimes introduce legislation that they know is not likely to be passed as initially drafted. Whereas a noncontroversial item might follow the formal steps in the legislative process to the letter, ideas that generate considerable debate may be negotiated behind closed doors outside the public scrutiny of a committee hearing or a floor session. In legislative parlance, this informal approach is known as negotiating a moving target. After an agreement is struck in private, the resulting compromise is amended into a measure (known as a vehicle) that is at an advanced stage in the legislative process. The integrated waste management legislation of 1989 and the oil spill response bill of 1990 were both negotiated behind the scenes and then rammed through the legislative process in great haste.

The method of cutting deals in private and then manipulating the formal legislative process to enact the informal agreement has several drawbacks. If the contents of a bill are completely replaced during floor consideration, or if a bill containing a deal is rushed through three committees in one day, committee review essentially is circumvented. Given the staff analyses prepared on all bills heard in committee, and given the opportunity for public input at committee hearings, bypassing committees should not be taken lightly. Private negotiating sessions do not involve coverage by the press corps and may not involve all persons with an interest in an issue. On the other hand, defenders of informal negotiations contend that following formal legislative procedures closely may produce weak legislation or none at all. If every lobbyist has the chance in committee to water a bill down with amendments, the resulting legislation may be little improvement over existing law. Likewise, why follow the formal legislative process carefully only to have the governor veto the enactment? If representatives of a governor have not been active on a given bill during committee review, it may be necessary to meet privately with individuals in the executive branch to find out what the chief executive must have in the measure to guarantee a signature on it. No doubt informal negotiations have produced accomplishments, but at what price? When a major legislative package is hastily adopted in the waning hours of a session, a close reading of such a compromise after the legislature has adjourned may reveal surprises for legislators and lobbyists who were not invited to the private negotiations.

Powers of Leadership _____

Given the nearly 7,000 bills, two annual budgets, and assorted confirmations to be dealt with in a typical 2-year session, decisions must be made concerning which members will have primary responsibility for what measures and how business will be routed through the legislative labyrinth. Organizational decisions by those in power in the assembly and in the senate have a great bearing on the outcome of legislation. In discussing legislative leadership, it is important to distinguish between positions with real power and those offices that are more ceremonial than influential.

Speaker

The speaker of the assembly is extraordinarily powerful because the occupant of this post makes pivotal decisions at every point in the legislative process.

- The speaker determines the number and the titles of standing committees, special committees, and subcommittees.
- The speaker establishes the schedule for committee meetings.
- The speaker appoints (and removes) members of the assembly to standing committees, special committees, and subcommittees, *excluding* the Assembly Rules Committee.

- The speaker appoints (and removes) chairs and vice chairs of all assembly committees, *including* the Assembly Rules Committee.
- The speaker provides guidelines to the Assembly Rules Committee regarding the referral of bills to particular committees.
- The speaker is an ex officio nonvoting member of all assembly committees.
- The speaker is presiding officer of the assembly and, as such, recognizes members during debate, renders opinions on points of order, names members to temporarily perform the duties of speaker, and clears the gallery when necessary.
- The speaker assigns members their office space in the Capitol.
- The speaker appoints the *majority floor leader* who expedites floor proceedings by making appropriate motions and points of order.
- The speaker appoints three members of the assembly to serve on conference committees in the event the senate has not accepted assembly language on certain bills.

This combination of leadership powers may be deployed to promote or to hinder the passage of bills, as well as to help or to hurt the careers of individual members. Mindful of the vast powers available to the presiding officer, members of the lower house ordinarily cooperate with the speaker. Should members of the assembly defy the speaker, they run the risk of losing their committee assignments, their office space, and their

Figure 7-2 Speaker Willie Brown, Jr. (Photograph by Adam Gottlieb.)

staff—not to mention any of their bills that are pending. Speaker Willie Brown (D, San Francisco) removed three Republican chairs of standing committees in 1986 when they broke with him by voting to hear a controversial bill that the speaker opposed. Brown also removed five fellow Democrats from committees in 1988 when they challenged his leadership.

Beyond their formal powers of office, modern speakers have assumed an informal responsibility (i.e., this task is not mentioned in legislative rules) to raise large amounts of campaign money and then dispense it to their party's candidates for assembly seats. During the 1986 legislative elections, Speaker Brown raised approximately $3.5 million to help Democrats win Assembly races. The transfer of campaign funds from one legislative candidate to another was outlawed in 1988 with the passage of a campaign reform initiative (Proposition 73). Since a portion of Proposition 73 has been invalidated in federal court, it is unclear as of this writing whether the prohibition against campaign transfers will remain in effect or not. Even if a speaker is not allowed to transfer his or her campaign funds to another person, there is nothing to prevent a leader from strongly suggesting that campaign donors give to certain candidates. When Speaker Brown was fighting the so-called Gang of Five in his own party in 1988, he actively discouraged interest groups from giving to their campaigns. Guiding money to, or away from, candidates for office is yet another weapon in the speaker's potent arsenal of powers.

Assembly Minority Leader

Whereas the speaker is elected by a majority of the entire (both parties) membership of the lower house, the minority leader is chosen by a majority of his or her own party members. To understand how many votes are needed to occupy certain leadership posts, we must digress for a moment to discuss *party caucuses*. When all the members of a given party in one chamber meet together, they constitute a party caucus. Overlooking the occasional independent legislator, there are four party caucuses in the California legislature: Assembly Democrats, Assembly Republicans, Senate Democrats, and Senate Republicans. (Besides party caucuses, there are separate caucuses of rural legislators, women legislators, and ethnic minority legislators.)

The minority leader speaks for the minority caucus on the Assembly floor. He or she also negotiates with the speaker concerning committee assignments, support staff, and office space for the members of the minority party. Although Assembly rule 26(e) clearly confers on the speaker the power to appoint all members to committees, Speaker Brown on occasion has accepted the list of GOP committee preferences prepared by the minority leader in exchange for pledges of cooperation on other issues.

Speaker Pro Tempore

The occupant of this office exercises the powers of the speakership whenever the assembly's regular presiding officer is absent. Although this post is formally filled by vote of the full assembly, it is customary for the speaker's choice for this post to be ratified by the chamber. The speaker pro tem commonly presides at the front of the Assembly chamber, so that the speaker is free to roam about the floor lining up support and negotiating with the opposition. The speaker may appoint an assistant speaker pro tempore to preside over floor sessions in the absence of the speaker pro tem.

Assembly Rules Committee

This committee operates as the executive committee of the lower house. It is responsible for hiring and firing legislative staff, recommending amendments to assembly rules and procedures, renovating assembly facilities in the Capitol, and referring bills and resolutions to committees. Prior to December 1980, the speaker had the power of bill referral, but one of the concessions Willie Brown made to the Republicans who helped elect him speaker was to shift this responsibility to the Assembly Rules Committee. Rare though it is for the speakership to lose control of anything, the presiding officer is not without means to influence bill referral. The Assembly Rules Committee is made up of nine members: four persons chosen by the minority caucus, four persons selected by the majority caucus, and a chairperson appointed by the speaker. A strong speaker (not one dealing with a divided majority caucus) should be able to control five of the nine members of the Assembly Rules Committee.

President of the Senate

The lieutenant governor of California serves as president of the senate on the basis of a provision in the state constitution. This post is largely ceremonial. The lieutenant governor may cast a vote in the senate only when it would be *decisive*—that it, in cases where there is a 20–20 tie. (Since it takes 21 votes to pass measures in the senate, the lieutenant governor's vote is not decisive in cases of ties at lower numbers.) A legislative constitutional amendment to drop the presidency of the senate as one of the lieutenant governor's constitutional duties was defeated by the electorate when it appeared as a ballot measure in June 1982. Since the upper house is saddled with a president that is not of its own choosing, senators have revised their rules to strip the post of its once formidable powers. Prior to World War II, the senate president assigned members to committees and referred bills to panels as well. In 1939 and 1940, these duties were shifted to the Senate Rules Committee.

President Pro Tempore

In the absence of the president of the senate, the president pro tempore (abbreviated to "pro tem" around the Capitol) becomes the presiding officer of the upper house. The president pro tem may name any senator to preside over meetings of the senate provided the lieutenant governor is not present. Serving as presiding officer is not the president pro tem's most significant responsibility; chairing the five-member Senate Rules Committee is. Senate rules provide for decisions on work flow and committee appointments to be made collectively by members of the Senate Rules Committee, but the 1980s have witnessed a transformation in senate leadership behavior. President pro Tem David Roberti (D, Hollywood) has taken a page from the speaker's book by raising much larger sums of campaign money than any of his predecessors. Roberti distributed $1.8 million to Democrats running for the senate in 1986. Though a lesser sum than Speaker Brown's $3.5 million in campaign help for the same year, remember that only 20 senate seats were being contested in contrast to 80 seats up for election to the assembly. Even if the prohibition against campaign fund transfers remains in effect, the pro tem will be able to help candidates win election to the senate by dispatching veteran campaign managers to their races. In addition to managing the work load of the chamber by chairing the Rules Committee, the pro tem is the leader of the majority party in the upper house and as such is expected to provide electoral assistance on a partisan basis.

Senate Minority Leader

Unlike the president pro tempore who is elected by a majority of the entire senate, the minority leader is chosen by a majority vote within the minority caucus only. Because of the power of the minority members on the Senate Rules Committee, this post is not as pivotal as its counterpart in the lower house in terms of dispensing benefits to party members. Committee assignments for senators from the minority party are overseen by the minority members on Rules Committee. However, the electoral role of the minority leader is becoming increasingly significant.

The minority leader and chair of the minority caucus are expected to assist members of the minority party in winning election to the senate. Minority leaders coordinate activities with the state's chief executive when the governorship is in the hands of their party.

Senate Rules Committee

This five-member executive committee of the upper house is composed of two senators nominated by the minority party caucus, two senators nominated by the majority party caucus, and the president pro tempore serving as chair. After nomination by the party caucus, all five members must receive 21 votes on the floor of the senate to be placed on the Rules Committee. (If a nominee fails to secure the necessary votes, the appropriate party caucus submits another name.) Because of the composition and the responsibilities of the Senate Rules Committee, leadership in the senate traditionally has been more collective and less partisan than that found in the assembly. Recent changes in the senate are making this generalization less applicable than it once was. As a review of the committee's duties demonstrates, the Senate Rules Committee undertakes what amounts to the work of both the speaker and the Assembly Rules Committee.

- Senate Rules Committee appoints (and removes) senators to standing committees, subcommittees, select committees, and conference committees.
- Senate Rules Committee designates (and removes) the chair and vice chair of each committee.
- Senate Rules Committee refers bills to committee.
- Senate Rules Committee proposes amendments to the senate rules to help expedite legislative business.
- Senate Rules Committee grants requests to waive the rules (or withholds approval of the same).
- Senate Rules Committee employs and discharges all senate staffers.
- Senate Rules Committee approves payment of studies prepared at the request of the senate and its committees.
- Senate Rules Committee assigns senators their offices and committees their hearing rooms.
- Senate Rules Committee supervises renovation of senate facilities.
- Senate Rules Committee reviews gubernatorial appointments before they are set for confirmation votes on the senate floor.

Since Senator David Roberti became president pro tem in December 1980, the power of the chair of the Senate Rules Committee has grown. The pro tem is now far more than one-fifth of the executive committee of the upper house. In addition to his electoral support role, the pro tem is the central leader in reviewing gubernatorial appointments and a key player in the policy compromises fashioned in the State Capitol.

Leadership Selection

In contests for the posts of speaker and president pro tem, the majority party caucus in each house is the key battleground. If this caucus is able to unify behind one candidate for speaker or pro tem, the choice of chamber leadership will be the majority party's alone. If the majority caucus splits into opposing camps during leadership selection, then a bipartisan coalition involving the minority party will be needed to elect a presiding officer. California moves back and forth between these two methods (selection within the majority party versus bipartisan coalition) in the election of speakers and presidents pro tem.

Assembly

At the end of each 2-year session, the speakership is automatically vacated to be filled once again when lawmakers come to the Capitol after their successful campaigns. New and returning members of the assembly gather in Sacramento in December of even-numbered years to select their speaker for the forthcoming session. It ordinarily takes a minimum of 41 of the 80 votes in the assembly to be elected speaker. Having garnered 41 votes at the start of a session is no guarantee that a speaker will remain in that post until the beginning of the next session. After Speaker Bob Moretti lost the Democratic gubernatorial primary in June 1974 to Jerry Brown, Assemblymembers Leo McCarthy (D, San Francisco) and Willie Brown (D, San Francisco) vied to replace Moretti as speaker in *mid*session. Assemblymember McCarthy prevailed (26–22) in the Democratic caucus, whereupon Assemblymember Brown released his Democratic supporters so that a united majority party could select Moretti's replacement in the vote on the assembly floor. Six months later, when the office of speaker was automatically vacated at the conclusion of the 1973–1974 session, the Republican minority in the assembly endeavored to revive the practice (common in the 1940s and 1950s) of bipartisan selection of the speaker. The GOP legislators decided in December 1974 to throw their support to Willie Brown in his second try for the speakership. Unwilling to allow minority party participation in choosing the presiding officer, assembly Democrats responded by voting as a bloc in favor of Leo McCarthy to continue as speaker. For this second attempt in 1974 to become presiding officer, Assemblymember Brown was punished by being removed as chair of the powerful Ways and Means Committee.

In both 1976 and 1978, McCarthy was returned in routine fashion to the speakership without open opposition in the majority caucus. Halfway through the 1979–1980 session, however, Assemblymember Howard Berman (D, Los Angeles) challenged McCarthy for the speakership. Perhaps thinking of the unified party votes cast after the speakership fights of 1974, Berman made a fatal assumption as he took on McCarthy. The challenger assumed that he needed to win only a majority in the Democratic caucus to gain a bloc vote by his party on the assembly floor. Despite the fact that Berman won slightly more support (26–24) than his opponent in the caucus, McCarthy did not follow the 1974 precedent by stepping aside and releasing his supporters to this opponent. When the Berman forces moved on the assembly floor in January 1980 to declare the speakership vacant, they could muster only 26 or 27 votes (far short of the necessary 41) on behalf of the motion. Even though McCarthy had lost control of his own caucus, he could not be removed without 41 votes being cast against him. By refusing to vote on motions to vacate the speakership, assembly Republicans in effect helped McCarthy stay on as speaker until after the general elections of 1980. With the speakership automatically vacated at the end of the 1979–1980 session, McCarthy realized that he would not be able to muster the 41 votes needed to remain presiding officer in the next session.

With Howard Berman on the verge of becoming speaker and with redistricting on the legislative agenda for 1981, assembly Republicans were receptive to Willie Brown's overtures concerning the formation of a bipartisan coalition to elect him speaker. In an informal agreement of two year's duration, then Minority Leader Carol Hallett (R, Atascadero) and Willie Brown agreed to the following in exchange for GOP votes for speaker:

- Republicans would be allowed to chair six standing committees.
- Republicans would become vice chairs of 19 standing committees.
- Minority Leader Hallet would list, and Brown would accept, the names of Republicans to serve on each committee.
- Equal money would be provided both major parties to prepare redistricting proposals.
- Bill referral would be shifted from the speaker to the Assembly Rules Committee.

On December 2, 1980, Assemblymember Willie Brown (D, San Francisco) was elected speaker for the 1981–1982 session with 51 votes (23 D, 28 R) to Berman's 24 votes (23 D, 1 R) with 5 abstentions (1 D, 4 R).

McCarthy's supporters went with Brown, but the new speaker actually received more votes from Republicans than he did from his own party. The bipartisan coalition was not to last for long, however. Speaker Brown carried out his promises to the Republicans regarding committee assignments and chairpersons, yet at the same time he wisely began mending fences within the majority caucus. By giving Democrats safe boundaries for their districts during the 1980s, acceptable committee assignments, additional staff assistance, and plentiful campaign money, Speaker Brown consolidated his support throughout the majority caucus.

With a solid Democratic caucus behind him, Willie Brown easily retained the speakership after elections in 1982, 1984, and 1986. During the 1987–1988 legislative session, however, the number of Democrats elected to the lower house had declined to 44. In the months prior to breaking Jesse Unruh's longevity record for service as speaker (7 years, 3 months, and 6 days), Brown lost control of a working majority in his chamber. During a fishing trip together in Mexico, Assemblymembers Steve Peace (D, Chula Vista), Gary Condit (D, Ceres), Rusty Areias (D, Los Banos), Charles Calderon (D, Whittier), and Gerry Eaves (D, Rialto) realized that by casting their five votes with the 36 Republicans on occasion, they could control the business of the Assembly. These dissident Democrats liked to refer to themselves as the Five Amigos, but most everyone else referred to them as the Gang of Five. They began to make their presence felt by voting with Republicans in committee against bills favored by most of the members of the Democratic caucus. Later, the gang voted with Republicans to bring bills to the floor that the Democratic leadership had purposely wanted to leave in committee. These were serious acts of defiance given the unwritten norms of the legislature. Although he was speaking of committee chairpersons, Jesse Unruh's words (spoken during his speakership) express the kinds of loyalty that leaders expect after giving good committee assignments to members.

> I never appoint anyone to a chairmanship who doesn't accept three conditions. The first is that they have to commit themselves to vote for me, in case anyone ever makes a move to try to dump me as speaker. The second is that they have to promise to vote against any motion to withdraw a bill from committee. If they want to be committee chairman, they have to support the committee system. The third thing they have to do is to pledge themselves to vote for the budget (Mills, 1987:108).

Members of the Democratic caucus, who were endeavoring to keep certain bills bottled up in committee, pressed Speaker Brown to discipline the dissident members of the party. Shortly after setting the longevity record for tenure as speaker in March 1988, Brown removed the members of the Gang of Five from their committee assignments. This led to loss of their staff support and subsequently to relocation into smaller office space.

Hoping to topple Willie Brown from the post of presiding officer, a motion was made on the floor in May 1988 to vacate the speakership. Before this motion could be voted on, a substitute motion was made to select then Minority Leader Pat Nolan (R, Glendale) as speaker. Steve Peace of the Gang of Five requested that separate votes be held on each motion so that he and his amigos could oust Brown without having to install a Republican as speaker. Peace's request was denied, and the motion before the chamber was whether to make Nolan the presiding officer. This motion received 36 affirmative votes—all from Republicans—five less than the votes needed to be elected speaker. Not unlike the refusal of Republicans in 1980 to join forces with Howard Berman in dumping Leo McCarthy as speaker in midsession, the Republicans in 1989 declined to join the Gang of Five in vacating the speakership. More precisely, the Assembly Republicans refused to oust Brown without winning the speakership for themselves.

With the speakership automatically vacated after the general elections in November 1988, the next hurdle for Willie Brown was securing enough votes to be elected speaker in December 1988. Fortunately for Brown, the Democrats captured two new districts in the assembly in the November election for a total of 46 seats. Even with the defection of the Gang of Five, Brown should have been assured the necessary 41 votes

Figure 7-3 The elephant man. (Dennis Renault, *Sacramento Bee*)

to be elected speaker. Then Assemblymember Lloyd Connelly (D, Sacramento) announced that he would be out of the country on the day of the speakership vote. Fortunately for Brown one member of the chamber had died, and a parliamentary ruling was made by the assembly chief clerk that 40 votes out of 79 members would be sufficient to become speaker. Forty votes is precisely the number Brown received to continue his record-breaking tenure as speaker into the 1989–1990 session.

After nearly toppling Speaker Brown in 1988, the Gang of Five was dismantled in the next legislative session. Gary Condit was elected to the U.S. House of Representatives on the resignation of Tony Coelho (D, Modesto), and Charles Calderon moved to the California Senate after the conviction of Joseph Montoya (D, El Monte). The rehabilitation of the former gang members was so complete by December 1990 that Speaker Brown appointed Steve Peace to chair the Committee on Banking and Rusty Areias to chair the Committee on Agriculture. Do you suppose Peace and Areias accepted the three conditions once set forth by Jesse Unruh?

Apart from his ability to retain his post, Willie Brown has been faulted for lacking interest in policy formation. Sherry Bebitch Jeffe, initially at USC and later with Claremont Graduate School, has distinguished what she calls the administrative speaker from the programmatic speaker (Jeffe, 1987:244). The former is known for providing the perquisites (perks) of office such as nice furnishings, plentiful staff, and ample travel funding. The latter is known for crafting policy and solving public problems. Compared to his predecessors, such as Jesse Unruh and Leo McCarthy, Speaker Brown has not generated many policy accomplishments. Brown was quoted in the *Sacramento Bee* in a manner that strongly suggests he accepts being characterized as an administrative speaker.

> I'm proudest of having made the job of being an Assemblyperson more comfortable for the membership—whether it was a health insurance policy that all the guys who have had (heart) bypasses are grateful to me for, whether it was the increase in salaries or the cost of transportation four times a month for the members between here and their districts. All of those things have made it financially and physically more comfortable and convenient for people to serve (Chance, 1988).

On the other hand, Speaker Brown periodically promises, "I'm going to devote more time to policy—period" (Smith, 1988). Brown did win approval of a mandatory seat belt bill and a pass-to-play measure requiring high school athletes to earn a "C" average in order to play sports. Though he claimed he would establish a program of affordable auto insurance for Californians, Brown has been unable to secure such an enactment. Columnist Dan Walters doubts Speaker Brown's desire to tangle with major campaign contributors. "None of the legislative accomplishments that Brown himself cites overcame serious opposition from moneyed special interests" (Walters, 1988).

Senate

In contrast to the more partisan lower house, the senate traditionally was known for its bipartisanship. The representation of both major parties on the powerful Senate Rules Committee contributed to this style. Also, the senate was regarded as a club where a live-and-let-live norm prevailed. Senators observed the bipartisan character of the upper house by not helping challengers try to unseat incumbent senators of the opposition party. The 10-year service of Senator James Mills (D, San Diego) as president pro tem well reflected the senate style of muted partisanship.

The 1980 general election results toppled Mills and produced a far more partisan president pro tem. Destroying what was once the senate norm, then Senator H. L. (Bill) Richardson (R, Arcadia) provided financial support to Republican John Doolittle in his upset victory over incumbent Senator Al Rodda (D, Sacramento). If the widely respected Rodda could be voted out of office, senate Democrats realized that they too were vulnerable to electoral defeat by well-funded Republicans. Unlike the 1-year-long battle for the assembly speakership in 1980, Senator David Roberti's rise to power was swift and sure. In the wake of Senator Rodda's unexpected defeat, Senator Roberti promised fellow members of the Democratic caucus that he would actively defend their seats if named president pro tem. He obtained such strong support within the majority caucus that Senator Mills stepped down without a protracted fight, and Roberti was elected president pro tem on December 1, 1980.

Senate Democrats have become accustomed to having a leader who is their protector come election time, but there is always the possibility that a bipartisan coalition could remove Senator Roberti as pro tem. At regular intervals, columnists speculate that Senator Robert Presley (D, Riverside) and his faction of conservative Democrats might join with Republican senators to end Robert's leadership. To counteract such a move, Senator Roberti took several steps in 1985 and 1986. The old Senate Finance Committee was broken in two, creating a new Budget and Fiscal Review committtee and a new Appropriations Committee. This allowed greater numbers of senators to be appointed to committees working on fiscal matters—a goal cherished by most members. It also permitted senator Roberti (through the Senate Rules Committee) to name a conservative Democrat to chair the newly created Appropriations Committee. Through adroit use of committee appointments and

Figure 7-4 President pro Tempore David Roberti. (Photograph by Adam Gottlieb.)

tenacious defense of incumbent Democratic seats, Senator Roberti has succeeded in holding 21 votes together inside the majority caucus to retain his post as pro tem. Should some Democrats try to form a leadership coalition with the GOP, Roberti can also cross party lines in search of the crucial twenty-first vote.

The two legislative chambers differ in several ways. The assembly is more high-tech as it has instituted electronic voting and television coverage of its proceedings, whereas the senate conducts roll-call votes and has been slow to televise its sessions. Although the advent of term limits (Proposition 140 in November 1990) may alter this, members of the lower house customarily have been more ambitious to move on to other offices than has been the case with senators. The upper house has the important constitutional power to confirm gubernatorial appointments that the assembly lacks. The Republicans in the assembly are known to have a far more tight-knit caucus than is the case with the Senate Republicans. Most importantly, though, the chambers differ in matters of leadership.

Traditionally, political history in California has focused on the interaction between the governor and the speaker. During the 1980s, this bilateral relationship has evolved into a truly trilateral one as the pro tem has grown in power. While Speaker Brown was contending with the Gang of Five in 1988, President pro Tem Roberti was instrumental in blocking the nomination of Representative Dan Lungren (R, Long

Beach) to become state treasurer. Roberti also was the key figure in resisting a change in the date of the state's presidential primary from June to March. (Though the California Senate ultimately may adopt such a date change, Roberti wanted to take the time to be sure that changing the presidential primary would not have an adverse impact on state legislative elections. Whatever the outcome of the issue, it demonstrated Roberti's power to single-handedly delay something that had widespread support among officeholders and the public.) No doubt hoping to control the damage from the Montoya and Carpenter convictions, the senate leadership pushed the adoption of a constitutional amendment (SCA 32) to restrict honoraria and outside income (later passed by the voters as Proposition 112). The major bond act relating to transportation funding (later passed as Proposition 111) and the outlines of the 1990 budget compromise both originated in the upper house. The fact that Senator Roberti received little criticism in the wake of the corruption trials indicated what a secure pro tem he was at the outset of the new decade.

Legislative Staff

Under the leadership of Jesse Unruh, Speaker of the Assembly from 1961 to 1968, the California Legislature entered the modern era. Sessions were lengthened to conduct more business. Legislative salaries were improved to decrease the need for additional gainful employment by legislators. Committee rooms and personal offices for members were constructed so that there would be ample locations for meetings to take place. Most importantly, legislative staffing was expanded in the hope of reducing reliance on the executive bureaucracy and interest groups for information needed during the lawmaking process. The intent behind these changes was to make the California Legislature as self-sufficient and as independent as possible and to increase its capacity to respond to public issues.

Since the late 1960s, widespread use of support staff has been one of the most noteworthy attributes of the California Legislature. Staff is provided for all manner of tasks. Personal staff (both in the Capitol and in the district) helps members with constituent relations and with legislative proposals. Committee consultants analyze bills prior to public hearings. Party caucus staffs do research on the opposition party, write speeches, and study voting trends. Each chamber has a floor staff to record roll-call votes, prepare legislative publications, and give parliamentary advice. Party leaders hire specialists in various policy areas to help them with the legislative agenda. When not responding to some immediate crisis, the Senate Office of Research and the Assembly Office of Research conduct long-range studies of California's future.

All of the above staff works for a portion, but not all, of the members of the legislature. Only a trinity of offices serves the entire membership of the legislative branch. First, as discussed earlier, the *legislative counsel* (created in 1913) drafts actual bills and amendments for all 120 members of both chambers. This office also prepares opinions on the constitutionality of various proposals. Should the legislature become involved in a court case, the legislative counsel (or outside attorneys retained by this office) handles the legal work in the judicial proceeding. The legislative counsel also helps in drafting language for initiatives if so requested by 25 citizens, but few backers of propositions take advantage of this service. Attorneys working in the office of legislative counsel are expected to be absolutely impartial and never to become involved in supporting or opposing pending legislation. Second, the *legislative analyst* (established in 1941) prepares a critique of the annual budget submitted to the legislature by the governor. This office is also expected to be impartial and to conduct a thorough examination of the budget regardless of the party affiliation of the governor or the partisan complexion of the legislature. In addition to work on the budget, the legislative analyst determines the fiscal impact of other legislative proposals and ballot measures. Third, the *auditor general* (founded in 1955) conducts both fiscal and management audits on behalf of the legislature. This office determines if state funds are being spent as authorized and if state agencies are being efficiently and effectively managed. All audits are public information after they have been submitted to the legislature.

Because of the loss of legislative overhead funds mandated by Proposition 140, some of the staffing that the legislature has become accustomed to will fall under the knife. Even with early retirements and the possible shifting of some legislative support functions into the budget of the executive branch, significant cuts in legislative staff will occur. It is still too early to tell which sorts of staff will be retained and which let go.

Term Limits

The California electorate approved Proposition 140 by a 52–48% margin in November 1990. The initiative limits Assemblymembers to three 2-year terms in office. After completing 6 years of service in the lower house, individuals are prohibited from ever running for the Assembly again. Former Assemblymembers are allowed to run for other offices. Members of the California Senate are allowed to serve two 4-year terms in the upper house, after which they may contest some other office if they like. Persons holding statewide executive posts are also limited to two 4-year terms. In addition, Proposition 140 abolished the legislative pension that members had been receiving; and the initiative reduced the annual overhead budget for the legislature from $176 million to $114 million (calculated at $950,000 per year per member).

There are a number of arguments on both sides of the term limits question. Those opposed to Proposition 140 make the following points:

- Term limits are indiscriminate. They remove exemplary public officials as well as the lesser lights.
- Term limits are undemocratic because they restrict voters' freedom of choice. Periodic elections provide adequate limits for curtailing the service of officeholders.
- Term limits reduce the power of legislators in comparison with other players in state politics. "Inexperienced legislators are less powerful in relation to legislative staff, executive branch bureaucrats, and interest group lobbyists" (Polsby, 1990). Not only are inexperienced legislators dependent on others to learn the ropes around the State Capitol, the role of money will be as crucial as ever. "Veteran members, proven vote getters, are much more powerful in relation to special interests than candidates who have to prove themselves in an uncertain and expensive campaign environment" (Polsby, 1990). Moreover, "legislators will find it difficult to cut ties to outside interests, since with term limits, each legislator would have to plan for his or her imminent return to the private sector" (Simmons, 1990).
- Term limits are likely to make the California Legislature less representative and less diverse than it already is.

> Who will run for these limited offices? Most likely wealthy professionals, who can afford to take time from the midst of their careers, retirees, and eccentric individuals who crave public recognition. Clearly, working people with families cannot afford to temporarily abandon their careers in midstream. Minorities and women would likely be shut out of these offices just as they are beginning to achieve representation (Simmons, 1990).

- Proponents of term limits fail to acknowledge that there presently is considerable turnover in the state legislature. As of 1990, "61 of 117 members (had) served for 10 years or less" (Matthews, 1990).

Those in favor of the limits imposed by Proposition 140 counter with the following arguments:

- Term limits increase competition for office. Entrenched incumbents ordinarily have a major advantage in raising campaign funds, and they are very difficult to oust from office.
- The 22d Amendment to the *U.S. Constitution* limits the President to two elected terms and over half the governors are limited in the number of terms they may serve.
- Term limits are not a new idea. Pennsylvania had term limits for its officials even before the constitutional convention in Philadelphia in 1787. For the first century of our nation's history, officeholders voluntarily stepped down so that a greater number of people could serve their country.
- "Indeed, the framers (of the constitution) would be distressed to discover that permanent legislatures have become a prominent feature of American politics in the late 20th century" (Petracca, 1990).
- There is no evidence that experienced, professional legislators are superior to amateur, citizen legislators. Incumbents with lengthy tenure in office tend to lose touch with their constituents. New blood and fresh thinking are needed in government.
- Contrary to the argument made by opponents of Proposition 140, "term limits will sever the stranglehold special interests (now) have on career politicians who seek financial support to stay in office" (Petracca, 1990).

Figure 7-5   "I'm just too busy to pick or prune!"
(Dennis Renault, *Sacramento Bee*)

Whether term limits turn out to be good for California or not, Proposition 140 has had consequences on state politics. Early retirements and layoffs for legislative staff have dealt a serious blow to morale in the State Capitol. If Proposition 140 is upheld, there no longer will be lengthy tenures in leadership as achieved by Speaker Brown and President pro Tem Roberti. State legislators traditionally have been interested in moving to the U.S. Congress, and Proposition 140 has intensified that desire. As members in the State Capitol reach their limits, there very well could be bruising primary battles for seats in the U.S. House of Representatives. Because of the lack of initiatives at the national level, the imposition of term limits on the U.S. Congress is not probable in the near future. Amendments to the *U.S. Constitution* originate through two-thirds votes of both houses of the Congress; it hardly seems likely that members would vote limits on themselves.

Other Reforms

When ethics standards were passed by the voters in June 1990 as Proposition 112 (see Chapter 3), the electorate also approved the creation of the California Citizens Compensation Commission. After a period of study and deliberation, this commission raised the annual salary of legislators from $40,816 to $52,500. Having given up income from honoraria as a result of Proposition 112, some legislators experienced a loss of total income as a result of the reforms. For some years, legislators have voiced support for the idea that they should be paid the same amount as superior court judges—some $96,000 per year. In addition to their salaries, legislators receive a leased automobile, a gasoline credit card, a telephone credit card, and per diem for lodging and food of $92 for each day the legislature is in session.

Since the Legislative Reform Act of 1984 (Proposition 24) was invalidated by the courts, there has been discussion of granting the Assembly Rules Committee the same powers as those currently held by the Senate Rules Committee—together with the speaker becoming the chair of this panel. During 1988, the Gang of Five held press conferences advancing this proposal. Another idea that is voiced from time to time is to increase the size of the legislature. The senate could equal the size of the California delegation in the U.S. House of Representatives (currently 52) and the assembly could be double that number (104). Additional seats might increase diversity in the legislature and decrease the cost of campaigning a small amount. Former Speaker Robert Monagan believes that the legislature should be able to conclude its work each year by July 1st so that members may return to their districts for extended periods (Monagan, 1990:132). With term limits, the end of honoraria, the loss of staff, and the possibility of still more alterations, the California Legislature is a changed place.

Summary

The modernized California Legislature did not achieve the independence that was envisioned for it. There are a number of reasons for this. First, the reforms of the 1960s focused more on informational independence than on electoral independence. With the creature comforts of the legislature enhanced, members worked harder to be reelected to the institution. Without public financing of campaigns, leaders of the party caucuses in the legislature spent increasing amounts of time raising money for reelection purposes—time that was not spent addressing the problems facing California. By raising vast sums from interest groups with business before the legislature, the independence of public decision makers was compromised.

Second, the degree to which the legislature could become independent of other sources of information was overestimated. Even as the legislature was increasing the size of its staff, there never was a realistic chance that the legislature could be uncoupled from the lobbying corps and the state bureaucracy in terms of obtaining accurate information quickly. Unlike the leisurely pace of academic research, political research has to be completed by deadlines. Legislative staffers naturally turned to the knowledgeable people who were nearby. Third, changes in technology enabled interest groups to pressure legislators as never before in history. With computerized bill-tracking services available to any group willing to pay a fee, it became very difficult for any legislator to hide a vote that was adverse to some interest. Having detected a negative vote, new computerized mailing techniques allowed groups to bring the hot breath of angry correspondence down on lawmakers. Rather than feeling independent, legislators were in a fish bowl under the vigilant gaze of attentive groups. Fourth, and perhaps most fundamentally, many legislators were never that interested in developing an independent institution. Lobbyists were personal friends, and they were potential employers after members retired from the legislature. And to repeat, lobbyists were the source of information and campaign contributions.

As a result of the ceaseless quest for reelection money, and finally the illegal solicitation of bribes for personal enrichment, the legislature's reputation was so severely damaged that it could not prevent the passage of term limits. The year 1990 marks the beginning of a new era for the California Legislature.

References: Chapter 7 _____

Cain, Bruce. *The Reapportionment Puzzle*. Berkeley: University of California Press, 1984.

Chance, Amy. "Willie Brown Fights to Keep Control of Assembly." *Sacramento Bee* (February 21, 1988).

Jeffe, Sherry Bebitch. "Can a Speaker Make Policy and Still Hold Power?" *California Journal* (May 1987).

Matthews, Jon. "Limiting Legislators' Terms Has Its Price." *Sacramento Bee* (July 1, 1990).

Mills, James R. *A Disorderly House: The Brown–Unruh Years in Sacramento*. Berkeley: Heyday Books, 1987.

Monagan, Robert. *The Disappearance of Representative Government: A California Solution*. Grass Valley: Comstock Bonanza Press, 1990.

Petracca, Mark. "Term Limits Will Put an End to Permanent Government by Incumbents." *Public Affairs Report*. Berkeley: Institute of Governmental Studies (November 1990).

Polsby, Nelson. "Limiting Terms Won't Curb Special Interests, Improve the Legislature, or Enhance Democracy." *Public Affairs Report*. Berkeley: Institute of Governmental Studies (November 1990).

Simmons, Charlene. "Term Limits Won't Achieve Political Reform." *The Davis Enterprise* (October 7, 1990).

Smith, Martin. "A New Version of Willie Brown." *Sacramento Bee* (November 22, 1988).

Walters, Dan. "Travails with Willie." *Sacramento Bee* (April 24, 1988).

CHAPTER 8

The Executive Branch

Given California's reputation as a pacesetter, the performance of the state's chief executive is of interest to a much wider audience than simply the residents of the Golden State. The governor of California is a figure of national importance. In the early months of 1991, there was speculation that Governor Pete Wilson would seek the presidency in 1996. Former Governor Ronald Reagan (1967–1974) won the presidency 6 years after he left the governor's office, and his successor, Jerry Brown (1975–1982), made two unsuccessful bids to capture the Democratic presidential nomination in 1976 and 1980. Two of California's governors who were famed for their progressivism, Hiram Johnson and Earl Warren, were candidates for the vice presidency. Even losers of gubernatorial elections in California can become president. After losing his race for governor in 1962, Richard Nixon was victorious on the national level 6 years later.

Important though governors may be in national politics, the executive branch in California involves much more than the operation of a single office. The governor, the most powerful and visible person, shares executive power with seven other elected individuals as well as the five-member Board of Equalization, which is also picked by the voters. This chapter begins with a description of the various components in the executive branch. The second part deals with the official and unofficial powers of the governor. The final part focuses on our present governor and his three predecessors in office. Contrasting these four chief executives illustrates the political styles of contemporary governors, compares their use of power as leaders of the most populous state in the Union, and shows how the dynamics of California politics can result in the election of very different type of governors.

Elected Executives

Prior service in elective office is ordinarily a prerequisite for those desiring to move to the governor's job. Hiram Johnson and Ronald Reagan are exceptions, although both were able to capitalize on the antipolitician sentiment of the voters in their eras. Of the contemporary governors since the 1930s, only Reagan lacked experience in elective office.

In addition to the governor, seven persons are elected to serve in individual office within what is known as the plural executive. The *lieutenant governor* is selected independently of the governor. Unlike the election of the president and vice president as a team from the same party, in California a governor and a lieutenant governor can be elected from different parties. As a result of the four most recent general elections (1978, 1982, 1986, and 1990), California has had lieutenant governors representing the opposite party from the governor. Some 22 states require the governor and the lieutenant governor to campaign together as one ticket, instead of running independently as is the case in California. On several occasions in 1989, Governor George Deukmejian expressed his strong support for changing the state constitution to require that these two officials run as a team from the same party.

The lieutenant governor becomes acting governor with full gubernatorial powers whenever the governor is unable to perform the duties of the office or is outside of the territorial limits of California. Lieutenant Governor Mike Curb (R) was acting governor for long periods in 1980 when Governor Jerry Brown (D) was campaigning for the presidential nomination in other states. Governor George Deukmejian (R) was visiting a new trade office in Frankfurt, Germany, when the Loma Prieta quake hit the Bay Area in 1989, thereby allowing Lieutenant Governor Leo McCarthy (D) to garner a great deal of publicity while responding to the emergency as acting governor. The state constitution also makes the lieutenant governor the president of the California Senate. This is not a significant role, however, because the only authority the president of the senate may exercise is to break 20-to-20 deadlocks by casting a tie-breaking vote. It has not been necessary to cast such a vote since 1975 when Lieutenant Governor Mervyn Dymally (D) did so.

Perhaps the most important ongoing function of the lieutenant governor is membership on the State Lands Commission (together with the state controller and the director of the Department of Finance). This commission regulates the use of over four million acres of state land and waterways, in addition to supervising onshore and offshore mineral leases. In the early 1990s, Lieutenant Governor Leo McCarthy (D) and Controller Gray Davis (D) used their votes on the lands commission to discourage offshore drilling in state waters extending 3 miles from the coast. The lieutenant governor also chairs the Commission for Economic Development, which is charged with improving California's business climate and attracting new businesses and employment to the state. The remainder of the duties of this office include memberships on the California Emergency Council, the Commission of the Californias, the World

Figure 8-1 Lt. Governor Leo T. McCarthy. (Photograph by Adam Gottlieb.)

Trade Commission, the Job Training Coordinating Council, the UC Regents, and the CSU Board of Trustees.

The position in the executive branch often considered next most powerful to that of the governor is the post of *attorney general*. This individual is the chief law officer for the state and head of the state Department of Justice. As such, the attorney general handles the legal work for civil cases involving agencies of state government. (Under certain statutory exceptions, for instance the Department of Transportation, some executive departments are allowed to hire their own lawyers to undertake legal cases.) The attorney general also is responsible for arguing all appeals that arise from criminal proceedings in the trial courts. To make sure that the laws of California are enforced in a uniform manner, the attorney general has supervisory power over all county district attorneys and sheriffs. The state attorney general may prosecute criminal cases in the event a county district attorney has declined to do so. When John Van de Kamp was the District Attorney of Los Angeles County, he did not bring the so-called Hillside Strangler to trial because he did not think he could win the case. Then Attorney General George Deukmejian assumed responsibility for the prosecution in July 1981 and eventually won the conviction of Angelo Buono, Jr. When running in the Democratic gubernatorial primary in 1990, Van de Kamp acknowledged that he made a mistake in not prosecuting Buono to the fullest extent.

More than the top cop, modern attorney generals have protected the general public in such areas as environmental law, consumer law, and antitrust law. Under the leadership of then Attorney General Van de Kamp, the Department of Justice won a ruling from the Public Utilities Commission requiring PG&E stockholders, as well as ratepayers, to shoulder the higher than expected costs of building the Diablo Canyon nuclear power plant. While serving as attorney general (1978–1982), George Deukmejian (R) did not maintain an environmental unit in the Department of Justice. On winning the office in 1982, John Van de Kamp (D) reinstituted an active environmental unit. With the narrow victory of Republican Dan Lungren in 1990, "the record clearly shows [he] likely will bring to an end, at least temporarily, the era of expansion in the attorney general's non-cop roles" (Dresslar, 1990).

The *controller* issues checks to pay state employees, lottery winners, and other bills against the State of California. It is the responsibility of the controller to audit the books of state government (and each of the localities therein) and to determine the legality of any financial claims against the state. By virtue of being controller, the occupant of this office serves on 52 boards and commissions in fiscally related areas. The controller chairs the Franchise Tax Board, which collects personal income and corporate taxes. Joining four other members each elected from districts encompassing one-fourth of the state, the controller is the fifth member of the Board of Equalization. This board collects the sales tax, gasoline tax, and taxes on liquor and cigarettes. As mentioned earlier in connection with the lieutenant governor, the controller serves on the State Lands Commission. The controller also is a member of a wide variety of commissions and boards dealing with public employee pensions, public construction projects (schools, hospitals, and community colleges), and bonded indebtedness. After serving as Governor Jerry Brown's chief of staff followed by a brief stint in the California Assembly, Democrat Gray Davis won election as controller in 1986 and 1990. Many assume that Davis will seek higher office in 1992 or 1994.

The *treasurer* is the state's banker, with the primary responsibility for selling state bonds, investing the state's funds in financial institutions, and paying out state funds when authorized by the controller. The interest from sound investments of state funds is considerable, and companies that are awarded contracts to sell billions of dollars of tax-exempt state bonds receive a fee from the state for their services. Jesse Unruh, the once-powerful speaker of the assembly who had strong ties to the legislature, held onto this office with little opposition from 1975 until his death in 1987. Under Unruh, this formerly obscure position was transformed into one of considerable financial clout. The treasurer serves on some 45 boards and commissions dealing with the investment of public funds and the financing of public projects through the use of bonds. On appointment by Governor George Deukmejian and confirmation by the legislature, Thomas Hayes (R) served the unexpired portion of Unruh's term. In the 1990 general elections, Hayes (46%) lost the treasurer's office to Democrat Kathleen Brown (49%). Of her prospects to follow Pat Brown and Jerry Brown into the governorship, it has been written that Kathleen Brown "is smoother than her father, more congenial than her brother, and as smart as her mother" (Smith, 1991).

The *secretary of state* is the chief elections officer, record keeper, and archivist for the State of California. This office is responsible for overseeing the qualification of initiatives, the printing of ballots, the preparation of the voters' pamphlet describing each proposition, and the tabulation of the vote. Corporations, lobbyists, and notaries public must all register with the secretary of state. This office also maintains a registry of vacant appointive positions within state government. The secretary of state serves as chair of the World Trade Commission, which promotes California's products abroad and encourages foreign investors to locate in the state. March Fong Eu (D) has held this post without serious challenge since 1974. Jerry Brown served one term (1970–1974) as secretary of state before winning the governorship.

The *superintendent of public instruction* heads the Department of Education and theoretically carries out policies set by an 11-member Board of Education appointed by the governor. As local school districts have had to turn to the state for increasing amounts of financial assistance in the wake of property tax reduction (Proposition 13 in 1978), the

Figure 8-2 Treasurer Kathleen Brown being sworn in by her father Governor Edmund G. Brown, Sr. (GQ Photography.)

superintendent has grown in power by exerting fiscal controls on the way money is spent. Bill Honig became superintendent in 1982 by ousting incumbent Wilson Riles. In major confrontations with Governor Deukmejian, Superintendent Honig vehemently argued for greater state funding for K–12 education. In 1990, Deukmejian's appointees on the Board of Education insisted on a greater role in reviewing Honig's departmental budget and in the naming of high-level personnel in the Department of Education. Honig resisted what he considered to be unwarranted intrusions into his domain. This political squabble brought forth the following editorial reaction from the *Sacramento Bee*.

> There's no doubt that California's arrangement is bizarre. The constitution gives the 11-member board policy direction over the schools; it gives the superintendent responsibility to carry it out.—As long as the superintendent is elected and the board is appointed, the superintendent will run the show, and should (December 11, 1990).

Of the eight executive officials elected by the voters of California, the superintendent is the only one to be selected on a nonpartisan basis. Candidates for this office carry no party label next to their name on the ballot.

With the passage of Proposition 103 in November 1988, the elected post of *insurance commissioner* was established. Former state Senator John Garamendi (D, Stockton) became the first occupant of this elected position. The commissioner is the head of the Department of Insurance. Garamendi moved boldly on assuming this office. He rescinded pro-industry regulations written by his appointive predecessor, and he froze all insurance rates in California. Garamendi has the difficult task of urging trial lawyers and insurance companies to agree on reforms that will be in the interest of consumers. The commissioner may levy fines on insurance companies for engaging in unfair business practices. As is the case for any elected executive in California, the commissioner may propose that new laws be passed by the California Legislature.

With eight independently elected executives, California voters have ample latitude in selecting the leadership of this branch of government. However, who is in charge? Who is responsible for the condition of California's schools? Who is responsible for instituting crime prevention programs? If an executive team from one party would help the executive branch operate more effectively, there are several possible means of achieving this objective. First, dropping the office-block ballot in favor of the party-column ballot might encourage voters to mark a straight-party slate. Second, party conventions or primaries could nominate seven individuals (omitting the nonpartisan superintendent) to run as a slate receiving just one vote for the entire group. Third, election of the offices other than the governor could be dispensed with all together in favor of gubernatorial appointment of these posts. It is true that the last suggestion would strengthen the hand of the governor, but does it make sense to convene governor's cabinet meetings, as is now the case, without the heads of the Department of Education, the Department of Justice, and the Department of Insurance being present?

Appointed Executives

The remainder of the high-level positions in the executive branch are filled by gubernatorial appointment. The governor's *cabinet* consists of the secretaries in charge of the superagencies in state government: (1) Business, Transportation, and Housing, (2) Health and Welfare, (3) Youth and Adult Corrections, (4) State and Consumer Services, and (5) Resources. Governors ordinarily invite the directors of such departments as Finance, Industrial Relations, and Food and Agriculture to attend cabinet meetings as well. Governor Pete Wilson added cabinet-level secretaries for children's services and education and for environmental protection. Individuals appointed as agency secretaries or department directors are the senior managers in the executive branch, and they usually possess considerable background in the program area they administer.

The governor's *personal staff* is not responsible for managing personnel in the various departments of state government, but instead provides the chief executive with close support in the performance of the daily routine in the corner office of the State Capitol. A press unit responds to inquiries from journalists. A constituent affairs unit answers the voluminous correspondence received by a governor. An appointments unit recommends individuals to fill vacant posts in state government. A legislative unit tracks the progress of various bills and suggests action to be taken by the governor. A scheduling unit arranges the daily events that a governor will attend. A legal affairs unit advises the governor whether or not to reduce sentences or to grant pardons to prison inmates. Personal staff usually is younger than members of the cabinet. Furthermore, while personal staff exhibits undivided loyalty to the governor, members of the cabinet endeavor to serve the interest of their agency's clients and employees as well as supporting the chief executive. Personal staff and the cabinet may not hold each other in high regard. An in-depth study of the administrations of Ronald Reagan and Jerry Brown found that "Reagan cabinet officers viewed the personal staff in much the same way as Brown cabinet officers, that is, as often inexperienced and politicized interlopers" (Hamilton and Biggart, 1984:217).

There is a wide assortment of some 402 *boards and commissions* that completes the appointed portion of the executive branch. The largest of these entities (e.g., Franchise Tax Board, Board of Equalization, Public Utilities Commission, Water Resources Control Board, State Lottery Commission, and the Air Resources Board) have budgets into the hundreds of millions and employees into the thousands. At the other end of the scale, there are bodies with no staff and little budget (e.g., Fig Advisory Board, Egg Commission, Fresh Carrot Advisory Board, Advisory Board to the Bureau of Home Furnishings, and the Automotive Repair Advisory Board). After conducting a study of boards and commissions in 1989, the state's Little Hoover Commission(!) issued the following conclusions.

> Some (boards and commissions) continue to exist even after they no longer have any budget, staff, or useful function.—Some of these organizations perform similar functions. This overlap in responsibilities at times leads to conflict between the organizations. Since there is not a single agency responsible for overseeing these various entities, coordination may often be minimal or even non-existent.—The overall pattern that emerges reflects a lack of oversight and, potentially, a lack of control. (Little Hoover Commission, 1989:3, 10).

The manner in which governors interact with these different types of appointees varies from administration to administration. During Ronald Reagan's years as governor, the cabinet met frequently (once or twice a week), and it was the focus of all major decisions in the executive branch. Issues were reduced to one-page memos in which the cabinet collectively recommended a course of action to Governor Reagan. When Jerry Brown assumed the governorship, the cabinet initially met nightly in unstructured discussions. As it became clear that the cabinet was a debating society not a decision body, it stopped meeting on a regular basis (Hamilton and Biggart, 1984:81–82, 203–211). Governor Brown relied on people whose ideas he valued, not on individuals because of the titles they held. Brown consulted with different groups of people in each issue area rather than placing his confidence in one entity like a cabinet.

Personal staff played the central role in the Deukmejian administration. This staff met every working day at 9:00 AM to assess the issues facing the governor. The chief of staff carried the advice of the personal staff to the chief executive. Even in a well-organized administration such as Ronald Reagan's, the personal staff did not meet on a daily basis. The Deukmejian cabinet met twice a month instead of the once or twice a week as under Reagan. Before having a meeting with Governor Deukmejian, his cabinet held a dress rehearsal with his personal staff. It initially appeared that the cabinet and personal staff were working as a team, but as the Deukmejian administration wore on it became clear that the personal staff had the upper hand. On the major compromise with the legislature in 1989 concerning the ballot measure to increase gasoline taxes, the key input to the governor came from personal staff not the cabinet.

Chief executives relate to the appointees on boards and commissions in different ways as well. If worthy of appointment in the first place, Governor Jerry Brown expected his appointees to have ideas for themselves and not to require guidance from others. Though careful research on this matter is lacking, it appears that Governor Deukmejian assigned staff members to monitor his appointees on various boards and commissions. On occasion, Deukmejian's appointees on a given board would be instructed to vote as a bloc by the governor's office. To the extent that boards and commissions were intended to provide a measure of distance or independence from the executive departments immediately under the governor's supervision, the practice of whipping appointees into line defeats the purpose of establishing supposedly quasijudicial bodies.

The Governor's Power

The state constitution establishes specific legal powers for the governor. Among these formal functions, the governor is required to give an annual report to the legislature, to make recommendations for future legislation, to cast vetoes, and to submit an annual budget covering anticipated expenditures by the branches of government. The governor has the power to fill vacancies created by death or retirement to a variety of offices (such as U.S. senators, statewide executive offices, and county boards of supervisors) until a successor is chosen in the next scheduled election. The governor may call the legislature into special session to consider a specific issue, and the chief executive is empowered to call special elections between regularly scheduled ones. He or she can embark on executive reorganization plans to restructure the state bureaucracy. Additionally, the governor is the commander of the California National Guard and has the authority to issue reprieves, pardons, and commutations to those convicted of a crime.

Budget and Veto

At the federal level, the chief executive must accept or reject bills in their entirety. In California, however, the governor can reject an entire bill (*general veto*); and, in bills involving appropriations, the governor can reduce or omit the sum of money agreed on by the state legislature (*item veto*). The item veto may be used only on monetary provisions of bills, and then only to decrease amounts contained in legislative measures. When a governor receives a bill during the middle of a legislative session, he or she has 12 days to either sign or veto the measure. If the governor does neither, the bill becomes law without his or her signature on expiration of the deadline. When the governor receives a large number of bills on the legislature recessing or adjourning at year's end, the chief executive is allowed 30 days to decide whether to sign or to veto measures.

The governor has a great deal of influence over the budget. It originates through consultation between the governor and the Department of Finance and is then handed to the legislature. Furthermore, it is returned from the legislature for the governor's signature before it can become law. Thus, the governor has the opportunity to structure the original document and the final say as to its shape when completed. While it is being debated in the legislature, the governor's key supporters there can use their influence to ward off drastic alterations. (See Chapter 9 for a detailed discussion of the governor's role as budget maker.)

Both the general and item vetoes may be overridden by a two-thirds vote in each house, although this seldom occurs. During his 8 years as the state's chief executive, George Deukmejian item vetoed over $7 billion from budgets approved by the legislature. He also cast a general veto 2,299 times to nullify the enactment of certain pieces of legislation. With strong backing from Republicans in the legislature, particularly from the Assembly GOP Caucus, it was never possible to obtain two-thirds votes in both houses to override any of Governor Deukmejian's general or item vetoes. Deukmejian's frequent use of the veto earned him the nickname of "Governor No."

Appointments

Authority to make appointments allows governors to make a broad and lasting impact on state government. Not only does a governor select the leaders of the executive departments, he or she also decides who will occupy judicial positions as well as those on boards and commissions. Some positions are known as "pleasure appointments" meaning that the occupant serves as long as the governor so desires. Other positions are known as "term appointments" meaning that there is a fixed period of service and the governor may not remove the appointee from the post. The term of a member of the UC Board of Regents is 12 years (as are the terms of appellate justices), so the influence of governors can last long after they have left office. As a general rule, the heads of super-agencies and departments are pleasure appointments, and the judiciary and the boards and commissions are term appointments.

Job seekers may check the registry of vacancies available at any county clerk's office. Individuals may submit applications for up to five positions with the appointments unit in the governor's office. After paper screening, interviews are held with members of the appointments unit and occasionally with the governor. Though most chief executives do not have the time, Governor Jerry Brown sometimes met with prospective appointees several times before deciding on an appointment. Roughly 400 appointments must be made at the beginning of a new administration. Thereafter, around 2,600 additional appointments will be required as terms expire on boards and judges retire from the bench.

Depending on the legislation that originally established a given board or department, some appointments require confirmation by the California Senate and some do not. When appointment requires confirmation, the Senate Rules Committee mails letters of inquiry to various groups in California to obtain reaction to the nominee. The committee holds hearings regarding appointments, and interested citizens are invited to testify on controversial appointees. Nominees are given the opportunity to defend their credentials. After committee review, an appointment must be approved by a majority (21 votes) of the full senate. In rare instances, such as appointments to the UC Board of Regents, a two-thirds majority (27 votes) is required for confirmation.

As is evident in Table 8–1, not all gubernatorial appointments are subject to confirmation. The governor may appoint whomever he or she pleases to personal staff. Governor Pete Wilson's appointment of state Senator John Seymour (R, Anaheim) to the U.S. Senate did not require any review. Appellate judicial appointments are confirmed by the Commission on Judicial Appointments not the California Senate. The overwhelming majority of gubernatorial appointments win confirmation, but the few appointments that are blocked understandably garner a great deal of press attention.

TABLE 8.1   Confirmaton of Gubernatorial Appointments

Type of Vacancy	Confirmation by California Senate
Judicial	No
U.S. Senate	No
County Supervisor	No
Governor's personal staff	No
Executive departments and superagencies	Yes
Boards and Commissions	Yes
Statewide, elected executive	Yes[a]
Board of Equalization	Yes[a]

[a]Both legislative chambers review confirmation; defeat in one house kills appointment.

Beyond Formal Powers

Formal powers, situational factors, and personal characteristics are interwoven in the performance of the governor's job. The formal powers of the governor are spelled out in the state constitution. However, just how successful the chief executive is in having budgets approved, vetoes upheld, and appointments confirmed by the senate depends on the two other sources of executive power. Generally, situational factors cannot be controlled by the governor. Rather, they provide the political context within which the governor has to operate. Clearly, if a Republican governor such as Pete Wilson has to contend with a Democratic majority in the legislature, much of the governor's energy can be sapped by political infighting. However, even when the governor's office and the legislature are held by the same party, personal factors can strain relations. Conflicts between independently elected executives can limit a governor's power, so too can budgetary constraints imposed by the initiative process.

A governor has personal resources that can be used effectively when the legislature appears reluctant to act. He or she can mobilize citizen support or leak favorable material to the news media. If the governor is assertive and charismatic, public opinion can be used to pressure obstinate lawmakers. On the other hand, a lethargic incumbent or one who uses a controversial issue for personal advancement may find that pub-

Figure 8-3 Governors Pete Wilson and George Deukmejian discussing the gubernatorial transition in 1991. (Governor's Office)

lic opinion supports the legislature. Stamina, intelligence, and family support contribute to successful governorships. Likewise, skillful use of the mass media and selection of top-quality appointees increase a governor's power immensely.

Because the constitutional responsibilities of the governor have remained largely the same over the years, the personal side of gubernatorial politics needs to be explored to understand how governors succeed and fail in convincing the electorate and the legislature of the wisdom of their ways. Rarely in state politics does one find as dramatic a difference among governors as with Ronald Reagan, Jerry Brown, George Deukmejian, and Pete Wilson. Examining their years as chief executive will make apparent four distinct styles of governing California.

Gubernatorial Contrasts

Ronald Reagan

Ronald Reagan graduated from a small midwestern college and worked for a while as a radio announcer before migrating to California. From 1937 to 1957, Reagan was at home in Hollywood. He appeared in numerous movies, was active in union politics, and served for 6 years as president of the Screen Actor's Guild. Reagan has characterized the early part of this period as one in which he was a "bleeding-heart liberal."

In the mid-1950s, Ronald Reagan polished the political philosophy that landed him in the governor's seat in 1966 and provided him with a national following in subsequent presidential elections. He moved from motion pictures into promotional work for General Electric in 1954. Reagan's pitch to GE workers and executives was later developed into "the speech" that he would give to citizens on behalf of Republican presidential nominees Richard Nixon in 1960 and Barry Goldwater in 1964. Essentially, "the speech" was a defense of the free-enterprise system in the face of the rising tide of socialism that threatened individual freedoms in the United States.

When Reagan challenged Pat Brown's third bid for election in 1966, he used the resources of the Spencer–Roberts public relations firm to his advantage. Reagan's potentially weakest point, his lack of political experience, became his greatest asset under the direction of Spencer–Roberts. To Reagan, career politicians such as Brown were responsible for the turmoil on college campuses and urban unrest. Reagan would present himself as a citizen candidate.

Although Reagan campaigned against big government, he was able to do little to curtail governmental spending and services after he became governor. He proposed that college students pay tuition in state-support-ed institutions. Although the tuition idea was dropped, this was an obvi-ous dig at the University of California students, many of whom Reagan thought were interested more in confrontation politics than education. He called for a dramatic cutback in state support for mental facilities, although this too was moderated. Above all, as a candidate opposed to increasing taxes, Governor Reagan soon realized that he would have to increase taxes to maintain essential services and to balance the budget in the wake of the deficit left by Pat Brown.

Reagan's relations with the legislature were strained during his 8-year incumbency, partly because of Democratic party control of the two houses for 6 years and partly because of Reagan's lack of programs for the legislature to enact. Reagan won reelection in 1970 easily, although not as impressively as in 1966. Reagan's Democratic challenger, Jesse Unruh, tried to pin a "do-nothing" label on the Reagan administration. However, with a divided Democratic party, Unruh's own image as a back-room politician, and a miniscule campaign budget, Unruh was unable to sway enough voters away from the Reagan camp. The Repub-licans swept the statewide offices with the exception of the secretary of state's position, which was won by Jerry Brown.

In his appointments to various positions, Reagan was oriented toward self-made Republican businessmen who shared his political philosophy. He stacked the important Public Utilities Commission with individuals who were viewed as favoring big business over the interests of the con-sumers, but the state's utility rates continued to remain among the low-est in the country. Just as his appointees reflected Reagan's political views, so too did they mirror his personal integrity. No judges or com-missioners were forced out of office because of scandalous behavior. Thus, it came as a surprise to many observers that a number of Rea-gan's advisers and appointees were embroiled in legally questionable actions during his two terms as president.

Prior to his second-term victory, Reagan announced that he would not be a candidate for a third term. Like other California governors, Rea-gan's eyes had been on the White House for some time, and he was increasingly touted as a Republican presidential candidate for 1976. Richard Nixon resigned the presidency in August 1974, and Vice Presi-dent Gerald Ford assumed the oval office. Reagan did well in several 1976 primaries but was unable to secure the nomination, which went to Ford, who in turn was defeated in the general election by former Gover-nor Jimmy Carter of Georgia. However, Reagan captured the Republi-can presidential nomination 4 years later. Using the same campaign style and themes familiar to California voters during his gubernatorial races, the 69-year-old Reagan emerged victorious over the incumbent Carter in the 1980 presidential election.

Lieutenant Governor Ed Reinecke was Reagan's choice to succeed him as governor in the 1974 state elections. Reinecke's legal problems stemming from the Watergate scandal resulted in his defeat in the Republican primary that year by State Controller and former Assemblymember Houston Flournoy. On the Democratic side, the familiarity of Jerry Brown's name and his clean image resulted in his securing the nomination with over 40% of the Democratic primary vote. In the 1974 general election, Brown, a 36-year-old bachelor, won the governor's position by less than 200,000 votes over Flournoy, then the closest gubernatorial election in over 50 years. Brown's wide lead in the early polls dwindled as the election drew closer. Had the election been held a week later, Flournoy might have won.

Edmund G. "Jerry" Brown, Jr.

In a span of 14 years, Jerry Brown was elected to a seat on the Los Angeles Community College Board (1968), became secretary of state (1970), succeeded Ronald Reagan as governor (1974), was reelected (1978), and was defeated in the 1982 U.S. Senate race. While governor, Brown ran unsuccessfully for the Democratic presidential nominations in 1976 and 1980. When Brown left the governor's office on January 3, 1983, after 8 years, he was only 44 years old, more than a decade younger than either Pat Brown or Ronald Reagan when they were elected governor for their first terms. During his years as governor, Jerry Brown's "lower your expectations" philosophy guided his approach to many of the problems facing the state. His message was that people have to assume more responsibility for their own well-being and become less reliant on the state to provide for them.

As an 18-year-old, Jerry Brown left the University of Santa Clara to enter the Jesuit seminary in Los Gatos to study for the priesthood. After three and a half years as a novitiate, he switched to the University of California at Berkeley, where he completed his undergraduate work. He subsequently received his law degree from Yale. Brown returned to California, where he clerked for the state supreme court briefly before joining a law firm in Los Angeles. Shortly thereafter, he entered politics in the community college board race.

Jerry Brown became a political celebrity because he captured the imagination of many Californians and expressed highly unconventional views. As governor, he flew tourist class, rode in a Plymouth rather than a Cadillac, refused to sign autographs, and lived in an apartment in downtown Sacramento rather than a lavish governor's mansion. Jerry Brown promised "a new spirit" during the 1974 gubernatorial campaign—an administration that would bring new people into government, be environmentally conscious, and be adapted to the technologies of the future.

One of the most far-reaching accomplishments in his first term was the passage of the Agricultural Labor Relations Act of 1975. Although the agricultural lobby did not support the Act, they reluctantly agreed to it under pressure from Brown. Under the provisions of the Act, a five-member Agricultural Labor Relations Board (ALRB) was created to monitor elections between farm workers and growers, and to mediate any disputes that arose over union affiliation. Brown's appointees to the ALRB were largely sympathetic to the workers.

One of the few projects where Brown achieved bipartisan support was the California Conservation Corps (CCC). For the CCC, adolescents between the ages of 18 and 20 are recruited to perform conservation work such as clearing brush from streams, maintaining fire trails, and aiding towns in the event of regional disasters caused by forest fires and flooding. The CCC was continued under the Deukmejian administration, but on a reduced budget.

One of the most significant aspects of Jerry Brown's administration was his appointments to state positions. This was especially evident with his appointments to judicial vacancies. He nominated the first women (Rose Bird), first black (Wiley Manual), and first Hispanic (Cruz Reynoso) to the state supreme court. His appointment of Adriana Gianturco to head the state Department of Transportation (Caltrans) irritated the highway lobby and the legislature. Brown reformed the traditional practice of appointing members of corporations and established professionals to state regulatory agencies. Thus, for example, instead of having only physicians on medical review boards to hear charges of unprofessional conduct against fellow doctors, Brown included lay members and chiropractors.

In a state where agribusiness and corporate enterprises wield considerable economic and political power, Brown began to flounder politically with his "small is better" philosophy during his first term in office. His opposition to nuclear power, empathy for farm workers, and pro-consumer appointments to key governmental positions earned him an antibusiness reputation in corporate circles. Moreover, when Dow Chemical scratched its plans to build a $500 million petrochemical plant northeast of San Francisco in early 1977, Brown's standing with the business community plummeted.

Jerry Brown became well known outside of the state not so much for the accomplishments of his administration, but because of his personal image as a highly unorthodox and imaginative politician. Brown attracted media attention wherever he went. With less than 2 years experience as governor, Brown entered the race for the 1976 Democratic presidential nomination. His "new spirit" attracted voters, but his entry into the race came too late to stop the nomination from going to Jimmy Carter.

After losing the presidential nomination in 1976, Brown won reelection as governor in 1978. Although the race was thought to be close at first, Brown won handily over his Republican challenger, Attorney General Evelle Younger. In spite of his reelection, there is little doubt that Brown was already planning a second run for the presidential nomination 2 years away. The governor's advisers urged that he spend more time tending to state affairs. Brown's public standing was weakening. Oblivious to what the polls indicated, Brown entered the 1980 presidential primary. After inglorious defeats in several states, Brown quit the race.

Back in California, Brown began to behave more like a conventional politician, cultivating ties with key legislators and party regulars, remembering legislators' birthdays, and signing autographs for kids. In spring 1981, an infestation of the Mediterranean fruit fly was discovered in the Santa Clara Valley. Because the Medfly posed an immediate threat to the agriculturally rich Central Valley region, farmers called for prompt aerial spraying of the area. Brown was reluctant to use pesticides over the populated area and instead used CCC workers and volunteers to strip the fruit trees. When the U.S. government threatened to quarantine California fruit, Brown reversed himself and allowed the spraying of Malathion from helicopters. Farmers were furious that Brown had delayed action, and Democratic legislators from the agricultural areas quickly separated themselves from Brown. Jerry Brown was unable to recover from the medfly crisis and his earlier absences from California while campaigning for the presidency, and he lost his race for the U.S. Senate to San Diego Mayor Pete Wilson by the margin of 51-to-46%.

Attorney General George Deukmejian and Lieutenant Governor Mike Curb vied for the GOP gubernatorial nomination in 1982. Although Curb stressed his experience as acting governor while Jerry Brown was campaigning out of state, Deukmejian's greater years of service to California (16 as a legislator and 4 as chief law officer) gave him the edge with voters in the Republican primary. Los Angeles Mayor Tom Bradley easily captured the Democratic nomination for governor by defeating state Senator John Garamendi (D, Stockton), and Mario Obledo, Brown's secretary of health and welfare. In one of the closest statewide elections in history, Deukmejian won the governorship by some 90,000 votes.

George "Duke" Deukmejian

On January 3, 1983, George Deukmejian was sworn in as California's thirty-fifth governor. In contrast to Jerry Brown's promise of "a new spirit," Governor Deukmejian pledged a pragmatic "commonsense society." Alluding to his predecessor, Deukmejian promised to appoint "a judiciary with a more balanced view" and to change "regulations which have choked off growth and progress."

George Deukmejian, the son of an Armenian rug merchant, was born in a small upstate New York town in 1928. He graduated with a bachelor's degree in sociology from Sienna College (New York) and received his law degree at St. John's University in Brooklyn. Following service in the army, Deukmejian moved to Long Beach in 1955, where he established a private law practice, married, and became active in local civic organizations. In 1962, he won an assembly seat campaigning on the themes of crime, big government, and the "trend toward socialism." Four years later he was elevated to the state senate, where he continued his reputation as an anticrime legislator. Senator Deukmejian authored a number of tough crime bills and the state's death penalty law. His only electoral defeat came in 1970, when he finished fourth in the GOP primary for attorney general, a race won by Evelle Younger.

In 1978, Deukmejian succeeded Younger as attorney general when Younger unsuccessfully challenged Jerry Brown's reelection bid. As attorney general, Deukmejian all but disbanded the environmental protection unit in the attorney general's office, argued several cases himself before the state supreme court rather than relying totally on staff attorneys, and formed a special "action group" within the agency to challenge what was regarded as pro-criminal decisions by the courts. Deukmejian invited reporters to accompany him as his agents made a helicopter landing on a suspected marijuana plantation in Mendocino County.

Attorney General Deukmejian was one of the three members of the Commission on Judicial Appointments, which reviewed confirmation of appellate court appointments made by the governor. Deukmejian voted against several of Brown's appellate nominees, although they were confirmed by the votes of the two other members. In one of his last acts as attorney general, Deukmejian voted against three of Brown's lame-duck appointees to a newly created appellate district in San Jose. Because this was a new judicial district, only two members of the commission were eligible to participate; thus Deukmejian's negative votes prevented Brown's appointees from attaining the bench and also left these three positions open for Deukmejian, as governor, to fill with his nominees.

The most pressing problem Governor Deukmejian faced in his first term in office concerned the state budget. Although the budget must be balanced when enacted into law, it can become out of balance if anticipated revenues fall short of state spending rates. The 1982–1983 budget (the last prepared by Jerry Brown) fell $1.6 billion into deficit. Deukmejian pledged he would not raise general taxes during the campaign, and he rejected even a temporary 1-cent increase in the sales tax proposed by Democratic legislators to offset the deficit. Loans from banks allowed the state to meet its obligations for the remainder of the 1982–1983 fiscal year, and these debts were repaid during the next fiscal year.

Governor Deukmejian lost three major appointment battles in his first term. His choices to head the Department of Finance, the Department of Industrial Relations, and the Department of Fish and Game were all rejected by the California Senate. The setbacks Deukmejian experienced during his first term in office were overshadowed by his accomplishments. Foremost among these was his image among the voters as a competent governor whose focus was on California, not on running for higher office. Deukmejian's policies had something for members of both parties. His pro-business appointments to state boards and agencies, advocacy of more freeways, efforts to reform the mammoth welfare system, and reduction in funds for the state's regulatory agencies pleased many Republican legislators. Conversely, Democrats supported the governor's calls to increase educational funding and his support of the University of California's divesting itself of investments in corporations doing business in South Africa.

Deukmejian's margin of victory over Tom Bradley in 1982 had been razor thin. In a rematch of the contestants 4 years later, Deukmejian was given another term by an impressive 61% majority of the voters. Bradley, unable to find an issue that would sway voters away from Deukmejian, carried only 2 of the 58 counties in the state—Alameda and San Francisco. As was the situation in 1982, voters then kept the same Democratic line-up in the other statewide executive offices and Democratic majorities in both houses of the legislature. However, Deukmejian's victory was sweetened by the defeat of Rose Bird and two other justices on the state supreme court whom he actively opposed in his reelection campaign.

George Deukmejian's second term in the governor's office involved a considerable amount of rough sledding. His principal accomplishments were recasting the California judiciary (Deukmejian appointed 67% of California's judges while he was governor) and keeping his campaign pledge not to raise general taxes. He also was able to establish international trade offices in Frankfurt, London, Tokyo, and Mexico City. With key members of his personal staff departing after his first term, Deukmejian lost close associates who were politically sensitive and closely tied to major figures outside of government. In 1987, Governor Deukmejian was strongly opposed when he curtailed Cal-OSHA (the state's worker health and safety program) and when he appointed U.S. Representative Dan Lungren as state treasurer. The governor could have expected organized labor to resist the demise of Cal-OSHA, but even the business community did not support the elimination of this program. With a number of GOP legislators in the State Capitol hoping to be appointed to the vacancy created by Jesse Unruh's death, the naming of Lungren did not sit particularly well with the members of either political party in the California Legislature.

> A sharp staff would have checked out the worker safety wipeout, cleared it with employers and others before making the move.—It [Lungren's appointment] was, if nothing else, another example of how Deukmejian operates, especially in his second term. He and his sycophantic aides make their decisions in secret, without consulting legislators or affected private interests, and then expect that they'll be ratified without question (Walters, 1988).

As discussed in Chapter 2, it was hoped that Governor Deukmejian's announcement in January 1989 that he did not intend to seek a third term as chief executive would lead to a more cooperative relationship with the legislative branch. Waste management reforms and the high-level agreement to place gasoline tax increases on the next statewide ballot (Proposition 111) were achieved in 1989, but the following year returned to pitched battles between the governor and the legislature. Realizing that he would be leaving his successor an even larger budgetary shortfall than he inherited from Jerry Brown, Governor Deukmejian called the legislature into special session in December 1990 to address the deteriorating fiscal situation. As the state's economy weakened and as revenue projections contained in the state budget were not met, Democrats in the legislature declined this last opportunity to work with George Deukmejian.

Without suffering a single veto override in his 8 years as governor, Deukmejian established new records for using general and item vetoes. Strong as his application of negative power was, he was faulted for lacking positive proposals to deal with the changing needs of California. Chief executives can help fashion legislative solutions, but it was Governor Deukmejian's style for the most part to stay out of the legislative fray and to either sign or veto whatever reached his desk. From the standpoint of his critics, Deukmejian did not provide adequate leadership for a large and dynamic state. After leaving office, the former governor defended his record in these terms.

> As governor, I did what I told the voters I would do, and that's how my administration should be judged.—I learned years ago that what the critics really meant when they said I lacked "vision" was that I wouldn't discard my agenda and adopt their agenda, the central element of which is always the same: more government and more taxes.—I always stood up for the average, law-abiding, working taxpayer (Deukmejian, 1991).

The 1990 Governor's Race _____

The race to occupy the corner office in the State Capitol after the departure of Governor Deukmejian pitted two individuals with similar views on many issues. Both Republican Pete Wilson and Democrat Dianne Feinstein opposed offshore drilling, supported capital punishment, were pro-choice concerning reproductive rights, and favored better programs for California's children. Neither made any sort of pledge not to raise taxes—the pledge that George Deukmejian made and honored with respect to general taxes. Perhaps the most notable differences between the two on the issues were Feinstein's support of Big Green (Proposition 128), which her rival opposed, and Wilson's backing of term limits (Propositions 131 and 140), which his opponent rejected. The main differences between these two candidates had to do with the conditions under which they waged their campaigns.

Lacking a strong GOP nominee then serving in state office, elders in the Republican Party prevailed on U.S. Senator Pete Wilson to return from Washington, D.C., and make the race for governor. Despite the fact that he had just won reelection to a 6-year term in the U.S. Senate over Lieutenant Governor Leo McCarthy (D) in November 1988, Wilson announced his candidacy for governor in February 1989. Republican leaders actively discouraged Los Angeles Police Chief Daryl F. Gates from entering the GOP primary against Wilson. This uncontested nomination may well have been the key to Wilson's selection as governor because it kept the Republican Party together, and it allowed the nominee to save his financial resources for the general election.

Dianne Feinstein, on the other hand, had to overcome a major opponent to secure the Democratic Party's nomination for governor. After serving 8 years as the state's top legal officer, John Van de Kamp attempted to move from attorney general to governor as Earl Warren (R), Pat Brown (D), and George Deukmejian (R) had done in the past. Over 4 months before the end of the primary campaigns in June, Feinstein aired a very effective television spot which contained actual footage of her informing the press of the assassinations of San Francisco Mayor George Moscone and Supervisor Harvey Milk in 1978. Soon dubbed "the commercial," the advertisement ended by saying that Feinstein was the only Democrat running for governor who supported the death penalty. The $600,000 that Feinstein spent airing "the commercial" boosted her into the lead in public opinion polls. In a serious miscalculation, Van de Kamp's strategists spent about the same amount (some $575,000) endeavoring to qualify three initiatives for the November ballot. These ballot measures on the environment, crime control, and political reform were to be centerpieces in Van de Kamp's fall campaign against the Republican nominee. The three initiatives made it to the November ballot, but Van de Kamp did not. Feinstein beat Van de Kamp 52 to 41% in the Democratic primary in June 1990.

Republican Wilson and Democrat Feinstein shared more than similar positions on many issues. Both were 57 years of age during the gubernatorial campaign, and both were undergraduates at elite universities (Yale for Wilson, Stanford for Feinstein). Both had angered members of their *own* political party earlier in their careers. To the outrage of many in the California Republican Party, Wilson had actively supported Gerald Ford during the GOP presidential primaries in 1976 instead of backing home-state hero Ronald Reagan for the nomination. (Wilson ran fourth in the GOP gubernatorial primary of 1978, but he was rehabilitated enough in the eyes of Republican voters to win the U.S. Senate nomination in 1982.) Feinstein irritated members of the Democratic Party by not supporting Leo McCarthy's race against Pete Wilson for the U.S. Senate in 1988 and by failing to back then Assemblymember Art Agnos (D) in his successful effort to succeed her as Mayor of San Francisco. Feinstein was even booed at the Democratic State Convention of 1990 when she expressed her support of the death penalty.

Although Feinstein's primary campaign was waged skillfully, she began the general election effort with some significant disadvantages. First, she lacked campaign funds having expended the bulk of her resources defeating Van de Kamp in the primary. Second, Richard Blum (her spouse) had loaned some $3 million to her successful primary outcome, thus establishing himself as a prime target for Wilson's attacks in the general election. Third, the California Democratic Party was so intent on defeating two redistricting reform initiatives in June (Propositions 118 and 119) and the two term-limit initiatives in November (Propositions 131 and 140) that money was drained away from Feinstein's gubernatorial campaign. Fourth, Feinstein lacked the statewide base enjoyed by Wilson. During her 10 years as mayor of San Francisco (1978–1988), Feinstein had not developed visibility throughout the state. On the other hand, Pete Wilson had conducted victorious statewide races for the U.S. Senate in 1982 (defeating Jerry Brown) and in 1988 (defeating Leo McCarthy). Fifth, the California Republican Party registered twice as many new party members in 1990 as the Democratic Party. In addition, the absentee voter program and the get-out-the-vote effort by the Republican Party were superior to those mounted by the Democratic Party.

To counter these disadvantages, Feinstein needed an outright win in the one televised debate she conducted with Wilson. She did not get it. Although initial press accounts of the debate claimed that neither candidate had blundered during the course of the event, subsequent analysis tended to favor Wilson. He received much attention for having endorsed term limits during the debate, whereas Feinstein was forced to explain why she wrote the words "choice," "education," and "growth" on the palm of her hand prior to

Figure 8-4 "Wait! I'm supposed to be running against your *husband*!" (Dennis Renault, *Sacramento Bee*)

the televised encounter. Wilson also challenged Feinstein's statement that she would make appointments according to the proportions of ethnic groups in California's population as a whole. In dealing with questions about her husband's business holdings, her debate performance, and the so-called "quota" issue, Feinstein was on the defensive during much of the campaign.

Though Feinstein trailed in voter surveys late in the campaign by eight or more percentage points, Wilson ultimately prevailed by 49 to 46% in the November election. Given the matters she had to surmount, and given the veteran staff working with Wilson, the narrowness of the victory margin allowed her supporters to suggest that Dianne Feinstein likely would enter another statewide campaign in the future—perhaps as soon as 1992.

Pete Wilson

Peter Barton Wilson was born in St. Louis, Missouri, and took up permanent residence in this state while attending Boalt Hall Law School at the University of California at Berkeley. On moving to San Diego, Wilson became active in Republican campaigns such as Richard Nixon's unsuccessful bid for the governorship against Pat Brown in 1962. Wilson was a candidate himself by 1966 when he won election to the California Assembly. He has not been out of public office since that year. After serving two terms in the lower house in Sacramento, Wilson was elected to three 4-year terms as mayor of San Diego (1970–1982). Though the mayor's office traditionally had not been viewed as a powerful post, Wilson built a major role for himself in land use decisions despite his lack of constitutional powers. After his unsuccessful run in the GOP gubernatorial primary in 1978, Wilson was elected to the U.S. Senate in 1982 and reelected in 1988.

Though both entered the governor's office facing budget deficits, Republicans Deukmejian and Wilson represented contrasting views and styles. Most fundamentally, Wilson never made the no-new-taxes pledge favored by his predecessor. Deukmejian opposed funds for family planning, whereas Wilson believed in reducing burdens on society whenever possible. Deukmejian liked having pesticide regulation in the pro-grower California Department of Food and Agriculture, and Wilson would suggest moving this responsibility to a newly created environmental protection agency. They also disagreed concerning the advisability of drilling for offshore oil.

Immediately on assuming the governorship, Pete Wilson began cultivating friendships in the legislative branch. He hosted a banquet for legislators and their spouses at which he toasted his guests and said he was proud to be in their company. A rare constellation of events in 1991 encouraged the executive and legislative branches to work together. Fac-

Figure 8-5 "Golly, thanks for the offer, Iron Duke, but I don't think it's going to fit me." (Dennis Renault, *Sacramento Bee*)

ing a recession, and with little prospect of the sort of economic upturn that saved Governor Deukmejian in 1983, California had to confront its budgetary deficit in a bold and decisive manner. In the wake of Proposition 140, the legislature had to restore its image as an institution. Moreover, 1991 was a redistricting year in which Governor Wilson had bargaining chips to influence reluctant legislators.

Saying that he was endeavoring to spread the pain, Governor Wilson delivered a $55.7 billion budget to the legislature in January 1991 that featured cuts in welfare and school spending, as well as hikes in automobile registration fees, university fees, and new taxes on items such as candy, newspapers, and bottled water. Though some Republicans opposed the tax hikes and some Democrats took exception to the cuts in welfare and education, many legislators of both parties called the governor's first budget a serious attempt to deal with California's fiscal crisis. As in his campaigns for public office, Governor Wilson was prepared to sacrifice votes at the extreme ends of the political spectrum to hold the center.

The pattern of Pete Wilson's early appointments had a moderate cast to it despite the number of former Deukmejian employees who joined the new administration. The appointments unit and the legislative unit working with Governor Wilson were virtually unchanged from the second Deukmejian administration. Henry Voss, director of California Department of Food and Agriculture, also stayed on with the new governor. These appointments rated little attention compared to a number of others. The appointment of Douglas Wheeler, formerly an executive director of the Sierra Club (1985–1987), as secretary of the Resources Agency was applauded by environmentalists. Though a Republican, Wheeler pledged to balance the interests of the environment and business in administering his agency. The education community was pleased with the governor's appointment of Democrat Maureen DiMarco to serve as secretary of children's services and education. Wilson also named a Democrat to head the Department of Alcohol and Drug Abuse Programs. In a gesture of bipartisan cooperation, Wilson named Bill Hauck to co-direct his gubernatorial transition. Hauck formerly had been on the staffs of Speaker Bob Moretti and Speaker Willie Brown— both Democrats.

Governor Pete Wilson named moderate Republicans to two high-profile vacancies. To sit in what had been his seat in the U.S. Senate, Wilson appointed state Senator John Seymour (R, Anaheim) to serve until the next general election in 1992. Even though Seymour lost the Republican primary for lieutenant governor in 1990 to state Senator Marian Bergeson (R, Newport Beach), Governor Wilson hoped that Seymour would be able to raise enough campaign money to be able to hold onto the U.S. Senate seat for the Republican Party. Because Seymour had changed his position from pro-life to pro-choice just before his campaign against

Bergeson, there were elements in the Republican Party that objected to this appointment. (Should a pro-life candidate successfully challenge Wilson's appointee in the Republican senatorial primary in 1992, Seymour could have one of the shortest tenures ever in the U.S. Senate.) Wilson also appointed Matt Fong in January 1991 to the seat on the Board of Equalization once held by the convicted Paul Carpenter. Republican Fong, formerly a Democrat like his mother Secretary of State March Fong Eu, was an unsuccessful candidate for Controller against Gray Davis (D) in 1990. Though this appointment may attract Asian-American voters to the GOP, hardline Republicans noted that Fong had been in their party for only 2 years before he received a plum position.

In his Inaugural and State of the State addresses after being sworn in as California's thirty-sixth governor since statehood, Pete Wilson provided Democrats with a rationale for reordering budgetary priorities. He urged lawmakers to support preventative spending to reduce the costs associated with maintenance and custodial programs. For example, programs for pregnant women to receive prenatal care should decrease expenditures for babies born with defects; and crime prevention programs should lessen the number of persons entering California's prison system. The initial reaction to the prevention theme was favorable, but only time will tell if the fiscal pain was spread fairly enough to forge a governing consensus.

Summary

In spite of the fact that executive powers are split among several elected officeholders in the executive branch, an arrangement that cuts into the leadership capabilities of any governor, voters hold the person in the top position responsible for the state of the state. If the economy is sagging, crime increasing, or a segment of the population openly rebellious, blame falls to the person in the most visible position—the governor. As Ronald Reagan, Jerry Brown, George Deukmejian, and Pete Wilson have all discovered, there is only so much a governor can do to effect governmental change. All recent governors have had similar constitutional powers to use in meeting the problems facing California, yet each of the governors has operated in a distinctive manner while in office.

A simple letter by Pete Wilson, just prior to his inauguration as governor, illustrates the type of personal touch that wins friends in the legislature. When the California Citizens Compensation Commission (CCCC) awarded the governor a raise from $85,000 to $120,000 per

Figure 8-6 Governor and Mrs. Wilson visit a classroom to underscore support for preventative spending. (Governor's Office.)

year, legislators were increased from $40,816 to $52,500. Wilson sent a letter to the CCCC requesting that legislators' pay be elevated in light of the loss of honoraria income (Proposition 112) and legislative pensions (Proposition 140). The CCCC did not comply with Wilson's suggestion, but his effort was duly noted inside the State Capitol. Particular events during the 4-year term and the personality of the chief executive must be considered when evaluating a governor's performance. The ability of the governor to rally citizens to the cause and to activate the legislature depends as much on the skillful use of informal powers that accrue to the governor as it does on the formal powers of office.

References: Chapter 8

Deukmejian, George. "My Approach as Governor." *Sacramento Bee* (January 14, 1991).

Dresslar, Tom. "Absentee Ballots Give Lungren the Edge." *California Journal* (December 1990).

Hamilton, Gary, and Nicole Biggart. *Governor Reagan, Governor Brown: A Sociology of Executive Power*. New York: Columbia University Press, 1984.

Little Hoover Commission. "Study on Boards, Commissions, and Authorities." Sacramento: Commission on California State Government Organization and Economy, 1989.

Smith, Martin. "The Democratic Alternative." *Sacramento Bee* (January 10, 1991).

Walters, Dan. "The Unmaking of a Governor." *Sacramento Bee* (June 19, 1988).

CHAPTER 9

Budgetary Politics in California

The budget impasse of 1990 brought forth a torrent of criticism of state government. First, approval of California's annual financial plan was delayed for 1 month into the new fiscal year. Second, the document ultimately produced was lambasted for not addressing the fiscal problems facing California. A leading columnist had this to say about California's 1990–1991 revenue and spending plan.

> As a budget package, it's a cruel joke. It does absolutely nothing about the structural problems that plague financing of public services in California.—This budget, at best, merely postpones the built-in problems until the next governor takes office (Walters, 1990a).

As annual budgets establish spending priorities for all of state government, it is a serious indictment when this process is flawed. The state's financial plan literally contains life or death decisions. Failure to spend public funds to reinforce an elevated freeway in Oakland cost 42 people their lives when an earthquake collapsed the upper roadway onto the lower lanes on October 17, 1989. Spending cuts in prenatal care yield children with preventable birth defects and lifelong health problems. Reductions in forestry and fire suppression budgets lead to the destruction of natural resources and structural improvements, as well as the loss of life.

The formal progression of events that supposedly culminates in the adoption of a state budget each year can be set forth with a fair degree of certainty. (Conversely, the informal negotiations that accompany the passage of the budget are fresh and unique each and every year.) Unlike budgeting at the national level, deficit budgets may not be enacted into law in California. That is, decision makers are not allowed to approve budgets in which projected spending exceeds anticipated revenue. On occasion, budgets are balanced on paper (not in reality) by accepting overly optimistic revenue estimates or depressed expenditure forecasts (Krolak, 1990:4, 37). After a state or local budget has been adopted, it may fall out of balance during its period of operation due to economic developments that generate less revenue than expected and/or greater program costs than originally projected.

The annual budget for the State of California is adopted as a legislative measure and signed by the governor. The budget bill, however, differs in significant respects from so-called policy bills that alter the state's statutory codes after enactment. Most importantly, the budget act is law for only 365 days. In contrast, policy acts usually remain in law books for many years until they are repealed or amended. The 1-year duration of a spending plan means that its replacement must be approved each and every year; a budget bill cannot be allowed to die. (Without a lawfully approved budget in place, the state controller is not authorized to pay the state's bills.) Whereas the budget bill must move through the legislature each year during a review period of slightly more than 5 months, policy bills may take the full 2 years of a legislative session to win approval. If a policy bill fails to win sufficient support during a particular 2-year session, it is simply reintroduced at the beginning of the next term. Despite pleas by their authors, it rarely is essential that policy bills be enacted by a given date to avoid calamity. Besides the annual requirement to produce a spending plan, budget and policy bills also differ with respect to authorship, committee referral, staff analysis, votes needed for passage, and veto prerogatives.

The budgetary or fiscal year (FY) in California begins on July 1st and ends on June 30th. To keep budgets in various stages of development from being confused with one another, it is sound practice to always identify by year (e.g., FY 1992–1993) which fiscal year is being discussed. State government deals with three different budgets each spring. The *current year* spending plan refers to an approved budget that is presently being spent by executive departments. As the end of the FY approaches, departments spend their accounts down toward zero and obtain approval from the Department of Finance to shift funds between accounts. The *budget year* spending plan is a proposed budget that is undergoing review by the legislature between the months of January and June. Departments testify before legislative subcommittees concerning this spending document. If necessary, the administration asks for late changes to be made to the budget bill. The *planning year* spending plan is the compilation of budget figures within the executive branch that have yet to be submitted to the legislature. Therefore, departments simultaneously administer (i.e., spend) one budget, seek legislative approval of a second budget, and plan the contents of a third budget to be sent to the legislature next year. To the extent that there is any rhythm to state government, budget making provides the beat.

The governor and key legislators are the central players in shaping the state budget, but there are other actors who also influence budgetary outcomes. By ruling on legal claims filed against the state and by interpreting the constitutionality of various revenues and expenditures, courts make an impact on the character of budgets. Likewise, activists who qualify ballot measures to increase or decrease taxes and appropriations play a major role in financial decisions in California. For private citizens, Howard Jarvis and Paul Gann certainly made profound changes in government budgets throughout the state. Those responsible for making federal budgets and for establishing the price of oil (which determines California's revenues from tideland wells) also contribute to budgetary decisions in California. Although a general description of how the state budget is created can be set forth, each year the budget cycle is unique due to changing economic and political circumstances.

The Budget Cycle

From origination to final approval, the state budget takes 18 months to prepare. The first 12 months of the process take place inside the various levels of the executive branch. The year-long period during which the administration arrives at requested budgetary amounts is not open to public view. After the governor's budget is made public and sent to the legislature in January, the proposed figures are reviewed in open legislative hearings during the next 5½ months. On legislative passage of the budget bill, the action once again returns to the governor's office where item veto decisions are made in private.

Executive Preparation

Even as the governor submits a spending proposal to the legislature on or before January 10th each year, civil servants throughout state government are considering what to ask the governor and the legislature for 1 year hence. Each bureau or division within the various executive departments calculates what spending levels will be needed to maintain current services. Since roughly 80% of the state budget consists of salary, close attention is paid to the number of positions authorized in each department. Any new position or personnel year (PY) must be fully justified both within the department and within the administration as a whole. Working with the department's own budget section, division chiefs gauge the staffing needed to maintain existing services or to provide for changed levels of service. Before agreement is reached to ask for a new position, a number of questions are asked. Might present staff be reassigned to cover the anticipated workload? Might seasonal or part-time workers be hired to avoid budgeting new PYs? Might present staff be paid overtime to provide the services in question? Is there any other way to deliver the services with the PYs currently authorized to the department?

After some 6 months (January–June) of discussion between division chiefs and departmental budget officers, determinations are made concerning the need to request new positions. Budget change proposals (BCPs) are drafted to justify any new PYs. After considerable negotiation among the various divisions within a department, a priority listing of BCPs is forwarded to the departmental director for approval or disapproval. The development of BCPs inside departments is well advanced by the end of June when the new state budget is enacted to fund state government for the next fiscal year. With a recently approved budget as well as BCPs in hand, departments are ready to take their financial requests up the hierarchy within the executive branch.

Before continuing with the next steps in the budget cycle, it is necessary to provide a short description of the role of the Department of Finance (DOF). In addition to developing population figures and economic projections, the main responsibility of DOF is to assist the governor in preparing and managing the annual budget for the State of California. DOF analysts are assigned to every department, or parts of departments, in state government. Depending on how close a DOF analyst is with his or her assigned department, it is possible that the analyst will be invited to participate in budgetary discussions inside the department. Since all BCPs and requests for new PYs ultimately are reviewed by DOF, it is advantageous for departments to provide full background information as soon as possible to the governor's fiscal watchdogs.

DOF is a force to be reckoned with throughout the budget process.—DOF staff members tend to have long memories. If, for some reason, department personnel are perceived as being less than forthcoming with DOF staff, it usually comes back to haunt the department somewhere down the road.—While DOF staff is sometimes seen only as naysayer, it will often work with department and agency staff to reconfigure or rewrite BCPs in order to meet the priorities of the governor. DOF staff can be creative and helpful when motivated to do so (Krolak, 1990:25, 26, 36).

Returning to the budgetary cycle, the most recently enacted budget for each department is referred to as the current services (or baseline) budget. In the usual course of events, departments are not required to justify their baseline budgets each year. (DOF may prepare BCPs of its own to cut certain services in a department. Should this happen, a department then would have to defend the base for the affected program.) Careful scrutiny is given, however, to all proposed changes in the current services budget. Shortly after the beginning of the fiscal year on July 1st, DOF sends what are known as price letters or budget letters to all departments. These letters establish the allowable size of inflationary adjustments for items commonly purchased by departments and for changes in salary and benefit levels. Using this information from DOF, departments adjust their baseline budgets.

Most departments in state government report to the governor through an intermediate (or agency) level. From 5 to 12 departments each are organized under such agencies as Business, Transportation and Housing; Corrections; Resources; Health and Welfare; and State and Consumer Services. (Departments that are not located under an agency report directly to DOF.) After preparation within departments, BCPs and adjusted baseline budgets are sent to the appropriate agency for review during July and August. BCPs may pass through the agency unchanged, be reduced in amount, or be rejected entirely.

Budget requests from departments throughout state government converge at the highest level of the administration in late summer. To handle the vast workload, early September is established as the deadline for receipt of departmental budget documents by DOF. From September through early November, DOF conducts hearings on the BCPs submitted by each department. These hearings are attended by department directors and their budget officers, personnel from the relevant agency at the intermediate level, and analysts and their superiors from DOF. Recommendations of approval or disapproval are agreed on for each BCP. Occasionally, certain BCPs are given no recommendation by DOF staff and left "open" for the director of DOF or the governor to decide. The outcomes arrived at during DOF hearings, together with decisions on open items, represent the spending levels contained in the governor's budget to be sent to the legislature in January. No matter what their original positions were on particular BCPs, departments are expected to defend the figures in the governor's budget once the spending plan leaves the administration and enters the legislative process.

Several pieces of last-minute business must be concluded before the budget exits the executive branch. In the middle of November, DOF schedules a conference in San Francisco (usually in facilities provided by a major bank) to hear from economists concerning likely business trends for the FY then being planned. Discussion of expected sales and employment levels helps DOF project the revenues and expenditures to anticipate for the FY that will begin over 7 months later on July 1st. Depending on how dignified a term one cares to use, these economic predictions can be called projections, estimates, or just guesses. Despite the precision suggested by listing numerical amounts, budgetary planning involves substantial uncertainty. Prior to the total holiday sales being calculated for the present year, economists are asked to predict what revenues will be generated by Christmas and Hanukkah purchases during the following year.

In November or early December, the governor may meet with the other independently elected executives to discuss spending plans for their agencies. In the case of the Superintendent of Public Instruction, the meeting with the chief executive is called the Education Summit. This event is significant in that over one-half of the state budget is devoted to education. Racing against the constitutionally imposed deadline of January 10th for submission of the budget to the legislature, the governor reviews DOF's recommendations on BCPs. Decisions are made on open items, and, in rare instances, the governor overturns DOF positions on particular BCPs. To reduce the crush on printing personnel, segments of the budget are sent to the state printer throughout December after their approval by DOF and the governor. In an effort to provide the legislature's budget analysts with additional time to prepare their report, confidential copies of the materials sent to the state printer are made available to the Legislative Analyst.

Apart from the need to pass a state budget each year, budget bills are unique for other reasons. Unlike nonfiscal bills where legislators and their staffers draft the contents, budget bills in their original form are not drafted by legislative personnel. Preparation of these massive bills is the responsibility of the executive branch, particularly the governor and DOF. Moreover, the state constitution instructs the governor to identify sufficient revenues to cover all planned expenditures. The governor may not present a budget bill containing a deficit to the legislature.

Legislative Amendment

On or before January 10th, the governor's budget is made public and presented to both houses of the California Legislature. Full press coverage attends the governor's submission of the proposed budget. Never again will as much space be devoted to the state's spending plan, despite the fact that the budget is over 5 months from final passage. Since the governor's plan is to be treated as a bill, the measure needs an author to introduce it as an official piece of legislative business. Unlike other bills which may be authored by any of the 120 members of the legislature, the budget bill is introduced by one of only two people—the chair of the Assembly Ways and Means Committee or the chair of the Senate Budget and Fiscal Review Committee. Authorship rotates from one chairperson to the other on a yearly basis. Before the members of these two committees hold hearings on the budget, there is a 6-week period during which legislative staff undertakes an examination of the governor's figures.

Since its creation in 1941, the Legislative Analyst's Office (LAO) has provided the entire membership of the legislature with an independent assessment of all proposals to spend public funds. In addition to its major task of analyzing the governor's budget, the LAO comments on the fiscal impact of ballot measures and statutory proposals being heard in the legislature. Each budget analyst at LAO is given the responsibility to examine the funding proposed for a certain department or for special programs within large departments. Areas of either inadequate or excessive funding are called to the attention of legislators. To allow members of the two committees ample time to hold public hearings on the budget, roughly 100 employees at LAO strive to finish their critiques of the governor's figures by the end of February. Despite the confidential preview of the proposed budget made available in December, the time crunch is so severe that LAO staffers may put in 20–25 hours of overtime per week during the peak months of January and February.

The past decade has seen considerable expansion in the staff assigned to Assembly Ways and Means and to Senate Budget and Fiscal Review. Some 10 to 15 consultants work for the chairs of each of these committees. They prepare analyses of the governor's budget largely from a majority party point of view. Though lesser in number, minority fiscal consultants to these two committees have been hired as well. Whereas LAO prides itself on being as objective and nonpartisan as possible, the staffers for these fiscal committees are partisan in character. William Hamm, who headed LAO from 1977 to 1986, has observed that, "We are not as influential as we were before the legislature had other voices it chose to listen to" (Gray, 1986:314). More than the presence of new players has caused an erosion in LAO's influence. During the early years of its existence, analysts from LAO were welcome each autumn to observe the DOF hearings on various departments' budgets. When this courtesy was withdrawn by DOF in the early 1960s, LAO lost an excellent means of gathering information on the financial status of executive departments. Furthermore, the confidential previews given to LAO at the time the budget is printed have been arriving later and later in the budget cycle. Of Governor Deukmejian's first term, Hamm has commented that, "This administration, particularly in the last 12 to 18 months, has turned very secretive and shown considerably less willingness to share information and to cooperate in helping us serve the legislature" (Gray, 1986:314). With less ample and less timely information from the executive branch, the depth of the LAO's "Analysis of the Budget Bill" may not be what it once was.

After release of the LAO's analysis to all members of the legislature in late February, public hearings are conducted on the budget for the next

$2^{1}/_{2}$ months. With regard to policy bills, it is customary for hearings to be scheduled by full committees. However, given the magnitude of the budget bill, it is broken into parts and then heard in various *sub*committees. Assembly Ways and Means and Senate Budget and Fiscal Review each has four to six subcommittees for the various segments of the budget such as education, health and welfare, transportation, and resources. (A legislator must be a member of a full committee to be seated on any of its subcommittees. After consultation with chamber leadership, the chairpersons of full committees appoint legislators to serve as subcommittee chairs.) These fiscal subcommittees are significant for two reasons. First, narrowing the number of departments under scrutiny allows subcommittee members to become more expert. Second, subcommittees concentrate budgetary decisions in the hands of very few legislators. With each subcommittee of Senate Budget and Fiscal Review consisting of only three members, just two votes in subcommittee are sufficient to recommend amendments to the budget bill in the upper house. With five to seven members assigned to each of the subcommittees of Assembly Ways and Means, it takes just three or four votes to recommend budgetary alterations in the lower house.

Although debate on any budget item is possible, the fiscal subcommittees ordinarily confine their attention to items highlighted in the LAO's analysis. Mindful of this practice, analysts at DOF prepare rebuttals to LAO criticisms. Each subcommittee will hold some 30 meetings between March and mid-May to hear testimony on its portions of the budget bill. Each subcommittee operates somewhat differently, but there is a conventional order of business that generally is followed. First, an analyst from LAO critiques a department's budget. Second, individuals from DOF and the department under review testify in favor of the governor's January figures (or in support of adjusted figures contained in Department of Finance letters sent to the legislature after release of the governor's budget). Third, legislators who are not seated on the subcommittee, but who are especially concerned about a particular budget item, may seek permission from a subcommittee chair to testify. Fourth, private citizens and advocates for interest groups may testify. Public testimony is much more common before policy committees than it is before fiscal subcommittees. The huge volume of budget items under review discourages lengthy discussion; however, some subcommittee chairs do entertain public input. (Unlike the budget hearings held inside the executive branch, members of the public are welcome to attend the hearings of the fiscal subcommittees in the legislature.) At any point, a subcommittee's own staff (on assignment from the parent committee) may be asked by panel members to comment on pending items.

Subcommittees generally do not take up items where the governor's requested figure is the same as that recommended by LAO and the fis-

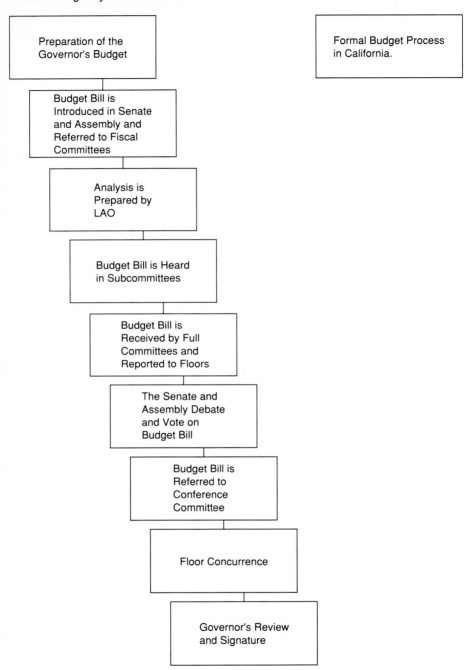

Figure 9-1 Formal budget process in California. *(Source:* DOF.)

cal committee staff. If the figures from these sources differ, the subcommittee is likely to cut or to increase the governor's figure. Easily resolved differences are agreed to in public, and the necessary changes in the budget bill are made. When agreement cannot be reached easily, negotiations move "behind closed doors." Relevant analysts from LAO, DOF, the line department, and the subcommittee staff meet privately in an effort to reach a consensus figure that can be presented to the legislators on the subcommittee. If the behind-the-scenes negotiation by the small circle of budget specialists bears no fruit, then a majority of the elected members of the panel will set the figure to be reported out of the subcommittee. Analysts from DOF carefully monitor all subcommittee changes to the governor's January figures. To keep track of the budget bill as it moves through the legislature, altered amounts are entered into a computer system operated by DOF.

Most legislators want to serve on Assembly Ways and Means or on Senate Budget and Fiscal Review (and subsequently be seated on a fiscal subcommittee) for the prestige and power such a committee assignment confers. Despite the heavy schedule of three subcommittee meetings per week, fiscal committee members like being in a position to influence state expenditures in every legislative district of California. When other legislators need state funds for highways, universities, parks, or prisons in their districts, they turn to their colleagues on the fiscal committees for assistance. Though not always appreciated outside the State Capitol, the chairperson of a fiscal subcommittee often exercises more power than his or her counterpart chairing the full policy committee in the related area. Changes to statutory law crafted by policy committees have little effect unless they are adequately funded by fiscal subcommittees.

To arrive at the most up-to-date projections possible as the beginning of the new FY approaches, DOF holds a second conference with private-sector economists during the spring. Fresh assessments of probable revenues and caseload costs are prepared by DOF. The so-called May Revision to the governor's January budget is sent to the legislature during the first week of May. With updated figures in hand, a flurry of last-minute decisions is made in subcommittee. By mid-May, fiscal subcommittees finish reviewing their segments of the budget bill and send a report of their recommendations to the full committee. Assembly Ways and Means and Senate Budget and Fiscal Review usually accept the reports of their subcommittees within a single day. Though changes in the budget bill can be made by the full committee, to question the work of one subcommittee might prompt protracted examination of the other subcommittee reports as well. Under current calendars, there is not sufficient time for the full committee to do anything more than a pro forma (for form's sake) review of subcommittee reports. The fiscal committees then send the budget bill together with recommended changes to the floor of each house. The annual spending plan for the state of California is rushed through the Assembly and Senate chambers on a two-thirds vote in about 1 hour before slowing once again as it enters conference committee. The brevity of the review accorded the budget bill both in full committee and on the floor reinforces the power of the small number of legislators seated on each fiscal subcommittee.

Given the wide variety of budget bill changes recommended by the subcommittees and subsequently adopted on the floor of each house, the Senate and Assembly versions of the annual spending plan no longer are identical. So that a bill with a single set of compromise figures may be sent to the governor, a conference committee is established consisting of three members named by the Speaker of the Assembly and three members appointed by the Senate Rules Committee. The majority party holds two of the three positions from each house. The conference committee's decisions must be approved by at least two conferees from each chamber. The chairpersons of Assembly Ways and Means and Senate Budget and Fiscal Review alternate each year as heads of the budget conference committee.

To finish its work in roughly 2 weeks, the conference committee allows no testimony during its deliberations; but it does provide one last chance for legislators to comment on the proposed budget. The six members of the budget conference committee hold Members' Day in late May so that the other 114 members of the legislature may plead for expenditures for their favorite programs or for projects in their districts. Legislators who have neglected to win support for their ideas at the subcommittee stage generally do not accomplish a great deal by making an appeal as late in the process as Members' Day.

The conference committee is presented with a massive agenda (some 1,000 pages) contrasting the figures adopted earlier on the floors of each house. If both the Assembly and the Senate have passed the same level of funding for certain programs, such matters are not considered conference items. Under Joint Rule 29.5c, the conference committee may agree to go *below* the lower of the two figures from the Senate and the Assembly, but the committee may *not exceed* the higher of the two figures. (The possibility that an expenditure might be reduced drastically in conference explains why departments go to great lengths to have identical figures passed in both houses.) As they move through the agenda, committee members resolve the less difficult discrepancies between the two houses first and pass over, for the time being, the more serious points of disagreement. Every 2 hours or so, the members of the conference committee recess to allow staff an opportunity to reconcile the status of the various accounts in the wake of the compromises agreed to by the six legislators. Round after round of compromise decisions, followed by staff reconciliation of the balances, narrows the number of remaining items still in dispute. Members of the budget conference committee meet informally outside the hearing room to engage in hard bargaining on the most difficult issues. The conferees may receive instructions from legislative leaders and the governor. Once agreement is reached on the remaining items, the committee members troop back into the hearing room to announce the resolution of the last matters on the agenda. The report of the conference committee hopefully arrives back on the floor of each house during the second week of June so that the legislature can approve a budget by a two-thirds vote and send it to the governor by the constitutional deadline of June 15th. If the wishes of the minority party have not received sufficient attention during the conference, achieving a two-thirds vote in each chamber can be difficult. Democrat Jesse Unruh, Speaker of the Assembly from 1961 to 1968, literally locked Republican members of the lower house inside the chamber 1 year until they provided the necessary votes to pass the budget bill.

"Big Five" Budgeting

The foregoing account describes the budgeting process when the projected revenues are able to cover anticipated expenditures. When a significant gap occurs between income and outgo, as happened for the budgets of FY 1990–1991 and FY 1991–1992, the normal method of adopting budgets is superseded by an informal process involving high-level negotiations among the Big Five. Not to be confused with the Gang of Five (Assembly dissidents) or with the First Five (Senate women), the Big Five consists of the governor plus the leaders of the four party caucuses in the California Legislature. After these five individuals arrive at a budgetary compromise in private, they expect the two houses of the legislature to adopt whatever measures are necessary to enact their agreement into law.

In the torturous summer of 1990, the ordinary role of the budget conference committee was not followed. With revised revenue and expenditure estimates in hand as of May, it became clear that the budget bill then under review (FY 1990–1991) was some $3.6 billion out of balance. In June 1990, the four top legislators (the Democratic and Republican leaders of each house) began negotiating with Governor Deukmejian concerning ways to produce a balanced budget. The governor initially favored closing the gap by making $3.6 billion in cuts to state programs. Democratic legislative leaders wanted some tax increases enacted to reduce the size of reductions in expenditures. The legislative process for the most part was put on hold during these high-level negotiations.

Figure 9-2 "Don't blame me, I'm only the captain of this tub!" (Dennis Renault, *Sacramento Bee*.)

Because of the lack of progress, the legislative leaders stopped meeting with Governor Deukmejian in early July, but the four top legislators continued to meet without the chief executive. Scheduled payments to some state workers, Medi-Cal providers, and local governments were missed during July. Negotiations with the governor resumed in late July when financial analysts let it be known that they were prepared to lower California's credit rating (thereby increasing interest rates on state bonds) in view of the lack of a state budget for nearly 1 month. The negotiators agreed to close three-fourths of the gap ($2.7 billion) with expenditure cuts and one-fourth of the gap ($900 million) with new taxes and fees (Legislative Analyst's Office, 1990b:8). Though many legislators of both parties found the specifics of this high-level agreement to be distasteful, both houses of the legislature approved bills containing the compromise budget of $55 billion on July 28th. Unlike the procedures in use most years, the final budget bills adopted on the Assembly and Senate floors in 1990 were not based on a report passed by the budget conference committee.

Governor George Deukmejian encountered serious budget deadlock in both the first and last years of his two terms as chief executive. In 1983, the legislature did not put a budget bill on his desk until July 19th—34 days after the constitutional deadline of June 15th for legislative passage. In 1990, the budget did not exit the legislature until July 28th—43 days past the constitutional limit. As of 1990, there was no penalty in the state constitution for late adoption of the annual budget.

Though the $3.6 billion budget gap in the summer of 1990 seemed large at that time, it was small in comparison to the $14.3 billion gap that hit the state during the following year. California was not immune from the effects of a nationwide recession that reduced state revenues collected from the sales and personal income taxes. This budgetary shortfall of unprecedented size would not have been closed even if California's leaders had decided to shut down all of the state's universities, prisons, and parks.

The fiscal crisis greeting Governor Pete Wilson as he entered office in January 1991 was so severe that he began face-to-face meetings with the other members of the Big Five immediately. Wilson's behavior differed dramatically from that of his predecessor. Rather than being forced to accept new taxes after the constitutional deadline for the passage of a budget, Wilson at the outset proposed to increase taxes and fees to cover approximately one half of the budgetary shortfall. Although Democrats would have preferred a hike in the personal income tax, Wilson opposed such an increase and opted instead to raise the sales tax. By exhibiting flexibility himself, Governor Wilson was able to obtain agreement from the Democratic leaders to cut welfare checks in the FY 1991–1992 budget and to suspend the law requiring yearly cost of living adjustments (COLAs) for public assistance recipients. Rather than breaking off negotiations with legislative leaders as Deukmejian did in 1990, Wilson kept bargaining with lawmakers of both parties until a budget compromise was reached.

Item Veto

After receiving the budget bill from the legislature, the governor has 12 days in which to act on the spending plan. As its name suggests, the item veto allows a governor to reduce or eliminate expenditure items line by line throughout the budget bill. To assist the governor in this final task, DOF has maintained a complete record of all legislative changes to the spending plan submitted in January. In making item veto decisions, the governor scans across several columns of figures: the executive branch figure of January, the figure passed by each house of the legislature in May, and the conference committee figure approved by the two chambers in June. Though frequent reference is made to using a "blue pencil" on the budget, the governor simply asks DOF staff to retain the conference committee figure or to lower it by a certain amount.

Governor George Deukmejian was not reluctant to exercise this power of office. During his first year as governor in 1983, Deukmejian item vetoed nearly one billion dollars from the legislatively approved budget—a total that approximated all of Governor Ronald Reagan's item vetoes for his 8 years in office. The yearly amount of Deukmejian's item vetoes slackened after 1983, yet he reached a combined figure of $2.5 billion in item vetoes for the 4 years of his first term. As is the case with the general or full veto of an entire statutory enactment, the legislature may override gubernatorial item vetoes by a two-thirds vote. Although Governor Jerry Brown did have a small number of his item vetoes overridden, Governor Deukmejian was never overridden during his 8 years in office. With the likelihood of an override being so remote, the item veto is one of the strongest tools available to a governor. Any legislative increases attached to a governor's January budget are subject to eradication by means of the item veto. A free-spending governor cannot increase amounts in a budget bill, but a fight-fisted governor has great power to cut expenditures.

In the last years of the Deukmejian administration, additional budget making took place after the governor exercised his item veto power. This phase of high-level negotiations occurs in August and September after the governor has signed the annual budget bill. This period is called the "second budget" by some and the "restoration process" by others. If the legislature has cut a program that was part of the governor's budget proposal made in January, the chief executive cannot unilaterally add funding for that program back into the budget bill. Governor Deukmejian, however, would item veto some part of the budget bill and label a particular cut as a "set aside." In his veto message explaining his use of the blue pencil, Deukmejian would offer to spend the set-aside funds in a certain way if the legislature would agree. If the legislature would not go along with the governor's proposal for use of the set-aside funds, the item-vetoed money would simply revert to the budget's reserve for economic uncertainties. The executive departments and the Legislative Analyst's Office do not prepare analyses during this restoration period. The set-aside negotiations are a last-gasp set of naked deals (devoid of technical analysis) through which the governor and legislative leaders attempt to secure funds for programs on their respective wish lists. It remains to be seen whether the set-aside process will continue under future chief executives.

Revenue Sources

Whereas expenditures undergo annual review, revenue laws need not be examined each year. If no bills are introduced and enacted to amend the tax codes of the State of California, then the same revenue provisions that were in effect the year before remain in force. Any alterations to California's revenue codes are carried as separate tax bills, not as part of the annual budget bill. (When tax code changes are enacted, the adjustment in revenues actually collected is reflected in the annual budget.) California employs a wide assortment of taxes to fund the operations of state and local government. Roughly 80% of the revenues at the state level are deposited in the *general fund*, which may be used to pay for programs in any department of state government. The remainder of the taxes collected by the state are placed in *special funds*, which may only be spent for purposes designated in the law creating the tax.

For many years, the state sales tax was the major source of revenue deposited into the general fund. As indicated in Figure 9–3, the sales tax contributed 40% of general fund revenues in 1970—some 11% more than the second largest tax source. In the past 20 years, however, the relative importance of the sales tax has declined. At 34% of revenues entering the general fund in 1990, the sales tax is still a significant aspect of state funding, but the personal income tax has become a more substantial source of revenue during the past two decades. From 1970 to 1990, the personal income tax has risen from 29 to 44% of the monies entering the state's general fund. The share of revenue generated by the bank and corporation tax has remained relatively stable at 12–13%.

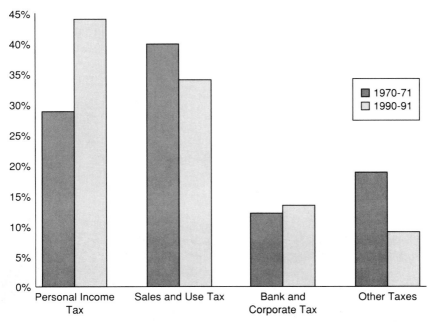

Figure 9-3 Change in revenue sources for general fund 1970–1971 and 1990–1991. *(Source:* DuBay: I–7.)

As of 1988, approximately 13 million Californians filed personal income tax returns—a figure roughly equal to the number of registered voters in the state. "California's personal income tax system is the most progressive in the nation, followed by Mississippi, New Mexico, Maine, and Rhode Island" (DuBay, 1990:1-24). A progressive tax takes a larger share of the income of a high-income individual than of a low-income person. The state sales tax, on the other hand, is considered regressive because it takes a flat percentage of a purchase price regardless of a taxpayer's ability to pay. Poor and wealthy alike pay the same sales tax (with additional fractions for local transit).

Figure 9–4 shows the various sources of revenue entering particular special funds in California. Governor George Deukmejian prided himself on not raising general fund revenues, such as income and sales taxes, during his tenure as chief executive. He did, however, approve of tax increases to the state's special funds. To help alleviate a fiscal crisis in 1983, Deukmejian supported raising motor vehicle registration fees. In 1990, he was one of many private and public leaders to urge voters to pass Proposition 111, which hiked gasoline taxes. In the aftermath of the Bay Area earthquake of 1989, Governor Deukmejian and the legislature agreed to add one-quarter of a cent to the state sales tax for a period of 13 months. Normally, the sales tax is considered a general fund revenue that may be expended anywhere in state government. In the case of the earthquake relief fraction of the sales tax, however, the enacting legislation created a special fund to make sure that these funds would be spent repairing the damage from this natural disaster.

The bulk of the cigarette and tobacco revenue shown under special funds in Figure 9–2 was approved by the voters under Proposition 99 in

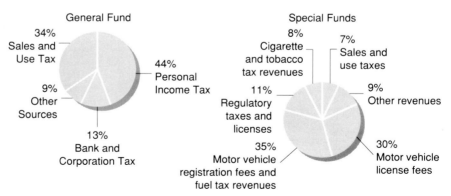

Figure 9-4 California's state revenue sources: 1990–1991. *(Source:* Legislative Analyst's Office 1990a:109, 130.)

November 1988. The revenue raised by this 25-cents-per-pack tax must be spent on specified health and natural resources programs. Similarly, revenues obtained from gasoline taxes and vehicle registration fees must be expended on transit agencies such as the Department of Transportation, the California Highway Patrol, and the Department of Motor Vehicles. By specifying how each special fund revenue source is to be spent, these earmarked taxes limit the decision-making discretion of elected officials. Though special fund revenues were only some 20% of state expenditures in 1990, the long-range consequence of increasing reliance on such taxes bodes ill for institutions of representative government. The popularity of skillfully drafted changes to special fund revenues can be considerable. Voters are able to know precisely what new services a tax change will buy. Moreover, to use the case of Proposition 99, nonsmokers could vote for a tax increase that they would not have to pay since they do not purchase tobacco products.

Aside from taxes already discussed, the property tax is the other major revenue source in California. During the first 60 years of statehood, the state and its localities shared the proceeds of the property tax. In 1910, local governments in California were given the exclusive right to collect property taxes. When the landmark Proposition 13 was passed by the voters in 1978, property taxes were cut by 57%. To ease the transition into an era with lower locally generated revenues, the State of California agreed to accept responsibility for funding a substantial portion of local school district expenses. Though the post-Proposition 13 property tax was raising slightly more revenue than the state sales tax as of 1990, the personal income tax is the most productive revenue source in California.

The property tax law enacted by Proposition 13 could face change due to pending legal cases. Under provisions of the ballot measure, property taxes are to be based on assessed values as of 1975–1976 (with annual adjustments of no more than 2%). If a property changes ownership, the assessed value is allowed to rise to the market price at the time of the sale. Under this arrangement, similar pieces of property in all respects are taxed at vastly different amounts depending on whether the property has had one or more owners since 1975–1976. Studies comparing properties of similar value show that recent buyers are paying property taxes 3 times, 5 times, or even 13 times higher than those paid by long-time owners (DuBay, 1990:I–74). Not only do similar properties receive different property tax bills, but it is also possible for a much less valuable piece of property (that recently changed ownership) to have higher taxes than a far more valuable parcel (that has not changed ownership). These disparities, or inequities, in taxation have spawned lawsuits claiming denial of equal protection of the law. These cases are on appeal. Depending on the outcome of these legal challenges, the State of

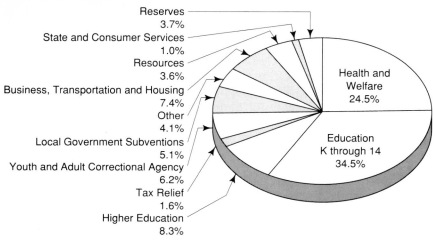

Reserves
3.7%
State and Consumer Services
1.0%
Resources
3.6%
Business, Transportation and Housing
7.4%
Other
4.1%
Local Government Subventions
5.1%
Youth and Adult Correctional Agency
6.2%
Tax Relief
1.6%
Higher Education
8.3%

Health and
Welfare
24.5%

Education
K through 14
34.5%

Figure 9-5 State of California expenditures by program area (general and special funds combined): 1990–1991. *(Source:* DOF 9/90.)

California could be forced to modify its local property tax collection methods.

What expenditures does the State of California make after collecting revenue from this variety of sources? Figure 9–5 shows that the preponderance of state expenditures is devoted to education. In the wake of Proposition 13 (1978), state educational funding now triples that provided by the local property tax. Health and welfare spending is the next largest portion of the state budget. Funding for California's correction system rose substantially in the 1980s; more of the state budget is now devoted to the state's prisons than to the University of California.

Budget Constraints

Ever since the late 1970s, public budgeting in California has become more and more constrained with limitations on the power of budget makers. This so-called fiscal corset requires highly creative maneuvering on the part of public officials to fashion legal, balanced budgets. As restrictions on the budgetary process mount, the ability of officeholders to shift funding in response to new public problems becomes increasingly difficult.

In addition to cutting property taxes, Proposition 13 (1978) also contained two key stipulations. First, the California Legislature would henceforth be required to enact state tax increases by a two-thirds vote. Second, local initiatives to raise special local taxes would need a two-thirds popular vote as well. (State initiatives to raise taxes were left at the majority vote level for the time being.) The net effect of these two changes was to make increasing taxes in California a very difficult, but not impossible, undertaking. Obtaining a two-thirds vote for higher taxes in the California Legislature is unlikely as long as a united Republican party controls at least one-third of the seats in one of the two legislative chambers. There have been some instances, however, when two-thirds popular votes have been obtained for local tax increases. Voters in 15 counties have agreed to raise the sales tax for specified purposes. Moreover, majority popular votes were achieved at the state level to raise taxes on cigarettes (Proposition 99 in 1988) and on gasoline (Proposition 111 in 1990). If drafted very precisely as to the uses to which new taxes will be put, and if a skillful campaign is waged, narrowly drawn revenue increases can be enacted. Hikes in the big revenue producers for the general fund (income and sales taxes) are difficult to obtain under the provisions of Proposition 13. That is to say, a majority popular vote or a two-thirds legislative vote is no easy task to raise these two general taxes.

Further restrictions on budget making arrived in 1979 with the passage of Proposition 4, also known as the Gann limit after its prime mover the late Paul Gann. This successful initiative required that annual state and local expenditures *from tax sources* not increase more rapidly than the rate of inflation and population growth. This expenditure ceiling is also referred to as the state appropriations limit or SAL. This limit was not confining in the early 1980s because the inflation rate was high enough to allow the state budget to move up steadily. However, state expenditures from tax sources did reach the SAL in 1987, and the state was required to rebate (return) $1.1 billion to California taxpayers in accordance with provisions contained in Proposition 4. With the size of certain caseloads (e.g., AIDs patients, prison inmates, and school children) growing much faster than the overall state population, the SAL has not increased as rapidly as some areas of need.

Pressure on appropriations limits at both the state and local levels resulted in two phenomena. First, since the limits applied only to expenditures from *tax* sources, much greater use began to be made of bond financing and user fees—both of which fall outside the Gann limit because they technically are not considered to be taxes. Second, a direct effort was made to loosen the expenditure limit by changing the formula enacted in 1979. Proposition 71 (June 1988) substituted California personal income for the U.S. consumer price index as the indicator of inflation to elevate the expenditure ceiling. This proposition, however, failed to receive the approval of the California electorate despite being supported by Bill Honig (Superintendent of Public Instruction) and the *Los Angeles Times*.

With the defeat of Proposition 71, Honig and the California Teachers Association (CTA) qualified Proposition 98 (November 1988) for the ballot. This measure was designed to assure that K–14 education would receive adequate funding as long as California intended to live with the original SAL. Proposition 98 provided that K–14 education receive either 41% of the *general* fund budget or the prior year's figure adjusted for enrollment growth and inflation—whichever was *higher*. This initiative also eliminated rebates to taxpayers of taxes collected in excess of the SAL. Henceforth, tax sources over the Gann limit would become part of education funding. Because Figure 9.3 combines general and *special* funds, the K–14 percentage is only 34.5% as opposed to the 41% required under Proposition 98. For the general fund alone, K–14 spending for FY 1990–1991 was 41%.

Critics of Proposition 98 contended that it would eventually cut into funding for other programs of state government. Opponents of the measure argued that it was a bad precedent to guarantee a certain percentage of the state budget to one area of spending. What would happen if other programs also were successful in locking up a portion of the state budget for their needs? Those in opposition to Proposition 98 believed such a measure would rob the budgetary process of its flexibility, and budget makers would no longer be able to shift funds to new spending priorities that might arise. Despite such arguments by Governor Deukmejian and others, Proposition 98 narrowly won approval at the polls in November 1988. The requirements of this initiative produced tremendous strife in the high-level budget negotiations that occurred in the State Capitol in the summers of 1989 and 1990. (Recall that Proposition 99 taxing cigarettes also passed in November 1988. Since it earmarked revenues to go to specified health-related programs, Propositon 99 did not provide budget makers with any revenue to be allocated as they saw fit.)

With statutory cost of living adjustments (COLAs) mandating increases in certain salaries and welfare benefits, with a guaranteed percentage of the budget allocated to K–14 education, with major new transportation funding needed to repair and expand California's rails and roadways, and with the SAL still in effect, the fiscal corset was pinching tightly at the end of the 1980s. The *Los Angeles Times* editorialized, "California leaders must begin untangling the fiscal pretzel that is paralyzing government" (March 16, 1989). After 12 private meetings between Governor Deukmejian and legislative leaders in June 1989, a grand compromise was reached on several budgetary matters. California voters accepted this compromise package called The Traffic Congestion Relief and Spending Limitation Act by narrowly passing Proposition 111 in June 1990. This initiative contained the following provisions:

1. Doubling of California's gasoline tax from 9 cents to 18 cents over a period of 4 years.
2. Placing these gasoline tax revenues outside the SAL so that there would be no restriction on their use.

3. Redefining "inflation" in the SAL as California personal income (instead of the U.S. consumer price index) to make a modest upward adjustment in the SAL.

4. Revising Proposition 98 so that any bonus K–14 education received one year (due to tax receipts exceeding the SAL) would not become part of education's budget base for the following year.

Proposition 111 was supported overwhelmingly by California's public officials and by the major newspapers in the state. Some $6 million was spent campaigning on behalf of the measure. There was practically no organized opposition to Proposition 111. When the initiative was approved by the slim margin of 52 to 48%, there was a collective sigh of relief in the State Capitol. It is noteworthy that the June election in 1990 featured very low voter turnout, perhaps due to the absence of a hotly contested primary race for governor in the Republic Party. Higher GOP turnout might well have led to the defeat of Proposition 111. In any case, the victory of the measure was so underwhelming that it cannot be interpreted as a clear signal from California voters that they are prepared to approve increases of other revenue sources.

With the revisions to the SAL contained in Proposition 111, it was hoped that the approval of the FY 1990–1991 budget would be easier than the deliberations on the FY 1989–1990 plan. This was not to be the case. Early in 1990, the taxes actually collected by the state began to fall below the revenue projections on which the Department of Finance had predicated FY 1990–1991 spending levels. Searching for a way to bring down expenditures to the actual level of revenues being received, Governor Deukmejian sought to have the funding guarantee for K–14 education (embodied in Propositon 98) waived by the legislature in recognition of fiscal emergency (Block, 1990:421). The governor persisted for 6 weeks in trying to obtain a suspension of Proposition 98 for the upcoming fiscal year, but the legislature held firm to the position that full K–14 funding be provided according to the provisions of the initiative. To break the impasse, Deukmejian finally settled for program cuts elsewhere and some modest tax and fee increases. Although Governor Wilson initially asked for the suspension of Proposition 98 during early 1991, he soon dropped this request when it became clear that the legislature would not comply.

Budget Reform

A number of ideas have been proposed for altering California's budget process. Only two other states besides California routinely require extraordinary legislative majorities to enact their annual budgets. Arkansas adopts its budget by a three-fourths vote, and Nebraska passes its annual spending plan by a three-fifths vote. (If the state budget is enacted after the beginning of the new fiscal year or as an emergency measure, then Illinois, Maine, and Oklahoma also require extraordinary majorities to pass the budget bill.) When the two-thirds vote rule was adopted in California in 1933, it was to be required only for expenditures in excess of a 5% growth limit then in effect. Through the years, the two-thirds vote rule gradually came to be applied to the entire budget instead of that portion over a particular growth limit. The state constitution was eventually amended in 1962 to conform to legislative practice. One historian of this issue has this to say.

> The two-thirds requirement for appropriations slipped into the state constitution incidentally, incrementally, and unintentionally.—If we were serious about budgetary reform in this state, we would adopt the budget by majority vote (Klein, 1990).

Since the extraordinary majority is required in both houses of the California Legislature, as few as 14 Senators *or* 27 Assemblypersons may block passage of the budget bill. To critics of the present rule, this amounts to minority rule—not majority rule. Should one-third of the membership of *one* house be able to frustrate the rest of the legislature

Figure 9-6 Old Mother Wilson went to the cupboard.
(Dennia Renault, *Sacramento Bee.*)

and possibly the governor as well? Extraordinary majorities are common for constitutional amendments and veto overrides. Does it make sense to have the same vote requirement for a bill of 1 year's duration (the budget) as for a change in the fundamental ground rules of state government (the constitution)? Should policy legislation passed by simple majority require a two-thirds vote to be funded?

The two-thirds vote for passage of the state budget does have its defenders. One student of the budgetary process argues as follows.

> While the ability of a small but determined minority to impact policy may be troublesome from a process perspective, it is also a fact that as a nation we have a long history of institutionalizing the rights of political minorities.—From a historical perspective, the "problem" has been with us for a relatively short time (Krolak, 1990:76–77).

As one columnist sees it, the problem is not with the two-thirds rule itself—rather it is with the failure to forge consensus and the inability to compromise. "It's only when the Capitol's political atmosphere becomes poisoned that the two-thirds vote becomes a major factor" (Walters, 1990b). California is one of very few states to require an extraordinary majority to pass the annual budget. This rule provides ample opportunity for mischief to enter the budgetary process.

If entirely eliminating the two-thirds vote in the budget process is too drastic a step, some other reforms might be more acceptable. California could drop the two-thirds requirement to three-fifths as is used in Nebraska. Following the example of Illinois, a simple majority could pass a budget that is enacted on time with an extraordinary majority required if a new fiscal year begins without a budget in effect. This approach would provide incentive for the majority party in the legislature to meet constitutional deadlines. Another idea would be to establish penalties for late adoption of the state budget, although it is not at all clear who should be penalized for missing a deadline. Should all legislators suffer the consequences of tardiness or just those voting against the budget bill?

As discussed previously, budget changes are that portion of the annual fiscal plan that are most carefully reviewed at this time. The budget base carried forward from the prior year is not thoroughly scrutinized. Examining the base (known as zero-base budgeting) is very labor intensive and costly, so it is seldom done. To conduct a zero-base analysis of an entire $55 billion budget would be a superhuman task, but a rolling schedule of certain departments having to undergo examination of the base might be feasible. With revenue increases becoming more and more difficult to pass, funding might be redirected from programs that can be identified as outdated or duplicative. The executive branch might foster a more cooperative relationship with the legislative branch by reinstituting some practices used in the past. For instance, members of the Legislative Analyst's Office could be allowed to attend Department of Finance hearings on departmental budgets and to receive copies of BCPs that have been rejected earlier in the budgetary process.

As mentioned previously, legal challenges may invalidate the property tax provisions of Proposition 13. More than that, the two-thirds vote required of a local electorate to pass initiative tax increases could be challenged as a denial of the one person—one vote principle articulated by the U.S. Supreme Court. If increases in general fund revenues are not forthcoming, the legislature could take a much closer look each year at the billions of dollars in tax exemptions and tax credits that state government has seen fit not to collect. Certain industries in California that have yet to become profitable may deserve preferential tax treatment, but how many tax exemptions have outlived their original purpose?

Summary _____

Approval of the annual state budget has become a major battleground in California politics. In 1983 and 1990, the governor and the legislature had sharp and prolonged confrontations in attempting to fashion a state fiscal plan. When deadlines are missed and political leaders grudgingly are forced to settle their differences, the outcomes of the budgetary process leave much to be desired. An editorial in the *Sacramento Bee* put it this way.

> The biggest immediate losers from the budget mess that emerged over the weekend are the old, the sick, and the children of California. The biggest long-term loser is the social and economic future of the state. This budget solves almost nothing (July 31, 1990).

In discussing budget making, it is easy to become preoccupied with procedural details and miss the major trends rolling over the state. As much as elected officials want to preserve their discretion and latitude in building budgets, it is clear that California voters of late favor dedicating (or earmarking) special taxes for specific purposes. This is a fundamental development that is likely to compound the problems in making California's public budgets in the future. Californians still have first-class appetites for public services even though the state now has a second-class revenue system. Reductions in revenues are not the whole story. Richard Dixon, chief administrative officer of Los Angeles County, has commented as follows.

I don't personally believe that the major change Proposition 13 brought in this state was the significant diminution of property taxes collected. The major change was it shifted most of the power to the state (Cox, 1988).

Faced with inadequate revenue sources and soaring demands for services, some local jurisdictions in California are on the verge of bankruptcy. At the point when Sacramento has acquired greater power over the course of local affairs, the effectiveness of the state's budgetary process has become highly suspect.

References: Chapter 9

Block, A.G. "Budget Deadlock Takes State to the Brink." *California Journal* (September 1990):420–424.

Cox, John D. "Local Power Shrinks with Budget." *Sacramento Bee* (May 16, 1988).

DuBay, Ann. *California's Tax Burden: Who Pays?* (Parts I and II). Sacramento: Senate Office of Research, 1990.

Gray, Thorne. "The Legislature's Skeptic." *California Journal* (June 1986): 312–315.

Klein, Charlie. "The Origin of 2/3 Vote on Budgets." *Sacramento Bee* (August 22, 1990).

Krolak, Richard. *California's Budget Dance: Issues and Process.* Sacramento: California Journal Press, 1990.

Legislative Analyst's Office. *The 1990–91 Budget: Perspectives and Issues.* Sacramento: February, 1990a.

Legislative Analyst's Office. *State Spending Plan for 1990–91.* Sacramento: August, 1990b.

Walters, Dan. "A Shameful State Budget." *Sacramento Bee* (July 29, 1990a).

———. "Supermajority Rules Capitol." *Sacramento Bee* (August 3, 1990b).

CHAPTER **10**

The California Judiciary

Once known for its stability and national leadership, the judicial branch in California encountered turbulence and criticism in the 1980s. The removal of three justices of the California Supreme Court by the voters in November 1986 was a most newsworthy event, but installing new judges on the high court by no means has solved the profound problems facing this branch. The three Ds of drugs, death-penalty reviews, and disciplining unethical attorneys have crowded other legal cases off court calendars altogether or have produced lengthy delays prior to court hearings. Professor Gideon Kanner (Loyola Law School) has observed that many Californians are not being well served by the judicial system at present.

> As things now stand, society's most unworthy members are making increasingly unbearable demands on the limited resources of the finite legal system, thus depriving deserving citizens of a proper share of the court's attention. At the rate we've been going, it won't be long before the California Supreme Court will become an institution operating principally for the benefit of convicted murderers and sleazy lawyers. A society that professes to live by the rule of law simply cannot so curtail its citizens' legal needs (Kanner, 1990).

During the 1980s, the number of drug arrests in California tripled. Drug offenses (i.e., manufacture, transportation, or sale) now constitute 60–65% of the criminal calendar in California's major cities, and drug-related charges (i.e., homicides from gang warfare and robberies to support drug dependency) make up an additional 20% of the criminal caseload in urban areas (Judicial Council of California, 1990a: Vol. 1:57–58). This vast number of drug cases has made it difficult for California's courts to adjudicate civil cases between residents of the state and has allowed lesser criminal offenses to go unprosecuted. Police are so busy with felony cases (punishable by serving at least 1 year in state prison) in the drug area that misdemeanor defendants (punishable by serving less than 1 year in county jail) skip court appearances knowing that there are not enough law enforcement resources to bring them to trial (Vargas, 1990).

The state constitution (Art. VI, Sec. II) requires that the California Supreme Court hear all appeals when a sentence of death has been pronounced by a trial court. California's intermediate level Courts of Appeal are not allowed to hear capital punishment appeals at the present time. The state's high court also hears appeals arising from disciplinary decisions imposed on unprofessional lawyers by the California Bar Association. Two different studies concluded that no more than one-fourth of the high court's decisions in 1989–1990 dealt with civil matters; the great preponderance of written opinions concerned capital punishment and lawyer discipline (Egelko, 1990). Professor Preble Stolz of Boalt Hall (U.C. Berkeley) has noted another aspect of the California Supreme Court's work load.

> The most destructive feature of government by initiative is that it crowds out other matters that might be on the court's agenda.—The power of the initiative began to be felt during Chief Justice Rose Bird's time; for much of her tenure the court's agenda was dominated by Proposition 13, the death penalty initiative, the reapportionment referendum (of 1982), and Proposition 8. The Supreme Court can decide only about 140 cases a year, and the justices would be less than human if they did not focus their attention on big cases.—The judicial preoccupation with ballot measures seems certain to continue (Stolz, 1990:10).

Under current procedures, the California Supreme Court has little time to devote to family law, corporate law, environmental law, labor law, consumer law, or a number of other areas of civil law.

John Arguelles, Marcus Kaufman, and David Eagleson, the three associate justices appointed by Governor George Deukmejian after voters removed the three members of the California Supreme Court in 1986, served 2, 3, and 4 years on the high court, respectively. For the 50 years prior to the appointment of these three justices, members of the state high court averaged 13.1 years of service (Uelmen, 1989). Short tenure on the Supreme Court means the panel has to deal with its workload with some justices that are still learning the job—a hindrance to its productivity. Hopefully, Arguelles, Kaufman, and Eagleson will prove to be exceptions to the rule and the replacements will remain on the high court for longer periods.

The Judicial System

The judicial system is divided into four levels as depicted in Figure 10-1: supreme court, courts of appeal, superior courts, and "inferior courts." These courts treat a variety of legal problems involving criminal behavior (misdemeanors and felonies) and civil matters (disputes between individuals such as divorces and suits for damages arising from automobile accidents). The inferior courts consist of the justice courts and municipal courts. The superior courts are the workhorses in the system, and it is here that most cases begin and end. Because the justice, municipal, and superior courts hear the cases first, depending on their

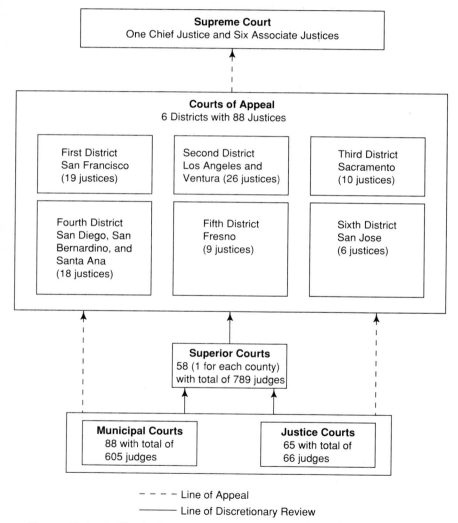

Figure 10-1   California Court System (July 1, 1989). (*Source:* Judicial Council of California, 1990 Annual Report, Vol. 2, page 18.)

severity, they have original jurisdiction. These courts are often referred to as trial courts, because this is where the two sides present their facts and argue their cases. Appellate jurisdiction refers to a higher court where the dissatisfied litigant (party to a legal suit) appeals the verdict hoping the justices will find an error in the original trial sufficient to warrant a new hearing. Although the superior courts can hear appeals from the two lower courts, the courts of appeal and the state supreme court are generally regarded as the appellate bodies. A litigant is entitled to have the fairness of an original trial reviewed by the level immediately above the trial court. Any reviews beyond the initial appeal are at the discretion of higher courts.

Justice Courts

These courts are holdovers from the days when the distance to the courthouse was great and the disputes relatively minor. Until 1974, justice court judges (generally referred to as justices of the peace in other states) were not required to have any legal training for office, and most did not. Since then, new justice court judges have to be lawyers. These courts generally operate on a part-time basis and are located in rural counties. The number of justice courts has declined from 224 in 1972 to 65 today, and urban counties have eliminated their use entirely. Minor civil matters (under $25,000) and petty misdemeanors such as public drunkenness fall within the jurisdiction of these courts.

Municipal Courts

There are 88 municipal courts in the state, predominantly in urban counties. Misdemeanor criminal matters, civil suits involving $25,000 or less, and small claims actions are heard in these courts, although the bulk of their caseload concerns traffic offenses. Persons accused of felony crimes can be arraigned before both municipal and justice court judges, however, their trials occur in superior court. Small claims actions involve civil matters of $5,000 or less, and these cases are resolved without the use of lawyers. Since the salaries earned by justice court and municipal court judges are now the same, and since judges at both levels must now be lawyers, the differences between these two systems are no longer significant.

Superior Courts _____

Each county has a superior court, although the number of judgeships varies, with the more populated areas having more judges. Los Angeles has more than 200 superior court judges, making it the largest trial court system in the nation. Contrary to the impression viewers get from watching television, felony criminal cases (punishable by more than 1 year in state prison) and juvenile delinquency matters constitute only about one-fourth of the cases filed in the superior courts. The bulk of the court's caseload is concerned with civil issues over $25,000, divorce, personal injury, probate, and guardianship petitions.

Courts of Appeal _____

In 1928 the legislature divided the state into five appellate districts with Sacramento, San Francisco, Fresno, Los Angeles, and San Diego as the district seats. In 1981, the legislature created a new sixth district appellate court in San Jose. These courts have appellate jurisdiction over matters coming out of superior court. In the most common setting, appellate court justices sit as a panel of three and decide whether or not to grant a new trial for a defendant claiming an error in the original hearing. Although everyone is entitled to one appeal, only about half of those eligible contest their verdicts. If the appellate justices determine that the trial judge erred in the handling of the case, then a new trial may be ordered. However, most trial proceedings are upheld. If the appeal is denied at this level, then one may appeal to the California Supreme Court—though the state's highest court exercises discretion by accepting some appeals and rejecting many more.

Supreme Court _____

The California Supreme Court is composed of six associate justices and one chief justice. The majority of the cases that come before the court are appeals from lower courts, although original jurisdiction exists for cases dealing with special writs such as *habeas corpus* (a petition asking for the reasons one is in custody) and *mandamus* (an order specifying an act to be carried out). Appeals from lower courts and original jurisdiction filings total over 4,000 pieces of business presented to the California Supreme Court per year. The high court typically will agree to accept some 7% of these items (Supreme Court of California, 1990:14). How does the court decide which items to accept? Items are assigned to each of the justices (likely to be forwarded to their staff attorneys) for preparation of a recommendation concerning whether or not to take the case. These recommendations are discussed at the court's weekly Wednesday conferences; at least four of the seven justices must accept a case for it to be taken up by the court.

Once an item is accepted for review, the chief justice assigns the case to a justice for preparation of another recommendation—this time a suggested resolution of the issues contained in the case. This proposed resolution of the case is circulated to all seven justices who thereupon give a preliminary response in agreement or disagreement with the suggested outcome. When four or more justices signify they tentatively agree with the proposal to resolve the issues in the case, the chief justice schedules the item for oral argument. (The practice of writing a proposed opinion before hearing oral argument has led some critics of the high court to argue that the jurists have already made up their minds before listening to the lawyers presenting the appeal.)

Excluding July and August, the California Supreme Court hears oral argument for 1 week of every month. Unlike trial court proceedings where evidence may have to be read into the record at considerable length, the oral portion of appellate review is very concise. Having read the trial court transcript, attorneys' briefs, and internal recommendations in advance, the justices on the high court know a great deal about a case before hearing oral argument. As a result, appellate jurists tend to interrupt lawyers making oral presentations to ask incisive questions pertaining to the most pivotal points in a case. Soon after hearing oral argument, the seven justices on the high court hold a conference. If the proposed resolution of the case that was prepared prior to hearing oral argument is still favored by four or more members of the court, the justice who prepared the initial resolution of the issues is responsible for writing the majority opinion in the case. Should the majority have shifted away from the initial recommendation as a result of hearing oral argument, the chief justice will ask one of the justices making up the new majority to draft the lead opinion. Once the majority opinion is prepared and circulated among all the justices, dissenting and concurring opinions may be written to accompany the release of the court's holding.

The Bird Court

Until the late 1970s, the court enjoyed a reputation as an independent, professional, and progressive body. It did not shy away from major social issues such as ordering equalization of per-pupil expenditures regardless of the local tax base (*Serrano v. Priest*, 1971) and identifying "reverse discrimination" brought about by affirmative action programs designed to equalize opportunities for minorities and women (*Bakke v.*

State Board of Regents, 1976). In 1972 and 1976, the court declared the death penalty in the state unconstitutional, although subsequent legislative action restored capital punishment.

However, the court's reputation declined during Jerry Brown's years as governor. Brown was accused of politicizing the court by appointing social activists who lacked the judicial credentials of previous justices when they were appointed. Brown did make several controversial appointments to the court, particularly Rose Bird as chief justice and Cruz Reynoso as an associate justice. Until Brown's administration, no minority group member and no woman had served on the court. Brown broke precedent with his appointments of the first woman (Bird), blacks (the late Justice Wiley Manuel and then Allen Broussard), and Hispanic (Reynoso) to the California Supreme Court.

Chief Justice Rose Bird was the most visible and controversial of Jerry Brown's many judicial appointees. She survived a close vote (51.7–48.3%) in 1978 when the state's citizens had their first opportunity to decide whether or not she would be retained in office. Bird's narrow victory at the polls was in part due to the controversy surrounding the supreme court's handling of the *Tanner* case. In 1975, the legislature passed what became known as the "use a gun, go to prison" law, which was authored by then Senator George Deukmejian. The intent of the law was to lessen the discretion normally available to judges in cases where guns were used in the commission of a crime. In the *Tanner* decision handed down in late 1978, the court narrowly ruled, with Bird in the majority, that the legislature did not intend to make this gun provision binding in all circumstances. Critics of Bird immediately charged that this unpopular decision was not made public until *after* Bird's election by the voters for fear that she would be rejected at the polls. Although Bird denied these charges, the uproar was sufficient to lead her to request an unprecedented investigation by the Commission on Judicial Performance as to the accuracy of the allegations. The commission's report neither rejected nor confirmed the charges. However, the investigation did reveal a court beset by divisions based on differences in personalities and political philosophies.

In one account of the events leading up to and including the investigation, Bird was faulted for being uncompromising and a poor administrator (Stolz, 1981). But this view was countered by another assessment that portrayed a competent Bird as the target of a vendetta campaign by right-wing politicians and organizations (Medsger, 1983). Partially in response to public criticism, the court agreed to review its ruling in the *Tanner* case and subsequently reversed its earlier decision. Still, even without the controversial Bird, it was clear that the public was becoming disenchanted with the activist thrust of the court's decisions over the previous 40 years.

In the 1986 general election, the voters decided by a 66–34% margin that Rose Bird should be denied another term on the court. This marked the first time any appellate court justice in the state had been removed from the bench by the public and the vote was made all the more dramatic when two other Jerry Brown-appointed justices, Cruz Reynoso and Joseph Grodin, were also denied reconfirmation. Governor George Deukmejian and all other Republican candidates in that year's general election made opposition to the three justices, especially Bird, key aspects of their campaigns. Anti-Bird organizations, led by the Victims for Court Reform, spent $8 million to defeat the three. Bird ran her own $2 million campaign, such as it was, through the Committee to Conserve the Courts. The thrust of her message was that the attacks against the justices represented an assault on judicial independence. The opposition focused on the three justices' reluctance to uphold death penalty convictions.

The desired balance of judicial independence and judicial accountability is a delicate one. If judges are denied additional years on the courts because their decisions run counter to public opinion, then they may well consider public feelings rather than constitutional obligations before rendering some decisions. On the other hand, the public has a right to expect that judges set aside their own personal feelings in deciding cases. Another problem presented in the effort to oust Bird, Reynoso, and Grodin concerned the way in which complicated legal issues were reduced to 30-second ads for television. Although judges are political figures, they have no vested constituency they can make promises to as do other politicians. Judges are prohibited by the canons of judicial ethics from campaigning in a partisan manner or discussing cases.

The Lucas Court

With the defeat of the three justices, Governor Deukmejian had the unprecedented opportunity to fill several vacancies on the court at one time. He chose one of his earlier appointees to the high court, Associate Justice Malcolm Lucas, to replace Bird as chief justice. Lucas, a former law partner of the governor's, had previously served on the state superior court and U. S. District Court. Deukmejian elevated appellate court judges John Arguelles, Marcus Kaufman, and David Eagleson to the other open seats on the high court. With five Deukmejian-appointed justices on the supreme court, the court as of 1987 had a judicially conservative majority for the first time since 1950. The differences in the opinions handed down by the Bird and the Lucas courts have been pronounced.

The Bird court reversed 58 death sentences and upheld just four during her decade on the bench. Under her successor, Chief Justice Malcolm

Lucas, the court affirmed 64 of 89 capital appeals it reviewed in just three years (LaVally, 1990:356).

The Lucas court has tended to hold that errors in trial court proceedings are "harmless." That is, even though the conduct of a trial may be flawed in some respect, the error is not viewed as sufficiently serious by the high court to warrant overturning a conviction or changing a sentence.

In addition to the change in opinions on the death penalty, the Lucas court has issued opinions favoring a number of California businesses. Although the Lucas court upheld the constitutionality of Proposition 103 (the measure narrowly approved by voters in 1988 to roll back car insurance rates by 20%), the court went on to say that rate reduction would be appropriate only where an insurance company could continue to receive a "fair and reasonable return" on its operations in California. Rollbacks have been forestalled due to this judicial language. Whereas the Lucas court has approved monetary awards to plaintiffs for the actual amount of losses they have suffered due to corporate misbehavior, the court has increasingly refused to award "punitive damages" in hefty amounts that would inflict significant financial penalties on businesses. "The threat of punitive damages discourages corporate misbehavior of all kinds, while the lack of this threat actually encourages it" (Schmitt, 1989).

Figure 10-2   Chief Justice Malcolm Lucas, California Supreme Court. (Photograph by Adam Gottlieb.)

There was speculation that Governor George Deukmejian had intended his three appointments to the state high court in early 1987 (Arguelles, Kaufman, and Eagleson) to be short-term or interim appointees (Egelko, 1990:348). All three were veteran jurists nearing the point when they would receive maximum pension benefits. On their resignations, Governor Deukmejian appointed Joyce Kennard (the second woman on the high court), Armand Arabian, and Marvin Baxter to the California Supreme Court. Kennard was born in Indonesia of Dutch descent; both Arabian and Baxter are Armenian-Americans like the governor who appointed them. Before being appointed to the Courts of Appeal in 1988, Baxter had served for 6 years in Governor Deukmejian's administration as his appointments secretary—a job in which he recommended hundreds of individuals for appointment as judges by the governor. With a former law partner (Lucas) and former appointments advisor (Baxter) placed on the high court, Deukmejian heard some complaints that he was installing his cronies on the court.

The Lucas court did exhibit its independence from Governor Deukmejian in striking fashion in 1988. The court disagreed with the governor on three significant cases. First, and most visibly, the court did not agree with the governor's contention that Representative Dan Lungren had won confirmation as state Treasurer by winning approval in a single house of the legislature. Second, the court refused to overturn the right of Californians to receive publicly funded abortions. Third, the court held that the governor exceeded his authority by exercising his line-item power on a nonbudgetary bill. The appointments of Kennard, Arabian, and Baxter to the high court are not expected to alter the fundamental shift that took place on the California Supreme Court beginning in early 1987. California begins the 1990s with five out of seven justices on the state high court having been appointed by Governor Deukmejian.

Judicial Selection

Originally all judges were elected on a partisan ballot. In 1911, however, party identification labels were dropped from the ballot in an attempt to insulate judges from electoral politics. In 1934, the constitution was changed again to provide for the system used today whereby appellate court judges are selected via a modified appointment system as described below.

Justice, municipal, and superior court judges are elected for 6-year terms on a *competitive* (more than one candidate) nonpartisan ballot. Because most citizens vote to retain the incumbent, it is important to realize that once a judge is on the bench, he or she usually will be there for some time. When midterm vacancies occur, the governor may appoint someone to serve the remainder of the term and thereafter stand for election. Although the election process cannot be dismissed, its value appears symbolic at best. Over 90% of the present superior court judges were originally appointed by the governor, not initially elected to the bench.

The appellate justices (the top two levels of courts) serve for 12-year terms. They face voters in a *noncompetitive* election (only one person listed on the ballot) in which the ballot asks, "Should Judge X be retained (yes or no) in office?" The selection process begins with the governor submitting the names of individuals he or she is considering for appointment to the State Bar's Judicial Nominees Evaluation Commission. This commission collects information from lawyers and judges about the suitability of the possible appointee. A confidential report is sent to the governor that characterizes the potential nominee as either qualified or unqualified. The governor is not bound by the contents of this report; but if the chief executive should proceed to appoint someone that the Nominees Evaluation Commission found unqualified, the State Bar is free to release its findings on the appointee to the public. Once the governor has made an appointment of an appellate justice, the three-member Commission on Judicial Appointments takes public testimony on the qualifications of the nominee. To be confirmed for membership on the appellate bench, nominees must receive at least two of the three votes on the Commission on Judicial Appointments.

Once confirmed, appellate justices must stand for election at the next-scheduled gubernatorial contest. Thereafter, justices again appear on the ballot when their predecessor's 12-year term of office was supposed to have expired. Presuming a justice survives these two electoral tests, he or she finally is ready to serve a full 12-year term. (The elections division of the Secretary of State clarifies when appellate justices must next face the voters—lest there be any question concerning how much of a particular judicial term has already been served.) Until 1986 when Bird, Reynoso, and Grodin were defeated, no appellate justice had ever been voted out of office in California. In 1990, all five of Governor George Deukmejian's appointees to the California Supreme Court (Malcolm Lucas, Edward Panelli, Joyce Kennard, Armand Arabian, and Marvin Baxter) were on the ballot and were retained in office. If a justice is rejected by the voters, then the process begins again with the governor nominating a candidate for the vacancy, followed by ratification by the commission and eventually an election.

The politics involved in staffing judicial vacancies are illustrated by the anger former Governor Reagan expressed over Donald Wright's reluctance to resign as chief justice of the California Supreme Court while Reagan was still governor. According to Reagan, Wright agreed that he would retire from the bench before the governor left office him-

Figure 10-3   "I can think of some other appointees I'd like to reconsider, Danny!" (Dennis Renault, *Sacramento Bee*.)

self. Wright indicated that he would not stay long in the post, and Reagan wanted to be able to appoint his successor. As it turned out, Wright enjoyed the job more than he anticipated and retired after Reagan left the governorship. This gave Democratic Governor Jerry Brown the opportunity to fill this strategic position with Rose Bird, a liberal Democrat who became the first woman on the state's high court. Moreover, Reagan thought he had the assurance of Wright that he supported the death penalty. Again Wright disappointed his benefactor by ruling the state's death penalty unconstitutional, not once but twice. It is unlikely that Chief Justice Malcolm Lucas will prove a major disappointment to George Deukmejian. Aware of Ronald Reagan's frustration with Donald Wright, judicial selection in the Deukmejian administration was done with great care and diligence. It would be a surprise indeed if there are any surprises among Deukmejian's high-level bench appointments. Every effort was made to appoint individuals who shared Governor Deukmejian's philosophy of government and constitutional interpretation.

The Judicial Bureaucracy

Besides the courts, there are three organizations that help in the transaction of business in the judicial system. First, the *Judicial Council* is the chief administrative agency in the state court system. The council enacts rules on court procedures and acts as the official statistician and record keeper for activities of the courts. The work of the Judicial Council is eased by the staff support provided by the Administrative Office of the Courts. This agency also monitors court-related legislation and organizes training workshops for trial and appellate court judges. The 21-member Judicial Council consists of 15 judges from all levels of the court system, as well as four lawyers from the State Bar and two state legislators. The chief justice chairs the Judicial Council.

Second, the *Commission on Judicial Appointments* has the authority to confirm or reject gubernatorial nominations to the courts of appeal and the supreme court. This three-member board consists of the chief justice of the supreme court, the attorney general, and a senior appellate judge. Clearly, this procedure is completely unlike the filling of vacancies at the federal level where U. S. Senate confirmation is required. The commission holds public hearings on the nominee at which time supporters and opponents may express their views. An appellate court judge cannot take office without majority confirmation. At first blush, it appears as if the commission serves as a check against a governor's appointment of unqualified individuals to the appellate courts. However, this is misleading because the state constitution prescribes no qualifications for nominees to the appellate courts aside from membership in the state bar association for 10 years.

The commission was created in 1934 and first rejected a nominee to the state supreme court in 1940, not because he was unqualified, but because he was deemed too liberal. It was not until late 1982 that the commission blocked other nominations, this time to the courts of appeal. This unusual action developed as a result of a disagreement between Governor Jerry Brown and Attorney General Deukmejian over the need for a new appellate district in San Jose. Because the new district of the Court of Appeals had no sitting member to participate on the Commission on Judicial Appointments, only the chief justice (Bird) and the attorney general (Deukmejian) voted on the appointees to this proposed district. Bird and Deukmejian cast their votes in opposite ways—no surprise there—so the nominees failed to win a majority of the commission. Attorney General Deukmejian also cast votes against Cruz Reynoso and Allen Broussard when Governor Jerry Brown nominated them to the Supreme Court. They took office, however, because the other two members of the commission voted for their confirmation.

There have been a number of proposals over the years either to enlarge the commission to include attorneys and private citizens or to abolish it in favor of state senate confirmation of appellate court nominees. The legislature might alter the composition of the commission in the future and also require that appellate court nominees have prior judicial experience (i.e., previous service on the municipal or superior courts) before becoming eligible for a position on the appellate bench.

Third, the *Commission on Judicial Performance* monitors the professional demeanor of the more than 1,500 judges in the state. The commission is composed of five judges, two attorneys, and two private citizens. Because judges occupy powerful positions in our society, the public has the right to expect that they conduct themselves in an impartial and professional manner. It is the intention of this commission to make judges aware that excessive drinking, chronic tardiness, verbal abuse, ethnic or sexual slurs of court personnel and litigants, or disability brought on by age or poor health will not be tolerated. The commission has the power to investigate charges of misconduct against judges and to recommend that the state supreme court remove, retire, or censure a judge according to the seriousness of the infraction. Additionally, the commission can privately admonish a judge on its own authority for lesser improper conduct. Although the public is not told which judges are admonished, this action by the commission probably would be sufficient to block the elevation of such judges to higher judicial positions.

For the calendar year 1989, the Commission on Judicial Performance received 848 complaints concerning judges on the California bench. The commission took action on only 54 cases during this year (Commission on Judicial Performance, 1990). Most of these actions were admonishments, not the more serious censures and removals. The most celebrated removal occurred in 1977 when Associate Justice Marshall McComb was dropped from the California Supreme Court after the commission found that he was not shouldering enough of the high court's workload due to his advanced age. Low productivity and unacceptable deportment are reasons for disciplinary action; the commission does not concern itself with complaints of a judge's "bad decision" made by a dissatisfied party to a suit.

Judicial Bias

Since the judiciary is expected to be the final arbiter in many disputes, it is important that the court operate in an impartial and fair manner. Male trial court judges have been removed from the bench in California for making lewd and suggestive comments to female attorneys (Judicial Council of California, 1990b: Sec. 4:13–15). In addition to sexual harassment, male judges are more likely to accept tardiness on the part of men lawyers than women advocates. The qualifications of women to practice law are more likely to be questioned than those of men. A female attorney has given the following account.

The judge asked that counselors state our name for the record. My opponent stated his name, and then I stated mine. The judge looked down at me from the bench, and in open court, asked me, "Are you an attorney?" I said, "Yes, sir." He then asked "Are you licensed to practice here?" I said, "Yes, sir." He continued to ask, "Will you provide me with your bar number after the trial?" I said, "Certainly sir."

All of this questioning of my credentials was done in open court in front of my client and my opponent, when it should have been done in a more discreet manner out of the hearing of my client and my opponent (Judicial Council of California, 1990b: Sec. 4:24).

Judges are the key to setting a tone of fairness in the courtroom. The behavior of court staff and male attorneys may be influenced by the example set by the judge. Court clerks and bailiffs are more likely to ask women lawyers "are you an attorney?" than they are to pose the same question to male lawyers. Gender bias exhibited by male attorneys can be more pronounced than that of male judges because it is not incumbent on lawyers to assure fairness in proceedings. (The primary responsibility of an attorney is to effectively argue their client's position.) Female litigants and female witnesses frequently undergo far more intensive cross-examination than is the case for their male counterparts. Outside of the courtroom, a male prosecutor offered to drop criminal charges against a woman defense lawyer's client if she would agree to accept a social engagement with him (Judicial Council of California, 1990b: Sec. 4:58).

A major study of ethnic and minority bias in California's courts is presently under way at the instigation of Chief Justice Malcolm Lucas. To paraphrase a quotation contained in Chapter 4, black Californians are 7 times more likely to be arrested than whites; and African Americans in the state are 12 times more likely to receive the death sentence than Anglos. Nonwhites receive longer sentences than whites for crimes of similar severity. Moreover, nonwhites serve longer portions of their sentences than do whites; and these disparities in time served cannot be explained by differences in behavior while in prison. Curtailing bias in California's judicial system will be hastened by altering the composition of the bench.

The bench in California must reflect the diversity and richness of California's social landscape.—It is true that one who experiences prejudice sees it and understands its pain and debilitations more readily than those who have never experienced prejudice. Those who experience prejudice are less likely to dismiss prejudice as just a joke, or call on the victim to toughen up (Judicial Council of California, 1990b: Sec. 4:88-89).

Lobbying the Judiciary _____

The judiciary is expected to be less politicized than the legislative and executive branches of government. To lessen political influences, judges run on nonpartisan ballots and are immune from being dismissed from their positions by governors, although they can be recalled by the voters. Whereas legislators may frequently appear as speakers before powerful groups that want certain bills enacted, judges are prohibited by a code of professional ethics from engaging in any activities that may be construed as a conflict of interest. However, it would be misleading to assume that judges operate in a vacuum free from their own personal biases or outside political pressures.

There are several ways in which groups can attempt to influence the judiciary. First, they may lobby the governor for the appointment of certain judges sympathetic to their cause. A potential judge's political ideology may not be common knowledge among the public, but local bar associations and interest groups usually are aware of a lawyer's position on certain policies such as capital punishment, regulation of business, and environmental quality standards. Furthermore, lawyers belong to organizations that give visibility to their political and social beliefs, such as the Sierra Club, NAACP, chambers of commerce, and fraternal lodges. Governors are well apprised of such affiliations, which influence appointments to the bench. Law enforcement organizations will write letters to the governor on behalf of a lawyer considered for a court appointment if that lawyer is regarded as a law-and-order proponent. Members of the Sierra Club urge appointments of attorneys who are viewed as environmentalists. Deukmejian's rejection of Jerry Brown's three appellate court nominees in San Jose (when the sixth district of the Court of Appeals was created) was based in part on critical letters he received from the state's agricultural lobby. It is unlikely that Ronald Reagan or George Deukmejian would appoint a judge who opposed the death penalty or that Jerry Brown would have appointed one who publicly advocated it. Of course, once on the bench, judges can exercise their independence by taking an unexpected stand on a controversial issue.

Second, in addition to lobbying original appointments, groups may help members of the judiciary when they stand for election. If a sitting judge is challenged at the end of a term or is the target of a recall, interest groups may contribute money, labor, and endorsements to the ensuing campaign.

Third, beyond influencing judicial elections, individuals and organizations who are not a party to a legal suit may file *amicus curiae* briefs in support of one side or the other. These "friend of the court" briefs usually broaden the scope of a lawsuit from a particular case to a general issue that can have a major impact. For example, if the use of a certain pesticide were to be challenged by farm workers in Fresno, it is likely that agricultural groups and environmentalists would be involved as *amicus* participants to argue that pesticide regulations should be broadened or narrowed for the state as a whole. It is difficult to measure the results of *amicus* activity in legal proceedings; however, it is certainly to the advantage of either side to muster outside support.

Fourth, interest groups shape the docket of court business by filing "test cases" concerning issues on which they have encountered unfavorable legislative or regulatory action. An example of such a successful action came about in the California Supreme Court's 1971 *Serrano* v. *Priest* ruling that school districts in the state must equalize public school per-pupil spending. The suit, brought by the Western Center for Law and Poverty on behalf of Mr. Serrano, was originally directed at the disparity in the level of per-pupil expenditures in Baldwin Hills ($580 per pupil in 1969) and the more affluent Beverly Hills school district ($1,230 per pupil in 1969). As a result of the court's decision, school districts throughout the state have to be financed on a relatively equal basis. This means that the state allocates additional funds to supplement public school budgets in those districts where property tax revenues are insufficient to operate the schools on an "equal" basis with school districts that generate more property tax revenues.

Fifth, a recent and controversial tactic in lobbying the judiciary is packing courtrooms during trials. Members of MADD (Mothers Against Drunk Driving) frequently appear in the courtroom where alleged drunk drivers are on trial, or convicted ones are about to be sentenced, for injury-and-death-related offenses. Their presence is a visible reminder to the judge and jury that many citizens are demanding harsher treatment for convicted drunk drivers.

Influencing the governor concerning judicial selection often involves communication out of public view, similar to inside lobbying of legislators. In contrast, the filing of test cases or *amicus* briefs is open to public view. Given adequate resources, other groups can respond to an open lobbying effort on a particular judicial decision. Attempting to influence judicial decisions is one of the more public displays of lobbying power.

The Administration of Justice _____

The functions of the criminal justice system are to prohibit certain types of behavior, enforce laws and apprehend violators, decide the guilt or innocence of the accused, and punish the guilty. Thus, in order of the above functions, participants in the system include the legislators (who pass laws), the police (who enforce the laws and apprehend violators), the judges and attorneys (who try cases), and corrections officials (who deal with those convicted).

In theory, the system is a rational one in which (1) citizens report crimes to the police, who (2) apprehend the suspects, who (3) are then brought to trial in the courts where the judge and/or jury weighs the evidence presented by the district attorney and the defense attorney before reaching a decision, and (4) if the accused is found not guilty, he or she is set free, or, if guilty, then punished in the appropriate manner. However, the criminal justice system operates neither smoothly nor efficiently, in part because of inadequate facilities, low budgets, changing rules, and a lack of consensus about how criminals should be treated. Additionally, the criminal justice system is set into motion after a crime has occurred; there is little it can do by itself to change the social conditions that encourage criminal behavior.

The main responsibility for preventing crime and apprehending culprits rests with the some 30,000 municipal law enforcement officers in some 460 city police departments in the state. Another 6,000 deputy sheriffs handle law enforcement duties in the unincorporated areas of the state's 58 counties. The California Highway Patrol, with about 5,000 officers, concerns itself primarily with traffic-related duties on the highways. The 225 state police officers provide security for state buildings, public officials, and visiting dignitaries in addition to doing investigative work on organized crime.

It was historically the responsibility of the state legislature and the state courts to establish the rules governing civil and criminal trials. Beginning in the early 1980s, two ballot propositions largely superseded the role of these two branches in determining courtroom procedures. The late Paul Gann, renowned ballot initiative sponsor, wrote of being thwarted in the legislature in attempts to strengthen the rules used to prosecute alleged criminals. In addition, "both National and State supreme courts rendered countless decisions which were widely, and largely accurately, perceived as pro-criminal and anti-victim" (Gann, 1988:69). While serving as executive director of the California District Attorneys Association and later as an assistant to then Attorney General George Deukmejian, George Nicholson drafted many of the provisions of the initiative constitutional amendment that became known as the Victims' Bill of Rights—Proposition 8—on the June ballot in 1982. Paul Gann used his network of supporters around the state to help qualify the measure and to carry it to a 56% victory at the polls. Proposition 8 included provisions that (1) established the right of all crime victims to seek restitution (financial compensation) from their criminal assailants, (2) required judges to consider public safety when setting bail, (3) created the right for all public school students and staff to attend and teach in safe schools, (4) abolished the exclusionary rule thereby allowing improperly seized evidence to be used in trials, (5) limited the use of insanity defenses, and (6) allowed a defendant's prior criminal record to be used in court. By placing these and other provisions in the California Constitution, Proposition 8 established rights for crime victims that were not recognized in constitutional law until the passage of this ballot measure. As the 1980s progressed, these rights of victims were implemented in legislative enactments and court rulings.

The second ballot proposition to alter the state's criminal justice system was the Crime Victims Justice Reform Act (Proposition 115) passed by 57% of the vote in June 1990. A major element of Proposition 115 was to permit criminal defendants only those rights granted in the U. S. Constitution and none of the defendant protections that had been developed through the years by the state courts citing the California Constitution as an independent source of rights. This proposition also allows trial court judges (not opposing counsel) to examine potential jurors, requires public defenders to be ready for trial on scheduled dates, and permits the use of hearsay evidence (a police account instead of an actual witness's testimony) in preliminary hearings. Proponents of this measure argue that its provisions will speed up the resolution of criminal cases in California and avoid the delay tactics often employed by defense lawyers. While upholding the remainder of Proposition 115 in December 1990, the California Supreme Court struck down the portion of the initiative that revoked defendant rights based on the state constitution. The justices ruled that such a charge amounted to a *revision* (not an amendment) of the state constitution, and initiatives may not be used to revise the state's basic law. Despite this setback, ballot measures have changed the administration of justice in California a great deal.

In civil matters, the courts are so bogged down that delays make out-of-court settlements standard procedure. It is not unusual for a delay of 2 to 5 years between the filing of a civil suit and the time when it comes to trial in the most populated counties in the state. Although civil cases lack the glamour associated with criminal matters, this side of the law is no less complex. Until 1966, the civil legal problems of the poor were treated sporadically by understaffed volunteer legal aid societies in some areas. In other places, there were no legal services for the poor at all. Such issues as wage garnishment, landlord–tenant disputes, welfare eligibility questions, divorce, and repossessions inflict a particular hardship on the poor, for they cannot afford lawyers to resolve these matters. Community-directed legal services programs were designed not only to deal with these problems but to engage in active law reform efforts to the advantage of the poor as a group.

One federally funded antipoverty program in this state is California Rural Legal Assistance. Created in 1966, CRLA was the most successful of the legal programs and the most controversial. Governor Reagan and CRLA were natural adversaries. Reagan supporters viewed CRLA as little more than a costly vehicle by which antiestablishment lawyers would sue state agencies for political purposes under the guise of helping the deserving poor. CRLA was impressive in its class action victories, although in reality most of its attention was devoted to more mundane legal matters. As president, Reagan sought to eliminate federally funded legal services programs such as CRLA; but congressional support for them prevented this action.

Another type of legal organization that developed from the political and environmental activism of the 1960s is the public interest law firm. Consumer advocate Ralph Nader spearheaded this effort nationally by calling for lawyers to devote a certain percentage of their time, or all if possible, to work in behalf of the public good. Most private citizens do not have the financial resources to challenge the building of a freeway, drilling for oil, or other massive projects that corporations or governments may seek to accomplish. The Center for Law in the Public Interest is one example. The center was founded in 1971 by four lawyers who left the largest law firm in Los Angeles. Among its successes, the center forced the Los Angeles Fire Department to hire more minority group members and Northrop Corporation (aviation) to reveal to stockholders the extent of illegal political campaign contributions. The Pacific Legal Foundation, based in San Francisco, is an example of a public interest law firm with a conservative orientation. Modeled after the Rocky Mountain Legal Foundation, the Pacific Legal Foundation has, among other activities, attempted to recover for taxpayers the extra costs of law enforcement officers during incidents of civil disobedience such as occurred at the Diablo Canyon nuclear power plant in the early 1980s when over 2,000 people were arrested.

Penal System

The California Department of Corrections, part of the Youth and Adult Correctional Agency, administers 21 major penal institutions and 41 work camps. As of 1991, some 100,000 felons were housed in these correctional facilities. (An additional 70,000 offenders are in county jails.) New sentencing laws (i.e., "use a gun, go to prison," "rob a home, go to prison," and Proposition 8 provisions) are adding some 100 people per week to these facilities. The two-man cells at San Quentin contain less square footage than the dog pens maintained by the San Francisco

Humane Society. The overcrowding increases tensions among the inmates, and several institutions are in almost perpetual "lock down" whereby prisoners are released from their cells only in small groups for brief periods of time during the day.

In 1982 and 1986 voters passed $995 million in bond measures to finance the construction of new prisons. It costs over $20,000 to keep an inmate in prison for 1 year. With tougher sentencing laws and a sharp increase in drug-related crimes, the Department of Corrections had to expand very rapidly in the 1980s to absorb many new inmates. California's state prison population tripled from 1980 to 1990. One of the major accomplishments of Governor George Deukmejian's administration was the construction of 14 new correctional facilities in California. Beyond building cells, the department has had to hire and train many new correctional officers. In a period when other departments have experienced cutbacks, the budget for the Department of Corrections has increased substantially in recent years.

About three of every four convicts who complete their prison sentences will be arrested within 3 years of their release from prison. Over half of these repeat offenders will be returned to prison. California's social problems exist just as much inside the penitentiary as outside. Prison violence associated with the growing Third World and black movements has resulted in the growth of various inmate gangs. The three prominent gangs in the prisons, the "Mexican Mafia," the "Black Guerrilla Family," and the "Aryan Brotherhood," are segmented along racial and ethnic lines. These gangs control drug activities in the prisons and the latter two are especially organized around racist and radical political philosophies.

Correctional authorities endeavor to protect inmates from each other, as well as isolating offenders from society. There are essentially two types of inmates: victims and predators. Prison gangs are known for their ability to carry out murders of inmates and sometimes guards. To control prison populations, wardens and their staffs continuously study the members of gangs at their institutions. Good behavior results in favorable work assignments in prison industries; bad behavior leads to loss of privileges (e.g., access to television, reading material, and athletics). Inmates that pose a threat to the general prison population lose all their privileges and are placed in a segregated housing unit (solitary confinement). Though it is possible for inmates to take educational courses and to learn job skills in prison, the correctional system is considered to be far more oriented toward protecting society than rehabilitating criminals. Aside from the added cost of conducting rehabilitation programs in prisons, some officials are skeptical of the overall value of rehabilitation. An employee of the Department of Corrections put it this way.

If you rehabilitate somebody, where are they going? You rehabilitate somebody right now, and you're going to put him down with no money in the
heart of Oakland in a skid row hotel with no job to go to, and the only
place he has access to cash is dealing drugs. Rehabilitation or not, you
have to be somebody really special to not get back into the same scene
(Cooper, 1988).

Capital Punishment _____

In April 1990, Robert Alton Harris very nearly became the 195th felon
to be executed in California. Harris had been on death row at San
Quentin State Prison for over 11 years after being convicted of killing
two 16-year-old boys to use their automobile in a subsequent bank robbery. At the last minute before Harris was to enter the gas chamber, a
federal judge ordered a stay of execution to allow an examination concerning whether defense psychiatrists had properly diagnosed Harris's
mental disabilities at the time of his crimes. Had the death sentence
been carried out on Harris in 1990, he would have been the first resident on death row to be executed since Aaron Mitchell was put to death
in 1967.

In 1972, first the California Supreme Court (*People v. Anderson*) and
then the U. S. Supreme Court (*Furman v. Georgia*) held that capital
punishment was unconstitutional (Zimring and Hawkins, 1986:37). The
courts found that the death penalty was being imposed arbitrarily. Poor,
nonwhite offenders were more likely to be executed than wealthy, white
felons. The courts ordered the states that wanted to legalize capital punishment to enact explicit sentencing standards that clearly distinguished which crimes were punishable by death and which by life
imprisonment. In 1973, then Senator George Deukmejian authored a
death penalty bill that passed the California Legislature and was signed
into law by then Governor Ronald Reagan. This enactment set forth specific "special circumstances" under which the death penalty could be
imposed. In addition to this legislative measure, the voters in California
approved a ballot proposition in 1978 that extended the list of special
circumstances that warranted capital punishment. Murder because of
race, religion, or ethnicity; murder of public safety officers, judges, and
elected officials; and murder-for-hire and multiple murders all qualify
as special circumstances. When former San Francisco Supervisor Dan
White assassinated Mayor George Moscone and Supervisor Harvey Milk
in 1978, he could have received the death sentence due to the multiple
killings and due to the victims being elected officials. Instead, the jury

returned a verdict of voluntary manslaughter based on White's "diminished capacity" caused by his sugar-rich diet (the so-called Twinkie defense). He was sentenced to 7 years and 8 months in prison.

With the passage of death penalty laws in 1973 and 1978, why have there been no executions since 1967? As mentioned earlier, the California Supreme Court must review all cases where capital punishment is imposed. The high court must examine the verdict of guilty of first-degree murder, the finding of special circumstances, and the fairness of the trial court proceeding. Multiple motions are made by defense attorneys to test every determination that the state's high court must make. As of mid-1990, there were 282 inmates awaiting execution on death row at San Quentin while multiple avenues of appeal were being pursued on their behalf.

Proponents of capital punishment argue that the death penalty serves as a deterrent to violent crimes and that it is society's only means of self-defense against the hardened criminal who shows no regard for the sanctity of human life. Opponents argue that it is not a deterrent, that it is applied only against the poor, and that taking a person's life puts the state on the same level as the condemned. Foes of the death penalty tout a study that concluded that 23 innocent persons have been put to death in the United States since 1900 (as cited in Hook and Kahn, 1989:92). Supporters of capital punishment argue that the execution of guilty persons in this century has saved many more than 23 lives by denying these offenders the opportunity to kill again. Two things are certain with the death penalty: the person who is executed will never commit another crime, and there is no way to correct the situation if the wrong person is executed.

Now that there are five Deukmejian appointees on the California Supreme Court, it is likely that executions will once again take place in California. The time-consuming appeals that accompany each capital case mean that there will be considerable delay between the imposition of the death sentence by the trial court and the implementation of the penalty at San Quentin.

Legal Reforms

Ideas to change California's legal procedures fall under two broad types: increasing system capacity and reducing system load. The six districts of the Courts of Appeal could begin to hear appeals in capital punishment cases instead of the present practice of sending all these reviews directly to the California Supreme Court. The state high court in 1989 completed review of 25 death penalty cases, but in the same year had 38 new capital cases sent to it. If this continues, the backlog of death penalty cases at the high court will expand—not contract. An alternative to using the Courts of Appeal to review capital cases is to split the high court into two five-member bodies called the California Supreme Court: Civil and California Supreme Court: Criminal. This arrangement would permit the judicial consideration of many civil issues that are now unable to be reviewed because of the backlog of capital cases at the high court. Associate Justice Stanley Mosk has been advocating this dual configuration, as now used in Texas and Oklahoma, since 1983 (Mosk, 1990).

For a number of years, retired judges have been brought back to the bench on a temporary basis to help deal with heavy work loads in the courts. Since the use of retired judges in this manner has reached its limits, the legislature might authorize the addition to the public payroll of adjunct judges who have not served as judges in the past. Given likely budget constraints at the state level, the prospects for adjunct judges are not high. Alternatively, the idea of instituting private judges (not on the public payroll) is being studied. If such an idea is adopted, litigants willing to pay court costs and unwilling to accept the delays in the state courts would have private judges adjudicate their disputes. By removing some work from the state courts, all cases would come to trial sooner. Critics of private judging are not without arguments.

> Others see it (private judging) as a harbinger of doom for an effective and fair legal system because it allows the rich to obtain speedy justice while the poor are relegated to an overworked public system. Moreover, critics worry that potentially high monetary rewards will woo the best judges from the bench into private judging (Judicial Council of California, 1990: Vol. 1,viii).

In addition to expanding the capacity of the court system, changes could be made to reduce the work load of the courts. There has been 80% public support among Californians for the death penalty according to most polls of late. However, a survey commissioned by the American Civil Liberties Union (ACLU) and conducted by the Field Institute found that there is also considerable support for life sentences without possibility of parole. Some 67% of Californians in this ACLU poll were in favor of life in prison without parole coupled with the requirement that convicts work in prison to pay the victim's survivors instead of the death penalty (Roderick, 1990). If California were to join the 13 other states that have abolished capital punishment (in favor of life sentences without parole) the kind of work undertaken by the California Supreme Court would be profoundly altered. Decriminalization of some types of drug cases would also reduce the load on the courts and the prisons.

In the 1980s, California attempted to build its way out of prison over-crowding by constructing thousands of new cells to hold offenders. Instead of expanding prison capacity, California could make more use of alternatives to incarceration. Trusted convicts could pursue employment outside prison in work-release programs. The whereabouts of these individuals can now be monitored by electronic surveillance devices that they would be required to wear. Another alternative to institutional confinement is to make violators accountable to victims or to the community by having vandals, for instance, scrub defaced school walls or work on environmental clean-up projects.

Summary

The power of the governor in California to appoint people to the bench makes an imprint on politics that far outlasts a chief executive's tenure in office. Through their opinions, judges set guidelines for prosecutors and law enforcement officials to follow in their contacts with defendants and other citizens. Unlike other areas of California politics where party loyalty is honored more in the breach than in fact, party affiliation and activism are significant considerations in making judicial appointments. Given ample financial resources, interest groups may attempt to influence court appointments through lobbying strategies and they can file suits to block or compel a particular government action. For those lacking the money to apply pressure on legislators and executives, use of donated legal services can be an effective means of placing issues on governmental agendas. The defeat of the three supreme court justices in 1986 signaled an end to the judicial activism of the high court. By appointing close associates such as Malcolm Lucas and Marvin Baxter to the top court, Governor George Deukmejian hoped to avoid any surprises in terms of the decisions made by his appointees to the California Supreme Court.

References: Chapter 10

Commission on Judicial Performance. *1989 Annual Report*. San Francisco, 1990.

Cooper, Claire. "Justice's Scales Way Out of Balance for Blacks." *Sacramento Bee* (March 6, 1988).

Egelko, Robert. "The Supreme Court's Revolving Door." *California Journal* (July, 1990).

Gann, Paul. "Justice for the Accuser: Proposition 8—The Victims' Bill of Rights." *Benchmark:* A Quarterly Review of the Constitution and the Courts (Winter, 1988).

Hook, Donald D., and Lothar Kahn. *Death in the Balance: The Debate over Capital Punishment.* Lexington, Massachusetts: D.C. Heath (Lexington Books), 1989.

Judicial Council of California. *1990 Annual Report* (Volumes 1 and 2). Sacramento, 1990a.

Judicial Council of California. *Achieving Equal Justice for Women and Men in the Courts:* Advisory Committee on Gender Bias in the Courts. Sacramento, 1990b.

Kanner, Gideon. "State High Court Hears Fewer Cases of Civil Litigation." *Sacramento Bee* (March 27, 1990).

LaVally, Rebecca. "Closing in on the First Execution In California." *California Journal* (July, 1990).

Medsger, Betty. *Framed: The New Right Attack on Chief Justice Rose Bird and the Courts.* New York: Pilgrim Press, 1983.

Mosk, Stanley. "A Civil-Criminal Split: Dual State Supreme Courts." *Sacramento Bee* (July 19, 1990).

Roderick, Kevin. "67% Favor Life Term over Gas Chamber." *Los Angeles Times* (March 1, 1990).

Schmitt, Richard. "Right Turn: California's High Court Denies Punitive Awards against Businesses." *Sacramento Bee* (July 16, 1989).

Stolz, Preble. *Judging Judges.* New York: The Free Press, 1981.

———. "Initiatives Sap Courts and Threaten Reform." *Public Affairs Report.* Berkeley: Institute of Governmental Studies (July, 1990).

Supreme Court of California. *Practices & Procedures.* San Francisco, 1990.

Uelmen, Gerald. "State Supreme Court and Death-Penalty Burnout." *Sacramento Bee* (December 9, 1989).

Vargas, Dale. "Crime But No Punishment." *Sacramento Bee* (September 9, 1990).

Zimring, Franklin E., and Gordon Hawkins. *Capital Punishment and the American Agenda.* London: Cambridge University Press, 1986.

CHAPTER 11

Local Governments in California

The institutional dilemmas we spoke of in Chapter 1 are nowhere more evident than in California's localities. County boundaries, some dating to the days of the Gold Rush and statehood, bear little relationship to the scope of present problems. New units of local government continue to proliferate, thus making coordinated responses to multijurisdictional issues more difficult to achieve. Counties have been given more responsibilities by state government, but they have less money to carry out their tasks because of the impact of Proposition 13 (1978). As the senior member of the California Assembly and as someone who has been an advocate before local government bodies in San Francisco, consider these remarks by Speaker Willie Brown as quoted in the *Sacramento Bee*.

> We do not have a rational system of local governments in California. What we have is a haphazard, random assortment of governing bodies all fighting over the same dollars and all contributing to a service delivery system that is more of a crazy quilt than a safety net (10-25-87).

Local institutions are markedly different from those at the state and national levels. Unicameral decision-making bodies are the rule at the local level instead of the bicameral legislatures found elsewhere. The relationship between the nation and the states is one involving legal equals (that is called federalism), whereas local units in this state are legally subordinate to the State of California (this is a unitary relationship). Since counties are technically subdivisions of the state that lack their own sovereignty, it is difficult for these units of government to resist the power of Sacramento. Local ordinances must not conflict with state statutes. When the state preempts a section of the law (e.g., narcotics control), local officials may not pass measures in that area. In addition, the clear separation of the executive and the legislative branches found at the state and national levels is not evident at the local level. The multimember boards, councils, and districts elected at the local level usually carry out both executive and legislative functions.

The electoral arena in local government differs as well. Unlike the partisan contests at the state and national levels, localities conduct nonpartisan elections. Whereas the upper levels of government feature legislative races from *districts,* it is still common at the local level to elect councilmembers and trustees *at-large*—that is, seeking votes throughout the entire geographic area of a local government instead of just a portion of it. Recall campaigns (see Chapter 6) are more common at the local than the state level. For the time being, term limits are a reality at the state level; but they are less common in local politics.

Aside from their unique attributes, local governments are crucial to the quality of life enjoyed by everyone in California. Land use, air quality, crime levels, traffic congestion, and K–14 education are but a few of the matters dealt with by local jurisdictions. We intend to devote considerable attention to the structural alternatives that are open to local units, but first it is important to understand that several other factors besides governmental structure contribute to the quality of life in a locality. For instance, decisions by industries to locate in (or to relocate away from) a certain area profoundly impact employment rates, revenues collected, and housing values. It is true that local governments try to attract and to retain businesses by creating industrial parks that offer low taxes and publicly subsidized waste treatment, but this does not refute the fact that it is fundamentally a private decision whether a business stays or goes. The role of community influentials (leaders in the realms of society, culture, and the media) likewise is central to the outcomes achieved in a locality.

In addition to the above matters, there are two other considerations that merit attention besides the structural components of a local government. First, what sort of local political culture exists in an area? Some communities are eager to attract new businesses and residents (the booster culture), others are content to provide minimal services to their citizens (the caretaker culture), and still others strive to enhance the surroundings with museums, parks, and libraries (the amenities culture). Second, what sorts of political organizations or coalitions exist in an area? U.S. Representatives Howard Berman (D, Panorama City) and Henry Waxman (D, Los Angeles) have organized the so-called Berman–Waxman machine that provides campaign assistance to Democrats throughout southern California. This operation helps candidates for local, state, and national offices. Similarly, until his death in 1983, Representative Phillip Burton (D, San Francisco) directed a campaign machine that boosted the careers of the slain Mayor George Moscone and Speaker Willie Brown, among other Bay Area Democrats. Keeping in mind industrial leadership, community influentials, political cultural, and campaign organizations, lest we overestimate the significance of public bodies, let us now turn to the structure of local governments in California.

County Governments _____

When California was granted statehood in 1850, 27 counties were created. Shortly after the turn of the century, the original boundaries were drawn to provide for 58 counties. Although this number has not changed for over 80 years, there have been recent attempts to increase their number by splitting some counties. In recent years, movements for new county formation have been mounted in Los Angeles, Santa Barbara, Sierra, and Fresno counties, among other places. Yet, since 1974, the attempts to create new counties have all failed to win voter approval. Indeed, the last successful county split occurred in 1907, when Imperial County was carved out of San Diego County. Nonetheless, discussions about splitting off new counties are still evident in Mendocino, Sonoma, Nevada, San Bernardino, and Monterey counties.

Unlike cities, which may be created solely by voters living within the new municipal boundaries, the process of forming a new county requires a dual majority. Not only must the voters in the area breaking away from an existing county approve a separation, but the voters residing in the remaining portion of the original county must consent as well. Although majorities have been obtained in some proposed new counties, the voters left behind in the remaining areas of preexisting counties have nixed these separations. With easier rules of formation, new cities have continued to be created in California despite the passage of tax-cutting Proposition 13 in 1978.

California counties vary as much in size as they do in politics and geographic setting. San Bernardino County, the largest in the United States, is 46 times as large in area as Santa Cruz County. Indeed, San Bernardino County is larger than three of the New England states combined. Alpine County, which borders on Nevada, south of Lake Tahoe, has a population of less than 1,500, whereas Los Angeles County is the most populous with close to 9 million residents. Only eight states in the Union have more citizens than reside in Los Angeles County. San Francisco has a unique identity in being the only city-county in the state, one of the few in the nation.

County governments, like other local governance units in the state, derive their operating authority from the state. The state constitution recognizes two types of counties: general law and charter. General law counties follow state law as to the number and function of elected officials in the county. Charter counties, of which there are 12, may establish elected positions and duties as local needs require, provided the state legislature approves. Charter status also contains revenue advantages in permitting more tax flexibility. In essence, a charter is a local constitution. A general law county can become a charter county if a majority of the the residents vote accordingly. The more populous counties such as Los Angeles, Alameda, and San Diego have secured charter status because of the need to serve their large constituencies. There are exceptions of course. Orange County is general law in spite of its high population, whereas Tehama County, with about 45,000 population, is a charter county.

Figure 11-1 California's 58 Counties.

The main governing authority at the county level resides with the board of supervisors. These 5-member boards (11 members in San Francisco) have varied legislative, executive, and legal responsibilities. Board members are elected for 4-year staggered terms by districts within the counties. The boards of supervisors are charged with the responsibility of delivering welfare and employment programs, providing health services, and operating municipal and superior courts. The boards can also provide additional services as county budgets and voter approval allow.

In addition to the boards of supervisors, the other major elected county officers include the following:

Sheriff: is responsible for law enforcement in unincorporated (noncity) areas, for maintaining the county jail, and serves as county coroner.

District attorney: prosecutes on behalf of the counties and represents the counties in legal suits.

Auditor, treasurer, assessor, and tax collector: are responsible for collecting revenues and disbursing county funds.

County clerk: is responsible for maintaining county documents and supervising elections.

Superintendent of schools: is responsible for county schools.

Most of the state's counties employ an appointed *county administrative officer* who is responsible for implementing board policies and coordinating county services. Boards of supervisors also appoint the *county welfare director* and the *county health officer* as well as members of advisory commissions. Commissions on the status of women, human relations commissions, and planning commissions report to the board on topics ranging from discrimination to zoning changes. New advisory boards and commissions may be utilized as the county voters desire. These boards and commissions are excellent avenues for citizen input. Residents can demonstrate their interest and knowledge of issues at commission and board of supervisors meetings. Because many positions on the commissions are filled by appointment, they represent an opportunity for local residents to influence policy guidelines and to begin careers in politics.

Cities and counties differ in more ways than the dual-majority requirement, previously discussed, to create a new county. Whereas counties must carry out certain state laws in areas such as public assistance and health, cities are less encumbered by state mandates. Citizens choose to establish a municipality (from unincorporated county territory) when they wish to collect additional taxes to pay for services over and above those provided by county government. In other words, cities deliver services their residents request, not programs ordered by the state. Further, the financial health of counties and cities is different. Most of the money expended by counties is transferred to them by the state and national governments, whereas cities are nearly self-sufficient financially. With the budgets in Sacramento and Washington, D.C., in deficit or at risk of being so, the transfers allocated to the counties have been squeezed and trimmed. In 1990, the state legislature and Governor Deukmejian agreed to assist the counties by allowing them to bill the cities for booking city prisoners in county jails and for collecting the local property tax. Not surprisingly, California's cities objected to these new county charges, and they moved to rescind the law.

Municipal Governments

Over three-quarters of the citizens of California are residents of some 460 cities in the state. The remainder of the population is located in the unincorporated areas of the counties. As counties are divided into general law and charter status, so too are cities. Some 84 of the more populous cities have charters, which permit them greater structural latitude than general law cities. A city may not occupy territory in more than one county.

There are two basic forms of city government: mayor–council and council–manager. About one-fourth of the cities in California employ a mayor–council form of government. Depending on charter language, a mayor may possess either strong or weak legal powers. A strong mayor has veto powers and a major role in budget preparation and appointments. A weak mayor has some ceremonial duties, but otherwise has little more legal power than ordinary members of the city council. In categorizing weak versus strong mayoral systems, the emphasis is not on the personal characteristics of the mayors but rather on the distribution of legal authority between the mayor and the council. Energetic and talented incumbents in weak mayoral structures can in fact be forceful leaders.

The council–manager combination is used in most of the state's medium-sized cities. Under this arrangement, the city council has the responsibility for policy making with the actual implementation of programs carried out by an appointed city manager. In the early years of this century, the progressives supported this form of city government because it emphasized the nonpolitical administration of municipal affairs by experts. The popularity of this form of local government, together with the nonpartisan elections for municipal offices, has made the "urban bossism" associated with cities such as Chicago, Kansas City, St. Louis, Boston, and New York rare in California.

Special Districts

The most prevalent form of government in the state is found in the special districts, such as mosquito abatement, cemetery, airport, fire, air pollution, transportation, flood control, and water districts. The establishment of special districts has to be approved by the Local Agency Formation Commission and the residents within the district. There are some 5,000 such special districts throughout the state, in addition to the more than 1,100 school districts. Special districts are established to provide services that are not made available by cities and counties. Unlike other types of substate governments, special districts are unique in two respects: (1) most are concerned with only one area of service, although some multipurpose districts perform a variety of functions; and (2) special districts create their own boundaries, which are permitted to transcend city and county lines. Thousands of single-purpose districts each with distinct borders create a jumble of local jurisdictions.

Special districts, like all forms of government in the state, have to conform to the state constitution and Local Government Code in terms of their operating authority. School districts, a type of special district, derive their authority from the Education Code. The operating revenues for special districts originate from the property tax or from special fees imposed such as landing charges for private planes at an airport.

Regional Governments _____

Because modern problems such as air quality and water contamination pay no heed to local boundaries, it has been necessary to establish regional bodies in an effort to cope with such issues. Some of these regional institutions are *advisory* in nature, and some possess strong *regulatory* powers. Councils of Government (COGs) are examples of the former. Counties, cities, and special districts may voluntarily join a COG to discuss mutual problems and make recommendations for the member governments to follow. Since member units may ignore the suggestions of the regional body, COGs have not been highly successful in addressing difficult issues. The Association of Bay Area Governments (ABAG) consists of 8 counties and 89 cities. The Southern California Association of Governments (SCAG) is made up of 6 counties and 175 cities. The Sacramento Area Council of Governments (SACOG) has 4 counties and 14 cities within it. The San Diego Association of Governments (SANDAG) involves some 14 cities, while the county initially opted not to join this COG. These are useful forums for sharing information, but they lack enforcement power.

Regional governments of a regulatory nature are becoming increasingly evident in California. The San Francisco Bay Conservation and Development Commission (BCDC) must approve any waterfront development in the Bay. Designed to stop the Bay from being filled in by construction projects, BCDC actually has been able to increase the amount of open water in the Bay by some 625 acres. The 27 member agencies in BCDC include the U.S. Environmental Protection Agency, the Army Corps of Engineers, the State Lands Commission, the California Resources Agency, and city and county officials from jurisdictions bordering the Bay. The California Coastal Commission (CCC) is empowered to grant (or withhold) permits for all development within the coastal zone (gener-

Figure 11-2 Air Quality Districts.

ally 1,000 yards from the shoreline). The CCC has improved public access to beaches, protected scenic views, and restored some wetlands. The 12-member CCC is appointed by the governor and the state legislature; local governments have resented not having control of land use decisions in the coastal zone. The CCC represents state preemption over local objection. With the crown jewel of the Sierra being polluted by sewage and by erosion related to development, the Tahoe Regional Planning Agency (TRPA) has been granted the authority to issue construction permits and otherwise maintain the water quality in Lake Tahoe. The regulatory powers conferred on these regional governments no doubt stem from the broad public consensus that these natural treasures need to be protected (Sanders, 1989:42–48).

Parts or all of four counties (Los Angeles, Orange, Riverside, and San Bernardino) make up the South Coast air basin. One county alone (Los Angeles) has 86 cities within it. Pollutants emitted from mobile and stationary sources make the air in this basin the worst in the United States. The South Coast Air Quality Management District (SCAQMD) is empowered to regulate emissions by businesses, local governments, and private citizens. The 12-member board of SCAQMD (selected by city governments in the air basin) is endeavoring to enforce new air quality standards that will require significant alterations in life-style. To reduce emissions from idling automobiles, SCAQMD is fostering mass transit, ridesharing, flexible working hours, and cleaner fuels. Excessive emissions from oil refineries and from ships purging their holds of pollutants result in stiff fines. The banning of liquid starters for barbecues set off a furious debate about the appropriate extent of SCAQMD's powers. Residents of this air basin realize they face major problems in achieving cleaner air. "The question is whether they also will agree that only big government can solve them" (Waldman, 1990:290).

The state's responsibility for the success or failure of regional government is undeniable. The state legislature established BCDC, CCC, TRPA, and SCAQMD. If local governments and COGs feel their powers have been usurped by these regional regulators, they should turn their wrath on the State Capitol that brought these agencies into being.

The Structural Debates _____

There have been ongoing controversies about various aspects of local government. One issue related to cities, school boards, community college districts, and special districts is whether elected members of these bodies should be selected at-large or from confined districts. As the 1990s began, some 23 of the state's 460 cities used district elections; the remainder followed the at-large approach. All large cities in California, except the City and County of San Francisco, which is at-large, conduct district elections for city council seats with mayors running citywide. The at-large approach is common for elections in special districts.

Advocates of at-large elections believe that officeholders chosen in this manner are more likely to represent the interests of the whole rather than those of a neighborhood. At-large voting does not prohibit two or more qualified candidates who happen to reside near each other from serving together on a local government body. The best qualified should serve regardless of where they live. A problem with district elections is that incumbents usually draw the districts, and this paves the way for gerrymandering.

Proponents of district elections counter that the at-large approach permits all officeholders to reside in the same area of a community, frequently the most affluent neighborhood. District elections encourage face-to-face canvassing by candidates walking one district; effective campaigns may be waged with less money than is the case with at-large races. Reduced financial outlays in district campaigns encourage a broader spectrum of citizens to run for office. District elections give residents the sense that a particular officeholder is "their representative" in case they should need to lodge a complaint or request government services. There is a symbolic advantage to district elections because they appear to include more diverse elements of a locality. One study of policy outcomes in at-large versus district municipalities found little change caused by the method of election employed. "Ultimately, however, the important political fact may not be whether change has taken place (due to district election), but whether it has been perceived to take place" (Heilig and Mundt, 1984:145).

A hybrid of the district and at-large approaches is now in operation in ten California cities. In places such as Pomona, Santa Ana, and Stockton, candidates are nominated from a specific district and they compete with opponents from that limited area, but they are voted on at-large throughout the entire governmental jurisdiction. This assures that each neighborhood in a city is represented, but it does not reduce campaign expenditures.

Another structural choice facing California's cities is the extent to which they rely on city managers or rejuvenated mayors. The traditional example of the former is Sacramento, where the appointed city manager has the power to appoint department heads, to propose the city's budget, and to negotiate land use matters with major developers. To underscore the strength of this position, the city manager in Sacramento may be removed by the city council only on a two-votes vote. Proponents of the strong manager arrangement believe that municipalities need professional, not political, administration. Although many council members are part-time public servants who have other forms of gainful employment, cities require full-time experts to manage their day-to-day affairs. Managers who are isolated to an extent from political pressure are capable of managing municipalities in the most efficient and business-like manner.

Opponents of strong manager systems argue that appointed officials are inherently less accountable to the public than elected ones. Mayors are more visible than managers, and the public is more likely to know where a mayor stands on the issues. Salaries are increasing for council-members and mayors, and elected city officials are spending more and more time at their public work. In large cities such as Los Angeles, council members actually are paid more than state legislators. In short, elected officials in some cities are becoming full-time participants in municipal governance. Because there are such high stakes involved in contemporary land use decisions, community influentials are unwilling to leave such crucial questions up to unresponsive experts (i.e., city managers).

City officials have the ability to create great wealth through land use decisions, and those in the land development business want friendly faces on city councils. —The result is increasingly well-financed and professionalized mayoral campaigns. And the candidate who works hard for a year raising money and campaigning door-to-door isn't about to play a ceremonial role once elected. The more money spent on a mayor's race, the more power the winner is likely to demand (Salzman, 1989).

Cities such as San Diego, San Jose, Oakland, and Fresno have all strengthened the powers of their mayors in recent years. If mayors run in a single district instead of citywide, are selected by other councilmembers, and have no special powers other than presiding at council meetings, then they are indeed ceremonial figures. Should they gain the ability to propose budgets, appoint department heads, and veto local ordinances passed by city councils, they can become formidable players in local politics. With the exception of Sacramento, most mayors in California's large cities are gaining increased power. If the urban landscape benefits from sound development decisions, the move to strong mayors will have been vindicated. If not, perhaps the expert managers of municipal government should have been left in charge.

In addition to the district/at-large and mayor/manager issues, there are fundamental structural questions involving the consolidation of existing governmental units. As anyone who has seen the word "unified" on the side of a school bus might guess, many small school districts in California have been consolidated in the past in hopes of improving services and saving money. Consolidation can occur in many forms. Similar types of governmental units (e.g., school districts or tiny counties) can be merged to achieve greater economies of scale. It is also possible to consolidate dissimilar government units. For example, following the model of the City and County of San Francisco, two different sorts of government entities can be brought together into one unit. A proposal to consolidate city and county government in Sacramento was put before the voters in November 1990, but it was defeated. Since much of the debate surrounding this vote concerned how powerful the mayor's office should be, it is not clear how much opposition there is to the idea of consolidation itself.

It is also possible to consolidate different special districts with each other or to join such districts with general-purpose governments like cities and counties. "There are now 72 federal, state, and local agencies issuing environmental decisions and regulations in Southern California" (Garcia and Remy, 1990). Proponents of consolidation argue that it makes no sense to have one agency make land use decisions about the location of housing, another authority make transportation policy, and still another body set air quality standards. Since the development of housing determines commutes, and the length of commutes impacts air quality, a consolidated government entity ought to be empowered to make coordinated policies in all these areas. Eliminating elective offices, however, is no easy task.

Seven Cities in California ————————————————————————

Discussions of city life in California can no longer dwell simply on Los Angeles and San Francisco—the long-time rivals. California now has 4 of the 13 largest cities in the nation. After New York City, the City of Los Angeles (3.4 million residents) is the second largest city in the United States. San Diego (1.1 million) is the sixth largest city in the country, while San Jose (750,000) and San Francisco (730,000) are the twelfth and thirteenth largest. Had the consolidation of Sacramento city and county been approved by the voters in 1990, the resulting jurisdiction of one million or more inhabitants would have placed the state capital in the top 10 cities in the country in terms of population. All of California's large cities are growing with the exception of one. Like Chicago, Cleveland, New Orleans, Detroit, and Washington, D.C., San Francisco's population declined in the late 1980s. With the emergence of Fresno and Sacramento, all of California's major cities are no longer situated along the coast.

Sacramento

The establishment of Sacramento was a direct result of the gold rush in 1849. At first, the major commercial center in the mother lode region, Sacramento's economy is now based on government-related jobs. Sacramento is the hub of state government with the legislature, regulatory agencies, executive departments, and lobbying firms located in the city. The *Sacramento Bee* is predominantly Democratic in its editorial policies, but a strong advocate of nonpartisan politics nonetheless. State employees are influential in city politics. This has provided a large talent pool of experienced professionals on which the municipal government can draw. Sacramento's cultural attractions include several excellent museums, a restored old town section, a ballet company, a city symphony orchestra, and a major jazz festival.

From 1921 to 1970, Sacramento was governed by a nine-member council and city manager. Traditionally, the council member receiving the largest vote in the at-large elections would be elected mayor by the council. From the 1940s to the mid-1960s, the council was largely representative of the business and real estate interests. Prior to 1965, only a few women had been on the council, whereas no ethnic minority group members ever had been. According to one observer, the Sacramento power structure governed the city through the "politics of acquaintance." Members of the council "[W]ere for the most part long-time residents with considerable influence; they represented a homogeneous group with common social and business ties which predated their service on the council. This facilitated easy informal communications between them at social events where their paths frequently crossed" (Mitchell, 1976:15).

In the late 1960s, the makeup of the council began to change. For the first time, minority representatives were elected to council seats. In earlier years, it was rare for a member of the council to be defeated for reelection, but in 1969 three incumbents with ties to development interests lost. With five new members elected in 1969, downtown business control of city hall decreased.

In 1970, voters approved a city charter reform measure allowing for district elections for council members and the separate election of a mayor by citywide voting. A liberal Democrat, Phil Isenberg, was elected mayor in 1975. Isenberg had the support of the *Bee* and reassured the business community that their expertise in management and government would be welcomed in his administration. The mayor did more than his predecessors in developing the central city, including spearheading the successful use of tax incentives to finance low-and-moderate-income housing projects in the metropolitan area. The popular Isenberg, reelected to the part-time position in 1979, was credited with skillfully handling council hearings and allowing the council to establish basic policy guidelines. He resigned as mayor in 1982 to enter the state assembly and was succeeded by Anne Rudin, a longtime member of the city council.

Rudin is a slow-growth proponent in a city that has grown tremendously—and the surrounding county areas even more rapidly—over the past two decades. With the arrival of a professional basketball franchise in Sacramento in 1985, prodevelopment business and financial leaders have exerted greater influence recently in both city and county politics. The revitalization of downtown Sacramento continues with the construction of a major hotel across the street from the State Capitol and the advent of a trolley system connecting suburbs to the central city. The sentiments of many local residents were expressed by the *Sacramento Bee* in an editorial supporting city–county consolidation: "Sacramento's fondest wish is not to become Los Angeles, an unplanned, ungovernable, polluted sprawl" (January 2, 1990). With the defeat of consolidation, however, Sacramento is facing the future without a comprehensive planning mechanism.

Oakland

The sixth largest city (population 350,000) in the state has long suffered an image problem. Located on the East Bay, Oakland's tawdry downtown area and early 1940s manufacturing architecture make the contrast with San Francisco across the bay all the more pronounced. World War II changed the structure of the city as thousands of migrants from the Midwest and South poured in to fill job openings in the defense plants. In 1940, less than 5% of the population was nonwhite. Today, the black population is almost 50%, and another 17% of Oakland's residents are Asian or Hispanic. Racial discrimination has played a major role in the deteriorating condition of the city. Restricted by segregated housing policies, African Americans and Mexican Americans were relegated to the flatlands of the city while whites moved from those areas into the surrounding hills. The city council ignored the plight of minorities throughout the 1950s and most of the following decade.

In a city with a heavily Democratic party registration, city politics were controlled by conservative Republican businessmen until the mid-1970s. The Knowland family, long prominent in local, state, and national politics, ignored minority problems in their influential newspaper, the *Oakland Tribune.* Joseph Knowland, the founder of the *Tribune,* was a leader in the attempt to halt the influence of the Hiram Johnson progressives in the early part of the century. The Kaiser family, of steel and shipbuilding fame, joined with the Knowlands in the 1950s as a political bloc to retain conservative control of the city. Joseph Knowland served in the state assembly and the U.S. House of Representatives and his son was a U.S. Senator. Bill Knowland gave up his Senate seat in 1958 to run unsuccessfully for governor against Edmund Brown in that year's gubernatorial race.

By the end of the 1960s, the black population began flexing its political muscle. The militancy of the Black Panthers in 1968 gave way to community organizing. By 1973, former Panther leader Bobby Seale was in an unsuccessful runoff election for mayor. In the 1977 municipal elections, Superior Court Judge Lionel Wilson became the first black to attain the mayoral position, thus succeeding Republican Mayor John Reading who had been in office for 11 years. And, with the adoption of district elections for city council seats in 1980, the previous decades of white voter domination of local elections ended.

There is a feeling of resurgence in Oakland today. The moderate Wilson, who was reelected in 1981 and 1985, is supported by white business leaders and black voters for emphasizing economic development in the city and for hiring local residents. Through changes in the city's charter, Wilson has increased the power of the mayor's office over the city council by exercising more control over department heads and the budget. The city's negative downtown image received a boost in 1966 with the completion of a $22 million sports complex. A major convention center project is under construction, although a long-anticipated downtown shopping complex has been slow to develop. The thriving Port of Oakland, fifth largest in the world, unloads more cargo than San Francisco docks. The city continues to battle a high crime rate, and financial woes hinder city services.

The mayor's race in 1990 (scheduled for the first time to coincide with statewide elections) featured three veteran African-American officeholders. The 75-year-old Wilson attempted to win his fourth term as mayor of Oakland, but he ran a disappointing third in the preliminary balloting. The runoff election was between Assemblymember Elihu Harris (D, Oakland), who had been in the state legislature since 1978, and 11-year Oakland city Councilmember Wilson Riles, Jr. Harris outspent Riles by a 3-to-1 margin and was elected mayor by a comfortable margin.

San Francisco

San Francisco is a picturesque city built on the hills overlooking the bay. The city boasts a multiethnic population, great diversity in lifestyles, the Golden Gate bridge, cable cars, numerous cultural attractions, and an overall ambiance considered lacking in other metropolitan centers in the state. The San Francisco area has also gained notoriety for its homosexual community, the urban sprawl associated with South San Francisco and Daly City, a high crime rate, and what many deplore as the transformation of an aesthetically appealing city into another urban center replete with uninspiring skyscrapers. In spite of very real problems, San Francisco is consistently rated as one of the most desirable cities in the country in which to reside.

The growth of San Francisco and the development of its politics have been functions of several factors peculiar to the geographic location of the city. Its harbor was the main departure for those heading into the mother lode country. This attracted migrants from foreign countries and provided the city with an international flavor unique on the West Coast. The influence of the various labor, neighborhood, ethnic, and economic groups in the city has superseded that of partisan politics.

Instead of two separate governments, the local charter sets out a combined city and county of San Francisco. This government has a mayor and a board of supervisors, thus adopting aspects of both city and county institutions to its structure. The political power of the old order—the financial district bloc and the Catholic Irish and Italians—has diminished. For over 25 years, Democrats have had a lock on city hall. Indeed, Republicans last occupied the mayor's office in 1963. Only about 20% of the city's voters are registered Republican.

From 1963 to 1975, Joseph Alioto controlled city hall largely on the strength of his policies, which favored the old European ethnic communities, labor, liberals, and black voters. Alioto's politics of compromise worked for a decade, but after the firefighter's strike in 1973, his appeal diminished. Alioto entered the democratic gubernatorial primary of 1974, but lost the race to Jerry Brown.

Liberal Democrat George Moscone, a former state senator, was elected mayor in 1975. Moscone lacked the flamboyance of Alioto, but he proved to be an effective leader of the divergent groups in the city that were demanding a voice in the political process. Moscone's service as mayor came to a tragic end in November of 1978 when he was assassinated in his office by former Supervisor Dan White, who also killed Supervisor Harvey Milk, the first self-acknowledged homosexual on the board. Fellow Supervisor Dianne Feinstein, an unsuccessful candidate for the mayor's post in the past, was chosen by the board to succeed Moscone as mayor.

Dan White's trial for the murders of Moscone and Milk resulted in his conviction for voluntary manslaughter, and he was sentenced to less than 8 years in prison. After the sentence was handed down on May 21, 1979, gays, outraged at the lenient punishment, rioted at city hall that night. White was released from Soledad prison in 1984 and paroled to Los Angeles County for a year. He returned to San Francisco in 1985 and subsequently committed suicide 10 months later.

Feinstein, a political science graduate from Stanford, first won a board of supervisor's seat in 1969, but was an unsuccessful mayoral aspirant in 1971 and again in 1975. She was elected mayor in 1979. Feinstein proved to be an astute politician, although her hard-driving administrative style and work habits irritated some of the board. She was regarded as a liberal on social and economic issues and as a conservative on crime. Her support of a controversial handgun control ordinance and veto of a gay-rights measure led to a recall move against her in 1983. She held her office with an 80% vote and was reelected mayor 7 months later by an equally impressive majority.

San Francisco's charter establishes a strong-mayor system. The mayor proposes the budget, makes key appointments, and may veto ordinances passed by the 11-member Board of Supervisors (chosen at-large). Feinstein used her budgetary authority to strengthen the police and fire departments and to fund the most comprehensive AIDS education programs in the world. Having served two full terms as mayor (plus a portion of Moscone's term), Feinstein was forbidden by the charter from running again for mayor in 1987.

Assemblymember Art Agnos (D, San Francisco), a member of the state legislature since 1976, defeated former Supervisor John Molinari in the 1987 mayoral race. Agnos promptly was confronted with a number of difficult problems. On leaving office, Feinstein bequeathed Agnos a budgetary deficit. The owner of the San Francisco Giants baseball team threatened to relocate the team unless a new stadium was provided by the city and county. The Loma Prieta earthquake in 1989 was a costly blow to a city that relies heavily on tourism. Mayor Agnos was a reassuring presence throughout the crisis, and he helped the city rebound as quickly as possible.

As the 1991 city election approached, Agnos received the welcome news that a most worthy adversary would not be making a race to deny him a second term. State Senator Quentin Kopp (I, San Francisco), formerly a member of the Board of Supervisors for 15 years, declined to run against Agnos. Unlike some major cities, three of the most important politicians in San Francisco actually are in state government: Assembly Speaker Willie Brown, Lt. Governor Leo McCarthy, and state Senator Quentin Kopp.

San Jose

San Jose has experienced more dramatic changes in this century than any other city in California. Founded in 1777 during the period of Spanish colonization of the Pacific Coast, the area was naturally blessed with abundant water, a mild climate, and fertile soil. The end of the gold rush turned many miners into farmers. The community was the commercial center of the Santa Clara Valley and for a brief time in the early 1850s served as the first capital of the state. By the 1880s San Jose politics was dominated by the Southern Pacific Railroad. As in the rest of the state, opposition mounted to the railroad dynasty, and progressive reformers captured city hall in 1902.

Past and present San Jose politics have revolved around growth. By 1940, the population of San Jose was 68,000, with agriculture as the primary economic base. During the war years and into the late 1940s a number of prominent companies, including IBM, General Electric, Pittsburgh Steel, and Kaiser, established major plants in the area. During the period through the 1970s, the dominant theme was growth—population and economic. By 1950 there were 95,000 people living in the 17 square miles that encompassed the city. By 1960 the city had enlarged to 64 square miles with a population of over 200,000. It more than doubled during the 1960s, into an urban center of 446,000 people in 149 square miles. Essentially the population of San Jose, now 750,000, had doubled three times in 35 years. With growth came an economic price tag in the form of schools, water and sewer services, public safety personnel, and highway costs to accommodate the new residents.

Growth was inevitable. San Jose was near San Francisco for commercial purposes, had a better climate than the bay city, and, unlike San Francisco, had no unions but did have space for new business expansion. The electronics industry hastened development, encouraged by Stanford engineers who, instead of heading east for their fortunes, established their own companies in the area beginning in the late 1930s.

The war years brought defense contracts to area companies. Business interests prospered, employment opportunities swelled, and the chamber of commerce aggressively promoted the hospitality of San Jose to businessmen interested in relocating to the area. Generally, what industry wanted, local business and political leaders delivered, whether it be capital improvements, zoning changes or more land for expansion. The major newspaper, the *Mercury News,* cheered on the growth advocates.

In 1962, residents rebelled against the growth-oriented city council by electing three antigrowth council members and in 1970 a new city manager abandoned annexation policies in favor of urban development. The following year, Janet Gray Hayes, an environmentalist, was elected to the city council. In the 1974 elections Hayes was chosen mayor and her allies on the council were retained despite being outspent 10 to 1 by the old guard.

The mayor appoints citizens to commissions and presides at the council meetings but, until recent changes in the city charter strengthened the position, lacked the power to direct city policies. Since the late 1970s, council members have been chosen by districts. Hayes was reelected in 1978 and then stepped down from office to be succeeded by Councilman Tom McEnery in the 1982 elections. McEnery, reelected in 1986, comes from a prominent San Jose family long active in local business and politics.

McEnery made good on his pledge to rejuvenate the downtown area. He doubled his staff and budget, gained approval for a $139 million downtown convention center, built libraries and parks, increased the size of the city's police force, initiated a trolley system, and improved the city's airport. He also increased the power of the mayor's office on budget matters. McEnery was criticized for slow action in dealing with the toxic waste problem and for not being responsive to the needs of the city's poor and minority residents. High housing prices and severe traffic congestion hamper further industrial expansion. As in San Francisco, the city charter prohibits an incumbent mayor from serving more than two terms in office.

After serving 10 years on the city council, Susan Hammer was elected mayor of San Jose in 1990. The race between Hammer and Frank Fiscalini, a local school superintendent, was very close (she won by some 1,200 votes) and extremely bitter. Hammer's election reinforced San Jose's reputation as the so-called "feminist capital" of American politics. Eight of 10 members of the City Council in 1990 were women, as were 3 of 5 members of the Santa Clara County Board of Supervisors.

Fresno

Politics in Fresno focuses more on agricultural and business issues than on partisan concerns. The city was incorporated in 1885 shortly after the completion of the rail link down the San Joaquin Valley. By 1900, Armenians, Yugoslavs, and other immigrants combined to make the county the major producer of wine in the nation. Today, Fresno County is the nation's number one farm county with more than 200 commercial crops in production.

Members of 85 different ethnic groups are included among the 320,000 residents in the city of Fresno. Local government is a weak-mayor system with the council responsible for the selection of a city manager. Ideally, this reform type of government is supposed to produce stable, expert management of local affairs. In Fresno, however, the council and manager have been at odds with each other for the last two decades. Like San Diego, Fresno has been plagued by embarrassing legal and political troubles affecting the city council and law enforcement officials.

In the mid-1950s, the business community began voicing concern over the haphazard development in the city and the deteriorating condition of the business district. The immediate response was to transform much of the commercial center of town into a mall conducive to attracting shoppers and new business. The mall was dedicated in 1966 and encompasses over 85 acres of land.

The mall has not been the panacea for Fresno's urban ills that many anticipated. Regional shopping centers continue to be built, and suburban development advances with few restrictions. Thus, rejuvenating the downtown area is still a problem. Another aspect of the urban sprawl concerns the prime agricultural land that is falling to development. One response to this, proposed by then Fresno Mayor Daniel Whitehurst, was to dissolve the current city government and incorporate a new city that would include the urbanized areas of metropolitan Fresno. The plan never made it off the drawing board. Whitehurst, an attorney, was voted on the city council in 1975 and two years later, with a 120-vote margin, was elected mayor at the age of 29. In 1982, he made an unsuccessful bid for the Democratic senate nomination. Whitehurst's successor, Doyle Doig, tried to bring new business opportunities to the area. The mayor and the city council did establish a 20-member Long Range Goal Setting Group to formulate new policy options for council consideration.

Former television newscaster Karen Humphrey was elected mayor of Fresno in 1989. Like Sacramento, Fresno has a weak-mayor system with a strong city manager. Humphrey and her opponent, attorney Tony Capozzi, disagreed concerning this structural issue. Capozzi urged residents of Fresno to follow San Jose's lead in switching to the strong-mayor arrangement, whereas Humphrey supported the existing weak-mayor approach. With moderate housing prices and the likelihood that the University of California will locate a new campus nearby, growth pressures in Fresno will continue.

Los Angeles

According to 1990 population figures, 3 of every 10 Californians live in Los Angeles County, a sprawling area of 4,000 square miles that contains 86 municipalities, 95 school districts, and 275 special districts. There are tremendous qualitative differences in how residents work, live, and generally survive in these communities. Some of the richest and the poorest suburbs in the United States are found in this county.

Politically, the county is run by a five-member board of supervisors and an appointed county administrative officer. With a population of nearly 9 million residents (i.e., more than live in 42 of the 50 states in the country), each board member represents 1.8 million individuals. Obviously, the economic costs of managing a county of this size are tremendous. In 1990, the Los Angeles County budget, at almost $10 billion, was larger than the entire budgets in all but the largest states in the nation. In recent years, the divisiveness among board members has increased as a result of the competition for limited funds for district projects and the changing demographic makeup of the districts themselves. Board members are reluctant to interfere in another member's district and they operate their own districts much like feudal lords.

In response to a lawsuit filed by the Mexican American Legal Defense and Education Fund (MALDEF), U.S. District Judge David Kenyon in 1990 ordered that the supervisorial district lines be redrawn in Los Angeles County. He found that the incumbent supervisors (all white males) had "intentionally discriminated against the county's three mil-

LOS ANGELES COUNTY
BOARD OF
SUPERVISORS

Se Habla Español

Sacramento Bee

Figure 11-3 (Dennis Renault, *Sacramento Bee*)

lion Latinos when drawing district lines in 1981" (Bucy, 1991:22). After new district lines were approved by Judge Kenyon, one district contained Latinos amounting to 51% of the registered voters. Gloria Molina, the first Latina to serve in the California Assembly as well as on the Los Angeles City Council, was elected to the Los Angeles County Board of Supervisors from this new seat in early 1991.

The center of the county is the city of Los Angeles. Established in 1781, the "City of Angels" is just as likely to be referred to today as "the capital of Kitsch." Some 3.4 million people live in the city, or about 12% of the state's population.

The *Los Angeles Times* has played an important role in the development of the southern California region since Colonel Otis Chandler bought the fledgling paper in 1886. Throughout the first half of the century, the paper championed population growth, was antilabor union, probusiness, and conservative in its political orientation. The political influence of the *Times* has remained strong for over the past 40 years. In the 1950s, the *Times* supported Mayor Norris Poulson through three terms in office and then his successor, Sam Yorty, for two terms. In 1969, the paper endorsed black city councilman Tom Bradley; but Yorty, running what some felt was a racist campaign, won anyway. Again with the *Times* support, Bradley successfully unseated Yorty in 1973.

In contrast to Yorty, Bradley's style was one of quiet mediation. The mayor avoided becoming enmeshed in the school-busing turmoil in the

1970s, but he actively pursued more civilian control of the Los Angeles Police Department. The department had enjoyed excellent relations with former Mayors Poulson and Yorty, largely because they provided department leadership with much insulation from outside interference. Even before the Rodney King beating in 1991, the department had been criticized for application of excessive force involving police shootings and use of "choke-holds" to subdue suspects. Bradley established a mayor's Police Commission to investigate alleged acts of police abuse of force. Police Chief Daryl Gates became so incensed over Bradley's actions that he considered running against him.

It would appear, at first glance, that Los Angeles is governed under a strong-mayor system. On closer inspection, it is evident that the mayor's powers have been constrained by the assignment of key duties to an assortment of commissions and civil servants. The mayor does not sit on the 15-member city council, which instead selects its own president to serve as presiding officer. The council members have been aptly characterized as "15 little mayors" given the manner in which they protect their own districts. The size of this body ensures disagreement on most issues, thus council members are constantly forming short-lived alliances to support (or oppose) each other on various projects. Council members serve 4-year staggered terms and are elected from districts. As of 1990, the council had nine white members, three African-American members, two Latin-American members, and one Asian-American member.

The elected officials constitute one aspect of political power in Los Angeles. Downtown business leaders are equally influential, although much less visible. The powerful business leaders include corporate officials from the large banks, oil companies, aviation, insurance, Southern California Edison, and the Chandler family. In general, they opposed Bradley when he was first elected in 1973. Early in his first term, Bradley began appointing business executives to key advisory posts. He realized that he needed the support of community influentials to run the city properly. Downtown business interests were vocal supporters of, and major contributors to, Bradley's subsequent reelections in 1977, 1981, 1985, and 1989. His advocacy of downtown construction projects, urban renewal, and the 1984 Olympics for Los Angeles has been profitable for the city and business alike. Bradley's long promised, but much delayed, mass transit system finally was begun in 1986. A 22-mile stretch of the Metro Blue Line linking downtown Los Angeles to Long Beach was opened in 1990. Additional construction on the 150-mile trolley system will take place into the next century. Cutbacks in federal financial support for the system may cause major changes in the scope of the project.

Though Mayor Tom Bradley lost two tries at the governorship (1982 and 1986), his success in municipal elections is undeniable. He forged a coalition between African-American voters and Jewish citizens in West

Los Angeles. This coalition was later expanded to include Latinos and organized labor. Winning five terms as mayor in such a diverse community signifies a rare ability to work with a broad spectrum of people. With the negative publicity stemming from the 1989 disclosures that he guided city deposits into banks on whose boards he sat, Bradley's spotless image as a former police officer took a pounding. It is difficult to foretell what the political fallout will be from the LAPD's beating of Rodney King.

San Diego

Located 16 miles from the Mexican border, San Diego bears all the trademarks of a midwesterner's conception of a California dream city. It is rich in history, affluent, young, situated on a natural harbor, and politically conservative. San Diego is a post-World War II phenomenon. In 1945, San Diego was California's thirty-first largest city; today it is the state's second most populous and the nation's sixth largest.

The aerospace boom in the 1960s bolstered the city's economy. The healthy economic climate attracted corporations from the East, which wanted to locate in a growing area with sufficient amenities to offset the disadvantages brought on by relocation. Although part of southern California geographically, San Diego is protected from the urban sprawl of the Los Angeles–Orange County area by the federal government's Marine Corps base at Camp Pendleton. However, the metropolitan San Diego area has been experiencing a growth rate twice as fast as Los Angeles County's for the past decade, a feat that concerns many longtime residents.

From 1945 through the early 1970s, San Diego politics were dominated by the landed gentry (established families, retired military officers, and business leaders), financial notables, and James Copley, publisher of the two main San Diego newspapers. During this period of rapid expansion, San Diego, in contrast to San Francisco, was a city where newly arrived business leaders were absorbed into the mainstream of civic affairs.

The power structure of San Diego has changed dramatically in recent years. Although the navy is a main factor in the city, retired navy personnel no longer constitute a major political force. James Copley died in 1973, and his wife, Helen, controls the Copley newspaper chain without the superpatriotic overtones characteristic of the papers during her husband's control. Scandals have also had an impact on city politics. The election of Pete Wilson as mayor in 1971, as a reform candidate, came on the heels of the acquittal of then mayor Frank Curran on charges of accepting bribes.

Pete Wilson served as mayor from 1971 to 1982 when he was elected to the U.S. Senate. Wilson orchestrated a number of changes in San Diego politics. In 1973 he unsuccessfully advocated a charter reform that would have changed the city's council–manager form of government to a strong mayoral system. Voters rejected this by a wide margin. Undaunted, Wilson took other action that effectively increased the powers of the mayor's office at the expense of the manager's authority. He assumed control of the council agenda, made key programs (e.g., the Planning Department) responsible to the mayor, and had Sacramento and Washington lobbyists report to his office. The manager's staff stayed the same while Wilson's and the council's increased. His election support for faithful council members and his appointment to key city posts of individuals who adhered to his programs solidified his power base.

Following Wilson's departure to the U.S. Senate, 36-year-old County Supervisor Rodger Hedgecock, a Republican and an environmentalist, was elected mayor in a special election in 1983. Mayor Hedgecock led efforts to redevelop San Diego's downtown area and to cope with the city's rapid growth, both plans initially begun by Wilson. No doubt, Hedgecock not only wanted to match Wilson's successes in area politics, but, like Wilson, he had his eye on higher office as well. Five days before his reelection in 1984, Hedgecock's political future was derailed when he was indicted on multiple counts of perjury and accepting illegal campaign contributions. He won reelection anyway. Hedgecock received a 1-year sentence to be served in local custody and, by law, had to resign his mayoral post.

With Hedgecock's resignation, city voters chose Maureen O'Connor as mayor. O'Connor, at age 39, became the city's first female mayor and the first Democrat to win the position in over 20 years. O'Connor had previously served two terms on the city council; she was the youngest person, at age 25, to ever win a council seat. O'Connor is an environmentalist, a fiscal conservative, and staunch advocate of campaign finance reform measures. Charter revisions strengthening the mayor's power, changes long sought by Pete Wilson, were finally adopted during O'Connor's tenure as mayor.

In spite of O'Connor's political leanings, the city and county are Republican strongholds. Organized labor is not a political force. The first black to be elected to the board of supervisors, an incumbent city councilman, won office on a pledge to economize city financing and to work for the construction of a new state prison in the area. San Diego gives San Jose a good race for the title of feminist capital. Besides Mayor Maureen O'Connor, women served in the late 1980s as chair of the San Diego County Board of Supervisors, chair of the school board, deputy mayor, chair of the local Chamber of Commerce, head of the downtown redevelopment agency, and chairs of the county central committees of both major political parties (Spivak, 1989:285). Outside of government, Helen Copley is the publisher of the city's two newspapers, and Joan Kroc owns the Padres baseball team as well as being a major stockholder of the McDonald's fast food chain.

The downtown rejuvenation effort has been under way for several years. The tattoo parlors and clip joints that catered to the sailors in the past are disappearing, and business construction is increasing. Office space is expected to double, and some forecasters are expecting the city to rival Los Angeles and San Francisco as a major financial center. To the dismay of other localities in the state, San Diego is attracting corporations already located in California. Manufacturing, the military, and tourism have provided the economic base for the city over the years. Increasingly, education, medical research, and electronics are regarded as lucrative industries.

San Diego politics is a high stakes financial venture. Pete Wilson proved that an area politician could win major statewide races. However, the fast track of San Diego politics is littered with the wreckage of others who were too ambitious.

Summary _____

Local governments provide political entry points to an increasingly wide range of Californians. Five of California's seven major cities have elected women mayors, and the two holdouts (Oakland and Los Angeles) have had African-American mayors for lengthy periods. The successful MALDEF lawsuit in Los Angeles County suggests that local district lines hereafter should not be as disadvantageous to minority candidates.

Much is expected of local governments in California. They are the front lines in terms of addressing educational needs, crime, pollution, congestion, and homelessness. As the creations of state government, the effectiveness of local boards and councils is a direct reflection of the performance of the State Capitol. The role of state government was central to localities before Proposition 13 passed in 1978; it has become doubly important since that blockbuster proposition became law. As local governments increasingly turn to Sacramento for financial support, are the institutions of state government up to the task? Further, it bears repeating that only the state can design incentives needed to consolidate the profusion of overlapping local jurisdictions.

In the end, we return to the question raised at the outset of this text: Are the institutions of state government in need of fundamental change at this time?

References: Chapter 11 ⎯⎯⎯⎯⎯⎯⎯⎯⎯⎯⎯⎯⎯⎯⎯⎯⎯⎯

Bucy, E. Page. "Redistricting By Lawsuit." *California Journal* (January 1991).

Garcia, Dan, and Ray Remy. "Consolidate California Sprawl by Regional, Responsible Government." *Los Angeles Times* (March 25, 1990).

Heilig, Peggy, and Robert Mundt. *Your Voice at City Hall: The Politics, Procedures, and Policies of District Representation.* Albany: State University of New York Press, 1984.

Mitchell, Evelyn. "The Impact and Effects of the 1970 Sacramento City Charter Reform." M.A. Thesis, California State University, Sacramento, 1976.

Salzman, Ed. "Enter Strong Mayors—Exit City Managers." *Sacramento Bee* (April 23, 1989).

Sanders, Steve. "Does California Need A Policy to Manage Urban Growth?" Sacramento: Senate Office of Research, 1989.

Spivak, Sharon. "Has San Diego Become a Matriarchy?" *California Journal* (July 1989).

Waldman, Tom. "A Colossus Astride Southern California." *California Journal* (June 1990).

Index